How Buddhism Acquired a Soul on the Way to China

Oxford Centre for Buddhist Studies Monographs
Series Editor: Richard Gombrich, Oxford Centre for Buddhist Studies

The Oxford Centre for Buddhist Studies promotes teaching and research into all Buddhist traditions, as found in texts and in societies, and is equally open to the study of Buddhism by methods associated with the humanities (philology, philosophy, history) and the social sciences (anthropology, sociology, politics). It insists only on using sources in their original languages and on aiming at the highest scholarly standards.

Recently published by Equinox

Richard Gombrich, *What the Buddha Thought*

Venerable Seongcheol, *Sermon of One Hundred Days: Part One*

Previously published

Buddhist Meditation: An Anthology of Texts from the Pali Canon
Sarah Shaw

Early Buddhist Metaphysics: The Making of a Philosophical Tradition
Noa Ronkin

How Buddhism Began: The Conditioned Genesis of the Early Teachings.
2nd edition
Richard F. Gombrich

Metaphor and Literalism in Buddhism: The Doctrinal History of Nirvana
Soon-Il Hwang

Mindfulness in Early Buddhism: New Approaches Through Psychology and Textual Analysis, of Pali, Chinese and Sanskrit Sources
Tse-fu Kuan

Miphamis Dialectics and the Debates on Emptiness: To Be, Not To Be, or Neither
Karma Phuntsho

Remaking Buddhism from Medieval Nepal: The Fifteenth-century Reformation of Newar Buddhism
Will Tuladhar-Douglas

The Biographies of Rechungpa: The Evolution of a Tibetan Hagiography
Peter Alan Roberts

The Origin of Buddhist Meditation
Alexander Wynne

How Buddhism Acquired a Soul on the Way to China

Jungnok Park

equinox

SHEFFIELD UK BRISTOL CT

Published by Equinox Publishing Ltd

UK: Unit S3, Kelham House, 3 Lancaster Street, Sheffield, S3 8AF
USA: ISD, 70 Enterprise Drive, Bristol, CT 06010

www.equinoxpub.com

First published 2012

ISBN: 978-1-84553-996-2 (hardback)
978-1-84553-997-9 (paperback)

British Library Cataloguing-in-Publication Data
A catalogue record for this book is available from the British Library.

Library of Congress Cataloging-in-Publishing Data
Park, Jungnok, 1971–2008.
How Buddhism acquired a soul on the way to China / Jungnok Park.
p. cm. — (Oxford Centre for Buddhist Studies Monographs)
"This book is based on his Oxford D.Phil. thesis, which he completed early in 2008"—Data view.
Includes bibliographical references and index.
ISBN 978-1-84553-996-2 (hb) — ISBN 978-1-84553-997-9 (pb)
1. Buddhism—China. 2. Buddhism—Sacred books—Translating—History. 3. Buddhism—China—Doctrines—History. 4. Buddhism—India. 5. Self—Religious aspects—Buddhism. I. Title. BQ628.P37 2012
294.3'422—dc22

2011006347

Typeset by S.J.I. Services, New Delhi
Printed and bound by Lightning Source UK Ltd., Milton Keynes

CONTENTS

Foreword: The Late Jungnok Park vii
Richard Gombrich

Preface ix

Introduction 1

PART I: CHINESE BUDDHIST TRANSLATION IN ITS CULTURAL CONTEXT

1. The Characteristics of Chinese Buddhist Translation 5
2. The Verification of the Traditional Attributions of Translatorship 37

PART II: THE DEVELOPMENT OF THE INDIAN BUDDHIST CONCEPT OF SELF

3. Self in Early Buddhist Soteriology 65
4. Development of a Buddhist Self 104
5. *Nirvāṇa* and a Permanent Self 126

PART III: THE DEVELOPMENT OF THE CHINESE BUDDHIST CONCEPT OF SELF

6. Chinese Ideas about Self before the Arrival of Buddhism 151
7. Non-self but an Imperishable Soul in Chinese Buddhist Translations 177

8. A Survey of Interpolations and Adaptations of an Agent in *Saṃsāra* 196

9. The Characteristics of the Chinese Buddhist Concept of Self 207

Conclusion 223

Appendix 225

References 232

Index 241

FOREWORD: THE LATE JUNGNOK PARK

Richard Gombrich

This book is closely based on the DPhil thesis 'The Translation and Transformation of the Buddhist Concept of Self between India and China', which Jungnok Park completed in March 2008. The thesis was supervised in the Faculty of Oriental Studies, University of Oxford, by Mr Lance Cousins and myself. The oral examination took place in July 2008, but Jungnok died tragically the next day, before the result could be determined. I have edited the thesis for publication with a very light touch: most of the changes consist of small adjustments to make the English read more smoothly. The change of title merely reflects the fact that the thesis title is unwieldy.

Jungnok Park was born in South Korea in 1971. From 1989 to 1999 he was a Buddhist monk in the Jogye Order; he disrobed because he found he could no longer accept all the required beliefs. In 1997 he entered the Philosophy Department of Seoul National University, where he took a BA in 2000 and an MA in 2002; his MA thesis was titled 'Nirvana and Buddhist Ethics'. From 1998 to 2001 the Korean Foundation for Advanced Studies awarded him a scholarship for classical Chinese studies; and in 2003 the same foundation gave him a scholarship of full support for his doctoral studies, which he pursued at Wolfson College, Oxford.

Though modest to a fault, Jungnok had to admit that his classical Chinese was good. He also read Japanese fluently. On the other hand, he arrived at Oxford knowing no Sanskrit or Pali, but acquired full competence within two years. The improvement in his English, which he came to write like a native speaker, was scarcely less remarkable. These achievements, however, pale beside his razor-sharp intelligence and his determination to take nothing on trust. He thought for himself every inch of the way. He was receptive to advice, and indeed sought it, but when it was given he never would accept it without question; he always had to mull it over and come to his own decision. As a monk, he had rebelled (as he himself recorded) against what he saw as injustice and corruption within the Order. Alluding to this, he wrote that the approaches he had adopted in both his theses were intended 'to reveal how a tradition of normative orders assimilates alien principles of social justice and develops into a new system, maintaining its "traditional" identity'. He had extensive plans for further research into the historical relations between Buddhism and the struggle for social justice in China.

Jungnok was one of the most gifted students I have ever encountered. His capacity for hard work was phenomenal. Moreover, he was no less remarkable for his kindness and sensitivity. His early death was a terrible blow to scholarship, and I shall never stop missing him.

PREFACE

This book starts with a question: why did some Buddhist translators in China interpolate terms designating an agent in *saṃsāra* which did not appear in the original texts? To answer this question, I first analyse the linguistic, philosophical and cultural differences between India and China that made it necessary for translators to have a free hand in order to adapt the exotic ideas of Buddhism to Chinese culture. Utilizing this freedom, many Buddhist translators before the time of Kumārajīva (344–413 CE) interpolated the idea of an imperishable soul into the body of the canonical translations. Although this tendency to interpolate waned at the canonical level after the early fifth century, learned Chinese Buddhists developed a sophisticated exegetical system advocating the concept of *shen* 神, a permanent agent of perception, which was popular and influential during the fifth and sixth centuries. After the late sixth century, highly educated Buddhist theorists, such as Jizang (吉藏: 549–623), came to avoid including the idea of an imperishable soul in their doctrinal system. However, we observe that the idea of a permanent agent of perception remained vividly alive even during the development of Chinese Buddhism after the seventh century.

In the course of this development, the Chinese basically made use of the raw material imported from India; however, they added some 'seasonings' that were peculiar to China and developed their own 'recipes' about how to construct the ideas of Buddhism. While Indian Buddhists constructed their ideas of self by means of empiricism, anti-Brahmanism, analytic reasoning, etc., the Chinese Buddhists constructed their ideas of self by means of non-analytic insights, utilizing pre-established epistemology and cosmogony. Furthermore, many of the basic renderings had specific implications that were peculiar to China. For example, while *shen* in philosophical Daoism originally signified an agent of thought which disintegrates after bodily death, Buddhists added to it the property of permanent existence. Since many Buddhists in China read the reinterpreted term *shen* with the implications of the established epistemology and cosmogony, they came to develop their own ideas of self.

INTRODUCTION

Being a central theme of Buddhist ontology, epistemology and soteriology, the doctrine of non-self (*anātman*) has been used as a slogan that characterizes Buddhism. As the structure of the compound *an-ātman* indicates, it is the antithesis of the doctrine of *ātman*, which posits a permanent agent going through *saṃsāra*. However, in T6 *Mahāparinirvāṇa-sūtra* 般泥洹經, we find the following Chinese translation contradicting the fundamental doctrine of non-self:

> Since the mind is attached to existence, [the body] arises dependent on conditions. Doing [karmic] actions repetitiously, one receives extraordinary suffering. Once one has been born, one must die; once one has died, one must be reborn. Although one comes and passes away through birth and death, [one's] *jingshen* 精神 does not cease. Therefore [you] should not [cry] like this! [1]

As I clarify in Chapters 7 and 8, the translator uses the term *jingshen* to signify the permanent agent of perception; doubtless, this concept of *jingshen* is incompatible with the doctrinal system of early Buddhism to which the *Mahāparinirvāṇa-sūtra* belongs.

Which Indian or Central Asian term in the original text would best correspond to the term *jingshen*? Comparing this Chinese translation with the Indian versions of the *sūtra* (MPP and MPS) and other corresponding Chinese translations (T5.1.172c26–27, T7.1.205c3–4 and T1451.24.400a15–18),[2] we find that the above translation is full of

1. 惟心猗有，從因緣起，以作復作，受非常苦，生輒有死，死則復生，生死往來，精神不滅，莫致是處 (T6.1.188c24–26). Unless otherwise stated, all translations in this book are by the author.
2. The *Mahāparinirvāṇa-sūtra* 遊行經 in T1 (*Dīrghāgama*) does not have a corresponding passage.

arbitrary interpolations. For example, the corresponding part of the Pali *Mahāparinibbāna-sutta* merely states:

> Oh, impermanent are [all] constructed things. How could it (i.e., permanence) be possible here at all?[3]

What I aim to do in this book is to explicate how the Buddhist translators in China interpolated certain terms indicating a permanent agent in *saṃsāra* into the canonical body of Buddhist translations, and how such interpolations influenced the formation of the Chinese Buddhist concept of self. In order to achieve this aim, in Part I, I elucidate the cultural characteristics of Chinese Buddhist translation that allowed the particular interpolations of a permanent self. In Part II, I analyse the critical features of Indian Buddhist ontology, epistemology and soteriology that constructed the ideas of self in early and later Buddhism, and find the momenta that facilitated the transformation of the Buddhist concept of self in India. In Part III, I introduce the Chinese ideas of self before the arrival of Buddhism, expound how the established Chinese ideas exerted an influence on the translators' adaptations and interpolations, explore the historical development of the Chinese Buddhist ideas of self, and analyse the basic premises and ways of thinking that constructed those ideas. The concept of self plays a pivotal role in the formation of Buddhist ontology, epistemology and soteriology. By examining how the Chinese understood the Indian Buddhist concept of self and developed their own idea of self, I hope to illustrate the cultural process through which the Chinese assimilated Indian Buddhism and created their own form of Buddhism.

---

3. *aniccā saṃkhārā, taṃ kut' ettha labbhā? ti.* (D.II.140_10). MPS §44.13 reconstructs this part from the Tibetan **Mūlasarvāstivāda-vinaya-kṣudraka-vastu* as follows: *prāg evâsmākaṃ Bhagavatâkhyātaṃ: 'sarvair iṣṭaiḥ kāntaiḥ priyair manāpair nānābhāvo bhaviṣyati vinābhāvo viprayogo visaṃyogaḥ' kuta etal labhyaṃ: yat taj jātaṃ bhūtaṃ kṛtaṃ saṃskṛtaṃ vedayitaṃ pratītyasamutpannaṃ kṣayadharmaṃ vyayadharmaṃ vibhavadharmaṃ virodhadharmaṃ pralokadharmaṃ na prarujyate? nêdaṃ sthānaṃ vidyate.* Waldschmidt's reconstructions throughout MPS are strongly justified, being compared with other corresponding Sanskrit fragments, such as MSD and MPS_BV. In this specific case, the reconstruction is supported by an internal comparison with §45.8, §14.21 and §31.70.

Part I

CHINESE BUDDHIST TRANSLATION IN ITS CULTURAL CONTEXT

PREAMBLE

In this Part, I examine the general characteristics of Chinese Buddhist translation and the system of producing an authoritative translation. Translation was the first step towards introducing the exotic thought of Indian Buddhism to the Chinese. In order to convey peculiar ideas written in an unfamiliar style, Buddhist translators in China had to handle the differences in language, culture, philosophy and ethics between India and China. Although more familiar with the differences than ordinary people, the translators themselves were never free from the obstacles they posed. Hence, we find misunderstandings or controversial adaptations permanently implanted in their translations. The quotation from T6 on p. 1 is one example of this petrifaction of the translators' misunderstanding or intended adaptation. Once it is promulgated, however, the entire translation attains the authority of truth. Since readers tend to lack the knowledge to extract baseless interpolations from a translated text, even arbitrary interpolations or controversial adaptations acquire the authority of truth. In this way, the personal opinions of translators have been crucially influential in the formation of ideas that are peculiar to Chinese Buddhism. Here, in examining the major features of the linguistic, cultural and philosophical differences between India and China, I intend to explore the cultural substructure on which Chinese Buddhists developed their own ideas of self.

I dedicate Chapter 2 to introducing my philological method, which is adopted for a chronological survey in Part III. Demonstrating the historical development of the Chinese Buddhist ideas of self, I there make a chronological survey of the interpolations and adaptations found in the canonical body of Chinese translations that posit the existence of a permanent agent in *saṃsāra*. In order to make such a survey reliable, accurate attributions of translatorship are vital, since these can pinpoint the time and place of translation. Although the Chinese produced plenty of Buddhist catalogues with considerable accuracy, their records are incomplete: there are many missing and incorrect attributions. In order to demonstrate my method of making the chronological investigation reliable, I present a case study, attesting the traditional attribution of T20, *Ambāṣṭha-sūtra* 佛開解梵志阿 經, to Zhi Qian (支謙: fl. 222–53).[1] This complicated and 'monotonous' task is irrelevant to understanding the logical structure of the Chinese Buddhist concept of self, but is vital to comprehending its historical development.

1. In this book, all dates are CE, unless specified as BCE.

Chapter 1

THE CHARACTERISTICS OF CHINESE BUDDHIST TRANSLATION

> Kumārajīva used to discuss the characteristics of Indian languages with Sengrui 僧叡. He remarked on the similarities and differences [between Indian languages and Chinese] as follows: 'Indian custom takes much account of the rhythm of sentences. The pitch and metre [of Indian languages] aim to match string music. Whenever there is an audience with a king, there must be panegyrics. And, among the rituals for an audience with the Buddha, praising [his virtues] in song is the highest. The verses in Buddhist scriptures have that formal character. However, when we translate Indian languages into Chinese, we lose the rhythm of the sentences. Although the overall meaning may be delivered, there is a great difference in literary flavour. It is like giving chewed food to others: the food not only loses its taste but also makes them vomit.'[1]

This is an admission by the celebrated translator Kumārajīva (344–413) of the difficulties associated with Chinese Buddhist translation. Many elements of Indian languages could not be translated into Chinese because of the cultural, philosophical and linguistic differences. To overcome such differences, Buddhist translators in China sometimes had to insert words or sentences that do not appear in the original texts, or remove words or sentences from the originals. However, as I discuss below, the addition or removal of words or sentences does not necessarily lead to distortion. In order to convey the correct meaning, it may be unavoidable so as to provide readers with some background knowledge, or remove some expressions that may mislead readers due to their different implications in the two traditions.

---

1. 什每為叡論西方辭體, 商略同異云: '天竺國俗, 甚重文藻; 其宮商體韻, 以入絃為善. 凡覲國王, 必有讚德; 見佛之儀, 以歌歎為尊. 經中偈頌, 皆其式也. 但改梵為秦,

Therefore, due to the nature of their work, Buddhist translators in China were generally given a free hand to use their abilities to overcome the immense differences between South/Central Asian and Chinese culture. Their relatively free translations were guided by their understanding. Since they were unaware of all the differences, their misunderstandings easily yielded unintended distortions and their intentional adaptations caused unexpected misunderstandings.

It is the aim of this chapter to provide insights into the linguistic and cultural circumstances in which the Buddhist translators in China could arbitrarily insert certain terms to indicate a permanent agent in *saṃsāra*.

CHINESE BUDDHIST TRANSLATION THEORIES

The earliest extant Chinese Buddhist translation dates from the mid-second century, and Buddhist translation work has continued ever since. In the process of translation, the Chinese encountered many difficulties, and some Chinese Buddhist scholars theorized about these difficulties and provided guidance on how to handle them. Here I shall introduce two widely known theories: firstly, that of Daoan (道安: ?–385),[2] who paved the way for the transition from the period of archaic translation (before 375) to that of old translation (376–617); and secondly, that of Xuanzang (玄奘: 602?–664), who introduced the period of new translation (after 618).[3]

Daoan's Theory

Daoan is honoured for his comprehensive survey of Buddhist texts. During the period 374–85,[4] he compiled a Buddhist catalogue entitled *Zongli zhongjing mulu* [ZZL] 綜理眾經目錄, which is not extant, but incorporated in T2145 *Chu sanzang ji ji* [CSZJJ] 出三藏記集. ZZL is one of the earliest catalogues, providing later Buddhist cataloguers with an

失其藻蔚. 雖得大意, 殊隔文體. 有似: 嚼飯與人, 非徒失味, 乃令歐穢也' (CSZJJ, T2145.55.101c7–13).

2. His birth date is uncertain. CSZJJ records that he lived for over eighty years (T2145.55.109b5–9).
3. I follow Ono's distinction of the three periods of Chinese Buddhist translation. For more details, refer to Ono, 1936: spec. vol., pp. 7–9.
4. Daoan's catalogue is said to include the texts published up to 374, and he died in 385. Therefore the compilation of ZZL must have been completed between 374 and 385.

archetypal model. Although he did not produce translations himself, he organized many gatherings for that purpose. Based on his experience of directing the translation procedure, Daoan suggested the following principles for translation work.

Firstly, he suggested 'the five cases for not following the original texts' 五失本. [1.1] When the word order of foreign languages[5] differs from that of Chinese, translators are to phrase the text according to the Chinese word order. [1.2] As to the literary style of the scriptures, foreigners make much of simplicity, but the Chinese make much of style. For a translation to attract the Chinese readers' interest, the use of style is inevitable. [1.3] In the recitation of foreign scriptures, there is excessive repetition. Although it is not necessary to be averse to such repetition, it is to be removed. [1.4] The rhetoric in foreign expository works appears verbose. Without any change in [the meaning of] the paragraphs, it rephrases what has already been said, even using up to fifteen hundred words. Translators are to remove this repetition. [1.5] Having finished one topic, [foreign scriptures] begin a new one by repeating what has been related previously. Translators are to remove the repetition.[6] In short, translators should follow the Chinese word order, create a stylish composition, and remove redundant repetition. These principles reveal that Daoan preferred a reader-friendly translation to a strictly literal one.

Secondly, he points out 'three difficulties [in Buddhist translation]' 三不易.[7] [2.1] Buddhist scriptures[8] were preached out of compassion by the Buddha, who saw future lives, knew all past lives and had extinguished all defilements. He preached according to situation, and

---

5. In this context, 'foreign' means South/Central Asian.
6. 譯胡為秦, 有五失本也. 一者, 胡語盡倒, 而使從秦. 一失本也. 二者, 胡經尚質, 秦人好文; 傳可眾心, 非文不合. 斯二失本也. 三者, 經委悉, 至於嘆詠, 寧反覆, 或三或四. 不嫌其煩, 而今裁斥. 三失本也. 四者, 胡有義記, 正似亂辭. 尋說向語, 文無以異, 或千五百. 刈而不存. 四失本也. 五者, 事已全成, 將更傍及, 反騰前辭, 已乃後說, 而悉除此. 五失本也. ('The Preface to the *Summary of the Mahāprajñāpāramitā-sūtra*' 摩訶鉢羅若波羅蜜經抄序; T2145.55.52b23–c2).
7. *Yi* 易 in *sanbuyi* 三不易 has two meanings: change and easiness, so *sanbuyi* can mean 'three cases not to change' or 'three difficulties'. The latter appears to suit the context in question.
8. The five cases for not following the original texts and the three difficulties [in Buddhist translation] are mentioned in 'The Preface to the *Summary of the Mahāprajñāpāramitā-sūtra*'. In this preface, Daoan attributes the three difficulties to the translation of the *Mahāprajñāpāramitā-sūtra*. However, following the tradition, I apply them to Buddhist translations in general.

situations change. However, translators are to follow [the decline of] the present, abolishing the elegance of the past. [2.2] Ignorant translators can never access the wisdom of the Buddha. They try to translate the profound words of a thousand years ago for the present ignorant people. [2.3] The recitation and transcription of scriptures were performed by *arhat*s soon after the death of the Buddha. Now translators translate with poor knowledge after a thousand years have passed. Those *arhat*s were skilled, whereas the present translators are mediocre. The latter cannot match the former.[9] In short, it is difficult for translators to recreate the situation in which the scriptures were preached, and it is impossible for ignorant translators to deliver the profound truth of the Buddha.

Xuanzang's Theory

Xuanzang, who is widely honoured as a figure who perfected Chinese Buddhist translation, suggested the principles of 'the five cases not to be translated' 五種不翻. [3.1] Esoteric words should not be translated into Chinese: e.g., *dhāraṇīs*. [3.2] A word with multiple implications should not be translated into Chinese: e.g., *bhagavat* 薄伽梵.[10] [3.3] Something not existing in China should not be translated into Chinese: e.g., *jambu* tree 閻浮樹. [3.4] A word that has traditionally been transliterated should not be translated: e.g., *anuttarasambodhi* (阿耨菩提: the highest awakening) can be translated, but it has always been transliterated since the time of Moteng 摩騰.[11] [3.5] If a transliterated word yields preferable effects, it should not be translated: e.g., the transliteration *banruo* (般若: *prajñā*) is respected while the translated word *zhihui* (智慧: wisdom) is not.[12]

---

9. 然般若經，三達之心覆面所演. 聖必因時，時俗有易；而刪雅古，以適今時. 一不易也. 愚智天隔，聖人叵階；乃欲以千歲之上微言，傳使合百王之下末俗. 二不易也. 阿難出經，去佛未久，尊大迦葉令五百六通，迭察迭書. 今離千年，而以近意量截. 阿羅漢，兢兢若此，生死人，平平若此. 將不知法者勇乎？斯三不易也 (*ibid.*, T2145.55.52c2–9).

10. T1530 **Buddhabhūmi-sūtra-śāstra* 佛地經論 (translated by Xuanzang in 650) explains *bhagavat* with the following six meanings: sovereign 自在, prosperous 熾盛, dignified 端嚴, glorious 名稱, fortunate 吉祥 and adorable 尊貴 (26.292a2415–28).

11. Moteng is a legendary figure to whom the first Chinese Buddhist translation is traditionally attributed. He is said to have arrived in China in 67 and translated the *Sishierzhang jing* 四十二章經.

12. 唐奘法師論五種不翻: 一祕密故, 如陀羅尼. 二含多義故, 如薄伽梵, 具六義. 三此無故, 如閻 (淨)[浮] 樹, 中夏實無此木. 四順古故, 如阿耨菩提, 非不可翻; 而摩騰以來, 常存梵音. 五生善故, 如般若尊重, 智慧輕淺 ('Preface to the *Mahāvyutpatti*' 翻譯名義序; T2131.54.1055a13–18).

These principles for Buddhist translation suggested by Daoan and Xuanzang mainly relate to the linguistic and cultural differences between ancient India and contemporary China and to the translators' capacity to handle them. Among them, [1.1] (different word order); [1.2] (different stylistic flavour); and [1.3], [1.4] and [1.5] (rhetorical redundancies) instruct how to handle linguistic problems. [2.1] points out the differences in the temporal and cultural situations between the original composition and its translation. [2.2] and [2.3] concern the differences in intelligence between the speakers, writers, translators and readers. [3.1] relates to the different cultural attitudes towards sounds: for the Chinese, sounds are a mere means of conveying meanings; however, for Indians, sounds in themselves are regarded as the truth or transcendental power. [3.2] (a word with multiple implications) is another example of a linguistic problem. [3.3] originates from temporal and spatial differences. [3.4] is a rule for maintaining consistency in translations for the convenience of the reader; [3.5] is a rule for choosing a word whose tone is more effective for the promotion of Buddhism.

The difficulties in Chinese Buddhist translation, as pointed out by Daoan and Xuanzang, show the different interests, cultural backgrounds, ways of thinking, moral demands, philosophical education, etc., between Indian and Chinese Buddhists, and these differences are the cardinal factors that drove the development of a Buddhism that is peculiar to China. Next, I demonstrate how these factors influenced the Chinese translation and interpretation of South/Central Asian scriptures.

THE TRANSLATION PROCEDURE

Unlike the great majority of contemporary translations, which are carried out by one or more bilingual individuals, Buddhist translation in China has been undertaken by groups of religious and linguistic experts, many of whom have been monolingual. Traditionally, a Buddhist translation has been attributed to one or a few principal figures among many participant experts; and the honour of translatorship has usually been attributed to a person who recited the original text from memory, who brought the text from South/Central Asia, or who provided an authentic reading of the original text.

Occasionally it happens that the officially honoured translators never participated in the activity of translation. For example, the *Tripiṭaka Koreana* [K] and the *Taisho shinshu daizokyo* [T] attribute T210

Dharmapada 法句經 to *Vighna 維祇難 *et al.*[13] However, the colophon to T210 in CSZJJ (T2145.55.49c20–50a28) and the biography of *Vighna in CSZJJ (T2145.55. 96a22–27) indicate that his contribution was merely the delivery of the text to China, and that the actual translators were Zhu Jiangyan 竺將炎 and Zhi Qian (支謙: fl. 222–53). Thus although Zhi Qian was one of the most celebrated figures in Buddhist society at that time, the honour of official translatorship was credited to *Vighna, who made no contribution at all towards the actual activity of translation. Such an attribution may be the result of the Chinese Buddhist inclination to credit more authority to the sources from India than to the Chinese ones.

It also happened that, although they provided an authentic reading of the original texts in South/Central Asian languages, the officially honoured translators could not speak Chinese when they took part in the translation. For example, the Indian monk Guṇabhadra arrived in China in 435. At that time, he needed an interpreter to communicate with Chinese people, as stated in his biography in CSZJJ (T2145.55.105b17–106b21). The colophon to T353 *Śrīmālādevī-siṃhanāda-sūtra* 勝鬘師子吼一乘大方便方廣經 (T2145.55.67a14–b9, 67b10–c4) states that it was translated in 436, and the biography adds that, soon after his arrival in China and before the translation of T353, he translated T99 *Saṃyuktāgama* 雜阿含經 at Temple Qihuansi 祇洹寺 and T270 **Dharmabherī-sūtra* 法鼓經 at Temple Dongansi 東安寺. This clearly means that he started his translation work before he was able to speak Chinese, let alone write in classical Chinese.

After the translators from India or Central Asia had been living in China for a few decades, they may have become fluent in spoken Chinese. However, in many of these cases it is not plausible that their knowledge of Chinese literature and culture could have developed sufficiently to translate Buddhist scriptures into classical Chinese. To undertake Chinese translation by themselves, they would have to be not only versed in the vocabulary and syntax of classical Chinese, but also familiar with Chinese literature, ethics, philosophy and history. Such an

---

13. For the reconstruction of South/Central Asian proper names from Chinese and Tibetan sources, I rely mainly on the *Indo bukkyo koyu meishi jiten* 印度佛教固有名詞辭典 by Akanuma (1967), the *Foguang dacidian* 佛光大辭典 by Ci (1989), the *Kanyaku taisho bonwa daijiten* 漢訳對照梵和大辞典 by Ogiwara (1964), the *Bussho kaisetsu daijiten* 佛書解說大辭典 by Ono (1936–78), and *The Korean Buddhist Canon: A Descriptive Catalogue* by Lancaster (1979).

amount of knowledge is quite beyond anything that a foreigner could achieve even after a few decades of living in China. Hence, except for a few bilingual translators who were born and educated in China, such as Zhi Qian, Zhu Fahu 竺法護, Zhu Fonian 竺佛念 and Xuanzang 玄奘, and linguistic geniuses, such as Kumārajīva,[14] the majority of South/Central Asian Buddhist translators were compelled to depend on Chinese interpreters and experts for the adaptation to Chinese philosophy and literature. This dependence on Chinese assistants in the translation process is an important mechanism whereby the Chinese developed their own Buddhism: the renderings adopted by the assistants had implications that the original terms did not, and the readers read the translation with implications that were not anticipated by the South/Central Asian translators.

There are some extant colophons, prologues and epilogues of specific translations that describe how the procedure of Buddhist translation was structured in China. To illustrate this procedure,[15] I introduce three translators' teams: that of Lokakṣema (支婁迦讖: fl. 178–89), that of Buddhayaśas (fl. 408–15) and that of Xuanzang. These three teams belong to each of the three periods of Chinese Buddhist translation respectively: that of archaic translation (before 375), that of old translation (376–617) and that of new translation (after 618). It may be worth observing how the colophons, etc., record the Buddhist translation procedure.

The colophon to T224 *Aṣṭasāhasrikā Prajñāpāramitā* 道行般若經 records:

> On the 8th day of the 10th lunar month, 179, Yuanshi Meng Fu from Louyang, Henan, [transcribed] what was recited by the Indian *bodhisattva* Zhu Shuofo. At that time, the interpreter and translator 傳言譯者 was the Yuezhi *bodhisattva* Lokakṣema; the scribes (侍者: lit. attendant) were Zhang Shaoan from Nanyang and Zibi from Nanhai; the supporters 勸助者 were Sun He and Zhou Tili.[16]

This colophon lets us know that there were at least five roles fulfilled by the participants in the translation during this first stage of Chinese

14. He could translate by himself because he had lived with Chinese people for almost twenty years before he started his translation work in 401, not just because he was linguistically talented.
15. For more details on the structure of the Buddhist translation system in China, refer to Hukaura (1938).
16. 光和二年十月八日， 河南洛陽孟元士口授天竺菩薩竺朔佛. 時傳言 (者譯) [譯者] 月支菩薩支讖; 時侍者南陽張少安・南海子碧; 勸助者孫和・周提立 (in CSZJJ; T2145.55.47c5–8).

Buddhism: 1) the reciter of the original text; 2) the transcriber of the original recitation; 3) the interpreter or translator 傳言譯者; 4) the scribe (侍 者, here for 筆受),[17] who writes down the oral interpretation or translation; and 5) (probably financial) supporters. Compared to the translation teams of later periods, many of whom were supported by the Chinese emperors, this translation team appears small in number and simple in structure. Nonetheless, it shows the typical way of organizing a Buddhist translation team. It was divided into three parts: one consisted of those versed in the original language, another of those who were bilingual, and the third of those versed in classical Chinese but not necessarily in the original language.

Buddhayaśas arrived in China in 408 and translated T1 *Dīrghāgama* 長阿含經, T1428 *Dharmaguptaka Vinaya* 四分律, and other works. The epilogue to T1 by Sengzhao (僧肇: 384–414) illustrates the constitution of his translation team at that time:

> The emperor of the Great Qin was ... especially fond of [General Yao Shuang] and always entrusted him with Buddhist affairs. In 410, he (probably Yao Shuang) requested the Kashmirian monk Buddhayaśas, the Master of the Buddhist canon, to recite 出 the *Dharmaguptaka Vinaya* in 40 fascs.; it was finished in 412. In 413, he finished reciting this *Dīrghāgama*.[18] [At that time] the monk Zhu Fonian from Liangzhou interpreted (or translated) 譯 it; Qin Daoist Daohan put it in writing 筆受. At that time, renowned monks from all over China gathered at the translation place and participated in the correction 挍定.[19]

Through this epilogue, it emerges: 1) that the translation was supported by an emperor; 2) that there was a government officer who administered the translation procedure;[20] 3) that Buddhayaśas was the reciter, i.e.,

17. In classical Chinese, *shizhe* 侍者 literally means an attendant. However, with the help of the colophon to T418 **Pratyutpanna-buddha-saṃmukhâvasthita-samādhi-sūtra* 般舟三昧經, we know that *shizhe* 侍者 is a scribe. The colophon states, 'The attendant *bodhisattva* Zhang Lian, whose pseudonym is Shaoan, put it in writing' 隨侍菩薩張蓮字少安筆受 (in CSZJJ: T2145.55.48c12–13). The title for scribes was later established as *bishuo* 筆受.

18. Recitation is the first step in Buddhist translation. However, it also represents the whole process of translation. Therefore, the end of the recitation here means the end of the whole translation.

19. 大秦天王 ... 上特留懷每任以法事. 以弘始十二年歳上章掩茂, 請罽賓三藏沙門佛陀耶舍, 出律藏《四分》四十卷, 十四年訖. 十五年歳昭陽奮若, 出此《長阿含》訖. 涼州沙門佛念為譯, 秦國道士道含筆受. 時集京夏名勝沙門, 於宅第, 挍定 (in CSZJJ; T2145.55.63c9–18).

20. Later, this position was called *jianhudashi* 監護大使 or *jianyue* 監閲, which means inspector.

the nominal translator; 4) that Zhu Fonian 竺佛念 was the substantial translator; 5) that a Daoist took the role of scribe 筆受; and 6) that there was an assembly of renowned Chinese monks for the correction of the translation.

From the beginning, the promotion of Buddhism in China had some connection with royal families. However, during the period of archaic translation (up to 375), Buddhism was a minor religious movement. At that time, the normal life of Chinese people was not based on Buddhist principles. The Western Jin dynasty collapsed in 316, after which northern China was occupied by 'barbarians' throughout the period of old translation (376–617), except during the reign of the Sui 隋 dynasty (581–618). The 'barbarian' dynasties promoted Buddhism and adopted it as the governing ideology instead of the indigenous Chinese systems of thought, particularly Confucianism. Having made Buddhist translation a national affair, the 'barbarian' dynasties administered as well as supported the process of translation.

Although his translation procedure was not typical, the case of Kumārajīva (344–413)[21] is worthy of examination. It was not typical, in that he recited and translated by himself, and then gave lectures on the text in the course of the translation. It was through the lectures that he listened to his Chinese pupils' advice, verified what was said in the original text, corrected the Chinese translation, and embellished the Chinese composition. It is said (T2145.55.53b7–10) that five hundred celebrated Chinese monks attended the place of the translation and the lectures on T223 *Mahāprajñāpāramitā-sūtra* 摩訶般若波羅蜜經. None of the colophons, epilogues or prologues to his translations assigns a specific person to a specific position in the process of translation. However, the procedure of his translation reflects significant trends in the period of old translation. Firstly, from the scale of the assembly for the translations and lectures, we can infer the scale of royal support that the Buddhist translators enjoyed. This support boosted Buddhism as

21. GSZ tells that he died at Changan in 409 without mentioning his age at that time (T2059.50.333a3–5). However, 'the Memorial Statement for Kumārajīva' 鳩摩羅什法師誄, in the *Guang hongming ji* 弘明集 (T2103.52.264c18), records his death as occurring on the 13th day of the 4th lunar month, 413, at the age of seventy (in the Chinese calculation). If this memorial statement is correct, Kumārajīva was born in 344 and died in 413. The colophon to T1646 **Satyasiddhi-śāstra* 成實論 (T2145.55.78a6–10) supports the latter date for Kumārajīva's death. It records that its translation was finished on the 15th day of the 9th lunar month, 412. If so, Kumārajīva cannot have died in 409.

the governmental ideology and introduced it into the daily life of the Chinese. Secondly, it became a trend for a translation to be accompanied by lectures or discussions about it. In the case of the translation of T1 above, we note that there was an assembly of prominent Chinese monks for the verification of the translation.

In this specific case of the translation of T1 by Buddhayaśas, the fact that a Daoist took the role of scribe 筆受 is noteworthy. Scribes make the first composition of what is translated orally by the translators/interpreters. Therefore they greatly influence the selection of the Chinese renderings of Indian Buddhist terms. This important task was performed by a Daoist, which indicates that a mastery of Chinese literature and philosophy may have been a more important requirement for the position of scribe than an exact knowledge of Indian Buddhism, and that the overall translation aimed to attract Chinese readers' interest rather than to maintain literal accuracy to the Indian originals.[22]

Having travelled to India, learnt Indian languages and collected baskets of Buddhist scriptures from 629 to 645, Xuanzang 玄奘 returned to China 'with 657 Indian scriptures' (T2060.50.456b18–19). He was strongly supported by the Tang dynasty and translated 75 texts, all of which are preserved in T.[23] The epilogue to T1579 *Yogācārabhūmi* 瑜伽師地論 by Xu Jingzong 許敬宗 describes the grand scale and strict procedure of Xuanzang's translation team as follows:

> [Xuanzang] returned to Changan on the 6th day of the 2nd lunar month, [645]. By the ordinance of the Emperor, he was invited to stay at Temple Hongfusi, and the requisites were provided by government officers. The government invited twenty-one renowned monks, who were versed both in Buddhism and in other Chinese thought, and [let Xuanzang] translate the Buddhist Sanskrit manuscripts that he had brought with him. On the 15th day of the 5th lunar month, 647, he began the first translation of the *Yogācārabhūmi*. The Sanskrit text of this treatise consists of 40,000 verses, each of which consists of 32 syllables. It has five parts and aims to clarify the meanings of the 17 stages (地, *bhūmi*). Xuanzang, the Master of the Buddhist canon, respectfully held [i.e. recited] the Sanskrit manuscripts and translated them into Chinese. The monks Linghui, Lingjun, Zhikai and Zhiren

22. The dependence of Buddhist translation on other Chinese thought was probably deep-rooted. With reference to the translation of T224, Tang (1973, pp. 69–70) argued that Yuanshi Meng Fu, who transcribed the recitation by Zhu Shuofo, and Zibi, who was one of the two scribes 筆受, were inclined towards Daoism.

23. I exclude T2087 *Datang xiyu ji* 大唐西域記 from his translations because it is his own travelogue.

from Temple Hongfusi, the monk Xuandu from Huichangsi, the monk Daozhuo from Yaotaisi, the monk Daoguan from Dazongchisi and the monk Mingjue from Qingchansi put [the translation by Xuanzang] into writing 筆受, in accordance with the [correct] meaning. The monk Xuanmu from Hongfusi verified [the conformity of the translation with] the Sanskrit text 證梵語. The monk Xuanying from Dazongchisi did the proof-reading 正字. The monk Daohong from Dazongchisi, the monk Mingyan from Shijisi, the monk Faxiang from Baochangsi, the monk Huigui from Luohansi, the monk Wenbei from Hongfusi, the monk Shentai from Qiyansi in Puzhou, and the monk Daoshen from Fajiangsi in Kuozhou vindicated the meanings 證大義. The monk Daozhi from Puguangsi, in accordance with the meaning [of the original translation], embellished the composition 證文 of the 17 fascs. in 'the Part of Fundamental Stages', i.e. 'the Stage Associated with Five Consciousnesses' (*pañcavijñānakāya-samprayuktā bhūmi*), 'the Stage of Mind' (*manobhūmi*), 'the Stage Having both Ideation and Exploration' (*savitarkā savicārā bhūmi*), 'the Stage Having no Ideation but Exploration' (*avitarkā savicārā bhūmi*), and 'the Stage Having neither Ideation nor Exploration' (*avitarkāvicārā bhūmi*). The monk Xingyou from Pujiusi in Puzhou embellished the composition of the 10 fascs., i.e. 'the Stage of Concentration' (*samāhitā bhūmi*), 'the Stage of Non-Concentration' (*asamāhitā bhūmi*), 'the Stage Having Mind' (*sacittakā bhūmi*), 'the Stage Having no Mind' (*acittakā bhūmi*), 'the Stage Yielded by Learning' (*śrutamayī bhūmi*), 'the Stage Yielded by Thought' (*cintāmayī bhūmi*), and 'the Stage Yielded by Practice' (*bhāvanāmayī bhūmi*). The monk Xuanze from Xuanfasi embellished the composition of the 9 fascs., i.e. from 'the Stage of Gotra' (*gotra-bhūmi*) of 'the First Place of Yogācāra' to the end of 'the Second Place of Yogācāra', in 'the Stage of Learners' (*śrāvaka-bhūmi*). The monk Xuanzhong from Zhendisi in Bianzhou embellished the composition of the 5 fascs., i.e. from 'the Third Place of Yogācāra' to 'the Stage of Solitary Realizer' (*pratyekabuddha-bhūmi*). The monk Jingmai from Fuzhongsi in Jianzhou embellished the composition of the 16 fascs., i.e. 'the Stage of Bodhisattvas' (*bodhisattva-bhūmi*), 'the Stage with Residue' (*sopadhiśeṣa-bhūmi*) and 'the Stage without Residue' (*nirupadhiśeṣa-bhūmi*). The monk Bianji from Dazongchisi embellished the composition of the 30 fascs. in 'the Part of the Comprehension of Resolution' (*viniścaya-saṃgraha*). The monk Chuheng from Puguangsi embellished the composition of the 4 fascs. in 'the Part of the Comprehension of the Methods of Teaching' (*paryāya-saṃgraha*) and 'the Part of the Comprehension of Exposition' (*vivaraṇa-saṃgraha*). The monk Mingjun from Hongfusi embellished the composition of the 16 fascs. in 'the Part of the Comprehension of Subjects' (*vastu-saṃgraha*). I, Xu Jingzong, who am the Yinqing guanglu dafu, Xingtaizi, Zuoshuzi and Gaoyangxian kaiguonan,

> fulfilled the role of inspector 監閱 according to the ordinance. On the 15th day of the 5th lunar month, 648, the translation was completed, consisting of 100 fascs. in total.[24]

Xuanzang is a special figure in the history of Chinese Buddhist translation, since he simultaneously recited and translated the original texts by himself, as did Kumārajīva. However, unlike Kumārajīva, who did not follow the typical translation procedure, he established a strict system for his translation work. In the above case, we note that there were various positions relating to the translation procedure as follows: 1) the reciter 執梵文; 2) the translator 譯為唐語; 3) the scribes 筆受; 4) the verifier of [the conformity of the translation with] the original text 證梵語; 5) the proof-reader 正字; 6) the vindicators of the meanings 證大義; 7) the embellishers of the composition 證文; and 8) a government inspector 監閱. In this specific case, Xuanzang played the first and second roles simultaneously.

As we can see from the structure of the Buddhist translation teams, one of the most conspicuous characteristics of Chinese Buddhist translation is the cooperation between various experts. Even those translators who had sufficient knowledge of both Indian languages and Chinese, such as Kumārajīva and Xuanzang, set up a process whereby they consulted other experts on Buddhism, as well as experts on other areas of Chinese literature, philosophy, history, etc. This system of

---

24. ... 二月六日還至長安, 奉勅於弘福寺安置, 令所司供給. 召諸名僧二十一人學通內外者, 譯持來三藏梵本. 至二十一年五月十五日, 肇譯《瑜伽師地論》. 論梵本四萬頌, 頌三十二字, 凡有五分, 宗明十七地義. 三藏法師玄奘, 敬執梵文, 譯為唐語; 弘福寺沙門靈會 · 靈雋 · 智開 · 知仁, 會昌寺沙門玄度, 瑤臺寺沙門道卓, 大總持寺沙門道觀, 清禪寺沙門明覺, (烝)[承] 義筆受; 弘福寺沙門玄謩, 證梵語; 大總持寺沙門玄應, 正字; 大總持寺沙門道洪, 實際寺沙門明琰, 寶昌寺沙門法祥, 羅漢寺沙門惠貴, 弘福寺沙門文備, 蒲州栖巖寺沙門神泰, 廓州法講寺沙門道深, 詳證大義. 〈本地分〉中, 〈五識身相應地〉·〈意地〉·〈有尋有伺地〉·〈無尋唯伺地〉·〈無尋無伺地〉, 凡十七卷, 普光寺沙門道智, 受旨證文; 〈三摩呬多地〉·〈非三摩呬多地〉·〈有心〉·〈無心地〉·〈聞所成地〉·〈思所成地〉·〈修所成地〉, 凡十卷, 蒲州普救寺沙門行友, 受旨證文; 〈聲聞地、初瑜伽、種姓地〉盡〈第二瑜伽處〉, 凡九卷, 玄法寺沙門玄賾, 受旨證文; 〈聲聞地、第三瑜伽處〉盡〈獨覺地〉, 凡五卷, 汴州真諦寺沙門玄忠, 受旨證文; 〈菩薩地〉·〈有餘依地〉·〈無餘依地〉, 凡十六卷, 簡州福眾寺沙門靖邁, 受旨證文; 〈攝決擇分〉, 凡三十卷, 大總持寺沙門辯機, 受旨證文; 〈攝異門分〉·〈攝釋分〉, 凡四卷, 普光寺沙門處衡, 受旨證文; 〈攝事分〉, 十六卷, 弘福寺沙門明濬, 受旨證文. 銀青光祿大夫行太子左庶子高陽縣開國男, 臣許敬宗, 奉詔監閱. 至二十二年五月十五日, 絕筆, 總成一百卷 (T1579.30.283c1–284a3).

cooperative translation made it possible for an exotic religion to reach the minds of Chinese people; it bears a resemblance to Indian food cooked by Chinese chefs and served to the Chinese. Making use of the raw materials provided by experts in Indian Buddhism and languages, experts in Chinese culture developed various 'recipes' to arouse interest in Buddhist doctrine amongst their Chinese readership. However, some of the 'seasoning' added by experts in Chinese culture was peculiar to China, and the readers were apt to lack the knowledge to distinguish genuine Indian ingredients from Chinese ones. As a result, believing that the entire content of these translations had been derived from Indian sources, Chinese Buddhists came to develop their own form of Buddhism, not realizing that some of its premises were peculiar to the Chinese intellectual tradition.

THE LINGUISTIC CHARACTERISTICS OF BUDDHIST TRANSLATION

The Preference for Stylish Translation

The translation system consisting of a group of experts could pursue two aims: delivering the exact meaning of the Indian or Central Asian texts; and attracting Chinese readers' interest in conversion to Buddhism. Neither aim could be ignored; however, as the structure of Buddhist translation teams shows, Chinese Buddhist translation had a strong inclination to aim at touching the Chinese readers' hearts.

In order to attract the readers' interest and exert an influence on them, translators made use of all possible literary skills. Except for the few cases where bilinguals born in China took the roles of both reciter and translator, experts in Chinese culture normally provided these skills. A famous anecdote illustrates how Chinese experts performed this task. With reference to the translation of the Sanskrit sentence, *devā api manuṣyān drakṣyanti, manuṣyā api devān drakṣyanti* ('Deities too will see people; people too will see deities'), in the chapter 'Pañcabhikṣuśata-vyākaraṇa-parivarta' of the *Saddharmapuṇḍarīka-sūtra* (SP: p.129_12–13), it is said:

> At the place of Kumārajīva's translation, Sengrui 僧叡 also participated as a corrector 參正. In the 'Chapter of Prediction' 受決品 of [the previous translation of] the *Saddharmapuṇḍarīka-sūtra* by Zhu Fahu (i.e., T263 正法華經, tr. in 286), it is said, 'Deities see people; people

> see deities' 天見人人見天.[25] When Kumārajīva translated [the text] up to this point, he said, 'This translation [by Zhu Fahu] delivers the same meaning as the western text. But the expression is too simple [to be eloquent].' Sengrui proposed, 'How about [translating it as] "People and deities are in touch with each other, and see each other" 人天交接兩得相見?' Kumārajīva answered, in delight, 'Yes, indeed. Any insightful expression [in translation work] must be like this!'[26]

The Chinese expression, 天見人人見天 ('Deities see people; people see deities'), literally conveys the meaning of the Sanskrit expression, *devā api manuṣyān drakṣyanti, manuṣyā api devān drakṣyanti*. However, Kumārajīva points out that the literal translation fails to deliver the tone of astonishment which the speaker of the Sanskrit text shows, according to Kumārajīva's view, and he praises Sengrui's translation, 人天交接兩得相見 ('People and deities are in touch with each other, and see each other'), since it conveys not only the meaning, but also the tone of astonishment that the speaker of the text 'intended' to share with his readers.

Word Order

The syntax of classical Chinese differs completely from that of South/Central Asian languages. Even after selecting appropriate renderings for Indian words, the Chinese translators faced the problem of how to order them correctly. The classical Chinese composition of the twelvefold dependent origination may well demonstrate the difficulty of putting the renderings in order. Due to the grammatical apparatus of Sanskrit, there is no difficulty in reading the two links of the twelvefold dependent origination, *Ṣaḍāyatana-pratyayaḥ sparśaḥ* (Dhsk, p. 43) and *sparśa-pratyayā vedanā* (p. 45), with the correct meaning of 'contact is dependent on the six faculties' and 'feeling is dependent on contact': the varying terminations of the compounds ending in *-pratyaya* assure that they are *bahuvrīhi* compounds, literally meaning 'contact has the six faculties as its condition' and 'feeling has contact as its condition.'

---

25. The present T263 does not coincide with the statement in the quotation. It actually says, '[Deities] in heaven see [people] in this world; [people] in this world can look at [deities in] heaven. Deities and people visit each other in companionship' 天上視世間，世間得見天上．天人・世人往來交接 (T263.9.95c28–29). It is possible that some touches were added to Zhu Fahu's original translation, or that the quoted anecdote is not based on fact.
26. 什所翻經, 叡並参正. 昔竺法護出《正法華經・受決品》云: '天見人, 人見天.' 什譯經至此, 乃言: '此語與西域義同, 但在言過質.' 叡曰: '將非: 人天交接, 兩得相見?' 什喜曰: '實然. 其領悟 標出, 皆此類也' (GSZ: T2059.50.364b26).

Let us first consider the translation by Xuanzang: in his translation of the *Dharmaskandha*, he translates the sentences as 六處緣觸, 觸緣受 (T1573.26.502a19). Note that he did not change the word order of the Sanskrit sentences: 六處 (*Ṣaḍāyatana*) 緣 (*-pratyayaḥ*) 觸 (*sparśaḥ*), 觸 (*sparśa*) 緣 (*-pratyayā*) 受 (*vedanā*). We can find the same translation of these sentences in Kumārajīva's T262 *Saddharmapuṇḍarīka-sūtra* (9.25a6) in 406, Buddhayaśas and Zhu Fonian's T1 *Dīrghāgama* (1.61b20–21) in 413, Guṇabhadra's T99 *Saṃyukātāgama* (2.79b26) around 435, etc. However, because of the word order of the translation, ordinary Chinese readers who had no knowledge of Buddhism and who found no syntactic apparatus assuring a *bahuvrīhi* reading would read this translation as 'The six faculties are dependent on contact; contact is dependent on feeling' or 'The condition of the six faculties is contact; the condition of contact is feeling,' which is the opposite of the intended meaning of the original text. If someone reads the translation as 'Contact is dependent on the six faculties; feeling is dependent on contact' in accordance with the original meaning, it would not be their knowledge of classical Chinese but their knowledge of Buddhism that would lead them to do so.

There are various ways of rephrasing the sentences to avoid confusion. Kumārajīva, the translator of T262 above, phrases the sentences as 從六入有觸, 從觸有受 in T1564 *Madhyamaka-śāstra* (30.18a13–14), which literally reads 'From the six faculties, there is contact; from contact, there is feeling.' The aforementioned T1 phrases them also as 緣六入有觸, 緣觸有受 (1.60b26–27), which literally reads 'Because of the six faculties, there is contact; because of contact, there is feeling.' Note that the word order of the sentences has changed: 從/緣 (*-pratyayaḥ*) 六入 (*ṣaḍāyatana*) 有觸 (*sparśaḥ*), 從/緣 (*-pratyayā*) 觸 (*sparśa*) 有受 (*vedanā*). This simple re-ordering of the words removes any potential confusion. Nonetheless, Guṇabhadra and Xuanzang restored the original word order, which may mislead readers, throughout their translations.

The Loss of Metre

In Indian verses, metres are measured by the number of syllables or by morae. In any case, the cadence decisive to the metre is determined by a particular pattern of heavy and light syllables. Classical Chinese, in contrast, draws no distinction between heavy and light syllables. Therefore, the loss of the Indian metres in the course of translation is inevitable. For this reason, as quoted on p. 5, Kumārajīva clarifies the difficulty of translating verse: 'However, when we translate Indian languages into Chinese, we lose the rhythm of sentences. Although the overall meaning may be delivered, there is a great difference in literary flavour.'

Instead of the Indian use of heavy and light syllables, various metres in Chinese poetry are defined by the number of syllables and by the combination of rhyme, tone and antithesis. It would be impractical to follow all of these rules when translating the tens, hundreds or thousands of verses in a Buddhist scripture. Hence, the verses in Chinese Buddhist translations have been defined only by their number of syllables. Ever since the translations of Kumārajīva (401–13), each verse is usually, although not always, a quatrain of lines of five or seven syllables. However, during the period of archaic translation, each verse might be a quatrain of lines of four, five, six or seven syllables. In T184.3.468b29–69a10, Lokakṣema wrote a series of quatrains of nine syllables, and in some archaic translations we find quatrains with a varying number of syllables, e.g., T5.1.174a9–b7.

The Translation Procedure and Linguistic Misunderstandings

As we saw above, certain linguistic characteristics of the original texts have to be abandoned, e.g., word order, metre, etc.; otherwise, the translation will be awkward or incomprehensible for the Chinese. The main concern of the Chinese experts who were involved in the translation was the selection of the proper renderings and the creation of a beautiful composition. Once a draft had been produced by the interpreters/translators 譯語 and scribes 筆受, other translation procedures followed, depending on the draft. Only when some suspicious matters were found in the draft could the verifier of [the conformity of the translation with] the original text 證梵語, the proof-reader 正字 or the vindicator of the meanings 證大義 request an amendment. This meant that although there may have been mistranslations in the first draft, provided they made perfect sense, these could easily go undetected throughout the rest of the translation procedure.

For example, in the *Vimalakīrti-nirdeśa*, Vimalakīrti is praised for his virtue as *upāyakauśalyagatiṅgata* (VKN: p. 54_6–7). Among the three extant Chinese translations, i.e., T474 *Weimojie jing* 維摩詰經 by Zhi Qian, T475 *Weimojie suoshuo jing* 維摩詰所說經 by Kumārajīva and T476 *Shuo wugoucheng jing* 說無垢稱經 by Xuanzang,[27] there is no

27. By chance, all of the translators of these three translations were bilingual. They are celebrated for being qualified to recite and translate by themselves.

disagreement over the translation of the term *upāyakauśalya*, which means 'skilfulness in means', but there is disagreement over the translation of *gatiṅgata:* 'entering the places of rebirth' or 'having mastery of'. Zhi Qian translates *upāyakauśalyagatiṅgata* as '[one] who has far and wide entered the places of rebirth (*gati*) with skilful means' 善權方便博入諸道 (T474.14.520c27), whereas both Kumārajīva and Xuanzang translate it as '[one] who had mastery in [skilful] means' 通達方便 (T475.14.539a11; T476.14.560b10). Given that the word *gatiṅgata* is used only as an idiom meaning 'attaining', 'knowing', or 'mastering' in the Mahāyāna texts,[28] Zhi Qian's choice may be a mistranslation. Nonetheless, it makes perfect sense in that context: a *bodhisattva* enters various places of rebirth for the sake of saving living beings, although he or she is free from rebirth. Due to the fact that it makes perfect sense, the other assistants in the process of translation, who depended on Zhi Qian's first draft, may have had no way of detecting this possible mistranslation.[29]

Clearly, the translators, interpreters and scribes performed important roles. In most cases, the translators/interpreters were Chinese people or China-born children of immigrants who had been educated in China; the scribes were not necessarily expected to be versed in the original languages, but outstanding skills in Chinese literature and philosophy were required. They performed the first and most influential adaptations in the translation. When their adaptations made perfect sense, other Chinese experts and readers were apt to accept even the additional implications of the adaptations as the truth transmitted from the Indian texts.

Linguistic Apparatus and Unexpected Readings

It happens that, due to the language in which readers think, they may read something different from what the translators intended. The reading of

28. The Sanskrit-Japanese dictionary 漢訳對照梵和大辞典 by Ogiwara (1964, pp. 413–14) introduces the following Chinese renderings for *gatiṅgata*: 到 (to reach), 入 (to enter); 得 (to attain); 知 (to know); 通達 (to master), 通曉 (to know thoroughly), 已得通達 (having already mastered); 了 (to understand), 了達 (to understand thoroughly); 已窮盡 (having already exhausted); 究竟 (to complete); 究竟修已 (having completely practised), and 究竟得自在 (completely being as one wishes), which are found in the translations of the *Lalita-vistara*, the *Aṣṭasāhasrikā Prajñāpāramitā*, the *Saddharmapuṇḍarīka-sūtra*, the *Gaṇḍa-vyūha*, the *Samādhirāja-sūtra*, the *Sukhāvatī-vyūha*, the *Rāṣṭrapāla-paripṛcchā*, the *Laṅkāvatāra-sūtra*, the *Śikṣāsamuccaya* and the *Mahāvyutpatti*. None of these is translated as 'entering the places of rebirth'.
29. We find the same differences in the translation of *gatiṅgata* of VKN: p. 298_4–6 at T474.14.529b16–18, T475.14.548c29–49a2 and T476.14.575a5–7.

kongyixianse 空一顯色 may represent a typical example of this. Having listed twenty kinds of visible object (*rūpa*, 色) in the *Abhidharmakośa-bhāṣya*, Vasubandhu adds the following information:

> *kecit nabhaś câikavarṇam iti ekaviṃśatiṃ sampaṭhanti*. ('Some [masters] transmit the teaching that there are twenty-one [kinds of visible object], since the sky also has a colour.') (AbhK: p. 26_9–10, comm. to §1.10)

Here, I read *ekavarṇam* as a *bahuvrīhi* compound, not a *karmadhāraya*. However, since *varṇa* is sporadically used as a neuter, it may also be a *karmadhāraya* compound. In this case, we should translate *nabhaś câikavarṇam* as 'The sky is also a colour'. The concern now is that, in both readings, *nabhaś câikavarṇam* is a sentence, consisting of a subject (*nabhas*), a conjunction (*ca*) and a subjective complement (*ekavarṇa*).[30]

Paramārtha (真諦: 499–569) translates this as:

> 有餘師說: '空為一色, 故有二十一色.' ('Some masters say, "The sky is a colour. Therefore, there are twenty-one kinds of visible object."') (T1559.29.163a19–20)

Here, note, firstly, that *ekavarṇa* is read as a *karmadhāraya*, and, secondly, that the same character *se* 色 is read as 'colour' in the first location, but as 'a visible object' in the second.[31]

With reference to the same passage, Xuanzang translates: 有餘師說: '空一顯色, 第二十一' (T1558.29.2b28–29). Here Xuanzang's translation is ambiguous: we can read it as 'Some masters say, "A certain colour in the form of the sky is the twenty-first visible object,"' or as 'Some masters say, "The sky is a colour; this is the twenty-first visible object."' Since the Sanskrit expression, *nabhaś câikavarṇam*, is not a compound but a sentence, Xuanzang must have intended the latter reading, also regarding *ekavarṇa* as a *karmadhāraya* compound.

Paramārtha's translation makes it clear that the original expression is a sentence; however, it loses the distinction between *varṇa* (colour) and *rūpa* (visible object) by using the same rendering *se* 色 for both. Following the preference for the regularity of four syllables in a classical Chinese phrase, Xuanzang may have omitted the copula *wei* 為 and added the adjective *xian* 顯 before *se* 色 in order to distinguish *varṇa* (colour,

---

30. The commentary on the *Abhidharmakośa-bhāṣya* by Yaśomitra confirms that there was no corruption in the Sanskrit expression in question. The commentary still preserves *nabhaś câikavarṇam iti* (AbhK-vy, p. 25_15).
31. The Chinese word *se* 色 originally means colour. Only in the technical sense in Buddhist texts does *se* stand for material or visible objects.

顯色) from *rūpa* (visible object, 色). Xuanzang's amendment made the distinction clear, but it simultaneously made ambiguous whether the sequence of four words is a compound or a sentence. Xuanzang maintained consistency for the translation of *nabhaś câikavarṇam* as *kongyixianse* 空一顯色 throughout his translations, and it reads like a compound in many of the translations.[32]

In the field of Chinese Abhidharma, Xuanzang's renderings became the norm, and most of the later Chinese Buddhists read only his translation of the *Kośa*, rather than that of Paramārtha. Although Xuanzang may have expected his readers to read *kongyixianse* 空一顯色 as a sentence, even highly educated Buddhists have read it as a compound. Puguang 普光, the pupil of Xuanzang and renowned commentator on Xuanzang's translation of the *Kośa*, gives the following detailed explanation of *kongyixianse* in his commentary:

> Q: If the real nature 體 [of *kongyixianse* 空一顯色] is the colour of the space element (*ākāśa-dhātu*), why does the 11th fasc. of the *Abhidharma-vijñānakāya-pāda* announce, '*kongyixianse*: this is the same as the blue, yellow, red and white that are mentioned previously'?[33] If what the treatise announces is right, the real nature [of the *kongyixianse*] is the [colours] blue, yellow, red and white, [which have already been listed; therefore, there is no independent 21st visible object].
>
> A: What the treatise says, 'the same as the blue, yellow, red and white that are mentioned previously', signifies the respective colours that appear in the sky in the four directions surrounding Mt. Sumeru; it is called the colour of the space element. [There] 'the same as' means 'similar to'. This *kongyixianse* is similar to the blue, yellow, red and white that are mentioned previously; it is not the very [blue etc.]. Another possible answer is, 'Yes, it is.' [There] 'the same as' means 'the very'. This *kongyixianse* is the very blue, yellow, red and white which are mentioned previously.[34]

---

32. See T1537 *Abhidharma-dharmaskandha-pāda* (26.500a18), T1539 *Abhidharma-vijñānakāya-pāda* (26.583a16), T1545 *Abhidharma-mahāvibhāṣā-śāstra* (27. 64a7–9, 390b23), T1562 *Abhidharma-nyāyānusāra-śāstra* (29.334a11), T1579 *Yogācārabhūmi* (30.279b6), T1602 *Āryadeśanā-vikhyāpana* (31.483c18), T1605 *Mahāyānâbhidharma-samuccaya* (31.663c3) and T1606 *Mahāyānâbhidharma-samuccaya-vyākhyā* (31.696a24–29).

33. With the help of Sanskrit AbhK and AbhK-vy mentioned above, I would read the sentence in question, 空一顯色, 此即如彼青・黃・赤・白, as 'The sky has/is a certain colour; it is the same as the blue, yellow, red and white that are mentioned previously,' regarding *kongyixianse* as a sentence. However, here, Puguang read it as a compound.

34. 問: 若以空界色為體者, 何故, 《識身論》第十一云: '空一顯色, 此即如彼青・黃・赤・白'? 准彼論文, 即以青・黃・赤・白為體. 解云: 彼論言:

We see that Puguang modifies *kongyixianse* with the pronominal adjective 'this' 彼. This modification indicates that Puguang evidently regarded *kongyixianse* as a compound which means 'a certain colour in the form of the sky'. For this specific translation and interpretation, no one deserves blame. Xuanzang did not mistranslate; he simply removed the redundant copula *wei*, in order to distinguish *varṇa* from *rūpa*. The readers did not misread; in Xuanzang's translations, *kongyixianse* is suggested to be a compound.

ADAPTATIONS AND INDIGENOUS WAYS OF THINKING

Cultural Understanding

Sometimes cultural differences, along with linguistic differences, cause misunderstandings. A good example of this is *dvipadôttama*, 'supreme among bipeds', one of the epithets of the Buddha. Chinese translators translated this as *liangzuzun* 兩足尊. However, the Chinese Buddhists interpreted *liangzuzun* in two ways: firstly, supreme among bipeds (兩足尊: two-foot-supreme) and, secondly, the supreme one who is perfect in two qualities (兩足尊: two-complete-supreme), i.e., in the quality of merit and that of wisdom:

> [The Buddha is called *liangzuzun*,] firstly, since the good places of rebirth, i.e. the world of human beings and the world of deities, are honourably appreciated for their being [the realm of] the bipeds, and since the Buddha is the most honourable among them. Secondly, since he perfectly possesses both merit and wisdom, Buddha is called '*liangzu*' ('two-complete').[35]

Interestingly, the second interpretation, which is irrelevant to the original meaning, prevailed among Chinese Buddhists, and the first remained unpopular among ordinary Buddhists; only learned Buddhists who knew Sanskrit or were versed in Buddhist doctrine made use of the first definition.

It is uncertain whether the second interpretation is a Chinese invention or a transmission of a minor exegesis that originated in South/Central Asian Buddhism, but the reason why the second interpretation finally

---

'如彼青・黃・赤・白'者, 謂妙高山四邊空中, 各現一色, 名空界色. '如'之言: 似. 此空一顯色, 似彼青・黃・赤・白, 非即是也. 或可. '如'之言: 是. 此空一顯色, 即是彼青・黃・赤・白 (T1821 Jushelun ji 俱舍論記: 41.17a4–11).

35. 一約: 人天善趣兩足為貴, 於佛天人中尊. 二約: 福・慧俱備, 名為兩足 (T1786.39.118c8–9).

prevailed among the Chinese Buddhists can be found in the different meanings of the Chinese rendering *zu* 足 and their cultural implications. The Chinese word *zu* has two meanings: the noun 'foot' and the verb 'to complete, satisfy or possess'. In India, the biped is regarded as the supreme form of creature, so *dvipadôttama* means 'the supreme among supreme beings'. However, the Chinese do not value bipeds; it is not what Chinese Buddhists would have expected as an epithet of the Buddha.

The prevalence of the second, irrelevant interpretation among Chinese Buddhists was probably facilitated by the common use of *zu* between the rendering *liangzuzun* 兩足尊 for *dvipadôttama* and the rendering *mingxingzu* (明行足: knowledge-conduct-complete) for *vidyā-caraṇa-sampanna*. Being one of the ten epithets, *mingxingzu* (明行足: *vidyā-caraṇa-sampanna*) has more frequently been cited; and it must have been in Chinese readers' minds when they encountered *liangzuzun* (兩足尊: *dvipadôttama*), so they interpreted the *zu* in both epithets as 'complete'.

This is a trivial example of a Chinese Buddhist misinterpretation. Yet, the way in which it came about is crucial to understanding the development of Buddhism in China: Chinese readers read Buddhist terms with their Chinese implications. When this kind of misinterpretation happened to critical terms, such as *ātman*, *nirvāṇa*, *śūnyatā*, it was inevitable that Buddhism would develop in a way peculiar to China.

Adaptations and Unexpected Implications

Some passages in T210 *Dharmapada* 法句經 may well demonstrate how the kindness of translators could produce unexpected side-effects. For example, while the Sanskrit *Udānavarga* §1.35 states:

> Soon this body shall lie on the earth.
> Being insensible, without consciousness, like a cast-down stick.[36]

---

36. *[aciraṃ bata] kāyo 'yaṃ pṛthivīm adhiśeṣyate,*
śūnyo vyapetavijñāno nirastaṃ vā kaḍaṅgaram (Ud §1.35).

The corresponding Pali *Dhammapada*, the Patna *Dharmapada* and the Gāndhārī *Dharmapada* read:

aciraṃ vat' ayaṃ kāyo paṭhaviṃ adhisessati,
chuddho apetaviññāṇo niratthaṃ va kaliṅgaraṃ. (Dhp_P §41)

acirā vata ayaṃ kāyo paṭhaviṃ dahiśehiti,
chūḍo apetaviṃnyāno nirātthaṃ vā kaṭiṃgaraṃ. (Dhp_Pat §349)

ayireṇa vada'i kayu paḍha'i vari śa 'iṣidi,
tuchu [avaka-]daviñaṇa niratha ba kaḍiġara. (Dhp_G §153)

it is translated at T210.4.563a14–15 as follows:

> All bodies shall return to the soil.
> The shape shall be destroyed and *shen* shall leave [the body].
> Why would we be attached to it?[37]

Of interest is the translation of *vyapetavijñāna*, etc., as *shenqu* 神去. Although *shi* 識 has been a standard rendering for *vijñāna* from the beginning of Chinese Buddhist translation, as well as in T210, the translators Zhu Jiangyan and Zhi Qian chose *shen* rather than *shi* for *vijñāna* in this particular context.

It appears that, while the Indian translator Zhu Jiangyan may not have fully understood the implications of *shen*, the Chinese translator Zhi Qian may have read *vijñāna* as indicating an agent in *saṃsāra*. As I argue in Part II, when reading *vyapetavijñāna*, etc., a learned Indian Buddhist would have envisaged the cessation of impermanent consciousnesses, a series of which succeeded one another in connection with the body, since *vijñāna* in Indian Buddhism is regarded as a momentary mental action rather than an abiding agent of thought. On the contrary, as I argue in Part III, reading *shenqu* 神去, a learned Chinese Buddhist would have envisaged the departure of a permanent agent of perception from the body, due to the implications of *shen* in Chinese Buddhist usage. Once the translation had been completed, the majority of Chinese readers could have read only the implications of *shen*, because they were isolated from the information that *shen* was indeed a translation of *vijñāna*, a momentary mental action. Apart from the original intention of the particular translators, the fact that the Chinese Buddhists read the implication of a permanent agent in *saṃsāra* from the rendering is certain, judging from their debates on the doctrine of an imperishable *shen*. Those I shall examine in Chapter 9.

Censorial Deletion through Cultural Considerations

Cultural differences may drive translators to fail to translate certain expressions, since these may have forbidden implications in the other culture. For example, in the *Sakkapañha-sutta* of the *Dīgha-nikāya*, the divine musician, Pañcasikha, recites 'the verses relevant to the Buddha, the teaching, *arahants* and love' (D.II.265). The following is one of those verses:

---

37. 有身不久 皆當歸土 形壞神去 寄住何貪.

Embrace me, O lady of beautiful thighs.
Embrace me, O [lady] of tender eyes.
Fully embrace me, O beautiful girl.
This is what I am longing for.[38]

Among Buddhist drawings and sculptures before the fifth century CE, we can see the female breasts exposed, but not their thighs, which are always covered by long skirts, unless they are such beings as demonesses. Given that the artistic works reflect the custom of that time, it seems inappropriate to call a lady who is under the protection of a father (king Timbaru) and who has fallen in love with another man a 'lady of beautiful thighs'; the expression may imply a lack of chastity, by indicating, 'I have seen your thighs'. This is the more so because it is uttered in the vocative.

We have four Chinese translations corresponding to this Pali text: 1) the *Shi tihuanyin wen jing* 釋提桓因問經, in T1 *Dīrghāgama* (1.62b–66a, tr. Buddhayaśas and Zhu Fonian in 413); 2) the *Dapin shi wen jing* 大品釋問經, in T26 *Madhyamāgama* (1.632c–638c, tr. Saṃghadeva in 397–401); 3) the *Dishi wen shiyuan* 帝釋問事緣 in T203 **Saṃyukta-ratnakośa-sūtra* 雜寶藏經 (4.476a–478b, tr. Jijiaye 吉迦夜 and Tanyao 曇曜 between 465 and 472); and 4) the *Dishi suowen jing* 帝釋所問經 (T15.1.246b–250c, tr. Faxian 法賢 between 973 and 1001). None of these four Chinese translations contains the expression, 'lady of beautiful thighs'. Since none of the original Indian texts of these Chinese translations remains, we cannot tell whether the translators intentionally left the expression in question untranslated or not. However, suppose that there were such an expression in the original text and that the translator omitted it. Should we regard the translator's failure to translate it as an intended distortion? Given that the Buddhist translators aimed to promote Buddhism in China, and that such a sensual expression, which might be compatible with the spirit of Buddhism in India, was never allowable in Chinese society, would it have been appropriate to translate the expression into Chinese?

Compare the English translation of the Pali verse by Mrs Rhys Davids (1899–1921: vol. 2, p.301):

Within thine arm embrace me, lady, me
With thy soft languid eyne embrace and hold,
O nobly fair! This I entreat of thee.

---

38. *vām'ūru saja maṃ bhadde, saja maṃ mandalocane,*
palissaja maṃ kalyāṇi, etam me abhipatthitaṃ.
(D.II.266. I read *vām'ūru* for *vāmurū* with PED.)

We note that she translates *vām'ūru* as 'thine arm', although, as the commentary to the Pali verse explains, *vām'ūru* means 'a beautiful thigh'.[39] She was surely aware of the sensual implication of the expression and so avoided translating the original meaning. The Chinese Buddhist translators, if there had been such an expression in the original texts, would have acted similarly to Mrs Rhys Davids.

THE PHILOSOPHICAL AND ETHICAL DEMANDS OF INTERPOLATIONS

In order to make the exotic teaching of Indian Buddhism understood by the Chinese, the Buddhist translators inserted certain terms and expressions of philosophical explanation, or rephrased some ethical utterances that were alien to the Chinese. We do find some cases where the translators arbitrarily interpolated their own opinions and distorted the whole context as if they were the spokesmen of the Buddha. I here examine the interpolations in T20 *Ambāṣṭha-sūtra* 佛開解梵志阿經, as a case study of this. However, T20 is an extraordinary example in terms of the extent of interpolation: the text is full of interpolations and systematic distortions. We should be aware that by contrast the great majority of Chinese Buddhist translations include merely fragmentary and sporadic interpolations; the extreme case of T20 should not be generalized to the whole body of canonical translations.

The Ambāṣṭha-sūtra

The *Ambāṣṭha-sūtra* is a dialogue between the Buddha and a brahmin pupil and master, Ambāṣṭha and Pauṣkarasārin. The *sūtra* starts with the Buddha's arrival at a forest near the village of Pauṣkarasārin in Kosala. Pauṣkarasārin hears of the fame of the Buddha as a fully awakened one in possession of 32 legendary bodily marks, and orders his pupil, Ambāṣṭha, to visit the Buddha and check the bodily marks which prove his status. During a visit to the Buddha, Ambāṣṭha shows arrogance as a member of the brahmin caste, and the Buddha brings shame on him by revealing his family origins: the lineage of Ambāṣṭha originated from a

39. *vām'ūrû ti vām'ākārena saṇṭhita-ūru, kadali-kkhandha-sadisā ūrû ti vā attho.* '*Vām'ūru* means '[having] thighs of beautiful shape' or '[having] thighs [that resemble] the trunk of a banana tree' (Sv.III.702).

slave of the Śākyas, the pure kṣatriya lineage of the Buddha. Further, the Buddha makes a general declaration that the kṣatriya is the highest caste, along with the declaration that one possessed of [perfect] knowledge and conduct is the highest among gods and people. When asked about conduct and knowledge by Ambāṣṭha, the Buddha presents the details of Buddhist conduct and knowledge, as described in the *Sāmaññaphala-sutta* (D.I.62–84). After Ambāṣṭha returns and reports the conversation to Pauṣkarasārin, the master visits the Buddha himself, apologizes for Ambāṣṭha's rudeness, serves a meal to the Buddha and monks, listens to the Buddha, and attains Buddhist knowledge.

As complete recensions of the *Ambāṣṭha-sūtra*, one Pali, one Sanskrit and four Chinese texts are extant.[40]

1. The Pali *Ambaṣṭha-sutta* [PA] (D.I.87–110) is the third *sutta* in the *Dīgha-nikāya*. Generally speaking, PA is the richest of the six texts: although it does not relate new information, its composition style is, however, wordy, repetitive and standardized. As to the order of its paragraphs, we find that PA frequently differs from the other four texts: e.g., §§1.2–3, §§1.16–19, §§2.6–9 and §§2.19–22. According to the order of *sutta*s in the *Dīgha-nikāya*, it refers back to the second *Sāmaññaphala-sutta* concerning the details about Buddhist precepts, meditation and knowledge.
2. According to the Sanskrit *Dīrghāgama*, as preliminarily transcribed by Cousins and Vasudeva,[41] the Sanskrit *Ambāṣṭha-sūtra* [SA] is the eleventh *sūtra* in the third and final section (*nipāta*).[42] The manuscript of the *Āgama* has been radio-carbon-dated to the eighth century. With few differences, SA coincides with the stories in T1451 and T1448, which are introduced below. This supports the view that the Sanskrit *Dīrghāgama* is a Sarvāstivādin recension.[43]

---

40. In this book, I am concerned only with Indian and Chinese recensions. For the two Tibetan recensions of the *Ambāṣṭha-sūtra*, refer to Meisig, 1993, p. 119, n.1.
41. I am grateful to L. S. Cousins and Somadeva Vasudeva for the use of their preliminary transcript of the manuscript of this *sūtra*. I also thank Dr Gudrun Melzer for her kind information about the Sanskrit and Tibetan recensions of the *Ambāṣṭha-sūtra*.
42. For more information about the manuscript of this *Dīrghāgama*, refer to Hartmann, 2004, esp. pp. 119–28.
43. For a Sanskrit fragment corresponding to PA §§2.12–14, see Hartmann, 1989, pp. 63–4. The content of this fragment is similar, although not identical, to SA.

3. T20 *Fo kaijie fanzhi aba jing* 佛開解梵志阿經 (T20.1.259c–264a) is possibly the translation by Zhi Qian or, more probably, his successor in the late third century, as I argue in Chapter 2. This text will be described in detail below.
4. The *Amozhou jing* 阿摩晝經 (T1.1.82a–88a) is the twentieth *sūtra* in T1 *Dīrghāgama*; it is the first *sūtra* of the third section of the *Āgama*, which consists of four sections. It was translated by Buddhayaśas and Zhu Fonian in 413 (T2145.55.63c). T1 is widely acknowledged to be an *Āgama* of the Dharmaguptakas.[44]
5. T1451 **Mūlasarvāstivāda-vinaya-kṣudraka-vastu* 根本說一切有部毘奈耶雜事 (24. 378b–80b), and
6. T1448 *Mūlasarvāstivāda-vinaya-bhaiṣajya-vastu* 根本說一切有部毘奈耶藥事 (24.34c–35a) were translated by Yijing (義淨: 635–713) in 710 and between 700 and 711 respectively. In T1451, the *Ambāṣṭha-sūtra* is narrated as the origin of the monastic precept that prohibits monks from consuming food while the *dakṣiṇāgāthā* (施頌: the song of gratitude for alms) is being recited.

The anecdote about an aged monk noisily chomping on a certain type of biscuit (乾餅, *śaṣkulikā*) after the meals of Pauṣkarasārin had been served is included only in SA and T1451 among the six texts. T1451 lacks a description of the general superiority of the kṣatriya over the brahmin, an introduction to Buddhist conduct and knowledge, and the Buddha's criticism of Pauṣkarasārin's teaching; T1448 describes everything up to the general superiority of the kṣatriya over the brahmin, but omits the stories after the introduction to Buddhist conduct and knowledge, referring to the *Amozhou jing* in T1.

The Distortions and Interpolations in T20

Of the six texts, only T20 announces that the dialogue took place in Yuezhi 越祇[45] rather than in Kosala. As for the writing style, T20 is the shortest of the six texts, not because it contains less information but because it is terse and lacks repetition. In contrast to its terse expressions, we sometimes find in T20 dramatic expressions which appear to be a form

44. For this attribution, refer to Waldschmidt, 1980, p.136, and Mayeda, 1985, p. 97.
45. Yuezhi probably designates the republic of Vṛji people (Pa. Vajjī), as we can see at T5.1.160b10 and T6.1.176a6.

of arbitrary rephrasing: e.g., the conversation between Pauṣkarasārin and Ambāṣṭha, when the master orders the pupil to visit and test the Buddha (259c10–21), and the conversation when Ambāṣṭha reports his visit to Pauṣkarasārin (263c1–11).

In PA, SA/T1451/T1448 and T1, we find a discrepancy in the voice of the storyteller:

1. Up to the part corresponding to PA §1.23, Ambāṣṭha humiliates the Buddha over the impoliteness of the Śākya youths; the Buddha defends himself, proclaiming the purity of the Śākya lineage, and brings shame on Ambāṣṭha, divulging that his lineage originated from a slave of the Śākyas; then the Buddha saves Ambāṣṭha from the criticism of his brahmin colleagues by stating that his ancestor, the son of the female Śākya slave, was a sage (*ṛṣi*) with awesome supernatural powers. The concern in this part is not the virtues of an individual, but the purity of a specific family lineage.
2. However, in the part corresponding to PA §§1.24–2.10, with a general declaration that the kṣatriya is superior to the brahmin, the Buddha proclaims that the most important factor is one's individual knowledge and conduct. Then he dismisses Ambāṣṭha's attack as worthless, since he and his master lack the highest conduct and knowledge in the Buddhist sense, and since they do not live as taught by the founders of Brahmanism. The voice of this part sounds reasonable and general.
3. Then, from the part corresponding to PA §2.11, the naïve and specific voice of the first part returns: the Buddha reveals the 32 bodily marks, which prove his status, and Pauṣkarasārin serves food to the Buddha and the monks, and becomes a Buddhist after hearing the teaching of the Buddha. Here, the authority of the Buddha's teaching is not acknowledged because of its truth, but because of his appearance, i.e., the legendary bodily marks.

Regarding this, the voice of T20 sounds consistent: (1) instead of criticizing the impoliteness of the Śākya youths, Ambāṣṭha asks why the Buddha has his head shaved, wears a motley-coloured robe (*kāṣāya*) and holds a bowl (*pātra*), and the Buddha replies in terms of Buddhist morality (1.260a4–12); (2) in PA, SA/T1451/T1448 and T1, Ambāṣṭha insists on the superiority of the brahmins without offering any supporting argument, whereas in T20 he insists on the superiority because only the brahmins dislike killing (260a12–25); (3) while the other texts relate the story of King Ikṣvāku as an argument to support the purity of the Buddha's own breed, T20 employs the story to justify the superiority of the practice of individual virtues to the continuation of the family lineage (260a25–b11); (4) when Ambāṣṭha is criticized by his own colleagues, the Buddha saves him, not by mentioning the power of his ancestral sage, but by mentioning Ambāṣṭha's own virtue (260b22–24); (5) when discussing the case of sons of mixed caste, PA, SA and T1 argue for the superiority of the kṣatriya over the brahmin, whereas T20 emphasizes the virtues of the sons, regardless of their caste (260b24–c6). In short, the voice in question throughout T20 is consistent: what is important is not the breed or caste of a person, but his/her own virtues.

Note that the aforementioned parts (1) to (5) are unique to T20, being different or absent from the other five texts, and that the difference makes the voice of T20 consistent with respect to the importance of individual virtues. Since the original text of the translation of T20 is no longer extant, it is impossible to provide textual evidence that this consistency of voice comes not from the original text but from the Chinese reworking of it. However, many facts in the unique parts of T20, especially the content of (1) to (3), show that it must include abundant interpolations that originated in China.

Chinese Concerns in T20

Above all, the unique parts are full of views and terms peculiar to Chinese culture. As for Chinese terms, (1) in 260a4–12, having explained why monks have their heads shaved, etc., the Buddha defines this as the representation of *wuwei* (無為: lit. non-action) and *qingjing* (清淨: purity). (2) In 260a12–25, the Buddha announces that he teaches *renyi* (仁義: benevolence and righteousness), a pair of technical terms that represent Confucianism. (3) In 260a25–b11, King Ikṣvāku sighs, 'Nothing to be hoped for in life; having no worry is the best way!' 人生無幾, 無憂乃長,[46] a popular slogan of the Daoist or Chinese folk view of life. Indeed, these kinds of Chinese terms and expressions occur occasionally in other parts, i.e., those that are also common to the other four texts. However, in the common parts, these interpolations are inserted through the selection of Chinese renderings in accordance with the Indian context, whereas the interpolations in (1) to (3) above are inserted in accordance with the major Chinese concerns of that time. We can detect these Chinese concerns through making a comparison of the topics of (1) to (3) with

46. 人生無幾 may also mean 'life is short,' but 'nothing to be hoped for in life' is more plausible in this context.

those of the *Mouzi lihuo lun* [MLL] 牟子理惑論 (T2102.52.1a–7a), whose exact date is uncertain, but whose content reflects the earliest features of Chinese Buddhism not as translated from the Indian texts but in the view of the Chinese themselves.[47]

1. In the other four texts, Ambāṣṭha humiliates the Buddha, brutally abusing the Śākyas for the Śākya youths' impoliteness to a brahmin. This is a serious attack on the Buddha in Indian culture. However, this matters little to the Chinese, since for the Chinese all Indians are 'barbarians' 胡, regardless of their caste.[48] Contrarily, in T20, instead of attempting to disgrace the Buddha over his lineage, Ambāṣṭha asks why the Buddha has his head shaved, etc., and the Buddha presents an apology on that topic. In the Indian context, these matters merely reflect the peculiar appearance of Buddhist monks, whereas from an influential Chinese perspective they represent the immorality of Buddhist monks. In particular, shaving one's head has been regarded as one of the most immoral aspects of Buddhist monks throughout the history of China, which since the Han dynasty (漢: 206 BCE–220 CE) was governed by the Confucian ideology of filial piety. A typical attack on Buddhism on this ground is presented in MLL:

> Q: The *Xiao jing* (孝經: *Scripture on Filial Piety*) announces, 'Any part of the body, even the body-hair and the skin, should not be damaged, since it is given by the parents.' And, in his final moments, Zengzi (曾子: 505–436 BCE) [summoned his sons and] said, 'Uncover my hands, uncover my feet. [Is there any part damaged?]' Now, Buddhist monks shave their heads. How could a person go against the saints' words and violate the duty of filial piety [so deeply]? You have always enjoyed discussing rights and wrongs and reviewing others' honesty and duplicity. Then, how could you contrarily praise it (i.e., monks' shaving)?[49]

---

47. As for the attribution of MLL to Mouzi, two points are debatable: firstly, is Mouzi a historical person? Secondly, is Mouzi the author of MLL? While raising no question about the second point, Tang (1973 [1938]: pp. 73–80) argues that the historical accuracy of the biography of Mouzi, at the beginning of MLL, verifies Mouzi's historical existence, and that the work may have been written in the late second or early third century. However, the content of MLL includes matters reflecting the situation in the mid-third century. For more details on the historical veracity of this text, refer to Keenan, 1994, pp. 3–7, and Zürcher, 1972, pp. 13–15.
48. The Buddha has occasionally been designated as 'the barbarian elder' 胡老, even in Buddhist texts in China.
49. 問曰：孝經言：'身體髮膚，受之父母，不敢毀傷.' 曾子臨沒：'啟予手，啟予足.' 今沙門剃頭，何其違聖人之語，不合孝子之道也? 吾子常好論是非・平曲直，而反善之乎? (T2102.52.2c).

In addition, the motley robe may look unusual, but never immoral, in Indian culture. However, some Chinese people regarded even the mere style of dress as an apostasy from the glorious heritage of China (T2102.52.2c23–28). Also, in India holding a bowl represents living on alms, and the custom of mendicancy was common among religious practitioners; but for some Chinese people this represents an excessive asceticism that conflicts with the teachings of the Chinese saints (T2102.52.4c1–4).

2. In the first half of T20.1.260a12–25, Ambāṣṭha proclaims the superiority of the brahmin to the kṣatriya 王 because of the former's love of non-violence. The Buddha replies, 'You brahmins pay lip service to benevolence. Although you don't kill with your hands, your hearts are full of killing. I am now a Buddha, my body, speech and mind are pure, and I never kill.' Note that the Buddha proclaims the superiority neither of the Śākya clan nor of the kṣatriya; instead, he argues for his own moral virtues. In other words, in T20, the superiority of a certain social group in a 'barbarian' society is not proclaimed, but that of a virtuous individual. With regard to this point, being full of apologetics against sinocentrism, MLL shows similar concerns. While Sinocentrists criticize Buddhism as barbarian teaching, Mouzi emphasizes the individual virtues, regardless of the superiority or inferiority of the social group to which one belongs (e.g., T2102.52.2b26–c8, 3a23–3b3, 3c10–26 and 5c11–24).

In the second half of 260a12–25, Ambāṣṭha proclaims the superiority of his teacher to the Buddha, since while the teacher continues his family lineage, the Buddha has forsaken his wife and son. The Buddha defends himself as follows: 'All meetings and separations that occur according to causes and conditions are illusory. In the beginning [i.e., in past lives], [my present] parents, wife and children were not my relatives; nor did I belong to them. Discriminating between mine and others', people in the world fall into sin and suffer painful results in return.'[50]

3. Then, in 260a25–b11, instead of proclaiming the purity of the Śākya clan,[51] as do the other five texts, the Buddha proclaims the meaninglessness of the householder life. Being worried that his four princes, who are already in conflict, may kill innocent subjects in order to attain

50. 因緣離合，一切如幻. 父母妻子本非我親，吾亦非彼有. 世人但以是我・非我，而為罪惡，為後受苦.

51. T1421 *Mahīśāsaka-vinaya* 彌沙塞部和醯五分律 (22.101a13 f.) also presents an anecdote of the beginning of the Śākya clan. The story of T1421 is similar to that of PA, SA/T1451/T1448 and T1.

the throne, King Ikṣvāku, who was the Buddha himself in a past life, becomes a monk, thinking, 'Now, being a king, I wished for offspring. But now that I have sons, contrary [to my wishes,] they want to attack each other. What use is it for people to have offspring like this?'[52] Having left the householder life, King Ikṣvāku encourages an ascetic called Mali 摩離, who left home in shame at having no offspring, to dedicate himself to religious practice. Finally, the Buddha concludes,

> In this way, Ambāṣṭha, no matter how wise a son is, he can neither stop the ageing, disease and death of his father, nor go to a hell instead of the father who committed sins while he was alive. For this reason, I always save all beings with thoughts of loving kindness (*maitrī*). [Having left family life,] I have realized truth (*dao*), have become the Buddha, and am saving all the creatures in the world.[53]

Superiority among castes is a problem that Indian Buddhists confronted to gain religious authority among Indian people. However, in the above two parts, the speaker deals with the problem of the superiority of monkhood to filial piety, which was the most critical difficulty in making Buddhism understood by the Chinese at that time. Hence, MLL introduces the attack:

> Q: In fortunes, nothing is more important than the continuation of the lineage; nothing is more unfilial than failing to have offspring. [Now] monks forsake their wives and children and discard their property. Furthermore, some of them never get married before they die. How could one go against fortune and filial piety [like this]? They [vainly] mortify themselves, which yields nothing extraordinary; they [drive themselves] to the extreme, which produces nothing wonderful.[54]

Compare the above Chinese attack on leaving the householder life (*pravrajyā*) with an Indian commendation of it in an early *Upaniṣad*: having praised knowledge of the great unborn *ātman*, the famous sage Yājñavalkya in the *Bṛhadāraṇyaka Upaniṣad* (IV.4.22) praises the life of the wanderer as follows:

> Wishing only for this [true] world [of *ātman*], wanderers leave the householder life. This is exactly why ancient wise men who knew it (i.e. *ātman*) did not desire offspring: they think, 'What shall we do

52. 今我為王, 欲得子姓; 既已有子, 還欲相伐. 有嗣如是, 何益於人?
53. 如是阿, 正使子賢, 父老病亡, 子不能却; 生時為惡, 死入地獄, 子不能代. 用是故, 我常以慈 心, 救濟人物, 道成得佛, 度脱天下.
54. 問曰: 夫福莫踰於繼嗣, 不孝莫過於無後. 沙門棄妻子, 捐財貨, 或終身不娶. 何其違福孝之行也? 自苦而無奇, 自極而無異矣 (T2102.52.3a).

with offspring, since this *ātman* is the world for us?' Then, abandoning desires for sons, wealth and [the mundane] world, they wander about as mendicants.[55]

This kind of praise is not restricted to this *Upaniṣad*; we frequently find the abandonment of householder life for religious practice fully respected in Indian literature. This means that the above conflict on the level of ideology in T20 and MLL is more likely to be a Chinese concern than an Indian one.

In sum, in T20 we find many interpolations that reflect the opinion of the Chinese translator or a later interpolator, which appear in the context of the main Chinese concerns of that time, being absent from the other five parallel texts. The way in which the author or later reviser of T20 baselessly inserts his ideas and distorts the context of the original text is extraordinary, compared to normal Chinese Buddhist translations. Nonetheless, T20 has never been classified as an apocryphon in any Chinese Buddhist catalogue. Rather, it must have been more familiar to Chinese readers than the five corresponding texts, in which exotic or bizarre Indian values are conveyed without censorship. The characteristics of Chinese Buddhist translation, as examined above, allowed even such extreme interpolations and distortions; and the personal opinions of the translators easily gained the authority of Buddhist truth, which resulted in the development of a Buddhism that was peculiar to China.

---

55. *etam eva pravrājino lokam icchantaḥ pravrajanti. etad dha sma vai tat pūrve vidvāṃsaḥ prajāṃ na kāmayante: 'kiṃ prajayā kariṣyāmo yeṣām no 'yam ātmā 'yaṃ loka' iti. te ha sma putrâiṣaṇāyāś ca vittâiṣaṇāyāś ca lokâiṣaṇāyāś ca vyutthāyâtha bhikṣācaryaṃ caranti.*

Chapter 2

THE VERIFICATION OF THE TRADITIONAL ATTRIBUTIONS OF TRANSLATORSHIP

When I examine the development of the Chinese Buddhist ideas of self in Part III, I shall survey which renderings are used for particular Indian Buddhist terms and concepts, verify the attributions of translatorship, put the uses of relevant renderings in chronological order, investigate how the renderings were interpreted by the Chinese readers, and analyse the ontological, epistemological and soteriological features that constructed Buddhist ideas peculiar to China. For all of these tasks, the most basic attestation is the verification of translatorship.

In the preface to his CSZJJ, Sengyou (僧祐: 445–518) points out the difficulty and necessity of the verification of translatorship as follows.

> Originally, scriptures were produced in western countries and brought to China. They were carried over a vast distance, and translated from foreign languages into Chinese. Due to the differences in the languages [among the western countries], there have been different texts (i.e. various western recensions of a scripture); since [different recensions of] a scripture have arrived [in China] more than once, there have been [a few translations of a scripture with] old and new titles. However, later scholars barely carry out critical investigation; as a result, transcribing a text time after time, they do not know the year when the text was translated; competing with each other in recitation and exegesis, they have no idea about who translated it. [Thus] the transmission and inheritance of truth have already become extinct. Even when the saints [who lived with the Buddha] gathered at one time [in order to compile all the teachings of the Buddha], they verified the scriptures with five authentications.[1] Further, [being aware that] a thousand years [after

1. More generally, the six authentications of Buddhist scriptures are: 1) truthfulness (信成就: *evaṃ* 如是); 2) witness (聞成就: *mayā śrutam* 我聞); 3) the date (時成就: *ekasmiṇ samaye* 一時); 4) the preacher (主成就: *Bhagavān* 佛); 5) the

the death of the Buddha] have passed for the translation, we should clearly know who translated it and when.[2]

For this reason, he compiled CSZJJ, the oldest extant catalogue of Chinese Buddhist texts, around 515.[3] In it, he not only surveyed and collated the titles of Chinese Buddhist scriptures, but also collected the colophons, prologues, epilogues and other records of the scriptures. These colophons, etc., provide us with precious information about who translated the text and when, who brought the text and when, who were the assistants with the translation, who were the sponsors of the translation, what the translation procedure was, etc. For this careful and meticulous effort, CSZJJ has been regarded as one of the most reliable resources in the field of Chinese Buddhist philology.

PREVIOUS RESEARCH

In the *Yakukyosi kenkyu* 『訳経史研究』, researching into the translations by An Shigao (安世高: fl. 148–71), Lokakṣema, Zhi Qian and Kang Senghui (康僧會: ?–280), Ui (1971) restricts his research to the translations attributed to them by Sengyou in CSZJJ. Since the renderings and transliterations adopted by those translators were the principal constituents of his research, his restriction to the texts listed in CSZJJ is reasonable, perhaps even inevitable. Otherwise, the possible adulteration of their translation works by other translators' renderings and transliterations would have seriously weakened his arguments. The number of translations by those four figures is listed in the major Buddhist catalogues in Table 2.1.[4]

---

place of the preaching; and 6) those who were present at the preaching. Some Chinese scholars have regarded 'the first and the second' or 'the third and the fourth' as one authentication so that they count five authentications in total.

2. 原夫經出西域, 運流東方, 提挈萬里, 翻傳胡漢. 國音各殊, 故文有同異; 前後重來, 故題有新舊. 而後之學者鮮克研覈, 遂乃書寫繼踵, 而不知經出之歲; 誦說比肩, 而莫測傳法之人. 授之受道, 亦已闕矣. 夫一時聖集, 猶五事證經; 況千載交譯, 寧可昧其人世哉? (T2145.55.1a).
3. For the list of Buddhist translations before 374 (for this date, see T2145.55.40a1–3), Sengyou depended on Daoan's ZZL, incorporating it into CSZJJ.
4. In this table, I take account only of their translations, not their own creations, such as commentaries: e.g., I exclude Kang Senghui's commentaries on the *Daoshu jing* 道樹經, the **Ugradatta-paripṛcchā-sūtra* 法鏡經 and the **Ānāpānasmṛti-sūtra* 安般守意經.

Table 2.1 Change in the number of translations among the major Chinese catalogues

	ZZL	CSZJJ	FJL	LDSBJ	YCL	DNL	GYTJ	KYL	ZYL
An Shigao	31 + 4	35	35	176	33	172	176	95	95
Lokakṣema	4 + 9	14	15	21	11	20	21	23	23
Zhi Qian	30	36	35	129	36	130	130	88	88
Kang Senghui	2	2 or 6[5]	7	11	3	11	11	7	7

ZZL: *Zongli zhongjing mulu* 綜理眾經目錄 (incorporated in CSZJJ, compiled by Daoan in *c.* 374–85). (In the column of Daoan's list, the second number is the number of Daoan's new attributions of anonymous translations through the examination of their renderings and composition style.)
CSZJJ: *Chu sanzang ji ji* 出三藏記集 (T2145, compiled by Sengyou 僧祐 in *c.*515)
FJL: *Fajing lu* 法經錄 = *Zhongjing mulu* 眾經目錄 (46 146, compiled by Fajing 法經 *et al.* in 594 ?)
LDSBJ: *Lidai sanbao ji* 歷代三寶紀 (T2034, compiled by Fei Changfang 費長房 in 597)
YCL: *Yancong lu* 彥琮錄 = *Zhongjing mulu* 眾經目錄 (T2147, compiled by Yancong 彥琮 *et al.* in 602)
DNL: *Datang neidian lu* 大唐內典錄 (T2149, compiled by Daoxuan 道宣 in 664)
GYTJ: *Gujin yijing tuji* 古今譯經圖紀 (T2151, compiled by Jingmai 靖邁 after 664)
KYL: *Kaiyuan shijiao lu* 開元釋教錄 (T2154, compiled by Zhisheng 智升 in 730)
ZYL: *Zhenyuan xinding shijiao mulu* 貞元新定釋教目錄 (T2157, compiled by Yuanzhao 圓照 in 800)

On inspecting this table, we find three groups of major Chinese Buddhist catalogues.[6] The first consists of CSZJJ (*c.* 515, incorporating ZZL), FJL (*c.* 594) and YCL (602); the second of LDSBJ (597), DNL (664) and GYTJ (after 664); and the third of KYL (730) and ZYL (800). In the first group, about 35 translations are attributed to An Shigao; in the second, about 176; and in the third, 95. As Tokuno pointed out (1990, pp. 43–7), many of the new attributions by Fei Changfang 費長房, the compiler of LDSBJ, appear arbitrary. Furthermore, although KYL and ZYL removed the obviously incorrect attributions by Fei, many of the attributions followed by KYL and ZYL still appear to be baseless (*ibid.*, p. 53). Considering this situation, Ui's restriction to the texts attributed by Sengyou appears inevitable. However, this does not mean that we

5. When he lists Kang's translations at T2145.55.7ab, Sengyou records only two translations: the *Wupin jing* 吳品經 and the *(*Ṣaṭ) pāramitā-samāsa* 六度集經. However, in the biography of Kang, he lists (T2145.55.97a) four further translations: the *Fa anan nianmi jing* 法阿難念彌經, the *Jingmianwang jing* 鏡面王經, the *Chaweiwang jing* 察微王經 and the *Fanhuangwang jing* 梵皇王經.
6. For more information on the Chinese Buddhist catalogues, refer to Ono, 1936 (spec. vol.), pp. 3–7, 26–9.

can rely on Sengyou's statements without doubt. Although CSZJJ may be the most reliable among the extant catalogues, it is not guaranteed either that all of the attributions by CSZJJ are correct or that the text available to Sengyou is the same as that extant today. Thus it is advisable to maintain a critical approach to the attributions by CSZJJ.

For example, Sengyou sometimes provides us with confusing information. Attributing the *Amituo jing* 阿彌陀經, a recension of the larger *Sukhāvatī-vyūha* in two fascicules, to Zhi Qian, Sengyou notes that the full name *Amituo sanye sanfo saloutan guodu rendao jing* 阿彌陀三耶三佛薩樓檀過度人道經 is used as a heading inside the book (T2145.55.6c25). This information may have led later Chinese Buddhist cataloguers and the modern cataloguers of T to attribute T362 阿彌陀三耶三佛薩樓佛檀過度人道經 to Zhi Qian. However, comparing the style of the composition, renderings, and transliterations with other works of Zhi Qian and Lokakṣema, Harrison (1998, pp. 556–7) and Nattier (2003, p.242, n.121) argue that T362 may be a translation by Lokakṣema rather than Zhi Qian, and that T361, *wuliang qingjing pingdeng jue jing* 無量清淨平等覺經, is the retranslation of the *sūtra* by Zhi Qian. Sengyou may have written down what he witnessed, but after one and a half millennia, the texts have probably undergone some changes in transmission. Therefore, it is natural for us to find that some of the information that he provides in CSZJJ is quite different from what we see in the extant texts.

It is well known that there have been additional touches to Buddhist texts and the mistranscription of glosses into the textual body. Therefore, even if Sengyou provided us with uncorrupted information, there is no guarantee that the present translation would contain the genuine renderings and transliterations of the translator to whom it is attributed. To verify the traditional attribution of the translatorship and the genuineness of the text, we must perform an external and internal comparison of the writing style and the use of renderings and transliterations. Concerning T225 *Aṣṭasāhasrikā Prajñāpāramitā* 大明度經, Lancaster (1969) adopted this method of internal and external comparison. With regard to Chapters 2 to 27 of T225, he compares the renderings, the use of transliteration and the writing style with Zhi Qian's other translations, and concludes that T225 is the handiwork of someone other than Zhi Qian, suggesting that An Xuan (安玄: fl. 181) is the person responsible (pp. 250–3). With regard to Chapter 1, he compares its style and renderings with the remaining chapters of T225 and concludes that someone probably added commentaries to Chapter 1 and reworked its content and renderings, and that the interpolator must have had access to an original text that was similar to that of Kumārajīva (pp. 253–6).

However, there is one critical problem with his external comparison.[7] While Lancaster compares these elements of Chapters 2 to 27 with other translations of Zhi Qian, he does not spell out which ones are the works of Zhi Qian. If we follow Nattier's list of Zhi Qian's translations (see Table 2.3 below), we can find renderings and retranslations of transliterated words which Lancaster asserts are not to be found among Zhi Qian's translations.[8] Being a pioneer before computer searches were available, it appears that Lancaster could not inspect Zhi Qian's renderings and transliterations throughout the translations attributed to him by CSZJJ. Due to the lack of this primary step to demarcate the 'authentic' translations by Zhi Qian, his arguments concerning Chapters 2 to 27 are weakened.

In his 'A New Look at the Earliest Chinese Buddhist Texts', Zürcher (1991) attempts to draft an authentic list of Chinese Buddhist translations in the Later Han period, i.e., from the mid-second century to the end of the Han dynasty (220). To make the list authentic: (1) he demarcates the texts that he deals with, depending on the information from Daoan's ZZL and some information drawn from the records by the bibliographer Zhi Mindu (支敏度: fl. 290–306); (2) he also depends on corroborative evidence drawn from textual glosses, contemporary colophons/prefaces and quotations in the earliest Buddhist commentaries, etc.; (3) on the basis of (1) and (2), he establishes some 'landmarks', unquestionably authentic products of certain translators, e.g., T224 *Aṣṭasāhasrikā Prajñāpāramitā* 道行般若經 for Lokakṣema's translations and T602 **Mahānāpānasmṛti-sūtra* 大安般守意經 for An Shigao; (4) he carries out a terminological and stylistic analysis of those 'landmarks' to define a number of distinctive lexical and stylistic features that are peculiar to certain translators' teams; and (5) with reference to the extant scriptures, he affirms or rejects the attributions by Daoan and Zhi Mindu to Later Han translators in the light of (4) (pp. 278–9). As a result, he presents a list of '29 texts that may be considered genuine Han translations, made at Louyang by five different translators' teams between 150 to 220 AC' (p. 279).

7. Jan Nattier is working on this topic [2008].
8. For example, the rendering of *bhikṣu* as *chujin* 除饉 is also found in T210, and *kaishi* 開士/闓士 is also found in T76, T493 and T533; and the retranslation as *yingyi* 應儀 of the word usually transliterated *arhat* is also found in T76 and T532. More details on this problem will be published by Nattier.

Zürcher's work provided a good model for later scholars to follow. In 'The Earliest Chinese Translations of Mahāyāna Buddhist Sūtras,' Harrison (1993) examines the translations of Lokakṣema. There, following the method introduced by Zürcher, he gives more detailed information on Lokakṣema's Mahāyāna translations and investigates the characteristics of Mahāyāna Buddhism at that time. In a later article (1998, pp. 556–7), as mentioned above, Harrison suggests that T362 may also have been translated by Lokakṣema.

Nattier (2003) applies this method to the translations by Zhi Qian. She concomitantly carries out the task of determining a provisional list of the authentic translations of Zhi Qian and the task of inspecting Zhi Qian's renderings and transliteration with regard to the ten epithets of the Buddha. For these tasks, she first considers the texts attributed to Zhi Qian in CSZJJ, then examines the renderings and transliterations of the ten epithets of the Buddha in those texts; simultaneously, she verifies the attribution of the texts to Zhi Qian from the results of the examination. She also adds four translations as 'candidate texts' for Zhi Qian's authorship, translations which are not attributed to him by CSZJJ, but whose renderings are in accordance with Zhi Qian's other works.

Concerning the attributions of translatorship, the works of the above scholars show how we can minimize the risk of adulteration by the renderings and transliterations in incorrectly attributed translations or by later retouches. However, we should be aware that Daoan as well as Sengyou compiled their catalogues as a personal project, unlike many cataloguers during the Tang period, who conducted national projects. Their finances and manpower must have been insufficient to cover all of the texts translated in China. This insufficiency would be serious if Daoan included in his catalogue only the texts that he saw himself, as Tang (1973 [1938], pp. 208–9) states. The result of the minimization of possible adulteration should be utilized as a foundation for the accumulation of authentic translations. I shall now illustrate how we can perform this critical attestation, by verifying the traditional attribution of the aforementioned T20 *Ambāṣṭha-sūtra*, which is one of Nattier's 'candidate texts' for Zhi Qian's authorship.

THE TRADITIONAL ATTRIBUTION OF T20 TO ZHI QIAN

In the major Chinese Buddhist catalogues, we find information about the translations of the *Ambāṣṭha-sūtra* (see Table 2.2). As mentioned before, the catalogues are divided into three groups: (1) CSZJJ, FJL and YCL; (2) LDSBJ, DNL and GYTJ; (3) KYL and ZYL.

1. In the first group, we find two recensions of the relevant scripture, neither of which is attributed to Zhi Qian. CSZJJ tells us that the first, *Aba jing* 阿拔經, which was no longer extant in Sengyou's time, was also registered in Daoan's ZZL, and that the second, *Fo kaijie fanzhi aba jing* 佛開解梵志阿經, is a summarized scripture (抄經). We can infer that the first *Aba jing* in CSZJJ is probably the *Fanzhi aba jing* 梵志阿跋經 listed in FJL and YCL, since they share the alternative name *Aba mona jing* 阿跋摩納經, and since they are not mentioned as a summarized scripture. I could find no further records of the summarized scripture in later catalogues.
2. In the second group, two recensions of the relevant scripture are mentioned: one translated by Zhi Qian and the other by Fayong or an anonymous author. The records of Zhi Qian's translation are identical in these three catalogues. LDSBJ and GYTJ attribute the second to Fayong, adding an annotation that they obtained the information from the catalogue of Zhao 趙錄, whereas DNL does not attribute it to any translator. In addition, DNL places it among the extant texts, and specifies that it covers 13 folios, which indicates that it cannot be a summarized scripture.
3. KYL and ZYL eliminate 41 texts from the list of 129 translations attributed to Zhi Qian by LDSBJ, and attribute 88 translations to him. The *Fanzhi aba jing* 梵志阿 經 survived the elimination process. In addition, KYL and ZYL inform us that Zhi Qian's translation, entitled *Aba jing* 阿拔經, has been listed in Daoan's catalogue, and that it covers 14 folios (T2154.55.691b7–8), which implies that Zhi Qian's translation is the *Aba jing* 阿拔經 in CSZJJ. They also inform us that the translation of Fayong was not extant at that time (T2154.55.509b4–5).

Summing up the information presented in the above catalogues, we may conclude that T20 *Fo kaijie fanzhi aba jing* 佛開解梵志阿 經 has been attributed to Zhi Qian since 597, and that it was listed in the Chinese Buddhist catalogues from around 374–85, when Daoan's ZZL was compiled. However, since CSZJJ follows Daoan's classification of the *Aba jing* 阿拔經 as an anonym, and since Fei Changfang 費長房, the first cataloguer who attributed the text to Zhi Qian, is notorious for arbitrary attribution to irrelevant famous figures, further investigation is required for the confirmation of T20 as one of Zhi Qian's translations.

Table 2.2 Translations of the *Ambāṣṭha-sūtra* in the major catalogues

Catalogue	*Date*	*Compiler*	*Title in the catalogue*	*Attributed translator*	*Misc.*
CSZJJ	*c.*515	Sengyou 僧祐	*Aba jing* 阿拔經 (= *Aba mona jing* 阿拔摩納經)	Anonymous	Ø, Daoan
			Fo kaijie fanzhi aba jing 佛開解梵志阿經 (= *Fanzhi aba jing* 梵志阿經)	Anonymous	Summ.
FJL	594 ?	Fajing 法經 *et al.*	*Fanzhi aba jing* 梵志阿跋經 (= *Aba mona jing* 阿拔摩納經)	Anonymous	
YCL	602	Yancong 彥琮 *et al.*	*Fanzhi aba jing* 梵志阿跋經 (= *Aba mona jing* 阿跋摩納經)	Anonymous	
LDSBJ	597	Fei Changfang 費長房	*Fo kaijie aba fanzhi jing* 佛開解阿拔梵志經 (= *Fanzhi aba jing* 梵志阿經)	Zhi Qian 支謙	220–26 魏文帝世
			Fo kaijie fanzhi aba jing 佛開解梵志阿經	Fayong 法勇	c. 418 晉末
DNL	664	Daoxuan 道宣	*Fo kaijie aba fanzhi jing* 佛開解阿拔梵志經 (= *Fanzhi aba jing* 梵志阿經)	Zhi Qian 支謙	220–26 魏文帝世
			Fanzhi aba jing 梵志阿跋經 (= *Aba mona jing* 阿跋摩納經)	Anonymous	◎ 13 folios
GYTJ	after 664	Jingmai 靖邁	*Fo kaijie aba fanzhi jing* 佛開解阿拔梵志經	Zhi Qian 支謙	222–80 吳孫氏
			Fo kaijie fanzhi aba jing 佛開解梵志阿經	Fayong 法勇	c. 418 晉末
KYL	730	Zhisheng 智昇	*Fanzhi aba jing* 梵志阿經 (= *Aba mona jing* 阿摩納經, *Aba jing* 阿拔經, *Fo kaijie fanzhi aba jing* 佛開解梵志阿經)	Zhi Qian 支謙	◎, 14 folios
			Fo kaijie fanzhi aba jing 佛開解梵志阿經	Fayong 法勇	Ø, c. 418 晉末
ZYL	799	Yuanzhao 圓照	*Fanzhi aba jing* 梵志阿經 (= *Aba mona jing* 阿摩納經, *Aba jing* 阿拔經, *Fowen fanzhi aba jing* 佛聞梵志阿經)	Zhi Qian 支謙	◎, 14 folios
			Fo kaijie fanzhi aba jing 佛開解梵志阿經	Fayong 法勇	Ø, c. 418 晉末

Ø not extant; ◎ extant; Summ.: a summarized text

AN ATTESTATION OF THE ATTRIBUTION OF T20 TO ZHI QIAN

In verifying the traditional attribution of T20 to Zhi Qian, I follow Zürcher's method, apart from the third step, i.e., establishing 'landmarks'. It is true that some philological records guarantee the translation of a certain text by a specific translator. However, these records do not guarantee that there has been no retouching by later interpolators, no mistranscription of glosses into the text, and no confusion of titles between similar recensions. There is no guarantee either that a translator retained the writing style, renderings or transliterations that are used in such 'landmarks' throughout his career as a translator. The establishment of 'landmarks' without such guarantees may exclude some genuine translations from the opus of a translator. It is safer and more practical to 'define a number of distinctive lexical and stylistic features peculiar to certain translators' teams', as Zürcher did through the overall inspection of the texts demarcated by his first and second steps.

As an initial step towards the verification of T20 as one of Zhi Qian's translations, we should find reliable evidence to identify his authentic translations in order to minimize the confusion caused by irrelevant attributions. For this specific case, the most trustworthy record would be CSZJJ, which incorporates Daoan's ZZL. As listed in Table 2.3, Daoan attributes 30 translations to Zhi Qian, and Sengyou adds six further texts to this list, depending on information from a catalogue entitled the *Bielu* (別錄: *Special Catalogue*) (T2145.55.6c–7a).[9]

Ui (1971, pp. 530–2) presents a list of 22 extant translations by Zhi Qian among his 36 translations listed in CSZJJ. In general, Ui follows the attributions by the editors of T. Apart from T6, the other 21 texts among the 22 on Ui's list are identified as Zhi Qian's work by the editors of T. It remains unclear why he excludes from his list T1011 **Anantamukha-ādhaka-dhāraṇī* 無量門微密持經, which is attributed to Zhi Qian by both Sengyou and the editors of T. In the case of T533, which is also attributed to Zhi Qian by the editors of T, it may have been excluded from his list because the title *Chamojie jing* (差摩竭經: **Kṣemaṃkāra-sūtra*) in CSZJJ differs from the title *Pusa shengdi jing* (菩薩生地經: **Bodhisattva-janma-bhūmi-sūtra*) in T. However, the major Buddhist catalogues have

9. *Bielu* 別錄 may be regarded as a general name, meaning 'another catalogue'; however, its systematic use in CSZJJ indicates that it is the abbreviated title of a specific catalogue.

traditionally identified them as the same text with different titles. It also appears that Ui failed to include T210 *Dharmapada* on his list, since it is attributed by the editors of T not to Zhi Qian, but to *Vighna 維祇難 *et al.* As Nattier has pointed out (2003, p. 241, n.119), CSZJJ lists T210 as one of Zhi Qian's translations, and adds the information that *Vighna merely brought the text to China, while the actual translators were Zhu Jiangyan 竺將炎 and Zhi Qian (T2145.55.6c10–13, 49c20–50a28, 96a22–27). Ui further argues (1971, pp. 519–23) that the T6 *Mahāparinirvāṇa-sūtra* 般泥洹經, which is classified by editors of T as an anonymous work, is also a translation by Zhi Qian.

Researching into the renderings that are peculiar to Zhi Qian, Nattier (2003, pp. 208–9, 241–2) includes 26 extant texts in the 'provisional list of the authentic works of Zhi Qian.' To the 22 texts on Ui's list, she adds T210, T533 and T1011 for the reasons mentioned above. She also adds T328, which is attributed to Bai Yan (白延: fl. 254–59) by the editors of T. Pending further study of this text, she points out that while two translations with the same title, *Xulai jing* 須賴經, are registered in CSZJJ, Bai Yan's translation is reported as not extant at the time of CSZJJ. Following the attribution by the editors of T, Ui attributes T362 to Zhi Qian; however, agreeing with Harrison (1998, pp. 556–7), Nattier points out that the attribution of T361 to Lokakṣema (支婁迦讖: fl. 178–89) and that of T362 to Zhi Qian have been mistakenly transposed.[10] She adds four further texts to the list of 'additional candidate texts.' The T20 in question is one of the candidate texts.

In order to explore whether or not T20 is one of Zhi Qian's translations, I depend on Nattier's research into Zhi Qian's works. However, a few emendations to her list appear necessary. Firstly, in a separate paper (Park, 2008), I have argued that T5 is probably one of the earliest translations by Zhi Qian and that T6 is a retranslation of T5, possibly by Zhi Qian but more probably by an anonym in his translation circle.[11] Based

10. For this attribution, also refer to Ono, 1936 (spec. vol.), pp. 33–4, and Hirakawa, 1968, pp. 76, 89.

11. I use the expression 'Zhi Qian's translation circle,' etc., in order to designate the anonyms whose translation works exhibit virtually identical lexical and stylistic features to those of Zhi Qian. For example, judging from the lexical and stylistic features, it is difficult to distinguish Kang Senghui's translation work from that of Zhi Qian, as I demonstrate below. Considering the possibility that there may have been other translators, like Kang Senghui, who were close in time and space to Zhi Qian, we should not attribute an anonymous translation to Zhi Qian merely because its composition style is virtually identical to his own.

Table 2.3 A provisional list of Zhi Qian's translations

CSZJJ	*Daoan*	*Ui*	*Nattier*	*Park*	*T*
大般泥洹經	O	X	X	O	(T5 佛般泥洹經 attr. to Bo Fazu)
		O	O	Δ	(T6 般泥洹經 anonymous)
X	X	X	Δ	Δ	T20 佛開解梵志阿經
X	X	X	Δ	Δ	T27 七知經
釋摩男經	O	O	O	O	T54 釋摩男本四子經
賴吒和羅經	X	O	O	O	T68 賴吒和羅經
梵摩渝經	O	O	O	O	T76 梵摩渝經
齋經¯	O	O	O	O	T87 齋經
月明童子經	O	O	O	O	T169 月明菩薩經
瑞應本起經	O	O	O	O	T185 太子瑞應本起經
義足經	O	O	O	O	T198 義足經
法句經	O	X	O	O	(T210 法句經 attr. to *Vighna *et al.*)
明度經	O	O	O	O	T225 大明度經
本業經	O	O	O	O	T281 菩薩本業經
須賴經	O	X	O	Δ	(T328 須賴經 attr. to. Bo Yan)
阿彌陀經	O	X	O	O	(T361 無量清淨平等覺經 attr. to Lokakṣema)
		O	X	X	T362 阿彌陀三耶三佛薩樓佛檀過度人道經
維摩詰經¯	O	O	O	O	T474 維摩詰經
阿難四事經	O	O	O	O	T493 阿難四事經
X	X	X	Δ	Δ	T507 未生冤經
X	X	X	Δ	Δ	T511 蓱沙王五願經
私阿末經	O	O	O	O	T532 私呵昧經
差摩竭經	O	X	O	O	T533 菩薩生地經
七女經	O	O	O	O	T556 七女經
龍施女經	X	O	O	O	T557 龍施女經
老女人經	O	O	O	O	T559 老女人經
八師經	O	O	O	O	T581 八師經
慧印經	O	O	O	O	T632 慧印三昧經
了本生死經	O	O	O	O	T708 了本生死經
四願經	O	O	O	O	T735 四願經
孛抄經	O	O	O	O	T790 孛經抄
微密持經	O	X	O	O	T1011 無量門微密持經
小阿差末經Ø	O				
優多羅母經Ø	O				
悔過經	O				
賢者德經	O				
佛從上所行三十偈Ø¯	O				
惟明二十偈	O				
首楞嚴經	X				
法鏡經	X				
鹿子經	X				
十二門大方等經¯	X				

Ø not extant; Δ candidate text.

on my examination of T5 and T6, I suggest that T5 should be included in the 'provisional list of the authentic works of Zhi Qian', and T6 among the 'candidate texts'. In the case of T328, I temporarily consider it as a candidate text, removing its name from the list of 'authentic' works, for a reason that I shall explain below. Hence, I suggest 25 'authentic' works and 6 'candidate' texts of Zhi Qian, as presented in Table 2.3.

A Comparison between T20 and Zhi Qian's Other Works

As the first generation of Chinese Buddhist translators, An Shigao and Lokakṣema laid the foundation for future Buddhist translation, such as the basic renderings, the system of transliteration and the structure of translation teams. However, being full of unknown technical terms and exotic transliterations, written in a clumsy style, their translations are difficult to read even for a specialist with technical knowledge of Chinese Buddhism. Hence, in that embryonic period, when a basic knowledge of Buddhism was hardly to be expected of the readers, the pressing mission for the next generation was to produce translations that enabled the readers to understand the texts by themselves, without any technical knowledge.

Zhi Qian was a layman of Yuezhi origin.[12] About the end of Emperor Xian's 獻帝 reign (190–219), there was a nationwide upheaval, and Zhi Qian moved (probably from Henan 河南 province)[13] to the territory of the Wu 吳 dynasty. Being supported by Lord Sun Quan (孫權: 182–252), he dedicated himself to translating Buddhist texts during the period 222–53. Zhi Qian's contribution to the history of Chinese Buddhist translation is conspicuous. Most importantly, his translations are far

---

12. The colophon to the *Collated Multi-Translations of the Śūraṃgama-sūtra* (合首楞嚴經記: T2145.55. 49a16–b17) by Zhi Mindu 支敏度 (fl. 290–306) states that his father immigrated to China during Emperor Ling's reign (168–88). On the contrary, Zhi Qian's biography in CSZJJ (T2145.55.97b13–c18) states that it was his grandfather Fadu 法度 who immigrated to China during Emperor Ling's reign. KYL (T2154.55.489b3–c12) and ZYL (T2157.55.786c2–87a11) follow CSZJJ. However, GSZ states that Zhi Qian himself immigrated to China from Yuezhi 月支: 'There was a layman, Zhi Qian. His pseudonym was Gongming; he was also called Yue. Being originally a Yuezhi man, he immigrated to China' 先有優婆塞支謙, 字恭明, 一名越, 本月支人, 來遊漢境 (T2059.50.325a18–19).
13. Daoan's prologue to T708 *Śālistamba-sūtra* 了本生死經 (T2145.55.45b) designates Zhi Qian as Henan Zhi Gongming 河南支恭明. Henan is the province where Luoyang, the capital of the Later Han dynasty, was located.

more readable for Chinese intellectuals than the works by the first translators. Furthermore, his classical Chinese composition reflects a sense of literary style; although they date from the middle of the archaic translation period, many of his works compare well with the works of the early period of old translation. The composition of T20 demonstrates this characteristic of Zhi Qian's work: the relatively polished classical Chinese in T20 does not hamper readers from understanding its meaning because of awkward sentence structure, exotic writing style, etc.

However, such improved linguistic devices as refined composition, proper renderings and suitable choices between Chinese names and transliterations were insufficient to produce a readable translation *per se*, since the very content to be conveyed was extremely exotic to the Chinese at that time. To solve this problem, Zhi Qian utilized or interpolated Chinese concepts in his translations.[14] For example, in T76 *Brahmāyuḥ-sūtra* 梵摩渝經, when Brahmāyus seeks refuge in the Buddha, Zhi Qian introduces the five precepts in the following Chinese style:

> I want to be a Buddhist follower. Maintaining benevolence, I will not kill living beings; being content, I will not commit theft; leading a chaste life, I will not have inappropriate sexual relationships; maintaining my reputation, I will not lie; practising filial piety towards my parents, I will not drink intoxicants.[15]

The justification of sobriety in terms of filial piety must be a Chinese adaptation; such a justification is alien to Indian Buddhism. Zhi Qian's interpolations in his translation work on the one hand helped Chinese readers to understand exotic Buddhist ideas in the familiar terms of Chinese thought, and on the other hand disguised bizarre Indian values, so that Buddhism became compatible with established Chinese moral principles, particularly filial piety and loyalty.[16] This characteristic is in accordance with T20, as I demonstrated in Section 1.5.

14. For a discussion of Zhi Qian's interpolations, refer to Asayama, 1993.
15. 願為清信士,守仁不殺,知足不盜,貞潔不婬,執信不欺,盡孝不醉(T76.1.886a9–10). In the corresponding Pali *Brahmāyu-sutta* (M.II.145) and the *Fanma jing* 梵摩經 of T26 *Madhyamāgama* (1.689b), only the threefold taking of refuge is mentioned, without reference to the five precepts.
16. Not to mention the abandoning of the householder life, for which the Confucians have blamed Buddhism throughout Chinese history, even the Indian Buddhist idea of donation was accused of ruining the values of the Chinese family system. MLL (T2102.52.1a–7a) discusses this topic.

The consistency of the renderings and transliterations between T20 and Zhi Qian's other works also supports the traditional attribution of the text to Zhi Qian.[17] In T20 (1.259c22), *cakkavatti dhammiko dhammarājā* ('a righteous *dharma*-king turning the [heavenly] wheel', D.I.88_33)[18] is rendered as *feixinghuangdi* (飛行皇帝: flying emperor), which was adopted by only a few translators during the period of archaic translation; shortly afterwards *zhuanlunshengwang* (轉輪聖王: wheel-turning saint king) became a standard rendering. We find the rendering *feixinghuangdi* in T5 (1.169b3 ff.), T76 (1.883c3), T185 (3.473b3), and T225 (8.490c12–13) on the list of 'authentic works'. Interestingly, T185 juxtaposes *zhuanlunshengwang* and *feixinghuangdi* as 轉輪聖王飛行皇帝. It is possible that this redundant juxtaposition is a wrong transcription of a gloss or a retouching by a later interpolator.

T20 (1.259c22–24) renders the seven treasures of the wheel-turning king, i.e., *cakkaratana, hatthiratana, assaratana, maṇiratana, itthiratana, gahapatiratana* and *pariṇāyakaratana* (D.I.89), as respectively *jinlunbao* 金輪寶, *baixiangbao* 白象寶, *ganmabao* 紺馬寶, *yunxbao* 玉女寶, *shenzhubao* 神珠寶, *lijiabao* 理家寶 and *xianjiangbao* 賢將寶. Among the 'authentic' works, T5 (1.170a1–4) renders them as *huangjinfeilun* 黃金飛輪, *shenlibaixiang* 神力白象, *ganseshenma* 紺色神馬, *mingyuezhu* 明月珠, *tianyunūqi* 天玉女妻, *zhubaoshengchen* 主寶聖臣 and *dianbingshengchen* 典兵聖臣; T185 (3.473b3–6) renders as *jinlunbao* 金輪寶, *shenzhubao* 神珠寶, *ganmabao zhumaoge* 紺馬寶(朱)[珠]髦, *baixiangbao zhumaowei* 白象寶(朱)[珠]髦尾, *yunxbao* 玉女寶, *xianjianbao* 賢鑒寶 and *shengdaobao* 聖導寶. We find that the renderings for the seven treasures and their order differ slightly between T5, T20 and T185.[19] The candidate text T6 (1.185c4–6) presents the

17. For the examination of renderings and transliterations, I rely on computerized data about the Chinese Buddhist scriptures: the *Chinese Electronic Tripitaka Collection* released by CBETA in February 2007.

18. In this book I use Sanskrit as standard among various South/Central Asian languages from which the Chinese produced their translations. However, when only Pali parallels to specific Chinese texts are available, I retain Pali terms in order to make the source of comparison clear.

19. T185 (3.473b), which redundantly juxtaposes *zhuanlunshengwang* and *feixinghuangdi* as 轉輪聖王飛行皇帝, also in explanatory forms renders the elephant treasure (*hatthiratana*) and the horse treasure (*assaratana*) as *baixiangbao zhumaowei* (白象寶 (朱) [珠] 髦尾: the white elephant treasure whose tail hair is made of jewellery beads) and *ganmabao zhumaoge* (紺馬寶 (朱) [珠] 髦: the dark-red horse treasure whose tail and mane are made of jewellery beads). These explanatory renderings *zhumaowei* and *zhumaoge* are probably information added by the translator or a later interpolator, or a wrong transcription of a gloss.

renderings most similar to those in T20. Only the last treasure is rendered with a slight difference: *shengdaobao* 聖導寶 instead of *xianjiangbao* 賢將寶. The renderings for the treasures appear to be unstandardized within Zhi Qian's works; these slight differences may not weaken T20's compatibility with Zhi Qian's authorship.

In T20, we find the Chinese technical term *jingshen* 精神 (1.260c13, 262b21) and *hunshen* 魂神 (262b10), which indicate an agent going through *saṃsāra*.[20] However, *jingshen* and *hunshen* are not translation terms; they are arbitrary adaptations or interpolations by Chinese translators, as I elucidate below (see page 186). We find the technical term *jingshen* in T87 (1.911c12, 912a5), T185 (3.472c7 ff.), T210 (4.563a2 ff.), T361 (12.294a20–21), T581 (14.965b18) and T735 (17.537a19–21) among the 'authentic' works, and in T6 (1.188c26, 190a14) among candidate texts. As for *hunshen*, we find it in T5 (1.162a15), T185 (3.475c23, 478b3), T361 (12.295c15), T493 (14.757a14 f.), T581 (14.965a20, 966a11), T735 (17.536c9 f.), T790 (17.735b13) among 'authentic' works, and in T6 (1.177a26 ff.) among the candidate texts.

In T20 (1.260c14–15, 262b4), the four achievements of practitioners, i.e., *srota-āpanna* (having entered the stream), *sakṛdāgāmin* (once more returning), *anāgāmin* (not returning) and *arhat* (being worthy), are respectively rendered as *gougang* (溝港: stream), *pinlai* (頻來: lit. visiting in repetition), *buhuan* (不還: not returning) and *yingzhen* (應真: worthy-true). Among these four terms, the renderings *gougang* 溝港 and *pinlai* 頻來, especially the former, are infrequent in other translators' works. We can find *gougang* in T5 (1.163b4 ff.), T87 (1.911b26–28), T198 (4.174c24 ff.), T225 (8.482b15 ff.), T474 (14.528a17) and T790 (17.729a10) among the 'authentic' works, and in T6 (1.178b25 ff.) among the candidate texts.

As for the renderings of *pañcaskandha* (the five aggregates), the author of T20 (1.261c28–29) adopts *se* (色: colour), *tong* (痛: pain), *xiang* (想: idea), *xing* (行: performance) and *shi* (識: discernment) respectively for *rūpa* (form), *vedanā* (feeling), *saṃjñā* (apperception), *saṃskāra* (mental activities) and *vijñāna* (consciousness). Among the 'authentic' works, only six texts list the complete set of five aggregates. In four of these, i.e., T225 (8.479a23 ff.), T328 (12.55a5, 60c6), T474 (14.526c25, 531b7–8) and T533 (14.814b29), Zhi Qian translates the five aggregates as *se* 色, *tong* 痛, *xiang* 想, *xing* 行 and *shi* 識, as in T20. In T185

20. The part where *jingshen* appears is unique to T20; it does not appear in PA, SA/T1451 or T1.

(3.471c7–8), he translates the five aggregates as *sexiang* (色像: lit. colour and form), *tongyang* (痛痒: lit. pain and illness), *sixiang* (思想: thought and idea), *xingzuo* (行作: performance and production) and *hunshi* (魂識: soul and consciousness); in these renderings, one in each couple of characters, which I have underlined, coincides with the renderings of the five aggregates in T20. By contrast, in T559, we find slightly different renderings: *se* 色, *tongyang* 痛痒, *sixiang* 思想, *shengsi* 生死 and *shi* 識 (14.912a2–7), which occur frequently in An Shigao's and Lokakṣema's translations. In addition, in T5 (1.163b12–23), T708 (16.815c1 ff.) among 'authentic' works, and in T6 (1.178c4–14), T328 (12.55a5–6) and T511 (14.779b21–26) among candidate texts, we find the list of the twelvefold dependent origination, which includes four of the five aggregates. These texts render *saṃskāra*, *vijñāna*, (*nāma-*) *rūpa* and *vedanā* respectively as *xing* 行, *shi* 識, (*ming-/zi-*) *se* (名/字)色 and *tong* 痛 in common with T20.

As for the ten epithets of the Buddha, i.e., *tathāgata*, *arhat*, *samyaksaṃbuddha*, *vidyācaraṇasampanna*, *sugata*, *lokavid*, *anuttarapuruṣa*, *damyasārathi*, *śāstā devamanuṣyāṇām buddha* and *bhagavat*,[21] the writer of T20 renders them respectively as *rulai* 如來, *zhizhen* 至真, *dengzhengjue* 等正覺, *mingxingcheng* 明行成, *shandao* 善道, *shijianjie* 世間解, *wushangshi* 無上士, *daofayu* 道法御, *tianrenshi* 天人師, *fo* 佛 and *zhongyou* 眾祐. No list of the epithets in Zhi Qian's other works is identical to this. However, except for the rendering of *sugata* as *shandao* 善道, all of the other renderings appear intermittently throughout Zhi Qian's other works. For the renderings of the ten epithets of the Buddha in Zhi Qian's works, see Nattier (2003, pp. 209–34).

In sum, in the light of the writing style and renderings of T20, we may conclude that the translation of T20 is highly compatible with Zhi Qian's other works.

A Comparison between T20 and the Works of Other Translators

The above examination of the writing style and renderings of T20 demonstrates that the text is compatible with Zhi Qian's other translations. However, this compatibility in itself is not enough to prove that T20 is

21. Among these eleven epithets, the first *tathāgata* is traditionally not counted. As for *anuttarapuruṣa* and *damyasārathi*, I followed Zhi Qian's reading as reflected in his renderings. However, *anuttara* is more frequently counted as an independent epithet and *puruṣadamyasārathi* as another. For more details, see Nattier (2003, p. 227).

a translation by Zhi Qian. It could be translated by any member of his translation circle or anyone who thoroughly succeeded to his distinctive lexical and stylistic features. Therefore, to argue that T20 was translated by Zhi Qian, we must prove that it is incompatible with the work of any other translator. In order to carry out this task efficiently, I lay down the following principles:

1. I restrict the examination of the compatibility of T20 with other translators' works to the period of archaic translation (until 375). The renderings used in T20 imply that these texts were hardly translated during the period of old or new translation.[22]
2. I do not consider translators before Zhi Qian, i.e., those working during the Later Han period (until 210). The writing style and renderings of T20 are far removed from the Later Han translation work.
3. Except for T5/T6, I restrict the domain of the translations to those texts that are attributed to particular translators by CSZJJ. This restriction is imposed in order to prevent any possible adulteration of the renderings and composition styles by the arbitrary attributions of later cataloguers.
4. In order to examine the writing style, renderings and transliterations, I am concerned only with the extant texts.

The candidate authors who satisfy these conditions are: Kang Senghui (康僧會: ?–280); Bai Yan (白延: fl. 254–59); Zhu Fahu (竺法護: fl. 266–308); Nie Chengyuan 聶承遠; Wuchaluo 無叉羅 (fl. 291) and Zhu Shulan 竺叔蘭; and Faju (法炬: fl. 308) and Fali 法立. Because of the marked problem of retranslation between T5 and T6, I also consider Bo Fazu (帛法祖, fl. 290–306) as a candidate.

KANG SENGHUI 康僧會 (?–280)

Kang Senghui was born in Jiaozhi 交趾 (now in northern Vietnam), Wu 吳. His ancestors moved from Kangju 康居 to India, then to Jiaozhi in his father's time. Having lost his parents, he became a monk at the age

22. For example, the rendering of *rājan cakravartin* as *feixinghuangdi* 飛行皇帝 occurs only twice among the translations after 375: (1) T309 *Zuishengwen pusa shizhu chugou duanjie jing* 最勝問菩薩十住除垢斷結經 by Zhu Fonian 竺佛念 juxtaposes the later, standard *zhuanlunwang* 轉輪王 and the archaic *feixinghuangding* 飛行皇帝 (T309.10.995a29); (2) T177 **Mahāmati-sūtra* 大意經, traditionally attributed to Guṇabhadra (by LDSBJ and editors of T), uses the rendering 飛行皇帝 (T177.3.447b27). However, this attribution is not certain; CSZJJ classifies T177 as an anonym.

of ten, and moved to Jianye 建業, the capital of Wu, in 247. With the support of the Wu dynasty, he made several translations and commentaries before his death in 280 (T2145.55.96b1–97a17). Given that Zhi Qian was active in the territory of Wu between 222 and 253, it appears that Kang Senghui was active in the same place, only one generation later. T152 **(Ṣaṭ)pāramitā-samāsa* 六度集經 has been attributed to Kang Senghui, satisfying the above four conditions.

As to the composition style, the prose of T152 is similar to that of T20. Both texts follow the regular style of classical *wenyan* 文言. The forms of the verses in T152 are also similar to those found in T20, being regular quatrains of four, five, six or seven syllables. T152 also shows an attitude towards interpolations similar to that of T20. In T152, we find most of the Chinese terms that T20 adopts in order to appropriate established values: e.g., *renyi* 仁義 (benevolence and righteousness, T20.1.260a18, 263c28; T152.3.27c13), *renxiao* 仁孝 (benevolence and filial piety, T20.1.260c7; T152.3.26a14), *qingren* 清仁 (clean benevolence, probably the rendering of *karuṇā* in both texts, T20.1.260c10; T152.3.19a3), and *ciren* 慈仁 (love and benevolence, T20.1.261a16; T152.3.45a11, 52a17–18).

We also find that the renderings of T152 are compatible with those of T20. The writer of T152 renders *rājan cakravartin* as *feixinghuangdi* 飛行皇帝 (3.1c15 ff.), *srota-āpanna* and *sakṛdāgāmin* as *gougang* 溝港 and *pinlai* 頻來 (3.2b22 ff.), and the five aggregates as *se* 色, *tong* 痛, *xiang* 想, *xing* 行 and *shi* 識 (3.43b10–11), as in T20. We find the Chinese term *hunshen* 魂神 in T152 (3.35c6, 48c26), as in T20. For the renderings of the seven treasures, T152 presents three slightly different lists (3.21c15–16, 48c7–9, 52a13–15); however, these are not very different from those of T20. While T20 provides us with a full list of the ten epithets of the Buddha, T152 provides only partial ones; the renderings of the partial epithets are inconsistent within the text T152. A few of the renderings of the ten epithets in T152 differ from those found in T20. However, they are still consistent with the renderings used in other works of Zhi Qian. In sum, an examination of the renderings of T152 reveals that the authorship of T20 is compatible with T152.

In the light of writing style and the use of renderings, T152 appears to be consistent with T20. This means that, if the attribution of T152 to Kang Senghui 康僧會 by CSZJJ is correct, and if we may disregard the attribution of T20 to Zhi Qian by LDSBJ, Kang Senghui may be regarded as the probable writer of T20, as plausibly as Zhi Qian.

BAI YAN 白延 (BO YAN 帛延)

Bai Yan is said to have been active around 254–9 in northern China. The editors of T attribute to him T328 *Xulai jing* 須賴經, which is one of three translations attributed to him by CSZJJ (T4215.55.7b3). His brief biography in CSZJJ indicates that he was not a creative but a revising translator 重譯出 (T2145.55.96a27–28).[23] His *Xulai jing* is also probably the revised translation of Zhi Qian's original work. However, as mentioned above, Nattier rejects the traditional attribution of T328 to Bai Yan and attributes it to Zhi Qian. Indeed, the renderings of T328 are in accordance with Zhi Qian's other works. However, in terms of writing style, we find a few factors that weaken her new attribution.

An examination of the renderings does not exclude the writer of T328 from the list of candidates for the translatorship of T20. The wheel-turning king, his seven treasures and the four achievements of practitioners do not appear in T328. Instead, we find in T328 renderings for the five aggregates (12.55a5) which are the same as those found in T20; and the renderings of the ten epithets of the Buddha (12.54a24–26) agree with those found in T20, except for that of *sugata* as *shanshi* 善逝 (T328), instead of *shandao* 善道 (T20). As Nattier points out (2003, pp. 225–6), the *shandao* 善道 of T20 is the only exception to the uniform rendering of *sugata* as *shanshi* 善逝 (T328) in Zhi Qian's works.

However, an examination of the writing style makes it doubtful whether T328 can be attributed to Zhi Qian. Although trivial, there is an odd discrepancy between the prose and verse style in T328. Its prose appears less strict in following the regular style of classical *wenyan* 文言, compared to T20. On the contrary, the verses of T328 are more standardized than T20: each of the 72 verses at 18 locations in T328 is a quatrain of lines of five or seven syllables; it contains no quatrain of lines of four or six syllables. Although sporadically found in the works of the archaic translation period (before 375), this form of verse became standard roughly from the start of the old translation period. On the contrary, the verses in T20 consist of regular quatrains of lines of four, five or six syllables, a stereotype for archaic translations.

Most importantly, in T328 we cannot detect interpolations reflecting Chinese values, such as characterize T20 and Zhi Qian's other works.

23. Both CSZJJ and GSZ (T2059.50.325a9–12) state that his origin and life are unknown 不知何(許)人. LDSBJ (T2034.49.56c16–18) describes him as a monk from the west; KYL (T2154.55.519a27, 631c14) describes him as a western monk who was the crown prince of Kucha 龜茲.

In T328 we cannot find any Chinese term indicating a permanent agent in *saṃsāra*, such as *jingshen* 精神 or *hunshen* 魂神. Furthermore, not to mention *yi* (義: justice or righteousness in the Confucian sense), we cannot find a single occurrence of *xiao* (孝: filial piety) in T328. As for *ren* (仁: benevolence), it is used only as a rendering of *karuṇā* in place of *bei* 悲, or as an honorific, meaning 'gentleman'. The author of T328 does not attempt to make the hero *Xulai* (須賴) a figure familiar to the Chinese by means of adaptations or interpolations.

CSZJJ attributes a recension of *Xulai jing* to Zhi Qian (T2145.55.6c) and another to Bai Yan. Zhi Qian was active between 222 and 253 in southern China, and Bai Yan was active around 254–9 in northern China. Since CSZJJ indicates that Bai Yan was not a creative but a revising translator, Bai Yan's *Xulai jing* is probably a revised version of Zhi Qian's translation. If the writer of T328 was in the circle of Zhi Qian, it would be odd that the standardized style of the verses in T328 appears a generation later than that of Zhi Qian's T210 *Dharmapada*, which consists entirely of verses and whose style is similar to that of T20. Thus we may infer that the present T328 is more likely to be a retranslation by Bai Yan than the original by Zhi Qian. This possibility is strengthened by the fact that T328 lacks the Chinese interpolations prevailing in Zhi Qian's works.

In short, the probability that the writer of T328 wrote T20 is far lower than the probability that the writer of T152 did. Above all, the attitude towards interpolations reflecting Chinese values in T20 appears incompatible with the authorship of T328. Hence, I omit his name from the list of possible candidates for the authorship of T20.

BO FAZU 帛法祖 (FL. 290–306)

Although none of Bo Fazu's works satisfies all four of the above principles, he should be considered an exception, since he has traditionally been regarded as the author of T5 *Mahāparinirvāna-sūtra* 佛般泥洹經. As mentioned above, T6 is attributed to Zhi Qian by Ui and Nattier, and, as Nattier pointed out (2003, p. 241, n. 118), there is no doubt that, regarding T5 and T6, one is dependent on the other, i.e., one of the two is a retranslation of the other. The problem here is that T5 and T6 share conspicuous characteristics of Zhi Qian's translation work. If T6 is Zhi Qian's translation, as argued by Ui and Nattier, and if T5 is by Bo Fazu, as is traditionally supposed, Bo may be a strong candidate for the translatorship of T20. In the aforementioned paper (Park, 2008), I undertook an examination of the translatorship. Instead of repeating the same task, I will summarize here the results of my examination. Firstly, an examination of the renderings in T5 and T6 reveals that both texts are translations by Zhi Qian or by those who thoroughly took over his distinctive lexicon and style. Secondly, the archaic writing style, particularly the style of the verses, and the renderings that are unique to Zhi Qian indicate that T5 is probably his work, and that it may be one of his earliest translations. Judging from the verse style of T5, it appears to have been composed earlier than T210 *Dharmapada*, which was translated by Zhi Qian around 224. Thirdly, the tendency of T6 to remove the interpolated expressions of filial piety in T5 and replace the archaic renderings of T5 with later, standard renderings indicates that the writer of T6 is probably not Zhi Qian himself, but a successor in his translation circle.

For these reasons, I suggested above that T5 should be included in the 'provisional list of the authentic works of Zhi Qian,' and that we should include T6 among the 'candidate texts.' Consequently, there are no grounds for regarding Bo Fazu as a candidate translator of T20.

ZHU FAHU 竺法護 (239?–316?)[24]

Zhu Fahu 竺法護 was born in China. His ancestors emigrated to Dunhuang 敦煌 from Yuezhi 月支, and he became a monk at the age of eight. During the reign Taishi 泰始 (265–74), he travelled to western countries, learnt many South/Central Asian languages and collected Buddhist scriptures. CSZJJ attributes 154 translations to him, LDSBJ 210 and KYL 175. Among the extant texts in T, 95 translations are attributed to him.

Having researched the prologues, colophons and Buddhist catalogues, Suzuki (1995) nominated forty texts as definite translations by Zhu Fahu, and classified them into five types according to their similarities in terms of renderings and transliterations. In order to explore whether

---

24. Zhu Fahu's biography in CSZJJ (T2145.55.97c–98b) records that he died on the road escaping a revolt that caused Emperor Hui 惠帝 to move his residence to Changan 長安. Since the movement happened in 304 and since Zhu Fahu is said to have been seventy-eight when he died (according to the Chinese calculation), he would have been born in 227. However, in listing Zhu Fahu's translations, Sengyou himself annotates that Zhu Fahu had been engaged in translation from the reign Taishi 泰始 (265–74) to the second year of the reign Yongjia 永嘉 (308) (T2145.55.9b27–c4). The colophon to T588 **Suvikrāntadevaputra-paripṛcchā* 須真天子經 (T2145.55.48b22–26) records that the text was translated in 266; and the colophon to T186 **Lalitavistara* 普曜經 (T2145.55.48b27–c1) records that it was translated by Zhu Fahu in 308. Therefore, the record of his death year in his biography appears to be incorrect.

Table 2.4 Suzuki's list of Zhu Fahu's translations

Type	*Zhu Fahu's translations*
A	T222 光讚經, T588 須真天子經, T636 無極寶三昧經
A′	T186 普曜經, T263 正法華經, T266 阿惟越致遮經, T285 漸備一切智德經, T291 如來興顯經, T292 度世品經, T310 大寶積經 · 密迹金剛力士會 (fascs. 8–14), T310 大寶積經 · 寶髻菩薩會 (fascs. 117–18), T345 慧上菩薩問大善權經, T398 大哀經, T403 阿差末菩薩經, T460 文殊師利淨律經, T461 文殊師利現寶藏經, T565 順權方便經, T606 修行道地經, T627 文殊支利普超三昧經, T817 大淨法門經
B	T585 持心梵天所問經
B′	T338 離垢施女經
C	T103 聖法印經, T170 德光太子經, T182AB 鹿母經, T199 佛五百弟子自說本起經, T283 菩薩十住行道品, T315ab 普門品經, T317 胞胎經, T342 如幻三昧經, T349 彌勒菩薩所問本願經, T378 方等般泥洹經, T399 寶女所問經, T425 賢劫經, T435 滅十方冥經, T459 文殊悔過經, T481 持人菩薩經, T589 魔逆經, T598 海龍王經, T737 所欲致患經

Zhu Fahu could be a candidate for the translatorship of T20, I restrict my examination to the forty texts studied by Suzuki. Her list and classification of the definite translations of Zhu Fahu are shown in Table 2.4.

Among the five types in the table, we find that Zhu Fahu copies many of Zhi Qian's renderings in works of Types A′, B, B′ and C, but not in works of Type A. However, we find that some renderings in T20 are not in accordance with those in any of these four types. For example, unlike T20, none of the forty translations by Zhu Fahu renders *rājan cakravartin* as *feixinghuangdi* 飛行皇帝. All use the standard rendering *zhuanlunshengwang* 轉輪聖王, which appears in T186, T222, T263, T285, T291, T310 (8–14), T310 (117–18), T378, T399, T403, T425, T461, T585, T588, T598, T606 and T627. As for the four achievements of Buddhist practitioners, neither of the renderings *gougang* (溝港 for *srota-āpanna*) or *pinlai* (頻來 for *sakṛdāgāmin*) of T20 appears in the above forty texts by Zhu Fahu.[25] There are several occurrences of *yingzhen* 應真 (T263, T266, T398, T403 and T481); however, it occurs separately, never in the sequence of the four achievements. For these four achievements, Zhu Fahu uses the transliterations *xutuohuan* 須陀洹, *situohan* 斯陀含, *anahan* 阿那含 and *aluohan* 阿羅漢 (T222.8.150b14–15, T460.14.449c17–19, T481.14.629b22–23 and T588.15.107a27–28)

25. *Pinlai* appears once in T425.14.43c. However, there it is not used as a technical rendering for *sakṛdāgāmin*.

or the renderings *daoji* 道跡 (or 道迹), *wanglai* 往來, *buhuan* 不還 and *wuzhu* 無著 (T263.9.118a27, T266.9.201a8ff., T342.12.146b3ff., T345.12.164c26, T398.13.419c10–11ff., T403.13.592c21ff., T585.15.9b3 and 598.15.143c22). This inconsistency between the renderings of T20 and those of Zhu Fahu reveals that Zhu Fahu could not be the writer of T20.

NIE CHENGYUAN 聶承遠

Nie Chengyuan was a Buddhist layman who participated as a scribe 筆受 in Zhu Fahu's translation teams for T222 *Pañcaviṃśatisāhasrikā Prajñāpāramitā* 光讚經, T263 *Saddharma-puṇḍarīka-sūtra* 正法華經, T285 *Daśabhūmika-sūtra* 漸備一切智德經, T398 **Tathāgata-mahākaruṇā-nirdeśa* 大哀經, T585 **Brahmaviśeṣacintī-paripṛcchā* 持心梵天所問經, T588 **Suvikrāntadevaputra-paripṛcchā* 須真天子經 and the lost translation of the **Śūraṃgama-sūtra* 首楞嚴經. CSZJJ attributes the *Chaoriming jing* 超日明經 to him and notes that it is a revised translation of Zhu Fahu's original version. T638 is identified with Nie's *Chaoriming jing* by the editors of T.

T638 copies the renderings of Zhu Fahu. It renders *rājan cakravartin* as *zhuanlunshengwang* 轉輪聖王 (T15.533a ff.); for the renderings of the four achievements, it follows Zhu Fahu's renderings: *daoji* 道跡, *wanglai* 往來, *buhuan* 不還 and *wuzhu* 無著 (15.535a, 536b). Therefore, given that he is the writer of T638, Nie Chengyuan should be excluded from the list of candidate writers of T20.

WUCHALUO 無叉羅 AND ZHU SHULAN 竺叔蘭

Zhu Shixing 朱士行, popularly known as the first Chinese ordained monk and the first traveller to western countries for the purpose of collecting Buddhist scriptures, departed from China around 260. He collected the *Pañcaviṃśatisāhasrikā Prajñāpāramitā* in Khotan and sent it to China. It arrived at Louyang 洛陽 in 282 and was translated at Suinan Temple 水南寺 in Chenliujun 陳留郡 in 291. The Khotanese monk Wuchaluo 無叉羅 recited the original text 執胡本, and Zhu Shulan 竺叔蘭, a Chinese layman of Indian origin, translated/interpreted 口傳 it. The text was revised again by Zhu Shulan and Zhu Faji 竺法寂 in 303–4. Considering the typical procedure of Chinese Buddhist translation, we may regard Zhu Shulan as the substantial translator of the text. T221 *Fangguang banruo jing* 放光般若經 is identified by the editors of T as the *Pañcaviṃśatisāhasrikā Prajñāpāramitā* attributed to Zhu Shixing *et al.* by CSZJJ.

An examination of the renderings in T221 quickly reveals that they are not candidates for the translatorship of T20. Instead of the *gougang* 溝港, *pinlai* 頻來, *buhuan* 不還 and *yingzhen* 應真 of T20, T221 (8.5c ff.) uses the standardized transliterations *xutuohuan* 須陀洹, *situohan* 斯陀含, *anahan* 阿那含 and *aluohan* 阿羅漢 for the names of the four achievements of practitioners. Unlike T20, in which Chinese renderings are more frequently used than transliterations, T221 prefers the use of transliterations; for example, *aweisanfo* (阿惟三佛: *anuttara-samyaksambodhi*), *anouduoluosanyesanpu* (阿耨多羅三耶三菩: also for *anuttara-samyaksambodhi*), *boluomi* (波羅蜜: *pāramitā*) and *ouhejusheluo* (漚惒拘舍羅: *upāya-kauśalya*) do not match the vocabulary of T20. Therefore I exclude Zhu Shulan *et al.* from the list of possible candidates for the translatorship of T20.

FAJU 法炬 (FL. 308) AND FALI 法立

The birth and death dates of Faju and his origin are unknown. The colophon to T186 *Lalitavistara* 普曜經 states that Faju was one of the scribes in Zhu Fahu's translation team in 308 (T2145.55.48b27–c1). CSZJJ attributes four texts to Faju, i.e., the *Loutan jing* 樓炭經, the **Dharmapada-nidāna* 法句本末經, the *Futian jing* 福田經 and the **Tathāgatagarbha-sūtra* 大方等如來藏經,[26] and notes that Fali 法立 is the co-translator of the second and the third of them. The first three texts are identified as T23 大樓炭經, T211 法句譬喻經 and T683 諸德福田經 by the editors of T.

As for the writing style, I could find no significant difference between T20 and Faju's three extant translations. The prose and verse styles in Faju's translations are similar to those of T20. As for the attitude towards interpolations, we find the Chinese-style emphasis on filial piety intermittently throughout T23 and T211.

There are several differences between the renderings of T20 and those of Faju's works. T23 preserves two slightly different lists of the renderings for the seven treasures (1.281a5–7 and 290b16–18). These differ slightly from those found in T20, although the differences are trivial. Instead of the Chinese renderings of *gougang* 溝港, *buhuan* 不還 and *yingzhen* 應真 for the first, third and fourth achievements of practitioners in T20, Faju's works present us with *xutuohuan* 須陀洹 (T211.4.575c8 ff.), *anahan* 阿那含 (T211.4.581a24, 29) and *aluohan* 阿羅漢 (T23.1.290b3 ff., T211.4576a19 ff.). Considering these differences

---

26. It is striking that the number of Faju's translations increases to 132 in LDSBJ.

in renderings, Faju and Fali are less likely to be the writers of T20 than Zhi Qian and Kang Senghui.

In sum, the writing style and renderings of T20 appear to be in accordance with those of Zhi Qian's other works. Therefore, the traditional attribution of T20 to Zhi Qian since LDSBJ may be valid in the light of the comparison between those elements. However, T152 *(Ṣaṭ)pāramitā-samāsa* 六度集經 shows the same accord with T20; therefore, Kang Senghui has the same chance of being the author of T20 as does Zhi Qian. Besides, we cannot exclude the possibility that an anonym in Zhi Qian's translation circle was the writer of T20.

Provided that T5 is probably one of the earliest translations by Zhi Qian around 224 and that T6 is a retranslation of T5, probably later than the writing of T152 by Kang Senghui (fl. 247–80), we find some clues to narrow down the possible period of the translation of T20. For example, an undoubted interpolation by the author of T20, 'No matter how wise a son is, he can neither stop the ageing, disease and death of his father, nor go to a hell instead of the father who committed sins while he was alive' (see Chap. 1, note 53), occurs in the part unique to T20 (i.e., not common to PA, SA/T1451/T1448 and T1). A very similar sentence, 'The evil deeds of a father cannot be redeemed by his sons; the evil deeds of a son cannot be redeemed by his father,'[27] occurs only in T6, while the corresponding part of T5 does not have it. (MPP, MPS/T1451, T1 and T7 lack the corresponding part itself.) This may indicate the close relationship between T20 and T6. This closeness is strengthened by the fact that the renderings for the seven treasures in T20 are the most similar to those in T6, differing much from any of Zhi Qian's 'authentic' works.[28]

Surveying the use of the archaic and later standard renderings in T5, T6, T20 and T152, we can obtain meaningful information to pinpoint the translation date of T20. Comparing the peculiar renderings of the older and later couplets, we have the results shown in Table 2.5. Provided that these four translations were produced in the same translation circle, the renderings of the left-hand column for each couplet may well be

---

27. 父作不善, 子不代受; 子作不善, 父亦不受. 善自獲福, 惡自受殃 (T6.1.181b1–2).
28. However, it is not likely that T6 and T20 were written by the same author. Compared to T5, the probably later retranslation T6 includes a smaller number of interpolations reflecting Chinese values, as I demonstrate in Park (2008); whereas T20 shows a strong inclination to intentional interpolation and distortion, as I demonstrated in Section 1.5. The closeness between T6 and T20 may rather originate from temporal closeness within the translation circle of Zhi Qian.

said to pre-date the right-hand ones. As expected, T5 has the oldest stratum; it uses archaic renderings most frequently. Then, although it is a work of a generation after Zhi Qian, T152 by Kang Senghui shows that it still preserves a considerable number of archaic renderings. On the contrary, T20 replaces the archaic renderings with later standard ones except for *rājan cakravartin*; and T6 replaces all of them. This implies that T20 and T6 are probably more recent than Kang Senghui's T152. This implication is also strengthened by the fact that the renderings for the seven treasures in T152.3.21c15–16[29] are closer to those of T5, differing from the more standardized ones of T20 and T6. Therefore, it appears plausible to pinpoint the translation date of T20 to the late third century, which implies that the author of T20 may not have been Zhi Qian himself. It is also possible that Zhi Qian's original translation was subjected to a systematic retouching during the late third century.

Table 2.5 Use of archaic renderings in T5, T152, T20 and T6

	piṇḍapātika		*brāhmaṇa*		*rājan cakravartin*	
	分衛	乞食	逝心	梵志	飛行皇帝	轉輪(聖)王
T5	7	0	29	2	13	1
T152	5	1	13	125	13	0
T20	0	2	0	9	1	0
T6	0	2	0	18	0	9

29. 飛金輪・力白象・紺色馬・明月珠・玉女妻・聖輔臣・典兵臣.

Part II

THE DEVELOPMENT OF THE INDIAN BUDDHIST CONCEPT OF SELF

PREAMBLE

As a first step towards understanding the transformation of the Buddhist concept of self between India and China, I now examine the Indian Buddhist conceptions of self which were introduced into China and there developed further. I begin by investigating the principal factors that underlie the early Buddhist concept of self, and build up a picture of how those factors are constructed in early Buddhist soteriology. Then I draw attention to some eccentric factors in early Buddhism whose implications are not in accordance with the concept of self in that soteriology, and illustrate the way in which those factors constructed new Buddhist conceptions of self, yielding a dramatic change in the Buddhist doctrinal system.

Illustrating how such factors construct and transform Buddhist conceptions of self, I demonstrate the logical structure of those factors within a doctrinal system, and trace their transformation between various doctrinal systems of Buddhism. Although I bear in mind the historical development of these conceptions, the order in which I present them in this book is a logical one; it does not necessarily concur with their chronological development. My aim here is to reveal the fundamental ways of thinking that made possible the dramatic development of the Buddhist concept of self in India and China.

Chapter 3

SELF IN EARLY BUDDHIST SOTERIOLOGY

The English word 'self', frequently capitalized, has been widely used to translate the Sanskrit word *ātman*. Since *ātman* refers to a permanent self in many contexts of Indian thought,[1] and since the doctrine of *anātman* or non-self has been a distinctive catch-phrase of Buddhism, many contemporary scholars avoid using the English word 'self' in an affirmative sense. This avoidance may, on the one hand, help readers to keep in mind the fact that Buddhists rejected the concept of a permanent self, but on the other hand it may spawn the misunderstanding that Buddhists rejected any concept of self at all. In this book, I use the word self as it is used in daily life, i.e., with no implication of eternality or changelessness, and examine how Indian Buddhists developed their conceptions of self while rejecting the concept of a permanent self.

Self in Buddhism is described, analysed and taught in inseparable connection with its soteriology. One peculiar characteristic of the concept of self in Buddhism is that understanding self as it is (*yathā-bhūta*) may well be regarded as equal to the complete soteriological practice in Buddhism: when one understands how a living being comes into being and how it stops coming into being, one reaches the destination of Buddhist soteriology. For this reason, I analyse various Buddhist conceptions of self ontologically, epistemologically and ethically within their soteriological contexts, and illustrate how the conceptions are structured in the development of Buddhist soteriology.

---

1. Collins (1982, pp. 71–8) presents a survey and analysis of the early Buddhist usages of the term *ātman* or *attan* in three categories: as reflexive pronoun, as religious exhortation and as theoretical construct. For another survey, see Harvey (1995, pp. 19–21).

AN IMPERMANENT SELF UNDERGOING INNUMERABLE REBIRTHS

The four noble truths form the soteriological framework of Buddhism, in that they explain why and how one should practise Buddhism. According to the four noble truths, we have to know that life is suffering, eliminate the origin of the suffering, realize the cessation of suffering, and practise the way leading to that cessation. However, this framework itself is not peculiar to Buddhism. It has been shared by major religious movements in India before as well as after the emergence of Buddhism: living beings suffer the painful chain of endless rebirth, they are confined in the chain due to their ignorance and desire, there is a state free from such suffering, and, in order to achieve such a state, one should have correct views, etc. We cannot characterize Buddhism by this framework alone.

Indeed, what makes Buddhism peculiar among religious or philosophical movements in India is the Buddhist view of self, the correct understanding of which constitutes the 'correct view' that characterizes Buddhism. In early Buddhism, the concept of self is constituted by three critical features: 1) a self is located in *saṃsāra,* the chain of innumerable rebirths, being subject to the law of karma; 2) the so-called self is impermanent: it is a compound, all of whose components are impermanent; and 3) the components of a self are constructed dependent on certain conditions.

Self in the Postulate of Saṃsāra *and Karma*

Around the time of the Buddha, there were materialists who were branded by the Buddha as *ucchedavādin,* 'nihilists'. They were branded thus because they held that a self is destroyed at death. In the *Brahmajāla-sutta* (D.I.34), the Buddha describes them as follows:

> Monks, there are some ascetics and brahmins who advocate nihilism. They proclaim the annihilation, destruction, non-existence of living beings on seven bases. ... Monks, here a certain ascetic or brahmin advocates thus and holds the view thus: 'Since, sir, this self is indeed material, composed of the four great elements and produced by parents, it is annihilated and perishes after the destruction of the body. It does not exist after death.'[2]

2. *santi, bhikkhave, eke samaṇa-brāhmaṇā ucchedavādā sattassa ucchedaṃ vināsaṃ vibhavaṃ paññāpenti sattahi vatthūhi. ... idha, bhikkhave, ekacco samaṇo vā brāhmaṃo vā evaṃvādī hoti evaṃdiṭṭhī: 'yato kho bho ayaṃ attā*

Based on this ontological postulate, those 'nihilists' adopted an amoral position in ethics: for example, King Ajātasattu reports the view of Pūraṇa Kassapa:

> ... Suppose that one comes along (or to) the south bank of the Ganges killing, making others kill, mutilating, making others mutilate, torturing and making others torture. There is no evil on that basis; no evil is accumulated. Suppose that one goes along (or to) the north bank of the Ganges donating, making others donate, offering sacrifice and making others offer sacrifice. There is no merit on that basis; no merit is accumulated. ...[3]

The critical point in Pūraṇa Kassapa's view is that skilful or unskilful actions in this life are irrelevant to good or bad results in future lives, and that, therefore, there is no reason to give up one's present benefits from moral motives.

The early Buddhists in India rejected both 'nihilist' ontology and its amoral implications. They placed the self in *saṃsāra*, and bound it to the law of karma. To put it another way, karma is an identifier of a person in *saṃsāra*: the future I is the very person who will suffer or enjoy the results of my present moral actions, and the past I is the very person the results of whose moral actions I am suffering or enjoying. The law of karma is a mechanical power that locates living beings in certain circumstances according to the being's moral actions; it is a function whose input is moral or immoral actions and whose output is the comfort or discomfort of living circumstances. The discrepancy between the nature of input (*kuśala* or *akuśala*) and output (*avyākṛta*) implies that Buddhism is not determinism. What are determined by past actions are merely the temporary circumstances of the present life; any present moral decision is never determined by past actions. In this sense, we ascertain that so-called free will is presupposed in the early Buddhist karma theory.

The most conspicuous characteristic of Buddhist karma is ethicization, as K. R. Norman (1993b, p. 276) summarizes:

---

rūpī cātummahābhūtiko mātāpettikasambhavo, kāyassa bhedā ucchijjati vinassati, na hoti paraṃ maraṇā.'

3. ... *dakkhiṇañ ce pi Gaṅgātīraṃ āgaccheyya hananto ghātento chindanto chedāpento pacanto pācento, n' atthi tatonidānaṃ pāpaṃ, n' atthi pāpassa āgamo. uttarañ ce pi Gaṅgātīraṃ gaccheyya dadanto dāpento yajanto yajāpento, n' atthi tatonidānaṃ puññaṃ, n' atthi puññassa āgamo* ... (*Sāmaññaphala-sutta*, D.I.52).

> The word *karman* is used in a Brahmanical context to refer specifically to the ritual act enjoined by brahmanical ideology. The Buddha stated that he would interpret 'act' to refer to intention, with the result that there is a shift from ritual to ethics. Whereas the performance of the ritual action of sacrifice gave an automatic result, this development in the interpretation of kamma meant that the quality of the next life is determined by the quality of the actions.[4]

The core feature in the Buddhist ethicization of karma theory lies in the emphasis on moral intention. Among the three kinds of moral action, i.e., bodily action, verbal action and mental action, the last has always been regarded as the most important.[5] Furthermore, karma itself is defined as intention (*cetanā*): for example, 'I (i.e., the Buddha) declare karma to be intention. Having intended, a person makes karma by means of the body, words and thought.'[6] As defined in the *Vibhaṅga*, 'Unskilful bodily action is unskilful bodily intention ...';[7] this definition of karma as intention became the standard exegesis in later Buddhism.[8] Thus, even in a worldly sense, the early Buddhists presume strong moral motivations: to be happy in our future lives, we should be moral from our own hearts; it is useless to offer ritually correct sacrifices or to pretend to be moral.

Rejection of Eternalism

Given that the early Buddhists placed a self in a chain of innumerable rebirths, it appears natural to expect it to be permanent. However, on the contrary, the early Buddhists strongly rejected any conception of a

---

4. For more information about the characteristics of early Buddhist karma theory in contrast to Brahmanic ideas, refer to Gombrich (1984, pp. 94–7) and Collins (1982, pp. 53–8).
5. Hence, responding to a Nigaṇṭha, who follows the teaching that bodily action is the most important, the Buddha declares that mental action is the most important among the three kinds of action: *imesaṃ kho ahaṃ, Tapassi, tiṇṇaṃ kammānaṃ evaṃ paṭivibhattānaṃ evaṃ paṭivisiṭṭhānaṃ manokammaṃ mahāsāvajjataraṃ paññāpemi pāpassa kammassa kiriyāya pāpassa kammassa pavattiyā, no tathā kāyakammaṃ, no tathā vacīkamman ti* (*Upāli-sutta*, M.I.373).
6. *cetanā 'haṃ, bhikkhave, kammaṃ vadāmi. cetayitvā kammaṃ karoti kāyena vācā manasā* (A.III.415).
7. *akusalā kāyasañcetanā akusalaṃ kāyakammaṃ* ... (Vibh.364).
8. We can trace back the use of the term *sañcetanā* denoting *karman* at A.II.157–58: *kāye vā, bhikkhave, sati kāyasañcetanāhetu uppajjati ajjhattaṃ sukhadukkhaṃ* ...

permanent self. The critical reason why they rejected the existence of a permanent self is that, in the context of Indian philosophy, the property of 'being permanent' implies the property of 'being unchanging'. Buddhists presumed a self or a person continuing but ever-changing in *saṃsāra*. Since they rejected any self or its essence that exists forever without changing, they rejected any conception of a permanent self.

In the aforementioned *Alaggadūpama-sutta*, the Buddha describes a person who is frightened on hearing of the absence of anything eternal, i.e., a permanent, unchanging self:

> Monk, one may have a view, 'The world (*loka*) is the self (*ātman*). After death, I shall be permanent, constant, eternal and not subject to change. I shall continue to be the same for all eternity.' He listens to the Tathāgata or one of his disciples who gives teachings which conduce to uprooting every view, prejudice, bias, inclination and propensity, and which conduce to tranquilizing all mental activities, to abandoning all attachment, to destroying craving, to dispassion, to cessation and to *nirvāṇa*. [Then] he thinks, 'I shall be annihilated, I shall perish, I shall not exist.' [For this,] he grieves, gets distressed, laments, beats his breast and falls into confusion.[9]

Here, in addition to the claim that the Buddhist soteriology, aiming at *nirvāṇa*, is incompatible with any view of a permanent self, we can read that the adherents of a permanent self regarded the teaching of *nirvāṇa* as nihilism, since there will be no more self after *nirvāṇa*. Then, in the *sutta*, having described in contrast the characteristics of those who are not frightened by the absence of something eternal, the Buddha announces,

> ... Monks, neither do I see any belonging that would be permanent, constant, eternal, not subject to change, and that would continue to be the same for all eternity. ... Neither do I see any doctrinal attachment to a [permanent] self whose adherent would not fall into grief, lamentation, pain, dissatisfaction and trouble. ... While neither a [permanent] self nor what [permanently] belongs to self is admitted to be truthful or to

9. *"idha, bhikkhu, ekaccassa evaṃ diṭṭhi hoti: 'so loko so attā, so pecca bhavissāmi nicco dhuvo sassato avipariṇāmadhammo, sassatisamaṃ tath' eva ṭhassāmī' ti. so suṇāti Tathāgatassa vā tathāgatasāvakassa vā sabbesaṃ diṭṭhiṭṭhānādhiṭṭhā-napariyuṭṭhānābhinivesānusayānaṃ samugghātāya sabbasaṃkhārasamathāya sabbūpadhipaṭinissaggāya taṇhakkhayāya virāgāya nirodhāya nibbānāya dhammaṃ desentassa. tassa evaṃ hoti: 'ucchijjissāmi nāma su, vinassissāmi nāma su, na su nāma bhavissāmī' ti. so socati kilamati paridevati urattāḷiṃ kandati sammohaṃ āpajjati"* (M.I.136–37).

> be established, is it not entirely foolish to have such a view, 'The world (*loka*) is the self (*ātman*). After death, I shall be permanent, constant, eternal and not subject to change. I will continue to be the same for all eternity'?[10]

From this conversation, we notice that, despite being branded as nihilists by the advocates of a permanent self, the early Buddhists held fast to rejecting any conception of a permanent self.

Self as a Compound of the Five Aggregates

In early Buddhism, a self is regarded as a compound of the five aggregates, i.e., form (*rūpa*), feeling (*vedanā)*, apperception (*saṃjñā*), mental activities [other than *vedanā, saṃjñā* and *vijñāna*] (*saṃskāra*s) and consciousness (*vijñāna*). Firmly based on this theory, they refuted any conception of a permanent self, asserting that this is a delusion originating in incorrect observation of the five aggregates. So, in the *Khandha-saṃyutta*, the Buddha declares:

> Monks, all the ascetics and brahmins who consider self in various ways are [in fact] considering the five aggregates or one of the five.[11]

Throughout the major *Nikāya*s, we find this proposition prevailing: nothing more than the five aggregates is to be regarded as a self.[12]

Postulating that there is no self beyond the five aggregates, the predominant Buddhist method of disproving any conception of a permanent self follows this scheme: form (is impermanent, so it is suffering, and so it) is not a permanent self (*ātman*), feeling is

---

10. ...*aham pi kho taṃ, bhikkhave, pariggahaṃ na samanupassāmi yvâssa pariggaho nicco dhuvo sassato avipariṇāmadhammo, sassatisamaṃ tath' eva tiṭṭheyya ... aham pi kho taṃ, bhikkhave, attavād'upādānaṃ na samanupassāmi yaṃ sa attavād'upādānaṃ upādiyato na uppajjeyyuṃ soka-parideva-dukkha-domanass'upāyāsā ... attaniye ca, bhikkhave, attaniye ca saccato thetato anupalabbhamāne yam p'idaṃ diṭṭhiṭṭhānaṃ: 'so loko, so attā, so pecca bhavissāmi nicco dhuvo sassato avipariṇāmadhammo, sassatisamaṃ tath' eva ṭhassāmī' ti, na ca kho 'yaṃ, bhikkhave, kevalo paripūro bāladhammo? ti* (M.I.137–38).
11. *ye hi keci, bhikkhave, samaṇā vā brāhmaṇā vā anekavihitam attānaṃ samanupassamānā samanupassanti, sabbe te pañc'upādānakkhandhe samanupassanti etesaṃ vā aññataraṃ* (S.III.46).
12. E.g., the *Cūḷavedalla-sutta* (M.I.299), the *Mahārāhulovāda-sutta* (M.I.421), the *Pañcattaya-sutta* (M.II.230), the *Mahāpuṇṇama-sutta* (M.III.17), the *Chachakka-sutta* (M.III.284), the *Saḷāyatana-saṃyutta* (S.IV.1 ff.), and so forth.

... apperception is ... mental activities are ... and consciousness (is impermanent, so it is suffering, and so it) is not a permanent self; [therefore, there is no permanent self.][13] For example, in the above-quoted *Alagaddūpama-sutta*, the Buddha leads a dialogue:

> 'What do you think, monks? Is form permanent or impermanent?' 'Impermanent, sir.' 'Is something impermanent suffering or pleasure?' 'Suffering, sir.' 'Given that it is suffering and subject to change, is it appropriate to consider that this is mine, I am this and this is my self?' 'No, it is not, sir.' 'What do you think, monks? Is feeling ... apperception ... mental activities ... consciousness permanent or impermanent?' 'Impermanent, sir.' 'Is something impermanent suffering or pleasure?' 'Suffering, sir.' 'Given that it is suffering and subject to change, is it appropriate to consider that this is mine, I am this and this is my self?' 'No, it is not, sir.'[14]

The context in which we find the early Buddhists announcing a self to be a compound of the five aggregates is usually negative: it is not presented as an illustrative model of a self, but as a polemic apparatus to dispute various conceptions of a permanent self. Only sporadically do we find them using the five aggregates positively to illustrate their conception of self, although the illustration is still in the wider context of disputing the existence of a permanent self. Hence, in the *Bhikkhunī-saṃyutta* (S.I.135), when Māra (Death) distracts the *bhikkhunī* Vajirā in a Brahmanic voice:

> By whom was this being created?
> Where is the maker of the being?
> Where was the being born?
> Where does the being cease?[15]

---

13. We find another simpler scheme that, since they are not permanent, the five aggregates are not [permanent] self, e.g., M.I.424, M.III.282, etc., and another one that, since they are suffering, the five aggregates are not [permanent] self, e.g., S.IV.2 ff.
14. *'taṃ kim maññatha, bhikkhave: rūpaṃ niccaṃ vā aniccaṃ vā?' ti. 'aniccaṃ bhante.' 'yaṃ panâniccaṃ, dukkhaṃ vā taṃ sukhaṃ vā?' ti. 'dukkhaṃ bhante.' 'yaṃ panâniccaṃ dukkhaṃ vipariṇāmadhammaṃ, kallan nu taṃ samanupassituṃ: etaṃ mama, eso 'ham asmi, eso me attā?' ti. 'no h' etam bhante.' 'taṃ kim maññatha, bhikkhave: vedanā ... saññā ... saṅkhārā ... viññāṇaṃ niccaṃ vā aniccaṃ vā?' ti. 'aniccaṃ bhante.' 'yaṃ panâniccaṃ, dukkhaṃ vā taṃ sukhaṃ vā?' ti. 'dukkhaṃ bhante.' 'yaṃ panâniccaṃ dukkhaṃ vipariṇāmadhammaṃ, kallan nu taṃ samanupassituṃ: etaṃ mama, eso 'ham asmi, eso me attā?' ti. 'no h' etam bhante.'* (M.I.138).
15. *kenâyaṃ pakato satto, kuvaṃ sattassa kārako*
    kuvaṃ satto samuppanno, kuvaṃ satto nirujjhatī? ti.

the *bhikkhunī* answers,

> What do you refer to, saying 'being'?
> Is it not that you, Death, have a [false] view?
> This is a heap of mere things [conditionally] constructed.[16]
> Here no being is found.
> As it is called a chariot because it is an assemblage of parts,
> In that way, when there are the aggregates, it is conventionally called 'being'.[17]

That is, just as a chariot is no more than an assemblage of its parts, a so-called self is no more than a compound of the five aggregates. In other words, as we cannot find a permanent, unchanging chariot in the assemblage of impermanent parts, we cannot find any permanent, unchanging self in the compound of the five impermanent aggregates.

The Theory of Dependent Origination (Pratītyasamutpāda)

While the theory of the five aggregates aims to argue for the impermanence of a self, the theory of dependent origination aims to explain how and why such an impermanent self goes through *saṃsāra*. Among the various formulae of dependent origination,[18] the standard version in reversed sequence describes the process of personal experience of suffering as follows:

> Monks, what is dependent origination? Monks, dependent on ignorance, [there happen] mental activities; dependent on mental activities, consciousness; dependent on consciousness, name-and-form; dependent on name-and-form, six [sense] bases; dependent on six bases, contact; dependent on contact, feeling; dependent on feeling, craving; dependent on craving, clinging; dependent on clinging, becoming; dependent on becoming, birth; dependent on birth, there happen ageing and death, sorrow, lamentation, pain, dissatisfaction and trouble. In this way, there is the origin of the whole aggregate of suffering. Monks, this is called arising.[19]

---

16. I discuss the threefold meaning of *saṅkhāra* below (see note 48).
17. *kin nu satto ti paccesi? Māra diṭṭhigataṃ nu te?*
    suddhasaṅkhārapuñjo 'yaṃ, na-y-idha sattûpalabbhati.
    yathā hi aṅgasambhārā hoti saddo ratho iti,
    evaṃ khandhesu santesu hoti satto ti sammuti.
18. For information about the various formulae of dependent origination, see Bucknell (1999).
19. *katamo ca, bhikkhave, paṭiccasamuppādo? avijjāpaccayā bhikkhave saṅkhārā, saṅkhārapaccayā viññāṇaṃ, viññāṇapaccayā nāmarūpaṃ, nāmarūpapaccayā*

In the same formula, the theory describes the process of eliminating the whole mass of suffering as follows:

> However, because of the complete detachment from and cessation of ignorance, mental activities cease; because of the cessation of mental activities, consciousness ceases; ... because of the cessation of birth, ageing, death, sorrow, lamentation, pain, dissatisfaction and trouble cease. In this way, there is the cessation of the whole aggregate of suffering.[20]

Note that the phrase 'the origin of the whole aggregate of suffering' (*etassa kevalassa dukkhakkhandhassa samudayo*) is the second of the four noble truths, and that the phrase 'the cessation of the whole aggregate of suffering' (*etassa kevalassa dukkhakkhandhassa nirodho*) is the third. For this reason, as Lamotte (1980, p. 119) points out, we find a version of the four noble truths in which the second truth is the dependent origination of the arising of suffering and the third truth is the dependent origination of the cessation of suffering (A.I.176–77).

In the theory of dependent origination, what is emphasized is the process by which impermanent mental and bodily factors construct or destroy the origination of suffering. In other words, no permanent agent involved in such a process is posited by the theory; rather, it is designed to refute such an agent. For this reason, when the Buddha is asked by the naked ascetic Kassapa (S.II.20 ff.) whether suffering is created by oneself, by another, both by oneself and by another, or neither by oneself nor by another, the Buddha answers, 'No, it is not so,' to all four questions. Nonetheless, when he is asked whether there is no suffering, the Buddha answers that there is suffering, and proclaims that he knows and sees suffering. The Buddha explains his negative answers: on the

---

saḷāyatanaṃ, saḷāyatanapaccayā phasso, phassapaccayā vedanā, vedanāpaccayā taṇhā, taṇhāpaccayā upādānaṃ, upādānapaccayā bhavo, bhavapaccayā jāti, jātipaccayā jarāmaraṇaṃ soka-parideva-dukkha-domanass'upāyāsā sambhavanti. evam etassa kevalassa dukkhakkhandhassa samudayo hoti. ayaṃ vuccati bhikkhave samuppādo (S.II.1).

For the translation and interpretation of the twelve factors of dependent origination, see Williams (1974) and Bucknell (1999, p. 313). Providing exegetic vindication of the Theravāda Abhidhammic three-life interpretation of the twelvefold dependent origination, Bhikkhu Bodhi (1998a;1998b) expounds several factors relevant to rebirth.

20. *avijjāya tv eva asesavirāganirodhā saṅkhāranirodho, saṅkhāranirodhā viññāṇanirodho, ... jātinirodhā jarāmaraṇaṃ soka-parideva-dukkha-domanass'upāyāsā nirujjhanti. evam etassa kevalassa dukkhakkhandhassa nirodho hotî ti* (S.II.1–2).

one hand, we cannot say that suffering is created by oneself, since such a proposition postulates a permanent agent—it is eternalism; on the other hand, we cannot say that suffering is created by another, since that means rejecting karmic law—it is nihilism.[21] Then, with the honorific epithet of the 'middle way', the Buddha presents the dependent origination of the arising of suffering and that of the cessation of suffering.

EXCURSUS: A SYSTEMATIC READING OF BUDDHIST TEXTS

Throughout Chapters 3 and 4 and 7 to 9, I aim to explicate the basic premises and principles on which the Indian and Chinese Buddhists constructed their conceptions of self. To do so, I normally put aside 'unsystematic' readings of self. By a 'systematic' reading I mean one which provides a consistent understanding of the text, consistent not merely within itself but within a wider textual context; by 'unsystematic' I mean a reading which accepts inconsistency. This concept is so important for my method that now, before going further, I shall devote several pages to exemplifying and clarifying it. For an example of what I mean by 'unsystematic' readings in Buddhism, let me consider the reading of the mind-only theory into the first and second verses of the *Dhammapada*. *Pāda*s a-b of Dhp_P §§1–2 read *manopubbaṅgamā dhammā manoseṭṭhā manomayā*. Without 'systematic' knowledge of Theravāda Buddhism, the most natural reading of this would be, 'The mind leads things (*dhamma*); the mind is the best [among things]; and [things] are made by (or consist of) mind.' The last phrase recalls the mind-only theory. However, systematic understanding of the *Dhammapada* as a text belonging to Theravāda literature discourages us from following that natural reading. Instead, in order to be 'systematic', we need to adopt an artificial interpretation.

For example, Norman (1997, p. 1) translates the passage as 'Mental phenomena are preceded by mind, have mind as their leader, are made by mind,' and Kalupahana (1986, p. 113) as 'Ideas have mind as their pre-condition, are dominated by mind and are mind-made.' Note that both of them avoid the possibility of reading in the mind-only theory, by interpreting *dhammā* as mental factors only, which is, to a certain

21. In the *sutta* it is not explained why the last two possibilities are rejected by the Buddha. We may understand that the third is rejected because it combines the first two mistaken propositions, and the fourth because it is casualism.

extent, in accord with the interpretation of *dhammā* by its Pali commentator.[22] These translations are not entirely baseless: frequently in the canonical Abhidhamma literature, we find the contextual use of *dhammā* to signify the totality of mental factors at a particular time.[23] Indeed, it is intelligent to avoid taking *dhammā* to refer to [all] phenomena both mental and physical, for that leads us to the mind-only theory, a teaching not to be found in a 'systematic' reading of early Buddhism. Nonetheless, it appears that the translations by Norman and Kalupahana are artificial and 'meaningless', for the following reasons:

1. If we regard *manas* as mind in general, following Norman and Kalupahana, it does not make sense to claim that *manas* leads, is the best among, and makes (or comprises) *dhammā*. Given that both *manas* and *dhammā* are the totality of mental factors, it is a meaningless tautology to say that the totality of mental factors leads the totality of mental factors, etc.
2. We cannot follow the Pali commentator who defines *manas* as *viññāṇa* only, and *dhammā* as mental factors other than *viññāṇa*, when we take into account that the verses are stated clearly in the context of saṃsāric causation: if one behaves with unskilful [or skilful] *manas*, suffering (*dukkha*) [or happiness (*sukha*)] follows the person. Speaking in terms of Abhidhamma, which is utilized by the commentator, *viññāṇa* itself is morally neutral, therefore karmically sterile. It becomes unskilful [or skilful] when it is

22. *tesu imasmiṃ ṭhāne nissatta-nijjīvadhammo adhippeto. so atthato tayo arūpino khandhā: vedanākhandho saññākhandho saṅkhārakkhandho ti.* 'Among these, in this case, what is meant [by the word *dhamma*] is the *dhamma* which lacks any substrate of soul. That is, the three non-material aggregates: feeling-aggregate, apperception-aggregate and formation-aggregate' (Dhp-a.I.22). Note that, in identifying *mano* as *viññāṇā*, the commentator excludes *viññāṇa* from *dhammā*, which is not explicitly implied in the translations of Norman and Kalupahana.
23. We also find this contextual use of *dhammā* in the major *Nikāyas*, in particular, when *dharma* is modified by *kuśala* or *akuśala* in the context of practice: e.g., the use of *dhamma* in the four kinds of *samyakprahāṇa* (or *samyakpradhāna*) appears to signify mental factors only (see MPS §10.10). In A.IV.338–39, we find the use of *dhammā* in the same context as in Dhp_P §§1–2. However, while Dhp_P §§1–2 states that [all] *dharmas* have the mind (*manas*) as their leader, chief and material, A.IV.338–39 announces that [all] *dhammas* have desire (*chanda*) as their root, attention (*manasikāra*) as producer, contact (*phassa*) as origin, feeling (*vedanā*) as one who merges, concentration (*samādhi*) as prominent (*pamukha*), mindfulness (*sati*) as governor, wisdom (*paññā*) as the highest, and liberation (*vimutti*) as essence.

associated with unskilful [or skilful] *cetasikas* such as ignorance, desire, etc. [or wisdom, mindfulness, etc.]; from the moral characteristics of those *cetasikas*, karmic results follow. Therefore, what is the best or leader of *dhammā* must be unskilful [or skilful] *cetasikas*, as announced in A.IV.338–39 (see note 23).

3. The suffering [or happiness] in these specific verses indeed includes a disadvantageous [or beneficial] material atmosphere along with the sensation of pain [or pleasure]; therefore, the *dhammā*, which follow *manas*, must be all material and mental things to be experienced in subsequent lives.
4. In Abhidhamma, no matter whether *dhammā* is interpreted as things in general or the totality of mental factors, they are not said to be made by (or consist of) *manas*, no matter whether *manas* is interpreted as *viññāṇa* only or as mind in general.

However, even with the above unsatisfactory consequences, I assert that it shows a better systematic understanding of early Buddhism to follow Norman, Kalupahana or the Pali commentator than to follow the natural reading; the mind-only theory implied by the natural reading is alien to a systematic understanding of early Buddhism. Personally, being convinced that *manas* in this context designates the total mind-set of a person at a specific time,[24] I suggest reading the word *dhammā* as the totality of karmic rewards, both mental and physical,[25] in Dhp_P §§1–2, and also in A.IV.338–39. This reading of mine is also an artificial one: I restrict the domain of *dhammā* to karmic results, and read *manomaya* figuratively as 'caused by the mind', not literally as 'made by/of the mind'. In any case, what is the most correct translation is not the present question; my concern is to highlight the situation that compels us to an artificial reading.

Interestingly, the corresponding verses of other South/Central Asian recensions, i.e., Dhp_G §§201–2, Dhp_Pat §§1–2 and Ud §31.23–24, have *manojava* instead of *manomaya* of Dhp_P §§1–2. Since *manojava* means 'as swift as mind', it does not imply the mind-only theory. However, this phrase does not match the juxtaposed compounds *manopubbaṅgama* and *manoseṭṭha*: while *manopubbaṅgama* and *manoseṭṭha* emphasize

24. In the context of karmic causation, the interpretation of *manas* as the total mind-set of a person appears most appropriate. For example, the *manas* in the beginning of the compound *manas-karman* ('mental karma') does not signify *vijñāna*; it designates the total mind-set which is dominated by a skilful or unskilful intention (*cetanā*) (cf. note 6).
25. In Abhidhammic terms, *rūpupādānakkhandha* and *vipākā dhammā*.

the causal domination of *manas* over *dhamma*s, *manojava* merely describes the similarity between *dharma*s and *manas*. Considering that the verses emphasize the role of skilful and unskilful *manas* in karmic causation, *manojava* destroys the consistency of the whole passage.

The corresponding Chinese translations T210.4.562a13–16, T211.4.583a7–10, T212.4.76a11–12/21–22 have 心為法本心尊心使, and T213.4.795c1–6 has 心為諸法本心尊是心 使, all of which can be translated as 'the mind is the origin of *dharma*s 法/諸法; the mind is the highest [among *dharma*s]; and the mind manages [*dharma*s]'. Since *fa* 法 is the technical rendering of *dharma*, there is no problem with the translation per se. However, in its natural reading, the Chinese Buddhist must have read *fa* 法 as meaning anything material or mental. Annotating Dhp_P §§1–2, Kalupahana (pp. 157–8) introduces three English translations of the passage in question; the first two of these are from Chinese, the third is from Tibetan.

> Mind is the origin of all that is; mind is the master; mind is the cause. (Beal)
>
> Mind is the origin of everything. The eminence of the mind is caused by the mind. (Willemen)
>
> Mind is the leader of its faculties (*dharma*); mind is swift; the mind is the ruler. (Rockhill)

Leaving aside the problems of these translations that Kalupahana points out, let us attend to how the Chinese word *fa* (法: *dharma*) in question is translated. Following the natural reading in the context of the major *Āgama*s, Beal and Willemen translate it respectively as 'all that is' and 'everything', whereas, conferring with the Pali commentary and other Indian and Central Asian recensions, Rockhill translates the Tibetan equivalent as 'its faculties', by which he appears to mean 'the other subsidiary members of it'. The translation by Rockhill is unnatural; however, it provides us with a systematic understanding of the passage in the wider context of early Buddhism.

It must be emphasized that the rejected natural reading may be what the speaker of the text originally intended. Since many Buddhist scriptures are collaborative products and since the great majority have suffered alteration in the course of their transmission, there has always been a potential for the interpolation of the personal opinions of minor thinkers. In these circumstances, however, we should not magnify such minority opinions as the true teaching of the text or the doctrinal system and discard the prevailing, normative teachings as mere expedients for the mediocre. In this sense, I regard a 'systematic' reading as an honest effort to understand the whole context of a text or its doctrinal system, proscribing minority interpolated opinions from appropriating the true voice of the whole text.

We occasionally encounter the same situation with reference to the Buddhist concept of self. Not to mention Mahāyāna texts, even in the major *Nikāyas* and *Āgamas*, we find some descriptions of self that can be interpreted as an eternalist *ātman*. For example, Horner (1954, vol.1, p. 177) translates the passage, *attani ca bhikkhave attaniye ca saccato thetato anupalabbhamāne yam p' idaṃ diṭṭhiṭṭhānaṃ: 'so loko so attā, so pecca bhavissāmi nicco ...' ti, nanâyaṃ bhikkhave kevalo paripūro bāladhammo? ti*, in the *Alagaddūpama-sutta* (M.I.137), as follows:

> But if Self, monks, and what belongs to Self, although actually existing, are incomprehensible, is not the view and the causal relation that: 'This the world this the self, after dying I will become permanent, ...'—is not this, monks, absolute complete folly?

Note that her translation appears to accept the existence of an eternalist self:[26] such a true, permanent self actually exists, but it may be folly to speak about it while it is incomprehensible. With reference to the same passage, as Harvey (1995, p. 24) notes, 'Again, K. Bhattacharya holds the passage as indicating that any self that can be objectively seized is not the true, durable Self (1973: 67, note 3).' In other words, he wants to insist that what the Buddha rejects is the conventional self imagined by fools, not the true Self that cannot be grasped through ordinary perception.

On the contrary, Bhikkhu Ñāṇamoḷi and Bhikkhu Bodhi (1995, p. 232) translate the passage as follows:

> O Bhikkhus, since a self and what belongs to a self are not apprehended as true and established, then this standpoint for view, namely, 'This is self, this the world; after death I shall be permanent, ...'—would it not be an utterly and completely foolish teaching?

In this translation, they understand that a permanent self is not apprehended since it does not exist in the true sense. In order to make a proper choice between these two contradictory interpretations, it is

---

26. For the Upaniṣadic implications of the sentence, 'This the world, this the self, after dying I will become permanent ...' (*so loko so attā, so pecca bhavissāmi nicco ... ti*), see pp. 85 f. below.

necessary to consider the passage in a 'systematic' way, regarding the whole context of the *Alagaddūpama-sutta*.

In the *sutta*, having scolded the monk Ariṭṭha through the similes of a snake and a raft for his misguided view that [sexual relations] are not obstructive to Buddhist practice, the Buddha announces (M.I.135–36) that, while an untaught ordinary person is seized with such an Upaniṣadic belief in the permanent self as, 'This is mine, I am this, this is my self,'[27] a well-taught noble disciple rids himself of such a misguided belief. The refuters of any permanent self in the Buddhist texts would regard this as evidence of the rejection of a permanent, true self, but the supporters of the true self in the Buddhist texts would claim that what the Buddha rejects here is merely the coarse view of self with reference to the five aggregates, not the true self *per se*.

Then, answering a monk, the Buddha states (M.I.136–37; see note 9) that those who believe, 'The world (*loka*) is the self (*ātman*). After death, I shall be permanent ...', i.e., those who believe in a true, permanent self as taught in the Upaniṣads, are scared after listening to the teaching of *nirvāṇa*, believing that the true self will be annihilated after *nirvāṇa*. However, the Buddha clarifies that such a fear is baseless, since such an internal self does not exist: the foolish person is worrying about losing something that he has never possessed. Here we ascertain that the existence of a permanent, true self is clearly rejected in the *sutta*.

Furthermore, the Buddha continues by saying (137–38) that he has never seen any belonging (*pariggaha*) that is permanent, that he has never seen any substantial basis for the doctrine of [permanent] self (*attavādupādāna*) or any support of this view [on permanent things] (*diṭṭhi-nissaya*) that does not result in suffering. Therefore, here again, we clearly see that any conception of a permanent self or thing, not to mention the Upaniṣadic one, is rejected in this *sutta* by the Buddha. The passage whose contradictory translations are quoted above immediately follows this teaching. Therefore, there is no way to interpret the passage in question, *attani ca bhikkhave attaniye ca saccato thetato anupalabbhamāne*, as insisting on the existence of a true, permanent self. This is the reason why we should follow the translation by Ñāṇamoḷi and Bodhi: the passage must mean that a permanent self and its belongings cannot be perceived, i.e., do not exist, in any true and trustworthy sense.

---

27. For the detailed implications of this expression in the Upaniṣadic tradition, see p. 85 below.

Then the way to attain the highest Buddhist achievement is announced (138–39). The way to reach the highest state is never by seeing one's true self in any esoteric way. The way is indeed, as is well known, by realizing that none of the five aggregates is *ātman*. For this reason, an *arhat* abandons the conceit of 'I am' (*asmi-māna*) and is no longer subject to further lives (140). This is the most crucial reason why a true, permanent self can never be allowed in a systematic reading of early Buddhism. The canonical body of early Buddhism is a system that describes the suffering of life 'as it is', points out the origin of suffering for its elimination, steers readers towards the cessation of suffering, and instructs people in how to achieve the cessation of suffering. Throughout the instruction of how to achieve the cessation of suffering, we find it taught that every practitioner must see that all of the five aggregates, which comprise the world and living beings, are suffering, impermanent and non-self. It has never been taught that a practitioner must see a true, permanent self beyond the five aggregates. Unless early Buddhist followers were esoteric practitioners who sought for what was not taught in any part of their canon, it is baseless to insist that the Buddha and early Buddhists presumed the mystical existence of a true, permanent self beyond the five aggregates.

There then follows (140) the teaching that the Buddha is not an advocate of nihilism. The supporters of a 'true' self in Buddhism may regard this as a supporting authority for their views. However, the fact that the Buddha rejected nihilism does not necessarily indicate that he acknowledged that he was an eternalist. As is well known, the Buddha named his teaching the middle way: it is not eternalism, since it rejects any permanent self, but it is not nihilism either, since it teaches that both suffering and the cessation of suffering are subject to dependent origination (*paṭicca-samuppāda*). In reply to any question whether he is a nihilist or an eternalist, he doubtless gives a flat refusal. Here, the denial that he is a nihilist is stated not in order to advocate the existence of a mystic self, but to defend the practice dependent on *paṭicca-samuppāda*, which aims at attaining *nirvāṇa*, emphasizing that the eternalist belief, 'The world (*loka*) is the self (*ātman*). After death, I shall be permanent ...', is folly.

For further discussion, a distinction should be made between: 1) a systematic reading within a canonical corpus; 2) a systematic reading based on a hermeneutic tradition; and 3) a systematic reading by a personal hermeneutics.

1. 'A systematic reading within a canonical corpus' means a reading that provides us with a consistent understanding of a text and

the reason why the text is located within a particular canon. The above critique of the passages from the *Dhammapada* and the *Alagaddūpama-sutta* shows how a systematic reading in this first sense works. Mind-only theory is a systematic reading of certain Buddhist texts and comprises a canonical body of thought found in those texts. However, if we read an implication of mind-only in the passage in question, we make the *Dhammapada* inconsistent and fail to locate it in the canon of Theravāda. In the same way, the reading of Upaniṣadic *ātman* in early Buddhist texts makes early Buddhism an esotericism: there is a hidden, true teaching of the Buddha that the great majority of its mnemonic and textual transmissions apparently reject. In Chapters 3 and 4 and 7 and 8, I analyse the principal premises and basic ways of thinking that 'systematically' comprise the textual bodies of the major types of Indian and Chinese Buddhism.

2. A good example of a systematic reading based on a hermeneutic tradition is the Abhidharma treatises. They systematically analyse the fundamental ideas of the early Buddhist *sūtra*s and construct a doctrinal system according to their sectarian affiliation. The great majority of individual commentaries and treatises that survived critical readings by numerous Buddhists for more than a millennium reveal the same tendency towards a systematic reading: with few differences, their reading of Buddhist texts is in accordance with the common reading of their tradition. In Chapter 9, I introduce a popular and influential exegetical system, advocating a permanent agent of perception, in China during the fifth and sixth centuries.
3. A typical example of a systematic reading by a personal hermeneutics is Bhattacharya's reading of an Upaniṣadic self into the Buddhist literature, as illustrated in his *L'ātman-brahman dans le bouddhisme ancien* (1973). I agree that his reading of sporadic passages is systematic in his way, being 'nevertheless challenging and well-documented' (Ruegg, 1989, p. 54); however, his arguments are not justified by the whole context of a canonical body or by any known party of hermeneutics in India before the late seventh century,[28] and his reading makes each text inconsistent or esoteric.

28. The great majority of translation work and the introduction of Indian Buddhism had almost been completed by the late seventh century, and then the Chinese developed their own Buddhism on the basis of what had already been imported: Xuanzang 玄奘 died in 664, and Yijing 義淨 (635–713) returned to China in

I have briefly illustrated the reason above, and present a fuller argument for this in Chapter 3. My use of the term 'systematic' refers to systematic reading in the first sense, unless it is specified as the second or third one.

Regarding the Buddhist concept of self, I argue in Chapters 3 to 5 that we seldom find textual support for the existence of a permanent agent in *saṃsāra*, if we hold fast to the 'systematic' readings in the first and second senses before the late seventh century. This is a critical feature that makes it possible to attribute an identity to various types of Buddhism, and differentiate them from other intellectual movements in India, while Buddhism underwent a dramatic change from early Buddhism to later Mahāyāna Buddhism. On the contrary, in Chapters 7 to 9, I argue that the concept of self as a permanent agent of perception has been strongly supported by certain systematic readings in the first and second senses in China, which were very popular, influential and sophisticated. I dedicate Chapter 6 to clarifying that such a popular systematic reading in China was not influenced by Indian Brahmanism but was a product of their 'creative' reading of Buddhism under the influence of indigenous Chinese thought.

Eccentric Factors Enfeebling 'Systematic' Readings

When we encounter such eccentric passages whose natural readings are incompatible with the doctrinal system of the texts, on the one hand we should look for interpretations such as are illustrated above, but, on the other hand, we should not brand such natural readings as mere misreadings. Considering that the textual body of any historical Buddhism has never been a monolithic system literarily, culturally or philosophically, we should bear in mind that some of them may reflect the real intention of a speaker of the text; the natural readings of such ill-matched passages would be better regarded as minority opinions that

---

694–95, which constituted the last of the massive imports of Indian Buddhist scriptures. For this reason, I restrict my concern to the cultural assimilation of Buddhism from India to China up to the late seventh century. After the eighth century, except for a few decades around 980–1000, the new import of Indian Buddhist texts and thought was in reality restricted to Vajrayāna Buddhism, whose influence on the Chinese Buddhist concept of self during the Song, Yuan and Ming dynasties is beyond the scope of this book. As for the relevant state of political affairs, the Chinese finally lost their control over Central Asia after their defeat in the Battle of Talas in 751.

survived the textual and doctrinal standardization process. In order to understand the logical structure of various Buddhist doctrinal systems, we should apply a 'systematic' reading to the literary corpus of a specific Buddhism. On the contrary, in order to understand the development of Buddhism, we must inspect carefully how some eccentric ideas motivated the development of a later doctrinal system. In this line of thinking, in Chapter 5, I examine how such ill-matched descriptions of self in early Buddhist texts are related to the creation of the later Mahāyāna conceptions of self.

BASIC PRINCIPLES THAT STRUCTURE THE BUDDHIST CONCEPT OF SELF

It was noted above (pp. 70–71) that the early Buddhists had a conception of self that is a sequence of mental and bodily elements, none of which is permanent, and that the arising of those elements depends on previous elements under the karmic and natural law. In this section, I aim to explicate the basic principles by which the early Buddhists constructed their concept of self.

Anti-Brahmanism[29]

In the Hindu tradition, the popular criterion for distinguishing between orthodox religious/intellectual movements and heterodox ones has been whether they acknowledge the existence of *ātman* and *brahman* as taught in the Vedic literature (including the *Vedānta*). Calling their own teaching the middle way, the early Buddhists classified wrong views into two categories (i.e., 'two extremes'): the views assuming a permanent self and the views rejecting (karmic) *saṃsāra*. For the convenience of discussion, I name the former eternalism, instead of the traditional term *śāśvatavāda*, and the latter nihilism, instead of *ucchedavāda*. Eternalism includes various 'orthodox' teachings that advocate the teaching of the Vedic literature as well as other 'heterodox' teachings, such as Jainism, which rejects the existence of the Creator *brahman* but acknowledges the existence of a permanent self, *jīva*.

29. I owe my knowledge about the relationship between early Buddhism and Brahmanic thought to Professor Richard Gombrich. He has taught and inspired me during reading classes in Oxford since 2003 and at the Numata lectures, at SOAS, in London, in 2006.

From the time of the early *Upaniṣads* and Buddhism, nihilism appears to have been a minority opinion in India. Hence the main adversaries of Buddhism, in terms of religious influence, were eternalists. For this reason, the doctrine of *anātman* has been the catch-phrase of Buddhism, with which nihilists had few reasons to disagree. However, although both the early Buddhists and Mahāyānists identified themselves as Buddhists advocating the *anātman* doctrine, the meaning of *anātman* differs between them: in many of the doctrinal premises on which their theories are established, the two traditions contradict each other. For example, the Mahāyāna ideas of *dharmakāya* and *tathāgatagarbha* would be regarded as eternalist ones by the Buddha of early Buddhism.

However, in standard exegesis, there was a consistent insistence on their *anātman* theories from the beginning of Buddhism to the fully developed Mahāyāna Buddhism up to the late seventh century in India: all major doctrinal systems in Buddhism rejected the concept of a permanent agent of perception, as taught in the *Upaniṣads*. I call this anti-Brahmanism. Here 'Brahmanism' includes various intellectual movements in India that acknowledge the concept of self as being permanent (*sat*), being conscious (*cit*) and feeling joy (*ānanda*), and the concept of *brahman*, the ultimate source of the creation and administration of the universe. This Brahmanism originates from the thought of the early *Upaniṣads*; many ideas found in the four *Vedas*, the *Brāhmaṇas* and the *Āraṇyakas* are excluded from my use of the term Brahmanism. This thorough rivalry with Brahmanism is a conspicuous difference between Indian and Chinese Buddhism. The Chinese Buddhists had virtually no accurate knowledge of Brahmanism; their information about it came almost exclusively from the translations of Indian Buddhist texts, in which Brahmanism is simplified, distorted and ridiculed. In Part III, I will discuss how the lack of a sense of rivalry with Brahmanism resulted in the development of the Chinese Buddhist ideas of self.

With this sense of rivalry, the early Buddhists reacted against Brahmanism in three ways: 1) they disputed the fundamental ideas of Brahmanism; 2) they redefined the basic concepts of Brahmanism in a Buddhist way; and 3) they designed their doctrinal system to attack basic Brahmanic doctrines.

1. In the *Chāndogya Upaniṣad* (VI.8.3–6), Uddālaka Āruṇi teaches his son Śvetaketu how to grasp the 'reality' of existents, pointing out that a bud cannot come out without its root, the root cannot be without food, and so one should look to water as the root of food, heat as that of water, and existence as that of heat, which is in accordance with its cosmogony. Then he declares that existence, or the root of all, is *ātman* (VI.8.7):

> It is that which is this subtle essence – this whole [world] has it as its nature; it is truth; it is the self. Śvetaketu, you are it.[30]

It is noteworthy that, throughout the major *Nikāyas*, the Buddha rejects the view 'this is mine, I am this, this is my self' (*etaṃ mama, eso 'ham asmi, eso me āttā*),[31] and that, as Gombrich has pointed out (1996, pp. 38–9), the rejected expression 'I am this' (*eso 'ham asmi*) in the *Nikāyas* is a transposition of 'You are it' (*tat tvam asi*). This Upaniṣadic self is the essence or the root of the whole world, and it is the 'real' existence of every self. Also, notably, the self in the former sense is expressed by 'the world' (*so loko*) and the self in the latter sense by 'the self' (*so attā*) in the previous quotation, where a person is frightened when he hears of the absence of a permanent self (see p. 69). If we consider how often the Upaniṣadic propositions 'This is mine, I am this, this is my self', 'The world (*loka*) is the self (*ātman*). After death, I shall be permanent ...', etc., are refuted in the major *Nikāyas* and *Āgamas*, we can see that the Upaniṣadic conception of a permanent self was a major target in the early Buddhist attack on eternalism.

One of the two fundamental senses of the Brahmanic self, which is considered as 'this whole [world]' in the above quotations, does not refer to the world in a merely physical sense. It signifies the supreme power that created the world and pervades it. The name of the supreme power is *brahman*. Before it became identified as the supreme power, the neuter *brahman* meant the sacred word, i.e., the word of the Vedas, with which brahmins, the possessors of sacred knowledge, wielded magical power over the physical world (Oldenberg, 1991 [1915], pp. 29–30). This sacred word, whose threefold knowledge (*trayī vidyā*) yields magical power, is elevated to the supreme power, as Oldenberg summarizes (*ibid.*, p. 32):

> Now 'the Brahman, the threefold knowledge' is the first creation, which the world-creator Prajāpati has released from himself taking pains and in fervent austerity and it has become the foundation of this universe. Now that creation merges with the creator, and it is taught, 'Prajāpati is verily Brahman, for Prajāpati is Brahman-nature.' 'The Brahman is the most ancient (highest), for there is nothing more ancient (higher) than

---

30. *sa ya eṣo '"ṇimâitadātmyam idaṃ sarvam, tat satyam, sa ātmā; tat tvam asi, Śvetaketo" iti.'*
31. For more information on the view of *etaṃ mama, eso 'ham asmi, eso me attā*, see Norman (1991 [1981], pp. 200–1).

this. The one who knows this will verily become the most ancient and the most glorious of all beings.'

When the word *brahman* is used in the sense of the supreme power, it declines as a neuter. In Buddhist texts, however, it generally declines as a masculine, referring to one of many gods. Gods wield considerable authority even in early Buddhism;[32] in particular, as one of the most powerful divine protectors, Brahmā plays an important role in many dialogues in early Buddhist *sūtras*. However, concerning the creation of the world, Brahmā has always been derided by Buddhists:

> At some time, monks, after a long time has passed, this world contracts [in the process of the destruction of the world]. As the world contracts, most beings are reborn in Ābhassara heaven. ... At some time, monks, after a long time has passed, this world expands [in the evolutionary process of the world]. As the world expands, an empty Brahmā-residence comes into being. When his merit or lifespan is exhausted, a certain being dies in the Ābhassara heaven and gets birth in the empty Brahmā-residence. ... Dwelling there alone for a long time, he becomes discontented and anxious, 'May other beings also come to be like this!' Then, because their merit or lifespan is exhausted, some beings die in the Ābhassara heaven, get birth in the Brahmā-residence and become his companions. ... At that time, monks, the being who first got birth there thinks, 'I am Brahmā, the Great Brahmā. I am the Conqueror, the Unconquered, the Only Seer, the Power-Wielder, the Lord, the Maker, the Creator, the Best, the Appointer, the Controller, and the Father of all beings that have been born and that will be born. These beings have been created by me. What is the reason? I previously thought, "Let other beings also come to be like this!" In this way I had this mental resolve and these beings came to be like this!'[33]

---

32. Gods read the mind of the Buddha. So a Brahmā named Sahampati dissuades the Buddha, who has just attained the complete awakening, from deserting the world without teaching the truth (Vin.I.5–6). And the Buddha knows about the lives of past Buddhas not only by his own knowledge, but also through being told by gods (D.II.10). Even Vessavaṇa Mahārājan, who is quite low in the hierarchy of Buddhist gods, transmits a protection-spell of past Buddhas to the Buddha (D.III.194–95).

33. *hoti kho so, bhikkhave, samayo yaṃ kadāci karahaci dīghassa addhuno accayena ayaṃ loko saṃvaṭṭati. saṃvaṭṭamāne loke yebhuyyena sattā Ābhassarasaṃvaṭṭanikā honti. ... hoti kho so, bhikkhave, samayo yaṃ kadāci karahaci dīghassa addhuno accayena ayaṃ loko vivaṭṭati. vivaṭṭamāne loke suññaṃ Brahmavimānaṃ pātubhavati. ath' aññataro satto āyukkhayā vā puññakkhayā vā Ābhassarakāyā cavitvā suññaṃ Brahmavimānaṃ upapajjati. ... tassa tattha ekakassa dīgharattaṃ nibbusitattā anabhirati paritassanā uppajjati: 'aho vata aññe pi sattā itthattaṃ āgaccheyyun' ti. atha aññatare pi*

As we read above, the masculine Brahmā in Buddhist tales is also subject to birth and death according to the merit and lifespan caused by past karma. A certain being, whose merit or lifespan had been exhausted first, probably because he had the least merit, falls into the empty Brahmā-residence and suffers loneliness. Accidentally, after his wish for a companion, other beings fall into the Brahmā-residence, since their merit or lifespan is exhausted. Misunderstanding this accident, he regards himself as the Creator. The teller of the above tale rejects the Brahmanic creation theory and ridicules the concept of *brahman* as the creator. Compare the above Buddhist tale with a Brahmanic one in the *Bṛhadāraṇyaka Upaniṣad*, I.4.1–3:

> In the beginning this world was just a single body (*ātman*) shaped like a man. He looked around and saw nothing but himself. The first thing he said was, 'Here I am!' and from that the name 'I' came into being. … The first being became afraid; therefore, one becomes afraid when one is alone. Then he thought to himself 'Of what should I be afraid, when there is no one but me?' So his fear left him, for what was he going to be afraid of? One is, after all, afraid of another. He found no pleasure at all; so one finds no pleasure when one is alone. He wanted to have a companion. Now he was as large as a man and a woman in close embrace. So he split (*pat*) his body into two, giving rise to husband (*pati*) and wife (*patnī*). … He copulated with her, and from their union human beings were born.[34] (Olivelle, 1996, pp. 13–14)

Note that in the above passage the self (*ātman*), i.e., *brahman*, first identifies himself, 'Here I am' (*so 'ham asmi*). Obviously, a substantially identical sentence is used as the second in the sequence of three sentences (*etaṃ mama, eso 'ham asmi, eso me attā*), which is the axiomization of

---

sattā āyukkhayā vā puññakkhayā vā Ābhassarakāyā cavitvā Brahmavimānaṃ upapajjanti tassa sattassa sahavyataṃ. … tatra, bhikkhave, yo so satto paṭhamaṃ upapanno tassa evaṃ hoti: 'aham asmi Brahmā Mahābrahmā abhibhū anabhibhūto aññadatthudaso vasavattī issaro kattā nimmātā seṭṭho sañjitā vasī pitā bhūta-bhavyānaṃ. mayā ime sattā nimmitā. taṃ kissa hetu? mamaṃ hi pubbe etad ahosi: 'aho vata aññe pi sattā itthattaṃ āgaccheyyun' ti. iti mamañ ca manopaṇidhi, ime ca sattā itthattaṃ āgatā' ti (*Brahmajāla-sutta*, D.I.17–18).

34. *ātmâivedaṃ agra āsīt puruṣavidhaḥ. so 'nuvīkṣya nânyad ātmano 'paśyat. so 'ham asmīty agre vyāharat. tato 'haṃ nāmâbhavat. … so 'bibhet, tasmād ekākī bibheti. sa bhāyam īkṣāṃ cakre: yan mad anyan nâsti, kaṣmān nu bibhemîti. tata evâsya bhayaṃ vīyāya. kasmād dhy abheṣyat? dvitīyād vai bhayaṃ bhavati. sa vai nâiva reme. tasmād ekākī na ramate. sa dvitīyam aicchat. sa hâitāvān āsa yathā strīpumāṃsau saṃpariṣvaktau. sa imam evâtmānaṃ dvedhā 'pātayat. tataḥ patiś ca patnī câbhavatām; … tāṃ samabhavat. tato manuṣyā ajāyanta.*

wrong views on self rejected throughout the *Nikāyas*.[35] Being alone, he feels afraid, desires companions, and creates beings. Exactly this process is clearly rejected and derided in the previous Buddhist tale. Such remade tales, which make use of Upaniṣadic materials to attack their doctrines,[36] provide us with vivid evidence of Buddhist rivalry with Brahmanism.

However, those Buddhist tales could merely be counter-narratives to disillusion people with Upaniṣadic tales; we scarcely find philosophical arguments disproving the existence of the Upaniṣadic *brahman* among early Buddhist texts. Instead, the early Buddhists focused on disproving the existence of the Upaniṣadic *ātman*, which in the context of Indian philosophy implies disproof of the Upaniṣadic *brahman*. The fact that the early Buddhists endeavoured to disprove the existence of the *ātman*, rather than the *brahman*, indicates their main concern: they were troubled by a self who suffers pain. If it is irrelevant to the suffering that people experience, any theoretical problem such as what the Creator is, who is eternal, what is boundless, etc., was no concern of theirs.

As for *ātman*, its original meaning is breath; it was regarded by Indians as 'the bearer of life, and as such, the existence of a person is based on it' (Oldenberg, 1991 [1915], p. 33). From the time of the Vedas to the time of the *Upaniṣads*, there developed the concept of *saṃsāra*, and Indian thinkers or yogis sought immortality in another world where there is no more suffering. Being expected to enjoy immortality in the other world, this Upaniṣadic *ātman*, i.e., the permanent and 'real' self, became identified with the neuter *brahman*, which is the eternal creator and which is the ground of the universe. However, employing various arguments and allegories, the Buddha refuted this Upaniṣadic idea of an immortal self and identified the realization of its absence with the correct path of Buddhist soteriology; for example:

> With regard to the view, 'The world (*loka*) is the self (*ātman*). After death, I shall be permanent, constant, eternal and not subject to change. I shall continue to be the same for all eternity,' he sees, 'This is not mine. I am not this. This is not my self.' Seeing in this way, he is not afraid of what does not exist.[37]

35. For the importance of disillusion with this self-awareness (*eso 'ham asmi*) in early Buddhist soteriology, see Harvey (1995, pp. 31–3, 40–2).

36. To see a typical way by which the early Buddhists satirically made use of Upaniṣadic materials to reject Upaniṣadic theories, refer to Gombrich (1992, pp. 163–76).

37. ... *yam p' idaṃ diṭṭhiṭṭhānaṃ: 'so loko so attā, so pecca bhavissāmi nicco dhuvo sassato avipariṇāmadhammo, sassatisamaṃ tath' eva ṭhassāmi' ti, tam pi: 'n' etaṃ mama, n' eso 'ham asmi, na m' eso attā' ti samanupassati. so evaṃ samanupassanto asati na paritassatî ti* (M.I.136).

When I examine early Buddhist empiricism and reductionism below, I will demonstrate the way in which the early Buddhists constructed their idea of self, challenging the Brahmanic conception of self.

2. On the one hand, the early Buddhists indirectly rejected the existence of the Upaniṣadic *brahman* by means of deriding and refuting its genesis; on the other hand, they reinterpreted the meaning of *brahman* in a Buddhist sense. Hence, in the *Aggañña-sutta*, popularly known as the *Buddhist Genesis*, the Buddha begins his teaching by advocating the superiority of virtues regardless of the caste to which the moral agent belongs. He says to two monks of brahmin origin who have been reviled by brahmins, 'Brahmins are the highest among castes ... [However] you two abandoned the highest caste and fell into an inferior caste, i.e., among shaven-headed ascetics who are menial, dark and born from the feet of Brahmā';[38] then, the Buddha appropriates *brahman* as one of his own epithets:

> Vāseṭṭha, for a person whose faith in Tathāgata is settled, rooted, established and firm, not to be taken away by any ascetic, brahmin, god, Death, Brahmā or anyone in the world, it is appropriate to say, 'I am a son of Bhagavant, belonging to [his] breast, born from [his] mouth, born of dhamma, created by dhamma and an heir of dhamma.' What is the reason? Vāseṭṭha, referring to Tathāgata, there are these epithets, 'Having the body of *dhamma*', 'Having the body of *brahman*', 'Being in the state of *dhamma*' and 'Being in the state of *brahman*'.[39]

From the common usage of juxtaposition in Pali, we can infer that *brahman* in the above quotation is used as a synonym of *dhamma*, i.e., the teaching of the Buddha, or truth.[40]

---

38. *brāhmaṇo va seṭṭho vaṇṇo ... te tumhe seṭṭhaṃ vaṇṇaṃ hitvā hīnam attha vaṇṇaṃ ajjhupagatā yadidaṃ muṇḍake samaṇake ibbhe kaṇhe bandhupādâpacce* (D.III.81).
39. *yassa kho pan' assa, Vāseṭṭha, Tathāgate saddhā niviṭṭhā mūlajātā patiṭṭhitā daḷhā asaṃhārikā samaṇena vā brāhmaṇena vā devena vā Mārena vā Brahmunā vā kenaci vā lokasmiṃ, tass' etaṃ kallaṃ vacanāya: 'Bhagavato 'mhi putto oraso mukhato jāto dhammajo dhammanimmito dhammadāyādo' ti. Taṃ kissa hetu? Tathāgatassa h' etaṃ, Vāseṭṭha, adhivacanaṃ: 'dhammakāyo iti pi, Brahmakāyo iti pi, dhammabhūto iti pi, Brahmabhūto iti pî' ti* (D.III.84).
40. We also find *brahmabhūta* to be an epithet of *nirvāṇa* at D.III.232, M.I.341, 411–412, II.159, and A.II.206, as Bhattacharya (1989, p. 17) points out. He also discusses (pp. 18–19) the relationship between *dharma* and *brahman* in the light of Pali commentaries. In general, Bhattacharya emphasizes the Upaniṣadic influence on the use of *brahma-* in the Buddhist literature.

Examining the use of Brahmanic terms in Theravāda Buddhism, Norman (1993b [1991], p. 274) summarizes the use of *brahman* in Pali Buddhist texts, 'There seems to be no occurrence in Pāli of the uncompounded neuter word *brahma* in the sense of the Upaniṣadic *brahman*, but the word *brahma* is used in compounds apparently in the sense of "excellent, perfect".' He also points out (*ibid.*, p. 279),

> Besides the convenience of taking over terms which were already known to his audience, albeit in a different sense, the Buddha possibly had other reasons for acting in this way. In part it may have been due to his desire to show that brahmanical Brahmanism was wrong in its basic tenets: a brahmanical *brāhmaṇa* was not as good as a Buddhist *brāhmaṇa*, brahmanical *śuddhi* was inferior to Buddhist *suddhi*, etc. If a teacher takes over his rivals' terms and repeats them often enough in his own meaning, he gives the impression that he is using them in the correct sense, and the original owners are wrong in their usage.

3. We frequently find that fundamental Buddhist doctrines inconspicuously, but probably intentionally, attack Brahmanic ideas. As Norman (1991 [1981], pp. 202–4) and Gombrich (1990a, pp. 14–15) illustrate, the early Buddhist doctrine of *trilakṣaṇa* (the three characteristics of any phenomenon: i.e., impermanence (*anitya*), suffering (*duḥkha*) and non-self (*anātman*))[41] challenges the Upaniṣadic concept of self (*ātman*) and its essential nature of permanence (*nitya* = *sat*) and joy (*sukha* = *ānanda*). The conflicting use of fire imagery between Brahmanism and Buddhism is also notable. Gombrich (*ibid.*, pp. 16–17) points out that, while fire represents something that must be kept alive in the Brahmanic tradition, in Buddhism it represents something that must be extinguished: i.e., passion (*rāga*), ill-will (*dveṣa*) and ignorance (*moha*), whose blowing out is *nirvāṇa*. In addition, Jurewicz (2000) elucidates several striking similarities between the twelvefold dependent origination (*pratītyasamutpāda*) and the Vedic ideas of creation, and carefully argues that the Buddha 'formulated the *pratītyasamutpāda* as a polemic against Vedic thought.' Her demonstration reveals the possibility that even such a fundamental doctrine as dependent origination is designed to rebut Brahmanic doctrines.

---

41. As mentioned before, the most frequent scheme for disputing eternalism in the early Buddhist texts uses the *trilakṣaṇa*: all of the five aggregates are impermanent (*anitya*); therefore, they are suffering (*duḥkha*); therefore, they are not permanent self (*anātman*).

Empiricism

In the *Mahāhatthipadopama-sutta*, Sāriputta states, 'The Buddha told, "One who sees dependent origination sees *dhamma*; one who sees *dhamma* sees dependent origination."'[42] In the early Buddhist texts, the term *dhamma* (Sk. *dharma*) has two basic meanings: firstly, the truth as taught by the Buddha, and secondly, phenomena as they are. Inspecting the context in which the statement is uttered, we find that both meanings of the term *dhamma* fit this statement perfectly. That is, if one sees phenomena arising and ceasing according to the law of dependent origination, one sees phenomena as they are, which is the truth as taught by the Buddha, and vice versa. Furthermore, the *sutta* as a whole provides us with the detailed context in which seeing dependent origination is identified with seeing phenomena as they are and with knowing the truth taught by the Buddha.

Sāriputta in this *sutta* starts the dialogue by eulogizing the four noble truths, the framework of Buddhist soteriology: 'Colleagues, whatever skilful teachings (*dhammas*) there are, all are included in the four noble truths,'[43] where 'skilful' (*kusala*) implies 'conducive to the cessation of suffering.'[44] Having expounded the four great elements (*mahābhūta*) of internal and external material, he explains the five clinging-aggregates (*upādānakkhandha*), the totality of which is defined as the first truth of suffering, as follows: the five aggregates are called clinging-aggregates when they come into being in such a way (*tathābhūta*) that the experience of consciousness (*viññāṇabhāga*) happens by means of the contact between objects, sense faculties and consciousness. Then, having proclaimed that seeing dependent origination constitutes seeing *dhamma* and vice versa, he repeats the four noble truths. To sum up, phenomena that arise and cease according to dependent origination are phenomena as they are ('real'): i.e., as they are experienced by consciousness. This is the truth as taught by the Buddha, and the understanding of it leads to the cessation of all suffering. I call this early Buddhist empiricism, since they identified what is real with what is experienced through consciousness.

---

42. *vuttaṃ kho pan' etaṃ Bhagavatā: 'yo paṭiccasamuppādaṃ passati, so dhammaṃ passati; yo dhammaṃ passati, so paṭiccasamuppādaṃ passatī' ti* (M.I.190–91).
43. *evam eva kho āvuso ye keci kusalā dhammā sabbe te catusu ariyasaccesu saṅgahaṃ gacchanti* (M.I.184).
44. For the meaning of *kusala* in Pali canonical texts, see Cousins (1996, pp. 143–8).

Concerning early Buddhist empiricism, we should bear in mind the fact that this empiricism admits specific extraordinary experiences, i.e., Buddhist meditative experiences. This meditative experience plays very important roles in Buddhist ontology, epistemology and soteriology. Past lives and future lives are not perceived by ordinary people, but are said to be observed through specific meditations. Without the knowledge attained through such meditations, the early Buddhists have no grounds for denouncing nihilist ontology or ethics. For the early Buddhists, the knowledge attained through meditation is regarded as a higher one (*abhijñā*) than that attained by ordinary perception. Therefore, when the early Buddhists say that something cannot be experienced, that implies that it cannot be observed even through meditation.

This empiricism of early Buddhism is not designed to grasp merely a lower truth; no knowledge, truth or reality beyond experience is accepted. Hence, the possibility is excluded that the 'ultimate' truth (*paramārtha-satya*) of non-dualistic insight or logical analysis ranks higher than the 'conventional' truth (*saṃvṛti-satya*) of normal perception and meditative observation. Internally, the whole system of soteriology and epistemology is constructed within the reach of our experience, and, externally, any ontological claim beyond our experience is rejected in a straightforward tone: 'Has anyone in the world seen it?'

For this reason, we find that 'everything' in the doctrinal system of early Buddhism is located within the reach of our experience. In the *Sabba-vagga* of the *Saḷāyatana-saṃyutta*, the Buddha announces:

> Monks, I will teach you about everything. Listen! Monks, what is everything? The eye and visible objects, the ear and sounds, the nose and smells, the tongue and tastes, the body and tangible objects, and the mind and mental objects—monks, this is called everything. Monks, a person may say, 'Having rejected this kind of everything, I will let you know another kind of everything.' But his words are groundless. Being [properly] asked, he would not be able to defend what he said; furthermore, he would fall into distress. What is the reason? That it is not within the reach [of our experience].[45]

45. *Sabbaṃ vo, bhikkhave, dessissāmi, tam suṇātha! kiñ ca, bhikkhave, sabbaṃ? Cakkhuṃ c' eva rūpā ca, sotañ ca saddā ca, ghānañ ca gandhā ca, jivhā ca rasā ca, kāyo ca phoṭṭhabbā ca, mano ca dhammā ca—idam vuccati bhikkhave sabbaṃ. yo, bhikkhave, evam vadeyya: 'aham etaṃ sabbam paccakkhāya aññaṃ sabbam paññāpessāmî' ti, tassa vācâvatthu-r-ev' assa, puṭṭho ca na sampāpeyya, uttariñ ca vighātaṃ āpajjeyya. tam kissa hetu? yathā tam, bhikkhave, avisayasmin ti* (S.IV.15).

This announcement contains three propositions. Firstly, 'everything' includes only our perceptive capacities and perceivable objects. Secondly, there is no 'other kind of everything', i.e., this Buddhist definition of everything is exclusive. It is clear that, in the context of the major *Nikāyas*, what is excluded from everything is such entities, advocated by eternalists, as *ātman*, brahman, etc. Thirdly, any insistence on such eternalist entities is unsound because they are out of the reach of our experience (*visaya*).

In the rest of the *Sabba-vagga* (S.IV.15–26), the Buddha lists everything that is to be abandoned, to be understood, burning, etc. There, everything includes only our sense faculties, their objects, consciousnesses, and other accompanying mental activities. Then, based on the same definition of everything, in the *Jātidhamma-vagga* (S.IV.26–28), the Buddha announces that everything is subject to birth, ageing, death, etc.; and, in the *Anicca-vagga* (S.IV. 28–30), the Buddha conclusively announces that all are impermanent, suffering, not [permanent] self, to be known, etc. Throughout the three *vagga*s, we find identified (1) what is experienced, (2) what is subject to birth, etc., and (3) what is impermanent, etc. This identification is expressed in a sentence, in a Mūlasarvāstivāda version of the *Mahāparinirvāṇa-sūtra*, as follows:

> How could it happen that something that is born, produced, caused, known, dependent-originated and subject to [destruction, decay, cessation, loss,] annihilation and [demolition] does not perish? Such a case is impossible.[46]

Here, anything to be known (*vedayita*), i.e., anything that can be experienced, is claimed to perish. From the context of the above quotation, we also read that this identification is adopted to support Buddhist soteriology in its rivalry with Brahmanism and any other kind of eternalism.

In addition, we find the same definition of everything in terms of the five aggregates. In the *Cūḷasaccaka-sutta*, the Buddha affirms that he teaches his pupils as follows:

---

46. *kuta etal labhyaṃ: yat taj jātaṃ bhūtaṃ kṛtaṃ saṃskṛtaṃ vedayitaṃ pratītyasamutpannaṃ [kṣayadharmaṃ vyayadharmaṃ vibhavadharmaṃ virāgadharmaṃ ni]rodhadharmaṃ [p]r[a]lo[kadharmaṃ na prarujyate]? nêdaṃ sthānaṃ vidyate* (MPS §45.8). The bracketed parts of this sentence are reconstructions by Waldschmidt (1980). For the justification of his reconstructions, see Introduction, note 3. MPP §6.11 does not list a word corresponding to *vedayita*: *taṃ kut' ettha āvuso labbhā: 'yan taṃ jātaṃ bhūtaṃ saṃkhataṃ palokadhammaṃ, taṃ vata mā palujjī' ti? n' etaṃ ṭhānaṃ vijjati.*

> Monks, form is impermanent, feeling is impermanent, apperception is impermanent, mental activities are impermanent, and consciousness is impermanent; monks, form is not [the permanent] self, feeling is not self, apperception is not self, [mental] activities are not self, and consciousness is not self. All things conditionally constructed (*saṅkhāra*) are impermanent; all phenomena (*dhamma*) are not self.[47]

In this announcement, we find identified (1) the totality of the five aggregates, (2) all things conditionally constructed (*saṅkhāra*)[48] and (3) all phenomena (*dhamma*). The difference between the definition of everything in terms of the five aggregates and that in terms of our sense faculties, etc., lies in the fact that the former mainly aims to dispute the ontological claims of eternalism, whereas the latter explains things in detail in terms of Buddhist epistemology and soteriology.

Whether a specific thing is included in everything is, in fact, determined by whether it is a mental object (*dharma*), i.e., an object of what the texts call mind-consciousness. Although it is not clearly announced in the major *Nikāya*s and *Āgama*s, we can infer from those texts that the sphere of mental objects is identical with everything, i.e., what is perceptible. The Buddha acknowledges that people think about a permanent self; however, he denies it to be an object of mind-consciousness or other consciousnesses: what is actually perceived by any consciousness is not the permanent self, but the five aggregates (see note 11). This means that the relationship between mind-consciousness and mental objects in early Buddhism is as vivid as the relationship between the five physical senses and their objects: it is observation rather than thinking. For this reason, we can infer that in early Buddhism mere names or concepts, e.g., the eternalist *atman*, etc.,

---

47. *rūpaṃ, bhikkhave, aniccaṃ, vedanā aniccā, saññā aniccā, saṅkhārā aniccā, viññāṇaṃ aniccaṃ; rūpaṃ bhikkhave anattā, vedanā anattā, saññā anattā, saṅkhārā anattā, viññāṇaṃ anattā. sabbe saṅkhārā aniccā, sabbe dhammā anattā ti* (M.I.230).

48. In the Buddhist texts, the term *saṃskāra* (Pa. *saṅkhāra*) is used in three senses. Firstly, it may mean mental activities in the karmic process, among which intention (*cetanā*) is representative. Secondly, it may mean all mental activities other than feeling, apperception and consciousness. Thirdly, it may mean anything conditionally constructed/constructive, in which case it is synonymous with the term *saṃskṛta*. In this quotation, the first two meanings can be applied to *saṃskāra*, when it is listed as one of the five aggregates. The last meaning is applied to *saṃskāra* in the last sentence. For the dual meaning of *saṃskāra* or *abhisaṃskāra*, see Collins (1982, pp. 200–3).

which do not signify anything that can be experienced in 'reality', are not included in 'everything' that exists.[49]

As mentioned above, the *Nikāyas* or *Āgamas* do not comprise a monolithic body of texts with a consistent philosophy. It is little wonder that we can find a few counter-examples to this general idea of 'everything' in the major *Nikāyas*. For example, in the *Mūlapariyāya-sutta*, the Buddha includes such abstract concepts as unity (*ekatta*) and diversity (*nānatta*) among all phenomena (*sabbadhamma*), and states that Buddhist practitioners and saints recognize (*abhijānāti*) them correctly (M.I.1–6).[50] However, such occasional statements should not be magnified as the hidden truth of early Buddhism. Otherwise the early Buddhists lose their grounds for refuting eternalist ideas.

When the early Buddhists rejected any eternalist idea, such as the Upaniṣadic *ātman*, their axiom was simple: if it is beyond the reach of our experience, it does not exist. For this reason, the Buddha argues in the *Poṭṭhapāda-sutta*:

> Poṭṭhapāda, there are some ascetics and brahmins who say and hold the view, 'After death, the self (*ātman*) is completely happy and free from illness.' ... I ask them, 'Elders, have you known or seen a completely happy world in your life?' They answer, 'No.' I ask them, 'Elders, have you perceived complete happiness in yourselves for one night or day, or for half a night or day?' They answer, 'No.' I ask them, 'Elders, do you know the way to experience a world of complete happiness?' They answer, 'No.' I ask them, 'Do you hear the voice of gods who have been born in a completely happy world, saying, "Behave well, and behave rightly in order to experience the completely happy world! Behaving in that way, we too have been born in a completely happy world"?' They answer, 'No.' What do you think, Poṭṭhapāda? In that case, doesn't the talk of those ascetics and brahmins turn out to be meaningless?'[51]

---

49. In this sense, *nirvāṇa* is the most controversial concept of early Buddhism. It is experienced by Buddhas and *arhats* or becomes the object of noble knowledge; but it is not subject to rising and ceasing. This controversial topic is beyond the scope of this book.

50. Note that, in the *Saḷāyatana-saṃyutta* (S.IV.29), we find 'everything' defined in terms of *abhiññeyya*, a gerundive form of *abhijānāti*.

51. *santi, Poṭṭhapāda, eke samaṇa-brāhmaṇā evaṃvādino evaṃdiṭṭhino: 'ekantasukhī attā hoti arogo param maraṇā' ti. ... tyāhaṃ evaṃ vadāmi: 'api pana tumhe āyasmanto ekantasukhaṃ lokaṃ jānaṃ passaṃ viharathā?' ti. iti puṭṭhā 'no' ti vadanti. tyāhaṃ evaṃ vadāmi. 'api pana tumhe āyasmanto ekaṃ vā rattiṃ ekaṃ vā divasaṃ upaḍḍhaṃ vā rattiṃ upaḍḍhaṃ vā divasaṃ ekantasukhiṃ attānaṃ sañjānāthā?' ti. iti puṭṭhā 'no' ti vadanti. tyāhaṃ evaṃ vadāmi: 'api pana tumhe āyasmanto jānātha: ayaṃ maggo ayaṃ paṭipadā ekantasukhassa lokassa sacchikiriyāyā?' ti. iti puṭṭhā 'no' ti vadanti. tyāhaṃ*

A permanent self? Complete happiness? We do not experience it. It is beyond the reach of our perception, so it does not exist. This is the simplest and the most powerful argument against eternalist ideas in the early Buddhist texts.[52]

When the early Buddhists dispute with other philosophers, they always postulate the principle that what exists is what we experience. This empirical principle is a fundamental premise; it is not questioned. When some topics incompatible with this principle were in question, they kept silent.[53] Being asked about the reason for their silence, they said, 'Friend, such a topic is not relevant to the benefit [of beings], the true teaching (*dhamma*) or the highest pure conduct. It does not lead to *nibbāna*, etc. Therefore, the Bhagavant did not expound it.'[54] To put it briefly, what is not based on our experience cannot yield *nirvāṇa*. However, the reaction of the early Buddhists is not always so passive. They are sometimes assertive on such topics. They declared that whatever topic is beyond the reach of our experience is an illusion projected onto the data we have perceived. Thus, having described sixty-two philosophical views, the majority of which are topics beyond the reach of our experience, in the *Brahmajāla Sutta*, the Buddha concludes that these views are 'dependent on [cognitive] contact' (D.I.43: *tad api phassapaccayā*), and that 'it is impossible to experience (i.e., know) them without [cognitive] contact' (D.I.44: *te vata aññatra phassā paṭisaṃvedissantî ti n'etaṃ ṭhānaṃ vijjati*).

---

evaṃ vādāmi: 'api pana tumhe āyasmanto yā tā devatā ekantasukhaṃ lokaṃ uppannā tāsaṃ bhāsamānānaṃ saddaṃ suṇātha: 'suppaṭipannattha mārisā, ujupaṭipannattha mārisā, ekantasukhassa lokassa sacchikiriyāya! mayam pi hi mārisā evam pi paṭipannā ekantasukhaṃ lokaṃ uppannā'?' ti. iti puṭṭhā 'no' ti vadanti. Taṃ kim maññasi, Poṭṭhapāda? nanu evaṃ sante tesaṃ samaṇa-brāhmaṇānaṃ appāṭihīrakataṃ bhāsitaṃ sampajjatī? ti (D.I.192–93).

52. It would be interesting to compare early Buddhist empiricism with the following Brahmanical argument in the *Mahābhārata* XII, 203, v. 6–7, as introduced by Frauwallner (1973 [1953], vol. 1, p. 81): although the other side of the Himālaya or the back of the moon has never been seen by men, one cannot on that account assert that it does not exist; in the same way, one cannot assert, on the ground that it is never seen with the eyes, that this fine subtle *Ātmā* in essence does not exist.

53. For early Buddhist silence on such topics, see Collins (1982, pp. 131–8) and Harvey (1995, pp. 83–90).

54. *na h' etaṃ āvuso atthasaṃhitaṃ na dhammasaṃhitaṃ na ādibrahmacariyakaṃ na nibbidāya na virāgāya na nirodhāya na upasamāya na abhiññāya na sambodhāya na nibbānāya saṃvattati. tasmā taṃ Bhagavatā avyākatan ti* (*Pāsādika-sutta*, D.III.136).

Reductionism

We have seen that the early Buddhist use of the five aggregates is contrived to refute the eternalist conceptions of a self, and that the early Buddhists insisted that all kinds of views about the self are, in 'reality', based on the five aggregates. However, even with such empiricism, the anti-eternalist proposition, 'there is no permanent self since all the five aggregates are impermanent', would be invalid, unless we postulate early Buddhist reductionism: the whole cannot have a specific property which none of its components has.[55] In his article, 'Anattā as *via Media*', Karunadasa (1987) acknowledges this principle, 'Stated in brief, what the Buddhist doctrine of *anatta* amounts to is that none of the constituents of the empiric individuality can be considered as one's self' (p. 2), and provides us with a soteriological justification of the principle:

> The non-identification of any of the constituents of the empiric individuality with self has given rise to the question whether there is a self over and above the constituents. As far as Buddhism is concerned, the question has no relevance. For Buddhism explains the totality of conditioned existence and deliverance therefrom in such a way that it simply rules out the very necessity of raising the question. In the first place, none of the Buddhist doctrines presupposes such a self and, in the second, none of the Buddhist doctrines becomes more meaningful by such an assumption. (*ibid.*, p. 3)

Agreeing with this soteriological justification, I argue that the early Buddhists applied this reductionist principle for the correct understanding of phenomena in general.

Indeed, we can see the reason why the early Buddhists came to have the principle: if a thing is dependent on another, the properties of the former are dependent on those of the latter. Hence, in the *Nandakovāda-sutta*, we find a simile:

---

55. To see what happens when this reductionism is not postulated in early Buddhism, refer to a brief introduction of the Pudgalavāda doctrine by Harvey (1995, pp. 34–8). In particular, on p. 35, he summarizes, 'The "person" is said to be related to the personality factors by the relation of *upādāya*: "derivation from", "relation to" or "correlations with" (Kvu.34, L'AK.V.323). It is like the relationship between fire and burning fuel; the fire getting its name from what it burns (SNS.182). Perhaps the most useful image, though, is one suggested by Venkataramanan (SNS.225). This is that of a whole (the person) and its parts (the personality-factors). That is, the Personalists held the "person" to be a kind of whole which was more than the sum of its parts. ... Such a "person" is said to be neither constructed nor unconstructed, neither eternal nor non-eternal (Kvu.24). It is "ineffable" (*avaktavya*).'

> 'If a person says, "Of that big tree standing full of heartwood, the root is impermanent and subject to change, the trunk is impermanent and subject to change, the branches and leaves are impermanent and subject to change. However its shade is permanent, consistent, eternal and not subject to change," does he say right?' 'No, he does not, sir. … The shade is even more impermanent and subject to change.'[56]

From the early Buddhist viewpoint, the whole is dependent on its parts, so its properties are also dependent on the properties of the parts. Given this reductionism of early Buddhism, a self cannot have a property that the five aggregates do not have: no permanence, joy or *ātman* can be attributed to it. In the same *sutta* (M.III.273), we find another simile: with regard to an oil lamp that is burning, we cannot say that, while its oil, wick and flame are impermanent, its light is permanent.

Throughout the *Nikāya*s and *Āgama*s, we find a strong tendency to utilize this principle. As is illustrated by the simile of a butcher's knife in the *Mahāsatipaṭṭhāna-sutta* (D.II.295) and in the *Puṇṇovāda-sutta* (M.III.274–75), the early Buddhists use their wisdom (*prajñā*) as a sharp knife. In order to proclaim that whatever is life is suffering, they announce that whatever comprises life is suffering: birth, ageing, sickness, death and, finally, the totality of the five clinging-aggregates, which are the result of the finest analysis. In the course of practice, when they observe their bodies, they do not observe the body as a whole; instead, they analyse it into its parts, such as head hair, body hair, nails, teeth, skin, etc. They do not observe their mind as a monolith, either; but divide it into its components: ignorance, craving, carelessness, awareness, concentration, wisdom, etc. For them, the cultivation of mind means the elimination of bad components and the accumulation of good ones, by plying the scalpel of wisdom.

THE EARLY BUDDHIST SELF AND NIRVĀṆA

Both the four noble truths, as the early Buddhist soteriological framework, and the twelvefold dependent origination, as a representative

56. *… yo nu kho evaṃ vadeyya: 'amussa mahato rukkhassa tiṭṭhato sāravato mūlam pi aniccaṃ vipariṇāmadhammaṃ khandho pi anicco vipariṇāmadhammo sākhā-palāsam pi aniccaṃ vipariṇāmadhammaṃ, yā ca khvâssa chāyā sā niccā dhuvā sassatā avipariṇāmadhammā' ti, sammā nu kho so bhaginiyo vadamāno vadeyyā?' ti.' no h' etaṃ, bhante. … pagev' assa chāyā aniccā vipariṇāmadhammā ti* (M.III.274).

model of the early Buddhist concept of self, deal with the topics in two domains: the accumulation of suffering and the cessation of suffering. In this section, firstly, concerning the latter domain, I discuss what the complete cessation of suffering means with reference to a person's state of being, and secondly, concerning the former domain, I inspect how suffering in *saṃsāra* is connected with *nirvāṇa* through the doctrine of non-self.

In early Buddhism, two kinds of *nirvāṇa* are distinguished: the *nirvāṇa* with residue (*upadhiśeṣanirvāṇa*) and the *nirvāṇa* without residue (*nirupadhiśeṣanirvāṇa*),[57] and there have been two kinds of distinction regarding these two. Firstly, the *nirvāṇa* with residue, where there still remains a bodily basis, is attained through the highest awakening by Buddhas or *arhat*s, whereas the *nirvāṇa* without residue, where there is no bodily basis, is attained after their 'death.' Alternatively, the *nirvāṇa* with residue is the soteriological achievement of an *anāgāmin* (non-returner), whereas the *nirvāṇa* without residue is that of an *arhat*.[58] In the discussion below, I make use only of the first distinction between the two *nirvāṇa*s.

---

57. For the difference in meaning between the Pali terms *sa-upādisesa-nibbāna* and *anupādisesa-nibbāna* and the Sanskrit terms *upadhiśeṣanirvāṇa* and *nirupadhiśeṣanirvāṇa*, refer to Cousins (1998, p. 10).

58. T125 *Ekottarāgama* defines the distinction: 'What is the state of the *nirvāṇa* with residue? It is a state where, after exterminating the five lower bindings (*pañcāvarabhāgīya-saṃyojanāni*), a monk will enter *nirvāṇa* in that world and never come back to this world. This is called the state of the *nirvāṇa* with residue. What is the state of the *nirvāṇa* without residue? It is a state where a monk extinguishes [corrupted] flows (*āsrava*), achieves freedom from [corrupted] flows (*anāsrava*), attains mind-liberation (*ceto-vimukti*) and wisdom-liberation (*prajñā-vimukti*), ... exhausts all birth and death, completes all pure practices (*brahmacarya*), receives no more existence, and knows things as they are. This is called the state of the *nirvāṇa* without residue.' (世尊告諸比丘: '有此二法涅槃界. 云何爲二? 有餘涅槃界・無餘涅槃界. 彼云何名爲有餘涅槃界? 於是, 比丘滅五下分結, 卽彼般涅槃, 不還來此世. 是謂名爲有餘涅槃界. 彼云何名爲無餘涅槃界? 如是比丘盡有漏, 成無漏, 意解脫, 智慧解脫, 自身作證, 而自遊戲, 生死已盡, 梵行已立, 更不受有, 如實知之. 是謂爲無餘涅槃界; T125.2.579a13–21).

   In the major *Nikāya*s, we do not find this second distinction between the two *nirvāṇa*s as clear as in the above *Ekottarāgama* passage. Instead, as indirect authorities, we find the following expression: 'One of the two fruits is to be expected [for the practitioner]: i.e. [firstly, complete] knowledge in this life, or [secondly, the state of] non-returner, if there remains clinging' (*dvinnaṃ phalanaṃ aññataraṃ phalaṃ pātikaṅkhaṃ: diṭṭhe va dhamme aññā, sati vā upādisese anāgāmitā*; D.II.314; M.I.62, 63, 481; S.V.129, 181, 236, 313; A.III.82, 143; V.108). For more details, refer to Hwang (2006, pp. 14–35).

According to early Buddhism, as the *Mahāparinirvāṇa-sūtra* tells us, even the Buddha after his highest awakening was subject to physical suffering.[59] The complete cessation of suffering can be attained only after the 'death' of Buddhas or *arhats*. If we attend to the definition of suffering (*duḥkha*) as the totality of the five clinging-aggregates in the first noble truth, the third truth, the cessation of suffering (*duḥkhanirodha*), must be attained along with the *nirvāṇa* without residue. However, in fact, the third truth more frequently relates to the *nirvāna* with residue, being representatively defined in terms of the cessation of craving (*tṛṣṇā*).[60] In other words, the cessation of suffering is more frequently defined in terms of the cessation of the origin of suffering (i.e., the second truth, see Chap. 3, note 65). In the same way, instead of the cessation of craving, we also find the cessation of enjoyment (*nandī*), e.g., in the *Puṇṇovāda-sutta* (M.III.267–68), and the cessation of passion (*chandarāga*), e.g., in the *Mahāhatthipadopama-sutta* (M.I.191), defining the cessation of suffering. In the doctrinal system of early Buddhism, the cessation of these particular mental factors is still compatible with the perception of physical pain.

The *Aṅguttara-nikāya* (A.III.410–17) juxtaposes a series of explanations about the origin, variety, result and cessation of soteriologically negative objects and about the path leading to their cessation. Those objects are: (a) desire (*kāma*) (410–12), (b) feeling (*vedanā*) (412–13), (c) apperception (*saññā*) (413–14), (d) [corrupted] flow (*āsava*) (414–15), (e) action [that causes rebirth] (*kamma*) (415–16), and (f) suffering (*dukkha*). There, the cessation of (a), (d) and (e) corresponds to the *nirvāṇa* with residue, whereas the cessation of (b) and (c) corresponds to that without residue. (The cessation of (f) can be interpreted in both ways.) Since the cessation of feeling and that of apperception cannot be attained while there are bodily bases and perceptions, they must signify the *nirvāṇa* without residue. For another example, in the *Devatā-saṃyutta*, the Buddha identifies liberation (*nimokkha*) not only with the cessation of enjoyment in becoming (*nandībhava*), but also with the cessation of apperception, consciousness and feeling.[61]

---

59. See MPS: §§14.1–6. For Pali, see D.II.99, and for Chinese translations, see T1.1.15a, T5.1.164c, T6.1.180a and T1451.24.387a.

60. That is, craving for sensual objects (*kāmatṛṣṇā*), craving for becoming (*bhavatṛṣṇā*) and craving for non-becoming (*vibhavatṛṣṇā*): e.g., in the *Sammādiṭṭhi-sutta* (M.I.48–49) and the *Khandha-saṃyutta* (S.III.158–59).

61. *nandībhavaparikkhayā saññāviññāṇasaṅkhayā vedanānaṃ nirodhā upasamā, evaṃ khvāham āvuso jānāmi sattānaṃ nimokkhaṃ pamokkhaṃ vivekan ti* (S.I.2).

We may regard the *nirvāṇa* with residue, i.e., the cessation of craving, etc., as cause, and the *nirvāṇa* without residue as its automatic result. Although there is a Buddhist practice of temporarily stopping feeling, apperception and consciousness (*nirodhasamādhi*), the complete cessation of those mental factors is not an aim of Buddhist soteriology. When they eliminate all ignorance and desire, there is no cause to produce the bodily bases in the next life (as is taught by the theory of dependent origination); as a result, there could be no more feeling, etc., after 'death', the attainment of the *nirvāṇa* without residue.

The above explanations describe *nirvāṇa* in terms of the cessation of specific factors that comprise a person; whereas we also find another description of *nirvāṇa* as the state of being: 'Birth is exhausted. ... There is no further [life] after this state of being,'[62] which is a representative description of the state that an *arhat* achieves. What does this sentence, 'There is no further [life],' mean? Dismissing the ten questions beyond the reach of experience, including whether the Buddha exists after his death or not, the Buddha in the *Aggivacchagotta-sutta* presents a simile:

> [The Buddha asks,] 'Vaccha, if you are asked, "When this fire is extinguished in front of you, towards which direction would the fire go from here: to the east, the west, the north or the south?" how would you explain it?'
>
> [Vaccha answers,] '[The question] is not appropriate, Sir Gotama, for fire burns depending on such fuel as grass or sticks. When its fuel is used up but no other fuel is supplied, [the fire] that has no food is generally considered to be extinguished.'[63]

That is, after the *nirvāṇa* without residue, there is no more basis for life activities: no body, no feeling, no apperception, no mental activities, no consciousness. The *Brahmajāla-sutta* explains this topic directly:

> Having eliminated what leads to becoming, the body of the Tathāgata remains. So long as his body remains, gods and human beings will

---

62. *khīṇā jāti, (vusitaṃ brahmacariyaṃ, kataṃ karaṇīyaṃ,) nâparaṃ itthatāyā (ti pajānāti)* (e.g., D.I.84).
63. *'sace pana taṃ, Vaccha, evaṃ puccheyya: "yo te ayaṃ purato aggi nibbuto, so aggi ito katamaṃ disaṃ gato puratthimaṃ vā pacchimaṃ vā uttaraṃ vā dakkhiṇaṃ vā?" ti, evaṃ puṭṭho tvaṃ, Vaccha, kin ti vyākareyyāsī'?' ti. 'na upeti, bho Gotama. yaṃ hi so, bho Gotama, aggi tiṇa-kaṭṭh'upādānaṃ paṭicca ajali, tassa ca pariyādānā aññassa ca anupahārā anāhāro nibbuto t' eva saṅkhaṃ gacchatī' ti'* (M.I.487).

> see him. After the destruction of the body, and once the life-span is exhausted, they will not see him.[64]

As I discuss further below, there has been a variety of views on the state of a self after the *nirvāṇa* without residue. However, given that early Buddhist empiricism allows 'in reality' no more than the five aggregates for any view of the self, the above descriptions of *nirvāna* imply that there is nothing to be designated as a self after that *nirvāṇa*. The acceptance of the existence of Buddhas after the *nirvāṇa*, no matter how mystically it is described, would deprive the early Buddhists of the majority of their core doctrines. They could not hold fast to empiricism, since there is an imperceptible form of Buddha beyond the five aggregates; this conflicts with the declaration throughout the major *Nikāya*s and *Āgama*s that the five aggregates are all that are to be perceived, and therefore all that exist. They lose reductionism, since the whole may have a special property that its parts do not have: e.g., a Buddha has the property of permanent existence that any one of his five clinging-aggregates does not have. The rivalry with eternalism would be pointless, since the Buddhist soteriological ultimate, i.e., *nirvāṇa*, would not be very different from the eternalist one, e.g., the attainment of the pure *ātman*.

The Buddhist conception of self lends a peculiar colour to its soteriological framework, which in itself is a pan-Indic one. The peculiar colour is the doctrine of non-self (*anātman*): since they do not realize that there is no [permanent] self, ordinary people are fettered to suffering innumerable rebirths, whereas, since they have realized that very fact, Buddhist saints are released from suffering.

For this reason, by definition, the origin of suffering is identified with 'the craving that yields further lives, that is accompanied by pleasure, and that finds pleasure here and there: i.e., craving for sensual objects, craving for becoming and craving for non-becoming';[65] and the cessation of suffering is the cessation of the craving, as introduced above. In addition, we find that the cessation of the three [corrupted]

---

64. *ucchinnabhavanettiko bhikkhave Tathāgatassa kāyo tiṭṭhati. yāv' assa kāyo ṭhassati, tāva naṃ dakkhinti devamanussā; kāyassa bhedā uddhaṃ jīvitapariyādānā na dakkhinti devamanussā* (D.I.46).

    The *Avyākata-saṃyutta* (S.IV.402) explains this topic, pointing out that there is no cause or condition to designate him. For more explanations on this topic, see Norman (1993a [1991]) and Karunadasa (1987, pp. 7–8).

65. *(idaṃ kho pana bhikkhave dukkhasamudayaṃ ariyasaccaṃ,) yā 'yaṃ taṇhā ponobbhavikā nandirāgasahagatā tatratatrābhinandinī, seyyathīdaṃ: kāmataṇhā bhavataṇhā vibhavataṇhā* (S.V.421).

flows (*āsravas*), i.e., the [corrupted] flow of sensual desire, that of [the attachment to] existence and that of ignorance, is identified with the attainment of *arhat*-ship. Among the three [corrupted] flows, 'the flow of [the attachment to] existence' is the desire for permanent self, 'the flow of ignorance' includes the view of a permanent self, and 'the flow of sensual desire' promotes the desire for a permanent self. In addition, we find in the *Khandha-saṃyutta* (S.III.157–58) a version of the four noble truths in terms of the view of a permanent self (*sakkāyadiṭṭhi*): i.e., the view of a permanent self, the origin of the view, the cessation of the view, and the path leading to the cessation of the view, in synonymizing juxtaposition with the typical version of the four noble truths, i.e., suffering, the origin of suffering, etc. (S.III.158–59).

It is probable that, due to the rivalry with eternalism, particularly with Brahmanism, Buddhists emphasized that ignorance of the absence of any [permanent] self and desire for immortality are the ultimate origin of suffering, and announced that the cessation of ignorance and desires is identical to the attainment of *nirvāṇa*. In this sense, Karunadasa (1987, p. 5) states, 'What is emphasized here is not deliverance of the self but deliverance from the self-notion which creates the duality between self and non-self.'

Chapter 4

DEVELOPMENT OF A BUDDHIST SELF

I will now briefly survey the development of the later Buddhist conceptions of self in India. Since Mahāyāna and non-Mahāyāna scriptures were introduced to China almost simultaneously, and Mahāyāna Buddhism became the mainstream in China from an early stage, it is essential to examine the later Buddhist conceptions of self, in order to understand how Chinese Buddhists came to form their own ideas of self. I cannot survey the whole development of later Buddhist ideas in detail, so I will focus on how the basic premises and principles that structured the early Buddhist conception of self were maintained, revised and abandoned by later Buddhists.

*DHARMA*S AND SELF: ABHIDHARMIC THEORIES

A strict systematization of doctrines is the main contribution of Abhidharmic scholars to the development of Buddhism: they defined the meanings of Buddhist technical terms, clarified the similarities and differences between overlapping categories, provided the classification of concepts and entities, presented a standardized cosmology, and so forth. This scholarship of systematization became more analytic and extensive as time passed: Abhidharma scholars around the fifth century aimed to make the system of Buddhist doctrines all-inclusive and consistent; nothing must remain unexplained by the Buddhist doctrinal system.

The principal attitude of the Abhidharmic scholars towards various early Buddhist doctrines is to preserve them as far as possible, unless they yield contradictions in their all-inclusive system. Hence, as regards the concept of self, we find them preserving the majority of early Buddhist ontological, epistemological and soteriological postulates.

As in early Buddhism, a self goes through *saṃsāra*; the so-called self is impermanent; it is a compound of the five aggregates, none of which is permanent; the components of such a self are constructed dependent on conditions; and the four noble truths still provide a soteriological framework, in which the concept of self plays a pivotal role.

Abhidharma Buddhists followed anti-Brahmanism, in that they also rejected any conception of a permanent self and any cosmogonic idea of *brahman*. However, we also find that internal sectarianism was rather stronger than anti-Brahmanism. For Sarvāstivāda and Theravāda, the main adversaries in the controversy regarding the concept of self were the Vātsīputrīyas, who were Buddhist 'heretics', insisting on the existence of an agent in *saṃsāra*, called *pudgala*.[1]

At first glance, Abhidharma Buddhists appear to maintain empiricism. However, they added one further source of truth, i.e., correct reasoning (*anumāna*), which caused them to lose empiricism in the early Buddhist sense. We can witness this change in the following statement of Vasubandhu, which rephrases the statement from the *Khandha-saṃyutta* quoted above, that any view on self is indeed based on the five aggregates (see p. 70), in Abhidharmic terms:

> Then how can we understand that this name *ātman* designates merely the succession of the aggregates and that nothing else [than the succession of the aggregates] is designated? Because there is neither direct observation nor correct reasoning [with reference to *ātman*]. When there are phenomena (*dharmas*), direct observation occurs unless it is hindered, e.g. [the perception] of the six perceptible objects and the mind; or [there must be] correct reasoning, e.g. [the reasoning for the existence of] the five sense faculties.[2] ... Since there is no such

1. Vasubandhu dedicates the *Pudgalaviniścaya* (*Clarifying [the Concept of] Pudgala*), the last chapter of the *Abhidharmakośa-bhāṣya*, to disputing the existence of *pudgala*. For English translations of this, see La Vallée Poussin and Pruden (1988–90 [1971–72], vol. 4, pp. 1313–55), and Duerlinger (2003). For the Theravādin rejection of *pudgala*, see Karunadasa (1996, pp. 11–12), Collins (1982, pp. 178–82) and Harvey (1995, pp. 34–8).
2. According to the Sarvāstivāda definition, the eye faculty, etc., is not the eyeball, etc., that we can see. The faculties are considered to be made of subtle material elements that cannot be seen (or [directly] pointed out): *uktaṃ ca sūtre: 'cakṣur, bhikṣo, ādhyātmikam āyatanaṃ catvāri mahābhūtāny upādāya rūpaprasādo rūpy anidarśanaṃ sapratighaṃ, evaṃ yāvat kāyaṃ ...'* (AbhK: p. 74, comm. to §1.35c). (The Pali Abhidhamma tradition also accepts that the five sense faculties cannot be seen (or pointed out): *pañc'indriyā anidassana-sappaṭighā, sattaras'indriyā anidassana-appaṭighā.* Vibh.127.) These faculties cannot be seen by sight, and other senses, such as hearing, etc., cannot

> [direct observation or correct reasoning] with reference to *ātman*, there is no *ātman*.[3]

They sharpened the Buddhist knife of wisdom. They analysed objects of perception to such an extreme that further meditative observation or theoretical analysis is impossible. As Karunadasa (1996, p. 6) witnesses, the critical Abhidharmic concept *dharma* (Pa. *dhamma*)

> assumes a more technical meaning, referring to those items that result when the process of analysis is taken to its ultimate limits. In Theravāda Abhidhamma, for instance, the aggregate of corporeality (of the *khandha*-analysis) is broken down into twenty-eight items called *rūpa-dhammas*. The next three aggregates – sensation, perception, and mental formations – are together arranged into fifty-two items called *cetasikas*. The fifth, consciousness, is counted as one item with eighty-nine varieties and is referred to as *citta*.

We also find Abhidharmists holding to a stronger form of reductionism: the components that cannot be analysed any further are real, whereas the whole is nominal. We find a felicitous illustration in the *Abhidharmakośa-bhāṣya*, showing how they apply this principle to the definition of technical terms. According to the early Buddhist definition, the aggregate of form (*rūpa-skandha*) means the totality of forms: 'Any form, no matter whether it is past, future or present, internal or external, gross or fine, low or excellent, or placed near or far away – this is the form-aggregate.'[4] So, applying strict reductionism to this definition, one Abhidharmic master challenges, 'If aggregate (*skandha*) means heap (*rāśi*) [of all form, etc.], the aggregates become nominal (i.e., they do not exist 'really'), since they are masses of various substances (*dravya*); [the aggregate is nominal] like a heap and like a person (*pudgala*).'[5] The issue of whether the aggregate is substantial or nominal is not agreed among

---

distinguish their existence; therefore, the existence of the five faculties is not supported by direct observation. Their existence can be proved by correct reasoning only.

3. *kathaṃ punar idaṃ gamyate: skandhasantāna ev êdaṃ ātmâbhidhānaṃ vartate nânyasminn abhidheya iti? pratyakṣânumānâbhāvāt. ye hi dharmāḥ santi, teṣāṃ pratyakṣam upalabdhir bhavaty asaty antarāye, tadyathā ṣaṇṇāṃ viṣayāṇāṃ manasaś ca; anumānaṃ ca, tadyathā pañcānām indriyāṇām. ... na câivam ātmato 'stīti, nâsty ātmā* (*Pudgala-viniścaya*; AbhK: pp. 923–4).
4. *yaṃ kiñci, bhikkhu, rūpaṃ atītânāgata-paccuppannaṃ ajjhattaṃ vā bahiddhā vā oḷārikaṃ vā sukhumaṃ vā hīnaṃ vā paṇītaṃ vā yaṃ dūre santike vā – ayaṃ rūpakkhandho* (*Mahāpuṇṇama-sutta*, M.III.16).
5. *yadi rāśyarthaḥ skandhârthaḥ, prajñaptisantaḥ skandhāḥ prāpnuvanti anekadravyasamūhatvāt rāśi-pudgalavat* (AbhK: 48, comm. to §1.20a).

Vaibhāṣika masters; however, there is no disagreement among the masters with the postulate that anything compounded is nominal and only components that cannot be analysed any further are substantial.

Dharmas *and Truth in the Highest Sense* (Paramārtha)

The *Abhidharmakośa-bhāṣya* by Vasubandhu has been read and honoured as a treatise comprehensively surveying and summarizing the Sarvāstivāda doctrines; however, in fact, in many cases Vasubandhu attacks Sarvāstivāda views, basing himself on Sautrāntika ideas. At any rate, his treatise came to have the most influence over the development of Chinese Abhidharmic understanding.[6] The structure of the treatise illustrates how Abhidharmic Buddhists systematized Buddhism as a whole, by means of (1) classifying the primary elements of which all things in the world are comprised, (2) explaining the twenty-two bodily and mental faculties that provide the bases for the perception or understanding of the phenomena surrounding a person,[7] (3) presenting a cosmology,[8] (4–8) expounding karma, defilements, soteriological progress, knowledge and meditations, and then (9) disproving the existence of any self other than the five aggregates.

We find here a shift in the concerns of Buddhist intellectuals. While the early Buddhists focused on personal experience in *saṃsāra* and extended their concerns to the phenomena that influence personal experience, Vasubandhu first expounds how 'everything' is constructed from primary factors (*dharmas*), and then extends his concern to personal experience and liberation. The shift of concern is reflected in the fact that the amount and detail of his explanation of general causation, i.e., the four kinds of condition (*pratyaya*), the six kinds of cause (*hetu*) and the five kinds of result (*phala*), greatly exceed those of twelvefold dependent origination. That is, the components of a self and their formation are dealt with rather as a section of the general topic of primary factors and their formation.

---

6. For more information on the *Abhidharmakośa* texts, refer to Willemen *et al.* (1998, pp. 269–78) and La Vallée Poussin *et al.* (1988–90 [1971–72], vol. 1, pp. liv-lxi).
7. Here, in the *Indriya-nirdeśa*, Vasubandhu also presents the list of 75 primary factors (*dharmas*) in five categories, the total of which is identical with 'everything'; then he expounds the four kinds of condition (*pratyaya*), the six kinds of cause (*hetu*) and the five kinds of result (*phala*).
8. Here, in the *Loka-nirdeśa*, he also expounds twelvefold dependent origination.

Regarding the importance of the concept of primary factors (Pa. *dhamma*), Karunadasa (1996, pp. 1–2) remarks,

> All the different modes of analysis and classification found in the Abhidhamma stem from a single philosophical principle, which gave direction and shape to the entire project of systematization. This principle is the notion that all the phenomena of empirical existence are made up of a number of elementary constituents, the ultimate realities behind the manifest phenomena. These elementary constituents, the building blocks of experience, are called *dhammas*. ... But the *dhamma* theory was intended from the start to be more than a mere hypothetical scheme. It arose from the need to make sense out of experiences in meditation and was designed as a guide for meditative contemplation and insight.

In the *Abhidharmakośa-bhāṣya,* Vasubandhu defines a *dharma* as something that bears its own characteristic,[9] i.e., a primary existent that withstands the highest meditative or philosophical analysis of specific characteristics. Then he classifies and systematizes everything in terms of *dharmas:* three *dharma*s as the unconditioned (*asaṃskṛta*) (AbhK: pp. 15–20, §1.5–6), eleven *dharma*s as form (*rūpa*) (pp. 24–38, §§1.9–14b), one *dharma* as mind (*citta*) (p. 41, §1.16), forty-six *dharma*s as mental factors associated with mind (*caitta*) (pp. 146–53, §§2.23–27), and fourteen *dharma*s as mental factors not associated with mind (pp. 165–220, §§2.35–48). In total, these comprise all that exist in the doctrinal system of Sarvāstivāda.

By contrast with early Buddhism, where *nirvāṇa* was seldom dealt with under the topic of what comprises 'everything', the Sarvāstivāda Abhidharmists regarded *nirvāṇa* as one of the *dharma*s and included it within 'everything'. The Sarvāstivāda Abhidharmists (and later the Yogācāra theorists also) classified the *nirvāṇa* with residue under the intended cessations (*pratisaṃkhyā-nirodha*) and the *nirvāṇa* without residue under the unintended cessations (*apratisaṃkhyā-nirodha*), both of which belong to the unconditioned (*asaṃskṛta*). This inclusion of *nirvāṇa* in 'everything' is a natural consequence for the Sarvāstivādins (and the Yogācārins), since they authorize correct reasoning in addition to direct observation as a means of grasping truth. Since *nirvāṇa* is

---

9. *svalakṣaṇadhāraṇād dharmaḥ* (AbhK, p. 11, comm. to §1.1). In Pali Abhidhamma, the term *dhamma* is defined: '*Dhamma*s are so called because they bear their own-nature' (*attano sabhāvaṃ dhārentî ti dhammā*. Vism.485). Karunadasa (1996, pp. 13–19) presents an informative examination of the meaning of *dhamma* and *svabhāva*.

defined in the Sarvāstivāda tradition as the cessation or absence of something, i.e., nothing, it cannot be the object of normal perception or meditative observation; therefore, it must be an object that is accessible only through reasoning, unless through mystical insight. On this point, such Abhidharma Buddhists as Vasubandhu lose the strongest weapon of early Buddhism against eternalism, i.e., naïve empiricism: if it is imperceptible, it does not exist. Accepting reasoning as a means of grasping truth, they cannot reject the existence of a permanent self and the creator of the universe, etc., merely on the grounds that they cannot perceive such things; otherwise, they have to reject the existence of *nirvāṇa* also.

We have seen that the early Buddhists acknowledged a higher knowledge (*abhijñā*) in contrast to the ordinary one: meditative observation can grasp a higher reality than ordinary perception does. Abhidharma Buddhists deepened the distinction between knowledge in the highest sense (*paramārtha*) and in the conventional sense (*saṃvṛti*). For the Abhidharmists, however, truth in the highest sense is closely related to correct analysis: as Karunadasa (1996, p. 12) remarks, 'This brings into focus two levels of reality: that which is amenable to analysis and that which defies further analysis. Analysability is the mark of composite things, and non-analysability the mark of the elementary constituents, the *dhammas*.'[10]

Abhidharmic wisdom in the highest sense performs analysis not only spatially but also temporally. The shortest temporal unit that can be observed in meditation or that cannot be analysed any further is called a moment (*kṣaṇa*). Based on this temporal analysis in the highest sense, later Abhidharma Buddhists insisted that all *dharma*s last for a single or a few moments, except for several *dharma*s among those belonging to the unconditioned, non-communicative forms (*avijñapti-rūpa*) and mental factors not associated with mind.

The Abhidharmic Conception of Self

As for the Abhidharmic concept of self, many of the fundamental ideas were inherited from the doctrinal system of early Buddhism. However, their sharp sword of wisdom, in particular that which analysed existence in its temporal aspect, yielded a conception of self that was peculiar

10. For more information about the Pali Abhidhammic distinction of knowledge or truth into two levels, see Karunadasa (1996, pp. 27–40) and Collins (1982, pp. 147–56).

to Abhidharma Buddhism. For example, with regard to a verse in the *Devatā-saṃyutta*:

> Life is led to the end, the life span is short.
> A person who is led to the end by ageing has no refuges.[11]

the Pali commentator comments:[12]

> Moreover, [the life span is] even as short as a moment. For, in the highest sense, the life-moment of living beings is extremely short, i.e., only as long as the operation of a single thought. Just as the wheel of a chariot moves on only a single point of a rim and stands on only a single point of it, in that way, the life of beings [lasts for] a single mind-moment. When the thought ceases, the being is also said to cease.[13]

A self is a compound of the five aggregates that undergoes *saṃsāra*. However, according to the above extreme analysis, the five aggregates last only for a single moment; therefore, in the next moment, the successive compound of the aggregates has different components from the previous one. It is said that the successive compound is neither the same as the previous one, since new components arise after previous ones have ceased, nor different from the previous one, since the arising of later components is dependent on the previous ones. In short, it is clear that no self can last more than one moment in the ontological sense. The identity of a person as a series of momentary compounds of the five aggregates can be designated by means of natural and karmic law as depicted in twelvefold dependent origination.

SELF IN THE *PRAJÑĀPĀRAMITĀ* LITERATURE AND MADHYAMAKA THEORY

For the Mahāyāna scriptures quoted in Chapters 4 and 5, I rely, wherever possible, on the texts written in Indian languages; this is in order to prevent the unconscious introduction of Chinese adaptations. However,

---

11. *upanīyati jīvitam, appam āyu,*
 jarûpanītassa na santi tāṇā. (S.I.2)
12. The commentator provides a few explanations of the passage, and that quoted is the last one. Normally, the best explanation 'in the highest sense' is given last in the Pali commentarial literature.
13. *khaṇaparittatāya pi. paramatthato hi atiparitto sattānaṃ jīvitakkhaṇo ekacittappavattimatto-y-eva. yathā nāma rathacakkaṃ pavattamānam pi eken' eva nemippadesena pavattati, tiṭṭhamānam pi eken' eva tiṭṭhati; evam evaṃ ekacittakkhaṇikaṃ sattānaṃ jīvitaṃ, tasmiṃ citte niruddhamatte satto niruddho ti vuccati* (Spk.I.22).

the relatively late dates of the manuscripts trouble me. While this book is concerned with Indian Buddhism no later than the late seventh century, the great majority of Mahāyāna manuscripts were produced far later than that. For example, the manuscripts of the *Aṣṭasāhasrikā Prajñāpāramitā* are from the eleventh to thirteenth centuries approximately (see AṣṭPr, p. ix). Considering textual developments in India, there must have been many interpolations by later Indian Buddhists. Moreover, we cannot but lose the textual development that may be reflected in a series of Chinese translations. For example, we have six extant Chinese translations of the *Aṣṭasāhasrikā Prajñāpāramitā*: T224 by Lokakṣema in 179–80, T225 by Zhi Qian (fl. 222–53), T226 (a partial translation) by Dharmapriya in 382, T227 by Kumārajīva in 408, T220 by Xuanzang in c. 660 and T228 by Dānapāla in 985. In general, the present Sanskrit text mostly agrees with the last two Chinese translations. For more information on the Chinese translations of the *Aṣṭasāhasrikā Prajñāpāramitā*, refer to Conze (1978, pp. 46–53).

Mahāyāna theorists adopted the same attitude as the Abhidharmists towards the inheritance of established theories from earlier doctrinal systems. They adopted a few new principles, or strengthened and generalized particular features among the established theories; however, applying their characteristic principles to old teachings, they minimized the number of abandoned authorities to the extent that they could retain the consistency of their new doctrinal system. It is closer to remodelling than creation. This is the reason why the new doctrinal systems are still called Buddhism, despite the fact that the application of those principles yields doctrines that would have been rejected by the Buddha of earlier Buddhism.

Those Buddhists who advocated the Prajñāpāramitā literature and Madhyamaka doctrines also frequently utilized established ideas of earlier Buddhism against their external adversaries. For example, when refuting the Brahmanic conception of a permanent self, Nāgārjuna, the founder of the Madhyamaka school, utilizes the early Buddhist principles, i.e., reductionism and empiricism, in his *Mūlamadhyamaka-kārikā* (MMK: p. 263 §19.1): if the self is identical with the aggregates, it must rise and cease (i.e., it is impermanent); if it were other than the aggregates, it would lack the characteristic of aggregates (i.e., it is not perceivable, so it does not exist).[14] Instead, they used their new ideas in

14. *ātmā skandhā yadi bhaved, udayavyayabhāg bhavet;*
skandhebhyo 'nyo yadi bhaved, bhaved askandhalakṣaṇaḥ.

order to counter their internal adversaries. Their new weapon targeted any conceptualization; in particular, Nāgārjuna himself strove to refute the Vaibhāṣika conceptualization of substances (*dravya*) and momentariness (*kṣaṇabhaṅga*).

Emptiness (śūnyatā)

The *Aṣṭasāhasrikā Prajñāpāramitā* starts with the Buddha's calling on Subhūti to preach to *bodhisattvas* about the perfection of wisdom (*prajñāpāramitā*). Subhūti begins his preaching with 'O Bhagavat, I do not observe such a thing (*dharma*) as a *bodhisattva*.'[15] I do not read the *Prajñāpāramitā* literature as upholding the view that there exists nothing in the world. Rather, it claims that, in 'reality', there is no such thing as is conceptualized by philosophers. Subhūti himself expresses the complexity as follows:

> 'O Bhagavat, while knowing, recognizing and observing neither what is named *bodhisattva* nor the perfection of wisdom, what perfection of wisdom will I teach to what *bodhisattva*? Bhagavat, this would be my anxiety: while not knowing, recognizing or observing an entity, I should make such a thing as a *bodhisattva* come into existence or pass away, merely by naming it.'[16]

In this extremity, we can designate neither an agent of karmic activity nor the surroundings in which karmic actions happen.

The proposition that, in 'reality', there is no such thing as is conceptualized by a name is described ontologically as follows:

> 'Buddha, *bodhisattva* and the perfection of wisdom are mere names. A [mere] name does not come into being. O Bhagavat, just as, although one speaks of the self (*ātman*), there is no self coming into being at all, in that way, while all things have no self-nature (*svabhāva*), what is form, feeling, apperception, mental activities or consciousness, which neither are to be grasped nor have come into being? In the same way, the non-self-nature of all these things does not come into

15. *nāhaṃ Bhagavaṃs taṃ dharmaṃ samanupaśyāmi yad uta bodhisattva iti* (AṣṭPr, p. 3).

16. *so 'haṃ Bhagavan etad eva bodhisattvanāmadheyam avindan anupalabhamāno 'samanupaśyan prajñāpāramitām api avindan anupalabhamāno 'samanupaśyan katamaṃ bodhisattvaṃ katamasyāṃ prajñāpāramitāyām avavadiṣyāmi anuśāsiṣyāmi? etad eva Bhagavan kaukṛtyaṃ syāt: yo 'haṃ vastv avindan anupalabhamāno 'samanupaśyan nāmadheyamātreṇa āyavyayaṃ kuryāṃ yad uta bodhisattva iti* (*ibid.*, p. 4).

> being either. Since nothing comes into being, there are no such things (*dharmas*).'[17]

Here, whatever we recognize is considered a mere name that has no self-nature, and therefore the existence of *dharmas*, which are conceptualized as primary factors, must be rejected, no matter whether they are temporary or eternal.

However, the Buddhists of the *Prajñāpāramitā* literature were never nihilists. If there is nothing, to what end do they advocate the practice of the perfection of wisdom? They based themselves firmly on the pre-established soteriological framework: living beings suffer endless rebirths; they do so since they are ignorant, i.e., in terms of the *Prajñāpāramitā*, they regard things conceptualized by names as real; there exists a state of cessation of suffering; the cessation of suffering can be attained by means of perfecting wisdom, i.e., by means of doing away with such conceptualization. They depict the state of doing away with any conceptualization as having nothing 'on which to take a position' (*sthātavya*). Hence, Subhūti reports to the Buddha:

> 'Furthermore, O Bhagavat, since a *bodhisattva* acts in the perfection of wisdom and practises it, on none of form, feeling, apperception, mental activities or consciousness is a position to be taken. What is the reason for this? If one takes a position on form ... or on consciousness, one does not act in the perfection of wisdom, but in the development (*abhisaṃskāra*) of form ... or consciousness. What is the reason for this? For, one who acts in the development [of the five aggregates] cannot comprehend, practise or achieve the perfection of wisdom.'[18]

---

17. *buddha iti ... bodhisattva iti ... prajñāpāramitêti Bhagavan nāmadheyamātram etat. tac ca nāmadheyam anabhinirvṛttam. Yathā ātmā ātmêti ca Bhagavann ucyate, atyantatayā ca Bhagavann anabhinirvṛtta ātmā; evam asvabhāvānāṃ sarvadharmāṇāṃ katamat tad rūpaṃ ... vedanā-saṃjñā-saṃskārāḥ ... vijñānaṃ yad agrāhyam anabhinirvṛttam? evam eteṣāṃ sarvadharmānāṃ yā asvabhāvatā, sā anabhinirvṛttiḥ. yā ca sarvadharmāṇām anabhinirvṛttir, na te dharmāḥ* (*ibid.*, p. 17).
18. *punar aparaṃ, Bhagavan, bodhisattvena mahāsattvena prajñāpāramitāyāṃ caratā prajñāpāramitāṃ bhāvayatā na rūpe sthātavyaṃ, na vedanāyāṃ na saṃjñāyāṃ na saṃskāreṣu na vijñāne sthātavyam. tat kasya hetoḥ? saced rūpe tiṣṭhati, rūpābhisaṃskāre carati, na carati prajñāpāramitāyām. evaṃ saced vedanāyāṃ sañjñāyāṃ saṃskāreṣu, saced vijñāne tiṣṭhati, vijñānâbhisaṃskāre carati, na carati prajñāpāramitāyām. tat kasya hetoḥ? na hi abhisaṃskāre caran prajñāpāramitāṃ parigṛhṇāti, nâpi prajñāpāramitāyāṃ yogam āpadyate, nâpi prajñāpāramitāṃ paripūrayate* (*ibid.*, p. 4).

This makes it difficult to clarify the position of the *Prajñāpāramitā* literature on empiricism. It still holds to empiricism, in that the existence of something beyond our experience is rejected; however, simultaneously, it appears to dissuade Buddhists from taking things as they are naturally experienced: the experience of ordinary people is regarded as being illusory.

Although it appears, at first glance, far removed from early Buddhist teaching, this principle of deconceptualization was an important practice from the time of early Buddhism, when it was called the emptiness concentration (*śūnyatā-samādhi*) and the signless concentration (*animitta-samādhi*), doing away with all notion (*-saṃjñā, nimitta*), ideation (*vitarka*) and intention (*saṃkalpa*). Generally speaking, the emptiness concentration focuses on the observation of the fact that any perceptive object is void of a permanent self,[19] whereas the signless concentration focuses on the process of not paying attention to any sign.[20] Hence, in the *Mahāvedalla-sutta*, Sāriputta differentiates between the two, as follows:

> What is, friend, the deliverance of mind through emptiness? Having gone to the forest, to the root of a tree, or to an empty village, a monk reflects, 'This is void of a [permanent] self or what [permanently] belongs to a self.' This is called the deliverance of mind through emptiness.
>
> What is, friend, the deliverance of mind through signlessness? Paying no attention to any sign, a monk enters and stays at the signless concentration. This is called the deliverance of mind through signlessness.[21]

---

19. For example, 'Since it is empty of a [permanent] self or what [permanently] belongs to a self, the world is said to be empty' (*yasmā ca kho, Ānanda, suññam attena vā attaniyena vā, tasmā suñño loko ti vuccati.* S.IV.54). Interestingly, while the *Cūḷasaccaka-sutta* (M.I.228) announces in a typical way that the five aggregates are impermanent, so suffering, and so non-self, its corresponding T125 *Ekottarāgama* states further: 'Form is impermanent, so suffering, so non-self, and so empty; being empty, it does not belong to me, and I do not belong to it. Feeling, apperception, mental activities, consciousness is ...' 色者無常, 無常即是苦, 苦者即是無我, 無我者即是空, 空者彼非我有, 我非彼有. 想・行・識 ... (2.715c).
20. Harvey (1986) presents a detailed discussion about the signless concentration.
21. *katamā c' āvuso suññatā cetovimutti? idh' āvuso bhikkhu araññagato vā rukkhamūlagato vā suññâgāragato vā iti paṭisañcikkhati: 'suññam idaṃ attena vā attaniyena vā' ti. ayaṃ vuccat' āvuso suññatā cetovimutti. katamā c' āvuso animittā cetovimutti? idh' āvuso bhikkhu sabbanimittānaṃ amanasikārā animittaṃ cetosamādhiṃ upasampajja viharati. ayaṃ vuccat' āvuso animittā cetovimutti* (M.I.297–98).

These two practices are closely related.[22] Their inseparable relationship is well reflected in the description of the practice of emptiness in the *Cūḷasuññata-sutta* (M.III.104–9). There, Ānanda asks the meaning of the Buddha's utterance that he frequently abides in emptiness, and the Buddha explains the meaning of emptiness virtually in the same terms as the signless concentration: there, the Buddha defines emptiness as not paying attention to the notion (*saññā*) of something.[23] Note that when independently used, *saññā* means apperception, an indispensable factor in our process of experience, whereas at the end of a compound it frequently means the notion of something attained by means of ideation (*vitarka*), or a component in the process of ideation.[24] Here the Buddha advises meditators to abandon the notions of things that are not present and inferior, and concentrate on the notion of something that is present and higher. The climax of this progress is the realization that any mental concentration is impermanent, which leads to the cessation of the [corrupted] flows (*āsava*s). Furthermore, we find in early Buddhist texts that ideation is regarded as a source of desire (*kāma, chanda*). For example, in the *Sakkapañha-sutta*, the Buddha announces that desire (*chanda*) originates from ideation, and that ideation originates from diffusion, conceptions and names (*papañca-saññā-saṅkhā*).[25]

22. Hence, after the above-quoted distinction, the *Mahāvedalla-sutta* continues to explain why these two practices can be understood as the same in meaning, being different only in name. Interestingly, on the contrary, the corresponding part of T26 *Madhyamāgama* (1.792a) clearly announces that the three concentrations on emptiness, signlessness and desirelessness are substantially different, both in meaning and in expression.
23. E.g., 'Not having paid attention to the notion of village and people, a monk pays attention to singularity based on the notion of forest': *bhikkhu amanasikaritvā gāmasaññaṃ, amanasikaritvā manussasaññaṃ, araññasaññaṃ paṭicca manasikaroti ekattaṃ* (M.III.104).
24. For example, in the *Alagaddūpama-sutta*, having reproached the evil understanding of Ariṭṭha, the Buddha states, 'Monks, there is no case where a person indulges in sensual desire without sensual objects, without notions of sensual objects and without the ideation of sensual objects': *so vata, bhikkhave, aññatr' eva kāmehi aññatra kāmasaññāya aññatra kāmavitakkehi kāme paṭisevissatī' ti n' etaṃ ṭhānaṃ vijjati* (M.I.133). Here, *saññā* means the notion (of sensual objects) and it is juxtaposed with ideation (*vitakka*) within the process between desire and ideation.
25. *chando kho, devānam inda, vitakkanidāno vitakkasamudayo vitakkajātiko vitakkapabhavo. ... vitakko kho, devānam inda, papañca-saññā-saṅkhānidāno papañca-saññā-saṅkhāsamudayo papañca-saññā-saṅkhājātiko papañca-saññā-saṅkhāpabhavo* (D.II.277). For this topic, see also previous note.

Moreover, we find ideation (*vitarka*) and intention (*saṃkalpa*)[26] playing the same karmic function, being used in the two equivalent triplets: the ideation towards desire, ill-will and violence (*kāmavitakka, vyāpādavitakka, vihiṃsāvitakka*) (e.g., D.II.186, M.I.11, S.II.151, A.I.148, etc.) vs intention towards them (*kāmasaṃkappo, vyāpādasaṃkappo, vihiṃsāsaṃkappo*) (e.g., D.II.312, M.II.27, S.II.151, A.III.428, etc.). In the *Vibhaṅga*, the antonyms of these three [ill] intentions (*saṃkappas*) are given as the definition of right intention (*sammāsaṅkappa*) at the *sutta* level (*suttantabhājaniya*) (Vibh.235), whereas speculation (*takka*), ideation (*vitakka*), intention (*saṅkappa*), fixing (*appanā*), firm fixing (*vyappanā*), applying the mind (*cetaso abhiniropanā*) and right intention (*sammāsaṅkappo*) are given as the register for the definition of right intention at the Abhidhamma level (*abhidhamma-bhājaniya*) (Vibh.237). Among the major *Nikāya*s, the *Mahācattārīsaka-sutta* (M.III.73) provides both definitions at the *sutta* and Abhidhamma level, adding linguistic activity (*vācā-saṃkhāra*) to the Abhidhammic register.[27] Their association with desire (*kāma*), etc., at the *sūtra*-level, indicates the karmic role of ideation (*vitarka*) and intention (*saṃkalpa*); their Abhidhammic association with fixing (*appanā*), etc., indicates their function in the process of thought; and their association with linguistic activity (*vācāsaṃkhāra*) in M.III.73 indicates their function in the linguistic process.

In short, we find the same concept of emptiness in the early Buddhist texts and in the *Prajñā-pāramitā* literature: it is a remedy for wrong notion (*-saṃjñā, nimitta*), ideation (*vitarka*) and intention (*saṃkalpa*), i.e., it eliminates conceptualization. Moreover, emptiness plays the same soteriological role in these two kinds of Buddhism: because they are attached to desired objects as conceptualized by ignorance, living beings suffer endless rebirth, whereas if they become detached from desired objects by means of deconceptualization, they are released from that suffering. However, while the early Buddhists held to a more natural kind of empiricism, in that they believed things to exist as we perceive them, the Buddhists of the *Prajñāpāramitā* texts sharpened the principle of deconceptualization to the extreme that any communication, as well as the personal experience of ordinary people, was considered illusory and defiled.

---

26. Cousins (1992, pp. 138–42) presents an informative analysis of the term *vitarka*.
27. However, the corresponding part of T26 *Madhyamāgama* (1.735c) provides only the *sūtra*-level definition, without the Abhidharmic register.

Nāgārjuna systematized the doctrine of emptiness in the *Prajñāpāramitā* literature and became a forerunner of the Mādhyamikas, whose name comes from the title of his monumental treatise, the *Madhyamaka-kārikā*. In the treatise, he confutes contemporary theories inside and outside Buddhism case by case, and his strategy is *reductio ad absurdum*. He argues that if we suppose the existence of such things as conceptualized by your side, and if we reason according to the rules and facts acknowledged by both sides, we fall into contradiction; therefore, things such as are conceptualized by your side do not exist.

Nāgārjuna sharpens his arguments when he challenges his internal adversaries: particularly the Vaibhāṣika theorists. For example, in the *Pratyaya-parīkṣā* of the *Madhyamaka-kārikā*, he argues that if anything exists as conceptualized by philosophers, it is impossible for a cause to yield its result. In particular, §§1.5–7 and §1.9 attack the Abhidharma (probably Vaibhāṣika) theory that a *dharma* in the form of a substance (*dravya*) lasts for a single moment (*kṣaṇa-bhaṅga*). He uses *reductio ad absurdum*: when such a conceptualization of time and substance is postulated, it is logically impossible for a cause to yield its result. While a cause exists, it cannot yield its result, since the result has not yet come into being, whereas after a cause has ceased, it cannot yield its result, since anything that has ceased cannot yield a result, as acknowledged by Abhidharma (Vaibhāṣika) theorists.

From his proofs by *reductio ad absurdum*, we read that Nāgārjuna is an empiricist no less than the early Buddhists. When he argues that if we admit the existence of such a concept, there cannot be any causation, there is no doubt that he postulates causation as agreed by both sides. Hence we read his arguments in the *Madhyamaka-kārikā* as aiming not at nihilism, but at the promotion of the Buddhist causation theories. In the *Āryasatya-parīkṣā*, Nāgārjuna announces,

> 'We call emptiness the fact that it arises dependent on conditions;
> It is a derivative concept; this understanding is the middle way.'[28]

Here he identifies the seemingly higher truth of emptiness with the easily ignored truth of dependent origination, and designates this identification as the middle way after which the monumental treatise and his school were named. This is to declare himself the real heir of the Buddha.

---

28. *yaḥ pratītyasamutpādaḥ śūnyatāṃ tāṃ pracakṣmahe,*
sā prajñaptir upādāya, pratipat sâiva madhyamā (MMK, §24.18).

Emptiness and Self

In the *Prajñāpāramitā* literature and Madhyamaka theories, we find nothing new added to the concept of self; they merely applied the idea of emptiness to whatever is conceptualized. Furthermore, there is a fundamental difference in attitude towards the concept of self. As we have seen, the early Buddhists rejected the concept of a permanent self, affirming that a self is comprised of impermanent factors. In contrast, the *Prajñāpāramitā* literature and Madhyamaka theories emphasize not being attached to any conceptualization, including such impermanent factors.

In terms of the five aggregates, while the early Buddhists affirm the arising and cessation of the five aggregates, in order to attack any conception of a permanent self, the Buddhists of the *Prajñāpāramitā* literature focus rather on attacking the conceptualization of the arising and cessation of the five aggregates themselves. Thus, in the *Aṣṭasāhasrikā Prajñāpāramitā*, Subhūti reports to the Buddha,

> 'Bhagavat, when a *bodhisattva* reflects on these things (*dharmas*) in the perfection of wisdom, he does not reach or obtain form, feeling, apperception, mental activities or consciousness; he observes neither arising nor cessation of form, feeling, apperception, mental activities or consciousness.'[29]

This affirms that the Buddhists of the *Prajñāpāramitā* literature abandoned the naïve empiricism of the early Buddhists. Not to mention the abstract concept of a permanent self, the naïve experience of the five aggregates is also illusory. For the complete liberation from suffering, it is not enough to realize that, in 'reality', there is nothing signified by such abstract names as *ātman*, etc. (in Madhyamaka terms, *pudgala-nairātmya*); it must also be realized that, in 'reality', such concrete names as *rūpa*, etc., signify nothing (*dharma-nairātmya*).

In short, the Buddhists of the *Prajñāpāramitā* literature and the Mādhyamikas rejected all kinds of self as conceptualized by the Indian philosophers, and strategically attacked the validity of the Abhidharmic terms that were precisely conceptualized. However, they did not present their own conception of self. They could not do so: if they had had their

---

29. *yasmin hi samaye, Bhagavan, bodhisattvo mahāsattva imān dharmān prajñāpāramitāyāṃ vyupaparīkṣate, tasmin samaye na rūpam upaiti, na rūpam upagacchati, na rūpasyôtpādaṃ samanupaśyati, na rūpasya nirodhaṃ samanupaśyati. evaṃ na vedanāṃ, na saṃjñāṃ, na saṃskārān, na vijñānam upaiti, na vijñānam upagacchati, na vijñānasyôtpādaṃ samanupaśyati, na vijñānasya nirodhaṃ samanupaśyati* (AṣṭPr, p. 13).

own ideas of self, they would have been contradicted by their own logical weapon. The swords in the hands of the Mādhyamikas have no hilt.

SELF IN YOGĀCĀRA THEORIES

While the Buddhists of the *Prajñāpāramitā* literature and the Mādhyamikas did not add new principles to Buddhism but applied the principle of deconceptualization universally to all established Buddhist ideas, Yogācāra Buddhists added two pivotal postulates: mind-only theory (*vijñaptimātratā*) and store-consciousness (*ālayavijñāna*). As other Buddhist developments do, the doctrinal system of Yogācāra inherited established Buddhist doctrines as far as was compatible with the new system. The two main Buddhist doctrines that the Yogācārins inherited were the emptiness theory of the Mādhyamikas and the Abhidharmic systematization.

Also, in the Yogācāra texts we find early Buddhist empiricism and reductionism still used in order to refute the existence of an eternalist self. For example, in the *Mahāyānasūtrālaṃkāra*, the prose commentary to §6.2 (MSA, p. 69) states:

> First of all, a mere view of a [permanent] self is not a sign of [the existence of] the self; [the mere view] does not yield [its] configuration [in reality]. For it is thus a void sign, because the token of the self is conceptualized. Furthermore, the view is [indeed based on] the five clinging-aggregates, since it is generated by coarse defilements. Apart from these two (i.e., the void sign and the five clinging-aggregates), there is no sign of [the real existence of] the self. Therefore there is no [permanent] self.[30]

Here we see that, at least when they challenge the eternalist conceptions of self, the Yogācārins make use of early Buddhist empiricism and reductionism: such conceptions are void, since they do not 'really' signify anything that we can observe; indeed, they are illusions imposed on the five aggregates that we experience.

As for reductionism, we find it sharpened more precisely in Yogācāra arguments. For example, in the *Triṃśikā-vijñapti-bhāṣya*, Sthiramati applies this principle to the following extent:

---

30. *na tāvad ātmadṛṣṭir evâtmalakṣaṇā, nâpi saṃsthitatā. tathā hi sā vilakṣaṇā ātmalakṣaṇāt parikalpitatvāt. sā punaḥ pañcôpādānaskandhaḥ kleśa-dauṣṭhulyaprabhāvitatvāt. nâpy ato dvayād anyad ātmalakṣaṇam upapadyate. tasmān nāsty ātmā.*

> 'Even an accumulation of atoms (*paramāṇu*) cannot be its (i.e., consciousness') object, since atoms do not have a shape. Given that [each atom] is not [the object of consciousness] when it is alone, accumulated atoms cannot [have a property] beyond their own [individual] natures. Therefore, like an individual atom, accumulated atoms are not objects [of consciousness].'[31]

Here Sthiramati argues that since an atom does not have the property of visibility, the mass of those atoms cannot have this property either.

The dependence of the Yogācārins on Madhyamaka doctrines is conspicuous when they expound the existential state of a phenomenon in three aspects, called the three natures (*trisvabhāva*):

> Whatever entity (*vastu*) is distinguished by whichever distinction,
>
> The self-nature [of that entity] is merely conceptualized. It does not exist.
>
> However, the distinction has the nature of depending on other things; it arises dependent on conditions.
>
> Its (i.e., dependent-arising's) perfect [nature] is constant separation from the previous one (i.e., the first illusory nature).
>
> Therefore, this [perfect nature] is neither different from nor identical to the nature of depending on others.
>
> [The perfect nature] should be explained as impermanence, etc. When [this perfect nature] is not comprehended, that [nature of depending on others] is not comprehended.[32]

(1) [There are only mental activities;] any entity (*vastu*) as distinguished is illusion since its ontological self-nature (*svabhāva*) is falsely conceptualized (*parikalpita*). (2) Mental activities arise and cease dependent on conditions (*paratantra*). (3) The fact that mental activities do not have such an illusory self-nature, i.e., emptiness, is their perfect nature (*pariniṣpanna-svabhāva*). As we have seen (pages 114–16), the second

---

31. *na ca paramāṇava eva saṃcitās tasyâlambanaṃ paramāṇūnām atadākāratvāt. na hy asaṃcitâvasthātaḥ saṃcitâvasthāyāṃ paramāṇūnāṃ kaścid ātmâtiśayaḥ. tasmād asaṃcitavat saṃcitā api paramāṇavo nâivâlambanaṃ* (TriṃśV, p. 28, comm. to §1).

32. *yena yena vikalpena yad yad vastu vikalpyate,*
parikalpita evâsau svabhāvo, na sa vidyate.
paratantrasvabhāvas tu vikalpaḥ pratyayôdbhavaḥ,
niṣpannas tasya pūrveṇa sadā rahitatā tu yā.
ata eva sa nâivânyo nânanyaḥ paratantrataḥ,
anityatâdivad vācyo, nâdṛṣṭe 'smin sa dṛśyate. (TriṃśV, pp. 116–22, §§20–22)

and third of the three kinds of nature are nothing new to Madhyamaka Buddhism. The first nature may be interpreted as being compatible with Madhyamaka theories; however, the Yogācārins, such as Vasubandhu, go further: what are referred to as having this threefold nature are mental activities only – there are no external objects.

Mind-only and Store-Consciousness (Ālayavijñāna)

As Schmithausen (2005, p.10) points out, statements indicating that there are no external objects are not found at all or, at best, only sporadically in some early Yogācāra works (especially the *Yogācārabhūmi*, but also others like the *Abhidharma-samuccaya*). However, after Vasubandhu's works, such as the *Viṃśatikā-vijñaptimātratā* and the *Triṃśikā-vijñaptimātratā*, the doctrine that there are no external objects became authoritative among the Yogācārins.[33] The Yogācāra that influenced Chinese Buddhism was in line with Vasubandhu's thought. Therefore I discuss Yogācārin theories of self by focusing on Vasubandhu's ideas.

While the *Triṃśikā* focuses on the explanation of the process by which our mind produces perceptions and external-object-like images and on how karmic activities create seeds in the store-consciousness and develop into results, the *Viṃśatikā* focuses on arguing that there are no external objects, and that the mind-only theory is the 'real' teaching of the Buddha. The commentary on the *Viṃśatikā* introduces those arguments:

> In Mahāyāna, it is established that the threefold world system is a mere imaging, since the *sūtra* says, 'O Jinaputras, the so-called threefold world system is merely mind.' The words mind, thought, consciousness and imaging are synonymous. Saying 'mind-only', it is intended to include [other mental factors] that are associated with mind. The word 'only' is intended to exclude external objects (*artha*).[34]

---

33. Schmithausen dedicates a short monograph (2005) to illustrating that it is baseless for some recent scholars to interpret the doctrine of mind-only not ontologically but merely phenomenologically, even with reference to fully fledged *vijñaptimātratā* texts, such as the *Viṃśatikā* and the *Triṃśikā* as well as Xuanzang's *Vijñaptimātratāsiddhi-śāstra* 成唯識論. For the problem of external objects in early Yogācāra texts, refer also to Schmithausen, 1987 (p. 32 and note 221).
34. *mahāyāne traidhātukaṃ vijñaptimātraṃ vyavasthāpyate, 'cittamātraṃ bho jinaputrā, yad uta traidhātukam' iti sūtrāt. cittaṃ mano vijñānaṃ vijñaptiś cêti paryāyāḥ. cittamātra[ṃ] sasaṃprayogam abhipretam; mātram ity arthapratiṣedhârtham* (ViṃśV, p. 1, comm. to §1).

This proclaims that only consciousnesses and other mental factors exist, not external objects independent of our mind.

Before the development of Yogācāra Buddhism, Buddhist doctrines were developed on the postulation of the existence of external objects; the belief prevailed that external objects exist as perceived by our ordinary or meditative experience. From this firm belief, some Buddhists, particularly the Vaibhāṣika-Sarvāstivādins, insisted that past and future things must exist; otherwise, the Buddha and meditators could not observe those things in meditation, since there cannot be any 'real' perception without 'real' objects.[35] However, we find this naïve empiricism, i.e., direct observation (*pratyakṣa*), abandoned by Vasubandhu. In the *Viṃśatikā*, a hypothetical opponent, probably an Abhidharmic scholar, challenges: 'By a valid means of knowledge (*pramāṇa:* i.e., direct observation, reasoning and *sūtras*), the existence or non-existence [of something] is determined. Among these valid means, direct observation is the most important. How [would you explain] the fact that there is the perception of external objects by direct observation?' To this challenge, Vasubandhu answers in verse: 'As is [the case of] direct observation in dreams, etc., when there is direct observation, there is no external object. How could such [direct observation] be regarded [as valid]?'[36] Earlier (page 105), we observed that Abhidharma Buddhists introduced correct reasoning as being as important as direct observation. Here we observe a Yogācārin completely abandoning the authority of the direct observation of ordinary people. This must have given crucial momentum for later Buddhists to develop metaphysics beyond our experience.

Regardless of the existence of past things, it is generally agreed among various Abhidharmic systems that only present things work, i.e., cause results. However, there are two instances to be explained in order to maintain this principle as universal. Firstly, how can the karmas that

---

35. 'When there is an object, there occurs a consciousness; it does not, when there is no object. If there were no past or future things, consciousness should have no perception of them': *sati viṣaye vijñānaṃ pravartate, nâsati. yadi câtītânāgataṃ na syād, asadālambanaṃ vijñānaṃ syāt* (AbhK, pp. 632, comm. to §5.25). For more information on this point, see Bareau (1991 [1957], esp. pp. 3–4).

36. *pramāṇavaśād astitvaṃ nâstitvaṃ vā nirdhāyate. sarveṣāṃ ca pramāṇānāṃ pratyakṣaṃ pramāṇaṃ gariṣṭam ity, arthe katham iyaṃ buddhir bhavati pratyakṣam iti.*

    pratyakṣabuddhiḥ svapnâdau yathā, sā ca yadā tadā
    na so 'rtho dṛśyate, tasya pratyakṣatvaṃ kathaṃ matam. (ViṃśV, pp. 18–19, §16)

have been done in the past work now?[37] Secondly, given that no material can be the cause of mental factors and that there is no mental activity at all during the achievement of cessation–concentration (*nirodha-samāpatti*), how could the last thought before entering the concentration cause the first thought after emergence from the concentration?[38] These problems can be solved by the introduction of store-consciousness (*ālayavijñāna*), which is a contribution of the Yogācārins as innovative as mind-only theory.[39]

According to Yogācāra theories, our karmic activities plant infusions (*vāsanā*) in our store-consciousness in the form of seeds (*bīja*). The seeds continue in succession (*saṃtati*) in the store-consciousness, and, when the circumstances mature, they manifest as karmic results.[40] This explains how past karmas cause future results. What directly cause the results are indeed not the past karmas but the present seeds that have come into being in succession after the implantation.

Here, 'to continue in succession' (*saṃtati*) is a technical term inherited from Abhidharma. According to Sarvāstivāda theories, a self, i.e., a compound of the momentary five aggregates, has a different set of components at every moment, but continues its identity in succession, since the present momentary components are the [karmic and natural] result of the previous ones. In the same way, a store-consciousness has a different set of momentary seeds at every moment, but continues its identity in succession, since the present seeds are the results of the previous ones. However, this is an explanation in the conventional sense. Since the Yogācārins also inherit the Madhyamaka doctrine of

37. This problem is used in order to support the existence of past things, just after the argument that past things are the object of our perception in the *Abhidharmakośa-bhāṣya* (see note 34). However, no explanation is found there of how karmas created in the past work in the present moment.
38. For the discussion of this problem in the *Abhidharmakośa-bhāṣya*, refer to AbhK, pp. 186–96, §2.43–44. Schmithausen (1987, Chap. 2) expounds the relationship between this problem and the introduction of store-consciousness.
39. For the relationship between the *bhavaṅga* theory of Theravāda and *ālayavijñāna*, see Harvey (1995, pp. 155–79). For the relationship between the *bīja* theory of Sautrāntika and *ālayavijñāna*, see Jaini (2001, pp. 219–37).
40. 'The infusions of karma along with the infusions of the two kinds of grasping produce another karmic result when the previous karmic result perishes' (*karmaṇo vāsanā grāhadvayavāsanayā saha kṣīṇe pūrvavipāke 'nyad vipākaṃ janayanti tat*;TriṃśV, p. 107, §19). Here, the 'karmic result' appears to signify the totality of the karmic results that constitute the parameters of a particular life. For the relationship between karma and store-consciousness, refer to Schmithausen (1987, chap. 3, esp. pp. 52–65).

emptiness, in the highest sense there cannot be any substance existing even for a single moment.[41]

Store-consciousness contains not only karmic seeds but also seeds of all phenomena that manifest as the world (*bhājana-loka*), the body (*sattva-loka*), consciousnesses and other mental factors.[42] This explains how the last thought before entering the cessation–concentration (*nirodha-samāpatti*) causes the first thought after emergence from the concentration: although none of the six consciousnesses can be active (*pravṛtti*) in that concentration, the seeds of consciousnesses and other mental activities remain in the store-consciousness and re-manifest from it when one re-emerges. Furthermore, the existence of store-consciousness explains how meditators observe past and future things. They observe the manifestation of the seeds of the past and future things, as ordinary people do in dreams. Thus, according to some Yogācāra masters, store-consciousness is the storehouse of all seeds that can possibly become manifest; if the store-consciousness of a person does not contain the seed of a specific phenomenon, that phenomenon never happens to the person. For this reason, if a person does not have the seed of flow-free knowledge (*anāsrava-jñāna*), the person has no possibility of becoming a Buddha; such a person is called *icchantika*.

Self and Consciousnesses

To sum up, the Yogācārins, at least after Vasubandhu, held the mind-only theory, refuting the existence of any external object. This ontological proposition is justified by the sacrifice of the authority of direct observation by ordinary people. This proposition lets each self swallow the world: nothing but other living beings is external to oneself.[43] In

41. In VimśV, p. 19, comm. to §16, we can read Vasubandhu's awareness of the contradiction pointed out by Nāgārjuna between the Abhidharmic (probably Vaibhāṣika) theory of time (*kṣaṇabhaṅga*) and the possibility of causation. In that context, he asserts that the possibility of perception implies the mentality of so-called external objects. Without postulating Abhidharmic theories on time and substance (*dravya*), his argument would be unsound.
42. In the *Triṃśikā*, Vasubandhu announces that the six consciousnesses manifest from store-consciousness (§§15–16), and that all external-object-like images, i.e., the objects of the six consciousnesses, also manifest from store-consciousness (§18).
43. The existence of other living beings is a primary premise that is not questioned in Yogācāra theories. Each person's store-consciousness stores the seeds of all possible phenomena. In the *Viṃśatikā* (§§18–19), Vasubandhu deals with the

order to explain how karmic and natural causation is possible without external objects, the Yogācārins introduced a new system: there is a special consciousness called store-consciousness that contains karmic seeds as well as the seeds of all phenomena, including past and future ones; this is the 'reality' beyond the experience of ordinary people.

Hence, a self in Yogācāra theories is a compound of momentary consciousnesses and other mental factors that continue in succession (*saṃtati*). The store-consciousness manifests or produces other consciousnesses as well as external-object-like images from the seeds stored in it. As in other Buddhist doctrinal systems, this compound of momentary consciousnesses is located in *saṃsāra*. However, unlike other Buddhist doctrinal systems, the compound of Yogācāra consciousnesses does not stop continuing in succession: they are still active even after the *nirvāṇa* without residue. While the Buddhas in other Buddhist doctrinal systems are depicted as not possessing any bodily and mental bases after *nirvāṇa*, the Yogācāra Buddhas are said to transform consciousness into transcendental knowledge (*lokottarajñāna*). This special *nirvāṇa* is called the *nirvāṇa* without abiding (*apratiṣṭhitanirvāṇa*). The introduction of this *nirvāṇa* caused a critical change in the Buddhist concept of self. I will discuss the implications of this *nirvāṇa* in relationship to its conception of self in the following chapter.

---

problem of how mutual influence among living beings, such as teaching and karmic activities, is possible when there are no external objects. The possibility of mutual influence is postulated as 'class-sharing' (*nikāya-sabhāga*): if we are in the same karmic class, our 'physical' and karmic activities automatically cause changes in others' consciousnesses of the same class; this is a matter of fact.

Chapter 5

NIRVĀṆA AND A PERMANENT SELF

In the *Mahāparinibbāna-sutta* [MP], the Buddha notifies monks of his final *nirvāṇa*, 'Ah, monks, I now bid you farewell. Conditionally constructed things are subject to decay; strive [for liberation], do not be careless! Soon there will be the complete *nirvāṇa* of the Tathāgata. Three months from now, the Tathāgata will attain *parinirvāṇa*.' Then he utters verses:

> I am old; little of my lifespan is remaining.
> I will leave you; I have made a refuge of myself. ...
> One who keeps this teaching and discipline without carelessness
> Will leave countless rebirths and put an end to suffering.[1]

Here the Buddha includes himself in the realm that is subject to decay and encourages the monks to leave *saṃsāra*. However, in the *Mahāyāna Mahāparinirvāṇa-sūtra* [MMP], we read a completely different teaching. In a Sanskrit fragment of MMP, having devalued the teaching of impermanence, the Buddha instead presents a eulogy on permanence:

> In just the same way, lady, do not conceive of me (i.e., the Buddha) as impermanent, [by thinking,] 'The Tathāgata will today enter *parinirvāṇa*.' Do not think in that way, [since it is as wrong] as conceiving of me as dead. The Tathāgata remains in the house of

---

1. *atha kho Bhagavā bhikkhū āmantesi: 'handa dāni, bhikkhave, āmantayāmi vo: vayadhammā saṅkhārā, appamādena sampādetha! na ciraṃ Tathāgatassa parinibbānaṃ bhavissati. ito tiṇṇaṃ māsānaṃ accayena Tathāgato parinibbāyissatī' ti.*
   paripakko vayo mayhaṃ, parittaṃ mama jīvitaṃ,
   pahāya vo gamissāmi, katam me saraṇam attano. ...
   yo imasmiṃ dhammavinaye appamatto vihessati,
   pahāya jātisaṃsāraṃ dukkhass' antaṃ karissatī ti. (D.II.120–21)

> those who always bear in mind: 'The Tathāgata is permanent (*nitya*), constant (*dhruva*) and eternal (*śāśvata*).'[2]

The last sentence, 'The Tathāgata is permanent (*nitya*), constant (*dhruva*) and eternal (*śāśvata*),' is one of the critical slogans of the MMP. Since a Buddha is permanent, for him there cannot occur the *nirvāṇa* without residue taught in the 'Hīnayāna' *sūtras*. Furthermore, not only Buddhas but also all living beings have a permanent nature, which is called *tathāgatagarbha* (the embryo of a Tathāgata), as discussed below.[3]

Can we call these two contradictory teachings by the same name of Buddhism? In this chapter, I trace the motivations and principal ways of thinking that yielded this dramatic change in the Buddhist ideas of self. In Chapters 3 and 4, I restricted my concern to the basic premises and principal ways of thinking that constitute the 'systematic' reading of the four major types of Buddhism; in this chapter, I highlight those factors that appear incompatible with a doctrinal system of established Buddhism and that facilitated a new development.

IMMORTALITY, HAPPINESS AND *NIRVĀṆA*

In early Buddhist texts, we occasionally find immortality praised and pursued by the Buddha and his disciples. For example, in the *Vinaya*, the Buddha introduces his first sermon by declaring: 'Monks, listen carefully! Immortality (*amṛta*) has been achieved [by me]. I will teach [it]. I will show the truth.'[4] What does 'immortality' mean? If what is taught by the Buddha is immortality, why would any eternalist, who believed, 'After death, I shall be permanent, constant, eternal and not subject to change,'

2. *evam eva, bhagini, mayā mā 'nityasaṃjña[ṃ] kārṣīt* [sic]*: 'adya Tathāgataḥ parinirvāsyati' ti, nâivaṃ kalpayitavyaṃ mṛtasaṃjñāvat! ye sadā 'nityo dhruvaḥ śāśvatas Tathāgata' iti dhārayanti, teṣāṃ Tathāgato gṛhe tiṣṭhati* (MMP_K: p. 18). This part corresponds approximately to the Chinese translation T374.12.385c26–86a1.
3. '... [He thoroughly understands the meaning of this *sūtra*: i.e.,] 'The Buddha is permanent, constant, eternal, immovable and happy.' He pronounces that all living beings possess *tathāgatagarbha*.' (*... nityo dhruvaḥ śāśvato hy acalaḥ sukho Bhagavānn iti, tathāgatagarbhaḥ sarvasattvānāṃ saṃprakāśyata iti.*) (MMP_SH, p. 73, has '(*... ani)ty(o) dhruvaḥ śāśvate(!) hy acala(ḥ) sukho Bhagavānn iti tathāgatagarbha : sarvbasatvānām* saṃprakāśyatīti*.' Here I read *nityo* for *anityo*.) This part corresponds to T374.12.399a6–7.
4. *odahatha bhikkhave sotaṃ! amatam adhigataṃ, aham anusāsāmi, ahaṃ dhammaṃ desemi* (Vin.I.9).

have fallen into despair after listening to the teaching of the Buddha or his disciples?

If we trust our understanding of the 'systematic' reading of early Buddhism, as described in Chapter 3, we should regard 'immortality' as no more than a rhetorical synonym for *nirvāṇa*. Recall its soteriological framework: knowing [whatever comprises life to be] suffering, eliminating the origin of suffering, realizing the cessation of suffering and practising the path conducive to that cessation, in which we find no space for 'immortality'. Moreover, in their irreconcilable rivalry with eternalism, the early Buddhists identified the ignorance of no [permanent] self (*anātman*) and the desire for immortality with the origin of suffering, and the thorough elimination of that ignorance and desire with the cessation of suffering.

Along with such definitions of the origin and cessation of suffering, it is said that, for the accomplishment of arhatship, a practitioner must remove the fear of eternal death, 'I shall be annihilated, I shall perish, I shall not exist,' or the desire for eternal life, 'The world (*loka*) is the self (*ātman*). After death, I shall be permanent, constant, eternal and not subject to change. I shall continue to be the same for all eternity.' Indeed, in early Buddhist texts, we frequently find the conquest of fear [of eternal death] regarded as a prerequisite for the attainment of the highest sainthood, as the *Cūḷataṇhāsaṅkhaya-sutta* describes:

> With regard to those feelings, he remains seeing impermanence, dispassion, cessation and abandonment. He is not attached to anything in the world. Not being attached, he is not afraid; not being afraid, he individually attains *parinirvāṇa*.[5]

To be brief, for the attainment of the ultimate soteriological aim, a practitioner should have neither attachment to eternal life nor fear of eternal

---

5. *so tāsu vedanāsu aniccânupassī viharanto virāgânupassī viharanto nirodhânupassī viharanto paṭinissaggânupassī viharanto na kiñci loke upādiyati, anupādiyaṃ na paritassati, aparitassaṃ paccattañ-ñ-eva parinibbāyati* (M.I.251–52).

The **Mahāriṣṭa-sūtra* 大品阿梨吒經 in the T26 *Madhyamāgama*, corresponding to the *Alagaddūpama-sutta*, describes this process: 'In all of these six viewpoints, a monk sees neither a [permanent] self nor what [permanently] belongs to a self. Not seeing them, he is not attached to this world; not being attached to this world, he has no fear. Having no fear, he attains *parinirvāṇa*' (所有, 比丘, 此六見處, 不見是神, 亦不見神所有. 彼如是不見已, 便不受此世; 不受此世已, 便無恐怖; 因不恐怖已, 便得般涅槃. 1.765c). The Pali *Alagaddūpama-sutta* lacks this part.

death. Following such a soteriology, one finds no place for immortality. It should never be pursued; it is a poisonous illusion to be dispelled.

In this context, it is interesting to compare two modern scholars' view on 'immortality'. With regard to the translation of *amata* in the Pali canon, Norman (1996 [1989], p. 165) argues,

> Once we realize that these epithets must refer to the condition of those beings who have gained *nibbāna*, then we can see that the translation 'immortality' for *amata* gives the wrong impression, because it implies that such beings live forever, which, as Kalupahana has made clear, is an untenable view. The correct translation must be 'where there is no death'.[6]

Against this, Bhattacharya (1989) points out that the term *brahma* as the first member of a compound is synonymous with *dhamma* and *nibbāna* in early Buddhist texts (pp. 17–19), and suggests that the early Buddhists used *amata* to refer to a property of *nibbāna* in a similar sense to its use in the *Upaniṣads*.

Regarding the 'systematic' reading of early Buddhism, I would follow Norman. However, in this chapter I am concerned with the trends that facilitated the further development of Buddhism. Note the use of the term immortal (*amṛta*) in the following passage from the *Bṛhadāraṇyaka Upaniṣad*, IV.4.7:

> When all desires that abide in his heart are banished,
> Then a mortal becomes immortal. He attains *brahman* in this world.[7]

The ideas in this verse support my argument that the Buddhist soteriological framework itself is not unique, but pan-Indic. In this Brahmanic text, life with repetitive death is considered as suffering, and desires are identified as the ultimate source of suffering. Then it announces that the cessation of desires yields 'immortality'.[8] The monk who feared 'I shall be annihilated, perish ...' and desired 'After death, I shall be permanent, constant, eternal ...' must have interpreted immortality in this Brahmanic sense. Although it is refused in that very *sutta*, such an interpretation

6. For this interpretation, also see Norman (1996 [1994], pp. 18–24, 27–9).
7. *yadā sarve pramucyante kāmā ye 'sya hṛdi śritāḥ,*
   atha martyo 'mṛto bhavaty, atra brahma samaśnuta iti.
8. Here we should pay attention to an inconspicuous but probably important difference between Upaniṣadic *amṛto* and Buddhist *amataṃ*. In the above *Upaniṣad*, *amṛto* is a masculine adjective, used as a subjective complement: he becomes immortal. However, in the previous Pali sentence *amataṃ* is a neuter in an impersonal sense: the Buddha achieved the impersonal deathless status.

appears to have been popular among early Buddhists. Leaving aside the fact that immortality is an official synonym for *nirvāṇa*, we find the prevailing use of 'immortal' as an epithet for Buddhist achievements. For example, compare the above quotation from the *Bṛhadāraṇyaka Upaniṣad* with the following sentence in the **Nirgrantha-sūtra* 尼乾經 of the T26 *Madhyamāgama*:

> Because of the bondage of sensual desire, the mind generates sorrow and suffering; when the bondage of sensual desire is removed, sorrow and suffering perish. Then he attains the ultimate in this life; he has no defilement or disturbance; he stays forever without change. This is to be known and to be seen by saints.[9]

If we separate this passage from the whole context of the *Āgama*, we fail to find a difference between this passage and the previous Upaniṣadic one.

I am not arguing that the Buddha or the early Buddhists in general aimed at eternal life. On the contrary, I agree that such an aim is contradictory to early Buddhist soteriology and other basic doctrines. However, it is true that here and there in early Buddhist scriptures we read of some Buddhists wishing for immortality, and I argue that such heterodox Buddhist wishes provided the momentum for the transformation of Buddhism.

While early Buddhist 'reality' is characterized by impermanence (*anitya*), suffering (*duḥkha*) and non-self (*anātman*), Upaniṣadic 'reality', i.e., *ātman* or *brahman*, is characterized by [permanent] existence (*sat*), consciousness (*cit*) and joy (*ānanda*). Among the three Upaniṣadic characteristics of 'reality', the second, i.e., being a permanent agent of perception, is never allowed by the 'systematic' reading of early Buddhism, as we can ascertain from the case of the monk Sāti in the *Mahātaṇhāsaṅkhaya-sutta*, where the Buddha reproaches his belief that 'this very consciousness runs through *saṃsāra*, not another'.[10] However, as discussed above, we observe that the terms synonymous with [permanent] existence (*sat*), such as immortal (*amṛta*), are used as the epithets of *nirvāṇa*; furthermore, we also find happiness or pleasure (*sukha*), synonymous with joy (*ānanda*), used as an epithet of *nirvāṇa*:

---

9. 因婬欲纏故，心生憂苦；除婬欲纏已，苦便滅. (因婬欲纏，生憂苦.) 現法中，而得究竟, 無煩無熱, 常住不變, 聖所知・聖所見 (T26.1.445a; the parenthesized sentence appears redundant). The corresponding Pali text, *Devadaha-sutta* (M.II.228), lacks this part.
10. ... *tad ev' idaṃ viññāṇaṃ sandhāvati saṃsarati anaññan ti* (M.I.256).

> Torturing neither himself nor others, he, in this life, has no cravings, [becomes] peaceful, cooled, and enjoys happiness (*sukha-paṭisaṃvedin*); he himself abides in the state of *brahman*. (*brahmabhūta*: see Chap. 3, note 39).[11]

Interestingly, Rhys Davids (1899, vol. 3, p. 223), Walshe (1995 [1987], p. 494) and Ñāṇamoli (1995, p. 445) do not translate *sukha* as happiness or pleasure, but as bliss. Their translations are astute; otherwise, they would contradict the soteriology of the major *Nikāyas* in general: while aiming at the cessation of all suffering, the early Buddhists regarded pleasure or happiness as being obstructive to reaching that cessation. As is well known, in the practice of the four meditations (*dhyāna*), the improvement in meditation is accompanied by abandoning particular feelings; a practitioner finally has to abandon pleasure both mental (*saumanasya*) and physical (*sukha*), retaining the neutral feeling of neither-pain-nor-pleasure (e.g., D.I.75).[12] Furthermore, as mentioned above, the cessation of feeling often represents entering the *nirvāṇa* without residue, the meaning of which becomes clear through the following description of an *arahant*'s awareness of the last moment:

> While he feels it, he knows that he is feeling the last moment of the body and the last one of [his] life. He knows that, after the break-up of the body because life has been consumed, all undesirable feelings will go cold right here, and physical remains [alone] will remain.[13]

This reluctance even for pleasure is more easily understood, considering that pleasure and pain represent karmic results.[14] Therefore, the happiness

---

11. *so anattantapo aparantapo diṭṭhe va dhamme nicchāto nibbuto sītibhūto sukhapaṭisaṃvedī brahmabhūtena attanā viharati* (*Saṅgīti-sutta*, D.III.232–33, *Kandaraka-sutta*, M.I.341, etc.).
12. *puna ca paraṃ, mahārāja, bhikkhu sukhassa ca pahānā dukkhassa ca pahānā pubb' eva somanassa-domanassānaṃ atthagamā adukkhaṃ asukhaṃ upekhā-sati-pārisuddhiṃ catutthajjhānaṃ upasampajja viharati.*
13. *so kāyapariyantikaṃ vedanaṃ vediyamāno 'kāyapariyantikaṃ vedanaṃ vediyāmī' ti pajānāti, jīvitapariyantikaṃ vedanaṃ vediyamāno 'jīvitapariyantikaṃ vedanaṃ vediyāmī' ti pajānāti. 'kāyassa bhedā uddhaṃ jīvitapariyādānā idh' eva sabbavedayitāni anabhinanditāni sītibhavissanti sarīrāni avasissantī' ti pajānāti* (S.II.83).
14. In early Buddhist contexts, pleasure (*sukha*) and suffering (*duḥkha*) are frequently used to denote karmic results: i.e., the comfort and discomfort of living circumstances. In this sense, the Buddha, in the *Devadaha-sutta*, rejects the Nigaṇṭhas' determinist view that all feelings, i.e., pleasure, pain and neither-pain-nor-pleasure, are caused by past actions. (*Bhagavā etad avoca: 'santi bhikkhave eke samaṇa-brāhmaṇā evaṃvādino evaṃdiṭṭhino: "yaṃ kiñcāyaṃ*

used as an epithet for *nirvāṇa* or for the highest saints cannot refer to the mental or physical pleasure of ordinary people.

By contrast to the above *arahant*'s testimony that there shall be no more [impermanent] feelings in connection with a bodily basis, we find a complete or permanent pleasure (*ekantasukha*) commended with reference to the highest soteriological state. So, in the *Mahāsīhanāda-sutta* the Buddha proclaims that he knows:

> 'Later, having destroyed the [corrupted] flows, such a person realizes in this life the mind-liberation and wisdom-liberation free from those flows by means of his own higher knowledge. Having attained [the liberation], he stays [in such a state] feeling complete pleasure.'[15]

Furthermore, we find in the *Bahuvedanīya-sutta* the Buddha defining the attainment of the cessation of apperception and feeling (*saññāvedayitanirodha*) as a higher pleasure than any other meditative achievement:[16] this particular cessation is a state where no feeling is sensed, but is praised as a higher pleasure. What then does pleasure during the absence of feeling mean? Whose pleasure is it?[17]

Recall the previous mention that 'complete pleasure' is the term used in the Brahmanic tradition, which is rejected by the Buddha himself in the *Poṭṭhapāda-sutta* (see Chap. 3, note 51). So the happiness of *nirvāṇa* must be a meaningless eulogy; otherwise, it must be a mysterious

---

purisapuggalo paṭisaṃvedeti: sukhaṃ vā dukkhaṃ vā adukkhamasukhaṃ vā, sabban taṃ pubbekatahetu.....” ti evaṃvādino bhikkhave nigaṇṭhā.' ;M.II.214.) We find the same use of pleasure and suffering in S.II.20 ff., where the naked ascetic Kassapa asks the Buddha whether suffering is created by oneself, by another, both by oneself and by another, or neither by oneself nor by another. Also recall the use of suffering and pleasure in Dhp_P §§1–2, which was discussed in detail above (pp. 75–7).

15. *tam enaṃ passāmi aparena samayena āsavānaṃ khayā anāsavaṃ cetovimuttiṃ paññāvimuttiṃ diṭṭhe va dhamme sayaṃ abhiññā sacchikatvā upasampajja viharantaṃ ekantasukhā vedanā vediyamānaṃ* (M.I.76).
16. *idh' Ānanda bhikkhu sabbaso nevasaññānâsaññâyatanaṃ samatikkamma saññāvedayitanirodhaṃ upasampajja viharati. idaṃ kho Ānanda etamhā sukhā aññaṃ sukhaṃ abhikkantataraň ca paṇītataraň ca* (M.I.400). At this point the Pali *sutta* stops listing ever-higher pleasures; however, the corresponding T99 *Saṃyuktāgama* announces that the pleasure of dispassion, seclusion, *nirvāṇa* and awakening is higher than that of the cessation of apperception and feeling: 若有異學出家作是說言: '沙門釋種子, 唯說想受滅, 名為至樂.' 此所不應. 所以者何? 應當語言: '此非世尊所說受樂數. 世尊說受樂數者, 如說: '優陀夷, 有四種樂. 何等為四? 謂離欲樂・遠離樂・寂滅樂・菩提樂” (2.124b11–16).
17. For a Theravāda answer to this question, refer to Ñāṇamoli *et al.* (1995, p. 1260, n.618).

experience contradicting early Buddhist empiricism. However, such descriptions of eternality and [complete] happiness with reference to *nirvāṇa*, intermittently found in the early Buddhist literature, are too vivid to be ignored merely as a meaningless eulogy. The emotion that we read there is a longing for the 'real' state as described in such eulogies, rather than a dry understanding of the 'naked truth.'

To sum up, neither immortality nor complete happiness is compatible with early Buddhist soteriology when it is armed with naïve empiricism. However, here and there in early Buddhist texts we observe that these two terms are used to refer to the state of *nirvāṇa* or to the highest saints. A 'systematic' reading leads us to consider such references as using established terms as metaphors, in order to attract Indian followers of Brahmanic background. However, we may well regard them as a reflection of the hopes of Buddhists who dreamt of such an ultimate state of being. By chance or by destiny, Buddhists came to demand that Buddhas should possess such properties out of moral necessity, as I argue in the following section. In other words, the state of being that originally they may have dreamt of became the state of being that they considered they ought to achieve.

MORAL DEMANDS AND A PERMANENT SELF

It may sound strange, but early Buddhist soteriology, based on the four noble truths, is compatible with rational egoism: it tells us why and how one removes one's own suffering, but does not tell why one endures suffering for others. It is true that the law of karma prohibits a practitioner from intentionally doing harm to others; otherwise, the practitioner cannot attain the *nirvāṇa* without residue, and so cannot be freed from physical suffering. However, within that soteriological framework, the law of karma says nothing about why a practitioner has to help others or even teach others the truth. Hence, if the soteriology based on the four noble truths were the whole of Buddhist ethics, we would find no grounds for blaming an *arhat* who committed suicide without teaching others the truth.[18]

---

18. We find many anecdotes about *arhats*' suicide just before and after the Buddha's *parinirvāṇa*. For example, Subhadra, the last disciple of the Buddha, enters *parinirvāṇa* as soon as he attains *arhat*-ship, saying that he cannot bear to take a last look at the Buddha entering *parinirvāṇa*: see MPS §§40.47–49,

Nonetheless, no form of traditional Buddhism has developed into egoism, because Buddhist ethics has loving kindness (*maitrī*) and compassion (*karuṇā*) as fundamental premises from its beginning. Without these ethical premises, the Buddha would not have started his mission of teaching, daring to suffer forty-five more years of physical pain;[19] therefore, there would be no Buddhism now. I argue that the emphasis on this ethical premise had a dramatic effect on the whole Buddhist doctrinal system.

There is a question that appears not to be solved if we hold firm to a belief in compassion: how could the Buddha have had the heart to enter the *nirvāṇa* without residue, leaving ordinary beings in the hell of *saṃsāra*? It is apparent that no early Buddhist assumed a Buddha to continue his teaching after he entered the *nirvāṇa* without residue. Then, given that he conquered Māra or Death so that he could prolong his lifespan if he wished,[20] how could the Buddha, the supreme embodiment of boundless compassion and loving kindness, abandon sentient beings in the hell of *saṃsāra*?

Of course, there is a traditional answer, which is explained in MPP: since the Buddha has already left his teaching to lead people to *nirvāṇa*, it is meaningless for the Buddha to maintain his life, particularly when he can endure the pain of ageing and disease only through a special concentration.[21] This answer may have satisfied some Buddhists, but not all. Being dissatisfied with the answer, Mahāyānists, such as the Yogācārins,

---

T5.1.172b, T6.1.187c, T7.1.204b, T99.2.254b, T100.2.413c, T125.2.752c and T1451.24.397a. (MPP lacks this part.) For the stories of *arhats'* suicide after the Buddha's *parinirvāṇa*, see T1451 **Mūlasarvāstivāda-vinaya-kṣudraka-vastu* (24.402c–3c) and T1425 *Mahāsaṃghika-vinaya* (22.490a–91a).

19. For the hesitation of the Buddha to teach ignorant beings the truth, refer to Vin.I.4–7. There, he confesses that the truth he has realized is so profound that it is burdensome to teach it to ignorant beings.

20. In MP, the Buddha endures a fatal disease and prolongs his life in order to take leave of his pupils (e.g., D.II.99). In addition, the Buddha hints to Ānanda three times that he can live for a *kappa* if he wishes. However, being obsessed by Māra, Ānanda fails to notice the Buddha's hint, which results in the *parinirvāṇa* of the Buddha (e.g., D.II.103). (There is disagreement on how long a *kappa* is. Some regard it as being as long as the current maximum longevity of human beings, i.e., around 100 years, but others regard it as a fabulous period of time. An (1998, pp. 1–9) presents a detailed discussion about *kappa* in this specific context.)

21. *yasmiṃ, Ānanda, samaye Tathāgato sabbanimittānaṃ amanasikārā ekaccānaṃ vedanānaṃ nirodhā animittaṃ cetosamādhiṃ upasampajja viharati, phāsukato Ānanda tasmiṃ samaye Tathāgatassa kāyo hoti* (D.II.100).

designed a new concept of *nirvana*: the *nirvāṇa* without abiding. In this *nirvāṇa*, Buddhas abide neither in *saṃsāra*, since they are completely freed from suffering, nor in *nirvāṇa*, since they never stop performing the mission of salvation.

The *Madhyāntavibhāga-śāstra* (MVibh, p. 139, comm. to §4.12) explains how consideration for others yields the new concept of *nirvāṇa* as follows: in the course of practice, the practitioners of the two vehicles (i.e., 'Hīnayānists') [practise mindfulness] with reference to their own successive bodies, etc., whereas Mahāyāna *bodhisattva*s [practise mindfulness] with reference to both their own and others' bodies, etc.; the practitioners of the two vehicles have in mind the impermanent aspect of the body, etc., whereas Mahāyāna *bodhisattva*s pay attention to the fact that there is no body, etc., to be obtained [therefore no body, etc., to be abandoned from the beginning]; the practitioners of the two vehicles aim to be liberated from the body, etc., whereas Mahāyāna *bodhisattva*s aim at the *nirvāṇa* without abiding, at being neither liberated from nor bound by [the body, etc.].[22] Here we read the reason why Mahāyānists brand pre-Mahāyāna Buddhism 'Hīnayāna'. They are proud of their boundless altruism: their Buddhas perform the duty of teaching and saving forever; and their *bodhisattva*s even postpone becoming a Buddha in order to engage in altruistic activities forever.[23]

Performing the mission of salvation forever in the *nirvāṇa* without abiding, a Yogācāra Buddha is described in terms of the threefold body and the four knowledges (*jñāna*). In the *Mahāyānasūtrālaṃkāra* [MSA], the description of Buddhas' four knowledges (MSA, pp. 138–42, §9.67–75) immediately follows the definition of the threefold body of Buddhas (MSA, pp. 134–8, §9.59–66), which I

22. *śrāvaka-pratyekabuddhānāṃ hi svasāntānikāḥ kāyâdaya ālambanam, bodhisattvānāṃ svaparasāntānikāḥ. śrāvaka-pratyekabuddhā anityâdibhir ākāraiḥ kāyâdīn manasikurvanti, bodhisattvās tv anupalambhayogena. śrāvaka-pratyekabuddhāḥ smṛtyupasthānâdīni bhāvayanti yāvad eva kāyâdīnāṃ visaṃyogāya, bodhisattvā na visaṃyogāya nâvisamyogāya yāvad evâpratiṣṭhitanirvāṇāya.*

23. The Buddhas' endless performance of teaching and the *bodhisattvas*' postponing becoming a Buddha appear to be contradictory. It is possible that there were two independent Mahāyāna movements. On the one hand, some Mahāyānists ascribed more value to *bodhisattva*s, who are endlessly engaged in salvation, than to Buddhas, who stop saving others after entering the *nirvāṇa* without residue; on the other hand, some did not allow the Buddha to enter the *nirvāṇa* without residue and demanded that he be active forever in the *nirvāṇa* without abiding.

discuss in detail below. The four knowledges are the transformation of bases (*āśrayaparāvṛtti*), i.e., the purified modes of the eight consciousnesses of ordinary beings: store-consciousness is refined into mirror-knowledge (*ādarśajñāna*), the seventh into equality-knowledge (*samatājñāna*), the sixth into examination-knowledge (*pratyavekṣājñāna*), and the first five into administration-knowledge (*kṛtyānuṣṭhānajñāna*). MSA (pp. 140–3, §§9.71–74) identifies the first two knowledges as *dharma*-body (*dharma-kāya*), the third as enjoyment-body (*saṃbhogika-kāya*), and the fourth as creation-body (*nairmāṇika-kāya*). These two ideas of the threefold body and the four knowledges are connected by the announcement (p. 138, §9.66) that the *svābhāvika*-body (i.e., *dharma*-body) is permanent (*nitya*) by nature (*prakṛti*), the enjoyment-body is in consecutive existence without interruption (*aviccheda*), and the creation-body is repeatedly (*punaḥ punar*) created.[24]

The ethical demand that Buddhas should perform the mission of teaching forever resulted in the abandonment of the concept that the ultimate *nirvāṇa* is unconditioned (*asaṃskṛta*). This abandonment, in turn, resulted in the obliteration of the distinction between what is conditioned (therefore productive) and what is unconditioned (therefore unproductive). As mentioned above, when a Yogācāra Buddha enters the *nirvāṇa* without abiding, a transformation of the bases (*āśrayaparāvṛtti*) of the Buddha occurs: the ordinary consciousnesses turn into the four kinds of extraordinary knowledge. In explaining the ten meanings of 'the transformation of the bases', MSA mentions,

> Since [a Buddha] abides neither in *saṃsāra* nor in *nirvāṇa*, [the transformation of the bases is] the conversion that has no duality of conditioned and unconditioned.[25]

This passage articulates that the *nirvāṇa* without abiding implies the obliteration of the distinction between the conditioned and the unconditioned.

Examining the term 'unconditioned skilfulness' (*asaṃskṛta-kuśala*), we can ascertain the process by which the altruistic concern of Mahāyānists finally yields this dramatic change in the Buddhist concept of self as

24. *prakṛtyā nityatā svābhāvikasya svabhāvena nityatvāt. asraṃsanena sāṃbhogikasya dharmasaṃbhogâvicchedāt. prabandhena nairmāṇikasyântardhāya punaḥ punar nirmāṇadarśanāt* (MSA, p. 138, comm. to §9.66).

25. *saṃsāranirvāṇâpratiṣṭhitatvāt saṃskṛtâsaṃskṛtatvenâdvayâvṛttiḥ* (MSA, p. 111, comm. to §9.14).

well as in the whole system of Buddhist doctrine. In the *Madhyānta-vibhāga-śāstra*, announcing the purpose of Mahāyāna practice, Maitreya and Vasubandhu, the putative authors of the verses and of the prose commentary respectively, state:

> [Commentary:] For what is it practised?
> For the sake of obtaining two kinds of goodness (*śubha*).
> [Commentary:] For the sake of conditioned and unconditioned skilfulness (*kuśala*).
> Always for the benefit of living beings.
> [Commentary:] For the benefit of boundless living beings.
> For the sake of the non-abandonment of *saṃsāra*.
> [Commentary:] If [a being] were not aware of the emptiness of endless, beginningless *saṃsāra*, he would forsake *saṃsāra* exhausted.
> And for the sake of non-exhaustion of skilfulness.
> [Commentary:] Even in the state of the *nirvāṇa* without residue, he does not throw it (i.e., skilfulness) off or give it up. The emptiness of it (i.e., skilfulness) is called the emptiness without abandonment.[26]

In many pre-Mahāyāna Buddhist doctrinal systems, *nirvāṇa* is definitely unconditioned and, in some sense, skilful (*kuśala*).[27] However, any pre-Mahāyāna *nirvāṇa* is not considered as unconditioned skilfulness as described above. In the context of the above quotation, unconditioned skilfulness is the skilfulness of altruistic activity, which is not abandoned even after the ostensible entrance into the *nirvāṇa* without residue. Unlike the pre-Mahāyāna Buddhist *asaṃskṛta*, which implies both 'unconditioned' and 'unproductive', the *asaṃskṛta* in this context is unconditioned in one sense, since Buddhas exist forever without suffering

---

26. *kimarthañ* ***ca*** *prapadyate?* ***śubhadvayasya prāptyartham*** *kuśalasya saṃskṛtasyâsaṃskṛtasya* ***ca. sadā sattvahitāya ca*** *atyantasattvahitârtham* ***saṃsārâtyajanârthañ ca*** *anavarâgrasya hi saṃsārasya śūnyatām apaśyan khinnaḥ saṃsāraṃ parityajeta.* ***kuśalasyâkṣayāya ca*** *nirupadhiśeṣe nirvāṇe 'pi yan nâvakirati nôtsṛjati. tasya śūnyatânavakāraśūnyatê ty ucyate* (MVibh, pp. 43–4, §1.19). The indented lines are verse, and are printed in this note in bold type.
27. Theravāda tradition regards *nirvāṇa* as something neither-skilful-nor-unskilful (*avyākṛta*) (*nirodhasaccaṃ avyākataṃ*; Vibh, p. 112), whereas the *Śāriputrābhidharma-śāstra* regards it as skilful (滅聖諦・道聖諦, 是名二善, T1548.28.577c2–3). The Sarvāstivāda summarized by Vasubandhu in the *Abhidharmakośa-bhāṣya* regards the intended cessation (*pratisaṃkhyā-nirodha*), therefore the attainment of the *nirvāṇa* with residue, as skilful, but the unintended cessation (*apratisaṃkhyā-nirodha*), therefore the attainment of the *nirvāṇa* without residue, as neither-skilful-nor-unskilful (... *pratisaṃkhyānirodhaś ca kuśala[ḥ] ... anyo 'vyākṛtaḥ*; AbhK, p. 66, comm. to §1.29).

from causation, but never unproductive in the other sense, since they continue to save living beings. Therefore, it is said, 'The emptiness of it (i.e., skilfulness) is called the emptiness without abandonment.'

In this context, in the last verse of the *Triṃśikā-vijñapti-kārikā*, Vasubandhu describes the state of self in the highest Buddhist achievement as follows:

> It is the uncorrupted realm, inconceivable, skilful and constant.
> It is happy and has the body of liberation;
> this is called the truth of the great saint.[28]

We may gather many astonishing implications from this concluding sentence. The ultimate state of a Yogācāra self is constant (*dhruva*); it is a compound of extraordinary knowledge (*lokottarajñāna*), as already mentioned; and it is happy (*sukha*). Now, it looks at first as if we find here, in the highest state of Yogācāra soteriology, all three characteristics of the Upaniṣadic *ātman*: existence (*sat*), consciousness (*cit*), and joy (*ānanda*).

To sum up, among Mahayānists there were two conflicting demands on Buddhas: Buddhas should be free from suffering, and they must perform the mission of salvation forever. In early Buddhism, even Buddhas after the highest awakening cannot avoid physical suffering. So they enter the *nirvāṇa* without residue, where there is no conditioned activity, so that there is no suffering at all. By contrast, Mahāyānists deny that Buddhas (even before the *nirvāṇa* without residue) suffer physical pain and hold that they, in 'reality', do not enter any death (or the *nirvāṇa* without residue); in this sense, Buddhas are free from the realm of the conditioned, i.e., the realm of birth and death. At the same time, they deny that Buddhas become inactive; in this sense, Buddhas do not find shelter in the realm of the unconditioned either.

However, this obliteration of the distinction between the conditioned and the unconditioned is not the invention of Mahāyānists. We can trace this trend in the early *Upaniṣads*, as Oldenberg (1991 [1915], p. 113) notes:

> The thinkers of the *Upaniṣads* would certainly not have thought of permitting some sort of movement of becoming, happening and action to enter those highest regions, where there is no duality, and hence no consciousness. They allowed, however, the Absolute to operate in this

---

28. *sa eva nâśravo dhātur acintyaḥ kuśalo dhruvaḥ,*
sukho vimuktikāyo 'sau dharmâkhyo 'yaṃ mahāmuneḥ (TriṃśV, p. 131, §30).

> world, in accordance with its pre-history, as an omnipotent creator and ruler. Thus an involvement of the *sat* in becoming remained.

However, although we clearly see some Mahāyānists moving towards ideas that were rejected by the Buddha of early Buddhism, we should not conclude that they came to have the same ideas of self as the Upaniṣadic ones. A 'systematic' reading of Mahāyāna Buddhism does not allow such an excessive interpretation, since we cannot understand the last verse of the *Triṃśikā* separately from the previous twenty-nine verses; rather, the truth of the last verse is dependent upon the veracity of the preceding twenty-nine verses. To understand thoroughly what was going on, we need to examine the theories of the threefold body (*trikāya*) and the embryo of a Tathāgata (*tathāgatagarbha*).

BUDDHISM OR BRAHMANISM?

The Three Modes of a Buddha's Body

We may interpret the threefold body of Buddhas as a result of Mahāyānists' efforts to include both the realm of the unconditioned and the realm of the conditioned in the domain of Buddhas. MSA (p. 135, §9.60) explains the threefold body as follows:

> The body of self-nature, that of enjoyment and that of creation;
> [These are] different modes of the bodies of Buddhas. The [latter]
> two depend on the first.
>
> [Commentary:] 'Buddhas have a body of three modes. The body of self-nature: [this is] the body of *dharma*, which marks the transformation of the bases. The body of enjoyment: with it, [a Buddha] enjoys *dharma* in the assembly grounds [of *dharma* teaching]. The body of creation: with this creation, [a Buddha] acts for the sake of living beings.'[29]

Here the *dharma*-body stands for what characterizes Buddhas in the realm of the unconditioned: being unchanging, it is the unconditioned substratum on which the transformation of bases is realized. Hence, the

29. *svābhāviko 'tha sāṃbhogyaḥ kāyo nairmāṇiko 'paraḥ,*
kāyabhedā hi buddhānāṃ, prathamas tu dvayâśrayaḥ.
trividhaḥ kāyo buddhānām. svābhāviko dharmakāya āśrayaparāvṛttilakṣaṇaḥ. sāṃbhogiko yena parṣanmaṇḍaleṣu dharmasaṃbhogaṃ karoti. nairmāṇiko yena nirmāṇena sattvârthaṃ karoti (MSA, p.135, §9.60).

other two bodies depend on it. As the *Ratnagotravibhāga* explains,[30] this *dharma*-body is defined in two ways: firstly, it is identified with the pure *dharma-dhātu*, or the pure nature of *dharmas*, which is frequently called *tathatā*, and secondly, it is identified with profound teachings [by Buddhas] because of which the pure *dharma-dhātu* can be realized. The enjoyment-body stands for the Buddhas performing the mission of salvation forever, beyond the distinction between the conditioned and the unconditioned. It is said that, after much practice, a practitioner can see the Buddha of this body, while others standing beside that practitioner cannot. The creation-body stands for the body of a Buddha in the realm of the conditioned, which appears to enter the *nirvāṇa* without residue.

While the creation-body is generated occasionally at will and the enjoyment-body is generated by the highest awakening (*anuttara-samyaksambodhi*), the *dharma*-body is not generated. If it is generated, by definition it cannot belong to the realm of the unconditioned. Rather, it is something found after the highest awakening, as one finds an object in a dark room after turning on the light. This means that all living beings are possessed of this *dharma*-body even before the highest awakening. MSA illustrates this feature as follows:

> As space is reckoned always to be omnipresent, in that way it (i.e., Buddhahood) is reckoned always to be omnipresent.
>
> As space is reckoned always to be omnipresent in the multitude of visible objects, it is omnipresent in the multitude of living beings.[31]

Hence, the *dharma*-body is not attained by Buddhas through practice, and ordinary beings possess the same *dharma-body* from the beginning. It is not to be produced, not subject to change and not to be purified; but it is always of such a kind (*tathatā*). The idea that all living beings are possessed of the nature of a Buddha is called the theory of *tathāgatagarbha* (the embryo of a Tathāgata): 'There is no difference in suchness among all [living beings]; for it is the self-nature of purity and [it is] Tathāgata. Therefore, all living beings are said to possess the *tathāgatagarbha*.'[32]

---

30. *dharmakāyo dvidhā jñeyo dharmadhātuḥ sunirmalaḥ,*
tanniṣyandaś ca gāmbhīrya-vaicitrya-naya-deśanā. (RGV, p. 70, §1.145)

31. *yathâmbaraṃ sarvagataṃ sadā mataṃ tathâiva tat sarvagataṃ sadā matam, yathâmbaraṃ rūpagaṇeṣu sarvagaṃ tathâiva tat sattvagaṇeṣu sarvagam.* (MSA, p. 112, §9.15)

32. *sarveṣāṃ nirviśiṣṭā tathatā, tad dhi śuddhisvabhāvaḥ ca tathāgataḥ. ataḥ sarve sattvās tathāgatagarbhā ity ucyate* (MSA, p. 122, comm. to §9.37).

Tathāgatagarbha

Among the three modes of a Buddha's body, the only permanent self is the *dharma*-body; the other two bodies are generated by practice; their components rise and cease in succession without interruption or are repetitively created according to conditions. The theory of *dharma*-body and *tathāgatagarbha* reveals that Mahāyānists came to have a permanent self; however, the fact that the other two bodies of Buddhas are generated by practice makes Mahāyāna Buddhists maintain anti-Brahmanism. Unlike the enjoyment-body and creation-body of Mahāyāna Buddhism, the properties of the Upaniṣadic *ātman* of being conscious (*cit*) and enjoying delight (*ānanda*) are not generated by practice. They are in full operation from the beginning, a theory derived from cosmogony.

Recall the Upaniṣadic account of genesis introduced above (see Chap. 3, note 34). The first manifestation of *brahman*, which is known as the 'large *ātman*' in the Brahmanic tradition, has self-awareness and claims 'Here I am!' Various accounts of cosmogony are presented in the early *Upaniṣads*. However, in all those accounts, the 'large *ātman*' is described in terms of self-awareness. With regard to this critical feature of the Upaniṣadic *ātman*, the research by Van Buitenen (1964) is worth quoting at length (pp. 109–10):

> Effortlessly the 'large ātman', itself resulting from and, in effect, identical with the creator's self-recognition, becomes involved in such speculations. No doubt there is (BĀUp. 4.4.22) 'this large unborn ātman which consists in cognition among the senses' (*vijñānamayaḥ prāṇeṣu*), but by the strange vacillation of perspectives this 'largeness' may also be a 'tininess': 'it lies within the space within the heart' (*ibid.*). This *vijñānamaya ātman* pinpoints itself there: 'When this person has fallen asleep, this person consisting in cognition, where does it then stay, where has it departed from?' 'Having taken consciousness with the consciousness of the organs (*prāṇas*), it lies in the space within the heart' (*ibid.* 2.1.16-17). This seeming reduction, however, does not decrease its amplitude: the perspective changes again: 'This person consisting in consciousness among the senses, luminous within the heart, does, being total (*samānaḥ*), pervade both worlds.' In this totality, this person or puruṣa or ātman equals brahman which is *vijñānamaya, manomaya, prāṇamaya, cakṣurmaya*, etc. (*ibid.* 4.4.5). Thus, however physically pinpointed (*tasya haitasya hṛdayasyāgraṃ pradyotate/tena pradyotenaiṣa ātmā niṣkrāmati ... savijñāno bhavati sa vijñānam evānv avakrāmati* ['The top of his heart becomes light; and through this light the ātman departs. ... He becomes possessed of knowledge; and he departs after knowledge alone'], BĀUp. 4.4.2), it remains total: *yatra tv asya sarvam ātmaivābhūt ... tat kena kam*

> *vijānīyāt/vijñātāram are vijānīyād iti* ('But where the ātman of him has become everything, ... whom would he know then and how? Indeed, he would know the knower'), declares Yājñavalkya.

The Brahmanic *ātman* of the properties *sat, cit* and *ānanda* is the great *ātman* of Upaniṣadic cosmogonic accounts. This view of the origin of *ātman* ascribes complete possession of the properties of *cit* and *ānanda* to the *ātman* of all beings.

On the contrary, the permanent self of Mahāyāna Buddhism, such as *tathāgatagarbha* in the state of ordinary beings, is a concept theoretically retro-abstracted from its soteriological result: the so-called eternal (in fact, incessant) activity of the Buddha has a permanent substratum, which does not rise or cease, which means that it has been 'possessed' by all beings from the beginning. Throughout Mahāyāna literature, this substratum is identified with the unconditioned entities (or concepts), such as *śūnyatā, nairātmya, tathatā, nirvāṇa*, etc., which are definitely inactive or unproductive. For example, the *Śrīmālādevī-siṃhanāda-sūtra*[33] defines *tathāgatagarbha* as the *dharma*-body that does not absent itself from [ordinary beings in] the realm of defilements.[34] This identification of *tathāgatagarbha* with *dharma*-body is found also in the *Ratnagotra-vibhāga* [RGV] §1.12, §1.24, § 1.84, §1.86, §1.152. It is also identified with *tathatā* (suchness) in MSA §9.37 and RGV §1.24, §1.152; with *satya* (truth) or *paramārthasatya* (truth in the highest sense) in RGV §1.12, §1.86; with *śūnyatā* in the *Śrīmālā-sūtra*[35] and the *Laṅkāvatāra-sūtra* [LAS] p. 33; with *śuddhi* (purity) in MSA §9.37;[36] and with *nirvāṇa* in RGV §1.86 and LAS p. 33. LAS (p. 33) also identifies *tathāgatagarbha* with *abhūtakoṭi* (non-existence), *anutpāda* (non-arising), *animitta* (signlessness) and *apraṇihitā* (desirelessness). It is clear from the above prevailing identifications that the so-called true self of all beings in Mahāyāna Buddhism is never an agent; it is an unconditioned entity or an abstract concept which does nothing.

---

33. The *Śrīmālā-sūtra* appears to be the mother of *tathāgatagarbha* theory; it is quoted throughout the *sūtra*s and treatises advocating the theory. Unfortunately, its Sanskrit version is not extant; here I introduce its ideas based on T353 勝鬘師子吼一乘大方便方廣經, translated in 436 by Guṇabhadra, who also produced the oldest extant translation of the *Laṅkāvatāra-sūtra* (T670).
34. 如是, 如來法身不離煩惱藏, 如來藏 (T353.12.221c10–11).
35. 'O Bhagavan, the knowledge of *tathāgatagarbha* is the knowledge of the emptiness of *tathāgata*.' 世尊, 如來藏智, 是如來空智 (T352.12.221c13).
36. MSA § 9.23 identifies the so-called *ātman* of Buddhas with *śūnyatā, viśuddhi* and *nairātmya*.

Reality and the Middle Way

In Chapter 3, I showed that for the early Buddhists reality meant what we experience, and that whatever we experience is subject to arising and ceasing. The *Śrīmālā-sūtra* shows that the concept of reality dramatically changed in Mahāyāna Buddhism. The *sūtra* announces that three of the four noble truths, i.e., the truth of suffering, origination and path, are impermanent, whereas only one, i.e., the truth of cessation, is permanent.[37] This classification itself may be interpreted to be compatible with early Buddhism. However, it further announces that the three truths are not the highest truth (*paramārtha-satya*); they are impermanent and not to be relied on,[38] and only the truth of cessation is the highest truth, which is permanent and to be relied on.[39] Clearly, the *sūtra* regards something permanent as being real and something impermanent as being illusory.

However, while asserting the reality of something permanent, the advocates of *tathāgatagarbha* did not fail to differentiate their theory from Brahmanism. To make this point clear, the *Śrīmālā-sūtra* announces that permanence, happiness, *ātman* and purity are properties of the *dharma*-body, [not of the other two bodies];[40] clearly, they were aware that the permanence of Mahāyāna 'reality' should not be the permanence of an agent [of perception or creation].

Here we ascertain the important role of anti-Brahmanism in the development of Buddhism. The concept of reality dramatically changed between early Buddhism and Mahāyāna Buddhism. However, the strong rivalry with Brahmanism always checked Buddhist movements from resembling Brahmanism. Instead of adopting the Upaniṣadic permanent agent of perception, the Mahāyānists identified the 'real' self with such unconditioned entities as *tathatā, śūnyatā, nairātmya, nirvāṇa, viśuddhi, dharmakāya, dharmadhātu,* (*paramārtha-*)*satya,* etc.; and the Mahāyānists also avoided attributing the property of creation to the 'real' entities, unlike the Upaniṣadic *brahman.*

However, we should constantly bear in mind that both the highest truth of permanent reality and the conventional truth of impermanent phenomena are meaningful only when located in the whole system of

37. 世尊, 此四聖諦, 三是無常, 一是常 (T353.12.221c25).
38. 是故苦諦・集諦・道諦, 非第一義諦, 非常, 非依 (221c27–28).
39. 是諦・是常・是依. 是故, 滅諦是第一義 (222a2–3).
40. 如來法身, 是常波羅蜜・樂波羅蜜・我波羅蜜・淨波羅蜜. 於佛法身, 作是見者, 是名正見 (222a23–25). RGV §§1.35–38 provides more detailed discussion to show that the four controversial properties belong to the *dharma*-body.

Buddhist soteriology, which follows the rule of dependent origination (*pratītyasamutpāda*): both the origination and cessation of suffering are subject to dependent origination. This soteriology of the middle way does not allow beings to be negligent just because they all possess original Buddhahood. Otherwise, Vasubandhu would have written only the last verse of the *Triṃśikā*, skipping the first twenty-nine verses. The reality of *tathāgatagarbha* is frequently expressed as a substantialized entity in its literature. However, the whole context of Mahāyāna soteriology tells us that it is a retro-abstraction from the highest soteriological achievement. There is no permanent, pure agent of perception which performs soteriological practice; a person, which is to say, a succession of impermanent components, goes along the soteriological path, and finally realizes that the unconditioned aspect of everything, i.e., *tathatā, śūnyatā, nairātmya, nirvāṇa, viśuddhi, dharmakāya, dharmadhātu* and (*paramārtha-*) *satya*, has always been there. The 'reality' or *tathāgatagarbha* is the expedient substantialization of this aspect.[41]

The Eulogies of the Activity of Tathāgatagarbha

However, just as we can find praise of immortality and complete happiness intermittently in the early Buddhist literature, we also find praise of the activity of *tathāgatagarbha* here and there in the literature. Indeed, this praise of the activity of *tathāgatagarbha* or *tathatā* is demanded by the doctrinal system of Mahāyāna. Such unconditioned ideas as *tathatā, śūnyatā, tathāgatagarbha*, etc., do not signify an entity that is independent from impermanent phenomena; they are indeed an aspect of every impermanent phenomenon. This is exactly implied by the three-nature (*tri-svabhāva*) theory of the Yogācāra (see Chap. 4, note 32). The Mahāyāna middle way allows neither the eternalism of an independent *tathāgatagarbha*, nor the nihilism of mere illusion or entire non-existence.

This middle way is not the creation of Mahāyānists. Recall the early Buddhist statement, 'One who sees dependent origination sees *dhamma*; one who sees *dhamma* sees dependent origination,' where *dhamma* may mean both truth as taught by the Buddha and phenomena as they are, which are identified with dependent origination itself. The Mahāyāna

41. For a detailed argument that the 'systematic' readings in the second sense (even after the eighth century), generally speaking, did not allow *tathāgatagarbha* to be an agent like the Upaniṣadic *ātman*, see Ruegg (1989), esp. pp. 19–44.

middle way has developed from this identification of truth, phenomena and dependent origination. Hence, having defined the middle way as the identification between emptiness and dependent origination (MMK, §24.18, see Chap. 4, note 28), Nāgārjuna continues:

> Because there is no *dharma* which is not dependently originated,
> For this reason, no *dharma* which is not empty is found.[42]

Clearly, Nāgārjuna adopts the truth of emptiness (*śūnyatā*) in order to explain the dependent origination of every phenomenon. To emphasize this close relationship between emptiness and dependent origination, he identifies the two under the honorific title of the middle way. This identification is also found intermittently in the later Mahāyāna literature. For example, in MSA (p. 104, §9.4), we find the identification between Buddhahood (*buddhatva*) and *dharmas:* 'Buddhahood is all *dharmas*' (*sarvadharmāś ca buddhatvam*). The plural form of *dharma* itself indicates that it means a thing; the whole context of the verse and its commentary indicates that it is truth or teaching. However, no matter whether it is a thing or truth, their identification is the emphasis on the middle way in Nāgārjuna's sense. 'Systematically' reading the eulogies of the activities of the *tathāgatagarbha*, we have to keep in mind that the eulogies are adopted not to advocate the action of a permanent agent, but to advocate the permanent truth of the middle way found in every impermanent phenomenon.

This middle way teaching, which emphasizes the inseparability between emptiness (or suchness) and dependent origination, yields another rhetorical expression: since there is suchness, etc., its virtues (*guṇa*) must exist. For example, 'With regard to that, because of their inseparable nature, the pure virtues of Buddhas do not differ at any time, even in the state of ignorant beings, which is entirely contaminated. Therefore, this state is beyond comprehension.'[43] Closely related to this rhetorical expression, there appeared another famous image of 'the mind shining by nature' (*prakṛtiprabhāsvara-citta*), which is frequently identified with *tathāgatagarbha*, as the *Ratnagotravibhāga* describes:

> Since the nature [of the *dharma*-body] is changeless, fine and pure, *tathatā* is compared to a golden disk.

---

42. *apratītyasamutpanno dharmaḥ kaścin na vidyate*
yasmāt tasmād aśūnyo hi dharmaḥ kaścin na vidyate. (MMK, §24.19)

43. *tatra vimalā buddhaguṇāḥ paurvâparyeṇâikāntasaṃkliṣṭāyām api pṛthagjanabhūmāv avinirbhāgadharmatayā nirviśiṣṭā vidyanta ity acintyam etat sthānam* (RGV, p. 22, comm. to §1.25).

> [Commentary:] The mind, due to its natural luminosity, though accompanied by endless defilements and sufferings, shows no instance of modification, so like fine gold it is called *tathatā*, meaning absence of change.[44]

This image is facilitated, firstly, by the idea that the prime virtue of Buddhas is their wisdom; secondly, by the idea that Buddhas' four knowledges are transformed from the eight consciousnesses of ordinary beings; and, thirdly, by the fact that throughout Buddhist history there was no distinction between the grasped truth and the wisdom that grasped it.[45]

However, when reading such rhetorical expressions, we should not substantialize the concept *tathāgatagarbha*, etc., and endow it with the properties of wisdom, happiness, etc. In doing so, we make Mahāyāna Buddhism a form of Brahmanism, which is rejected by the whole context of the Mahāyāna doctrinal and soteriological system. The above quotation should be understood to mean: the mind of ordinary beings also has the aspect of suchness, emptiness, non-self (*nairātmya*), etc., which is the permanent ground for the achievement of Buddhas' glorious virtues. Being fully aware of this problem, MSA (§13.19) articulates its identity as follows:

> Mind is thought to be shining always by nature,
> being defiled by incidental faults.
> Apart from the mind in the form of *dharmatā*,
> there is no shining by nature with reference to any other mind.

> [Commentary:] ... Apart from the mind in the form of *dharmatā*, there is no shining by nature with reference to any other mind, which has the characteristic of depending on other [conditions]. Therefore, here only the suchness of mind must be meant by 'mind.'[46]

---

44. *prakṛter avikāritvāt kalyāṇatvād viśuddhitaḥ,*
hemamaṇḍalakâupamyaṃ tathatāyām udāhṛtam.
yac cittam aparyantakleśaduḥkhadharmânugatam api prakṛtiprabhāsvaratayā vikārânudāhṛter ataḥ kalyāṇasuvarṇavad ananyathābhāvârthenatathatêty ucyate (RGV, p. 71, §1.148).

45. E.g., 'O Bhagavan, the highest correct awakening is a synonym for *nirvāṇa-dhātu*': *anuttarā samyaksaṃbodhir iti Bhagavan nirvāṇadhātor etad adhivacanam* (RGV, p. 3, comm. to § 1.1).

46. *mataṃ ca cittaṃ prakṛtiprabhāsvaraṃ sadā tadāgantukadoṣadūṣitaṃ,*
na dharmatācittam ṛte 'nyacetasaḥ prabhāsvaratvaṃ prakṛtau vidhīyate.
... na ca dharmatācittād ṛte 'nyasya cetasaḥ paratantralakṣaṇasya prakṛtiprabhāsvaratvaṃ vidhīyate. tasmāc cittatathatâivâtra cittaṃ veditavyaṃ.

This verse and its commentary make it clear that the mind shining by nature signifies only the *dharmatā* or *tathatā* of mind; in Yogācāra terms, it signifies only the perfect nature (*pariniṣpanna-svabhāva*), not the nature depending on other [conditions] (*paratantra-svabhāva*) (let alone the [falsely] conceptualized nature (*parikalpita-svabhāva*)).

An Eccentric Text

The *Laṅkāvatāra-sūtra* provides a good example of a sporadic text that cannot be read 'systematically'. The *sūtra* presents two contradictory ideas in itself. In Chapter 2, 'Collection of All *Dharma*s in 36000 Lines', its teaching of *tathāgatagarbha* is in accord with the above 'systematic' reading. For example, it articulates (LAS, p. 33):

> O Mahāmati, my teaching of *tathāgatagarbha* differs from the *ātman* doctrine of other religious teachers. On the contrary, Mahāmati, having taught *tathāgatagarbha* in terms of *śūnyatā* (emptiness), *abhūtakoṭi* (non-existence), *nirvāṇa*, *anutpāda* (non-arising), *animitta* (signlessness), and *apraṇihitā* (desirelessness), etc., Tathāgatas who are *arhat*s and who are completely awakened teach the realm that cannot be thought or expressed, through the instruction of *tathāgatagarbha*, in order to remove the ground for being frightened by the absence of *ātman*. However, Mahāmati, here the concept of *ātman* must not be adhered to by any *bodhisattva* in the future or the present.[47]

In fact, *tathāgatagarbha* has been explained by Buddhas in terms of *śūnyatā*, *nairātmya*, etc. However, having listened to the teachings of *nairātmya*, etc., which indeed conduce to *nirvāṇa*, ignorant beings think, 'I shall be annihilated, I shall perish, I shall not exist.' From this, 'they grieve, get distressed, lament, beat their breasts and fall into confusion.' To remove such a foolish fear, Buddhas give an expedient teaching of *tathāgatagarbha*. However, *bodhisattva*s with wisdom must not adhere to an eternalist concept of *ātman*.[48]

---

47. *Bhagavān āha: 'na hi, Mahāmate, tīrthakarâtmavādatulyo mama tathāgatagarbhôpadeśaḥ. kiṃ tu, Mahāmate, tathāgatāḥ śūnyatâbhūtakoṭi-nirvāṇânutpādânimittâpraṇihitâdyānāṃ, Mahāmate, padârthānāṃ tathāgatagarbhôpadeśaṃ kṛtvā, tathāgatā arhantaḥ samyaksaṃbuddhā bālānāṃ nairātmyasaṃtrāsapadavivarjanârthaṃ nirvikalpanirābhāsagocaraṃ tathāgatagarbhamukhôpadeśena deśayanti. na câtra, Mahāmate, anāgata-pratyutpannaiḥ bodhisattvair mahāsattvair ātmâbhiniveśaḥ kartavyaḥ.'*

48. LAS presents various arguments refuting the contemporary teachings of Brahmanism. Nakamura (1955,pp. 87–8, 93–102) introduces the various teachings reflected in LAS.

However, in Chapter VI, 'Momentariness', the natural readings of some of the sentences attribute the property of producing everything to *tathāgatagarbha*, and name it store-consciousness (*ālayavijñāna*):

> Bhagavat addressed him: 'O Mahāmati, *tathāgatagarbha* is the cause of good and bad things. It becomes the creator of all destinations (*gati*) of living beings, like a dancer on a narrow stage, without a [permanent] self or what [permanently] belongs to a self. … Therefore, in that case, Mahāmati, *tathāgatagarbha*, which is called store-consciousness, must be purified by *bodhisattva*s who pursue extraordinary [truth].'[49]

Doubtless, this natural reading of the passage made the *tathāgatagarbha* an agent, i.e., the creator of everything; being known as store-consciousness, it manifests or creates everything. If this natural reading of this sentence is the truth intended by the Buddha, the Mahāyāna system of soteriology entirely collapses: if whatever we experience is a manifestation or production by the true, pure self (*tathāgatagarbha* = *ālayavijñāna*), why should anyone strive or practise? In order to locate the *Laṅkāvatāra-sūtra* within the canonical body of Mahāyāna Buddhism, we have to forge an artificial interpretation of the passage. As emptiness is the ground for dependent origination, *tathāgatagarbha* is the ground for store-consciousness' manifestation of everything; in this sense, like a rhetorical identification between emptiness and impermanent phenomena, there may occur a rhetorical identification between *tathāgatagarbha* and store-consciousness.

To sum up, I have argued that, while the properties *sat, cit* and *ānanda* of the Brahmanic *ātman* are inherited from Upaniṣadic cosmogonies, the permanent self of Mahāyāna Buddhism, such as *tathāgatagarbha*, is theoretically retro-abstracted from its soteriological result; therefore, the latter does not have the properties of *cit* and *ānanda* in the Brahmanic sense. In Part III, I will demonstrate how a popular and influential 'systematic' reading of Buddhist self developed in China; I shall focus on the fact that in that 'systematic' reading the full properties of *sat, cit* and *ānanda* in the Brahmanic sense are attributed to the 'true' self.

---

49. *Bhagavāṃs tasyâitad avocat: 'tathāgatagarbho, Mahāmate, kuśalâkuśalahetukaḥ sarvajanmagatikartā pravartate naṭavad gatisaṃkaṭa ātmâtmīyavarjitaḥ. … tasmāt tarhi, Mahāmate, tathāgatagarbha ālayavijñānasaṃśabdito viśodhayitavyo viśeṣârthibhir bodhisattvair mahāsattvaiḥ* (LAS, p. 90).

Part III

THE DEVELOPMENT OF THE CHINESE BUDDHIST CONCEPT OF SELF

PREAMBLE

In Part II, I examined the doctrinal factors, fundamental ways of thinking and ethical concerns that formed the conceptions of self in early Buddhism, Abhidharma, Prajñāpāramitā-Madhyamaka and Yogācāra Buddhism. Then I theoretically reconstructed the process whereby the Buddhists came to attribute the property of permanence to a self, although it was strongly rejected by the Buddha of early Buddhism. In this last part, I examine how the complex Indian Buddhist conceptions of self were translated, interpreted and re-created by the Chinese.

Based on distinctive ontological, epistemological and soteriological postulates, the Indian Buddhists developed a series of conceptions of self. Struggling with the advocates of other religions, they maintained the slogan of 'non-self' (*anātman*) to identify themselves and differentiate themselves from others. By contrast, before the arrival of Buddhism the Chinese had no idea of a permanent self at all. This meant that, considering that the doctrine of non-self is the antithesis of the idea of a permanent self, there was from the beginning no reason to teach the doctrine of non-self to Chinese people. It is unreasonable to refute what has never been thought. Ironically, what the Chinese learnt from Buddhism was the concept of a permanent self.

For the specific subject matter of Part III, I cannot but emphasize how the Buddhist ideas of self developed differently from their original meanings in India. This emphasis may create the impression that Chinese Buddhism is by nature an indigenous Chinese philosophy, disguising itself as an Indian product. However, such an impression is incorrect. The fundamental premises of Chinese Buddhism differ greatly from those that prevailed in China before Buddhism was introduced. Furthermore, as we have seen, there were some indications in Indian Mahāyāna Buddhism from which the Chinese Buddhists could develop their particular ideas of self, although they were not systematized to form a mainstream view in India. In this part, I aim to reveal the grounds on which such distinct ideas of self could finally be systematized by the Chinese Buddhists.

Chapter 6

CHINESE IDEAS ABOUT SELF BEFORE THE ARRIVAL OF BUDDHISM

Some works of ancient Chinese literature, particularly the *Guoyu* 國語 and the commentaries on the *Chunqiu* 春秋, are treasure houses of the various Chinese ideas of self before the arrival of Buddhism in China. However, it is impractical to introduce all these ideas in a single chapter. Instead, I here restrict my concern to the philosophical ideas formed after the time of Confucius 孔子 (551–479 BCE). Moreover, since even the philosophical ideas that developed after Confucius are too varied and complicated to discuss, I here introduce only the mainstream thought that struggled with Buddhism for influence. In general, these mainstream ideas agree with the authorities frequently quoted in Neo-Confucian writings.

While the strongest adversaries of the Indian Buddhists were eternalists, the adversaries of the Chinese Buddhists were entirely 'nihilists.' Before the arrival of Buddhism, the Chinese believed neither in *saṃsāra* nor in a permanent self. The mainstream philosophers who influenced the later debates opposed to Buddhism were, in a sense, materialists: the mind is made of *qi* (氣: pristine material or vital energy). Indian Buddhist reductionism cannot be traced in Chinese thought before Buddhism, and analytic reasoning was frequently regarded as a fundamental obstruction to the realization of truth. The new matrix on which the ideas of Buddhism were to be cultivated was entirely different from its original one.

As for the Chinese concept of self before the arrival of Buddhism, one of its most conspicuous characteristics is that a self was considered in relationship with *dao* (道: way), the principle or power that creates and administers the universe in an ethico-cosmogonic sense. The Chinese identified the ethical principle with the principle of the creation; different ethical systems were justified by different conceptions of *dao*. In that identification between what ought to be done 所當然 and what it is 所以然, the Chinese focused on how one should act, rather than on what a person is.

THE SOCIAL SELF

Before the arrival of Buddhism, there were four major intellectual movements: Confucianism, Mohism,[1] Legalism[2] and Daoism. Among these, the first three movements aimed at realizing an ideal or wealthy society, and only the last was also concerned with individual liberation, although even this was within the matrix of politics. With regard to the concept of self, philosophical Daoism was the main adversary of Chinese Buddhists; therefore, my discussion of the Chinese Buddhist ideas of self will focus on their relationship with the Daoist ones. However, Confucianism, as the victor among the three politically oriented movements, became the governmental and social ideology from the Han dynasty (漢: 206 BCE–220 CE) onwards and it continuously wielded ideological power over China until the nineteenth century, although the degree of power fluctuated from time to time. Since the Confucian ideology regulated the whole social system, the Buddhists in China had to struggle against the overwhelming political power, as well as the ethico-philosophical attacks, of the Confucians.

---

1. Limits of space do not allow me to introduce Mohist doctrines and their ideas of self in detail. Their slogan 'universal love' reminds us of the Buddhist ideal of *maitrī-karuṇā*; however, aside from the question of their inner motivation, their apparent arguments for universal love are very different from Buddhist ones. They advocated universal love in order to realize the greatest benefit to society as a whole, i.e., to maximize the wealth and population of a country. According to their strict utilitarian principles, one should accept suffering if it helps to increase the wealth and population of society. For them, the cultivation of individual minds is to produce benefits for society. Indeed, they also developed an ethical cosmology which supposes the existence of *shangdi* (上帝: God) and *gui* (鬼: ghosts). However, such supernatural powers also exist for the benefit of this world. Individual liberation concerning the other world was not the Mohists' concern. For more details, see Feng (1952, vol. 1, pp. 76–105, 246–78) and Graham (1989, pp. 33–53, 137–70).
2. I cannot detect any significant influence of Chinese Legalism on the development of Chinese Buddhism. Hence, I shall seldom refer to Legalism. For details of the Legalist political philosophy, see Feng (1952, vol. 1, pp. 312–36) and Graham (1989, pp. 267–92).

The Proprieties

Confucianism has a long history even before Confucius. The critical term characterizing the tradition before Confucius was *li* (禮: ceremony, propriety), i.e., the code of social conduct. As conservatives, the Confucians 儒家 did not aim at reforming the social system into a better one; what they aimed at was the preservation of the ceremonial observances as established under the Zhou dynasty (周: 1122?–256 BCE). People were expected to act according to their social status, assigned by birth, which determined their detailed code of conduct. An ideal society, they held, can be achieved when the pre-established social codes are fully followed. For the pre-Confucius Confucians, the individual self was of no concern: whoever has a specific status should act according to the social code for that status, regardless of personality. In short, they pursued the mechanical operation of social codes, rather than the accomplishment of individuality.

As Confucius' work *Lunyu* (論語: *Analects*) became orthodox in Confucianism, the representative term for Confucianism changed from propriety 禮 to *ren* (仁: benevolence), which was frequently used as a synonym for *maitrī-karuṇā* (loving kindness and compassion) in the Chinese Buddhist literature. This was an important turning point, as a result of which the moral achievement of an individual became as important as the preservation of the old social codes.

As for the definition of *ren*, when Zhonggong 仲弓 asked, 'What is *ren*?', Confucius answered, 'Do not do anything to others that you do not want to be done to you!'[3] In a dialogue with Zigong 子貢, he also stated that '*Ren* means making others rise in the world as you yourself would wish, and letting others obtain the fame that you want yourself!'[4] This definition of *ren* by Confucius is strengthened by the adoption of the term *shu* 恕, the definition of which is also, 'Do not do anything to others that you do not want to be done to you,'[5] as in the above definition of *ren*. *Shu* has been regarded as the essential term penetrating the whole teaching of Confucius; [6] thus Mencius (孟子: 372–289 BCE) announces, 'For the accomplishment of *ren*, there cannot be any shorter path than the ardent practice of *shu* 恕!'[7]

---

3. 己所不欲, 勿施於人 (《論語 · 顏淵》, LY: §12.2).
4. 夫仁者, 己欲立而立人, 己欲達而達人 (《論語 · 雍也》, LY: §6.3).
5. 其恕乎! 己所不欲, 勿施於人 (《論語 · 衛靈公》, LY: §15.24).
6. 子曰: '參乎! 吾道一以貫之.' ... 曾子曰: '夫子之道, 忠恕而已矣' (《論語 · 里仁》, LY: §4.15).
7. 强恕而行, 求仁莫近焉 (《孟子 · 盡心上》, MZ: §13.4).

Let us compare the above explanation of *ren* and *shu* with the following explanation of *jianai* (兼愛: universal love) by Mozi (墨子: 470?–391? BCE):

> Regard others' states just as your own state, others' families as your own family, and others' bodies as your own body! Hence, there will be no battlefield when lords love each other, no usurpation when the chiefs of families love each other, and no hostility when all people love each other. There will be the grace [of lords] and the loyalty [of subjects], when lords and subjects love each other; the love [of the father] and the filial piety [of the sons], when fathers and sons love each other; and harmony and discipline, when brothers love each other. If all people in the world love each other, the strong will not hold sway over the weak, the majority will not threaten the minority, the rich will not humiliate the poor, the noble will not be arrogant towards the humble, and the cunning will not defraud the ignorant. It is through the rise of mutual love that disasters, usurpation, grudges and resentment in the world can be stopped. For this reason a virtuous person [lit. a man of *ren*] praises it [i.e., universal love].[8]

Here Mozi suggests that regarding others as much as oneself is the principle behind realizing the ideal of universal love. If the gist of Confucianism and Mohism is *ren* 仁 and *jianai* 兼愛, as explained above, I cannot find any fundamental difference between the two ethico-philosophical traditions. However, the two have a cat-and-dog history, blaming each other for deceiving people and distorting the *dao*.

A further inspection leads us to the conclusion that the ideas characterizing orthodox Confucianism have always been propriety 禮 and filial piety 孝, rather than *ren* 仁. Hence, in the *Lunyu*, we find *ren* also defined as 'overcoming [individual] self and recovering propriety' 克己復禮:

> When Yan Yuan asked about *ren*, Confucius answered, 'Overcoming [individual] self and recovering propriety is *ren*. If you overcome yourself and recover propriety even for one day, all people in the world will praise your *ren*. The practice of *ren* is for one's own [cultivation]. It is not for [pretending in the presence of] others, is it?' Yan Yuan asked, 'May I ask for details?' Confucius answered, 'If it is not [in accordance with] the proprieties, do not see, listen, speak or act!'[9]

8. 子墨子言: '視人之國, 若視其國; 視人之家, 若視其家; 視人之身, 若視其身! 是故, 諸侯相愛, 則不野戰; 家主相愛, 則不相簒; 人與人相愛, 則不相賊; 君臣相愛, 則惠忠; 父子相愛, 則慈孝; 兄弟相愛, 則和調. 天下之人皆相愛, 強不執弱, 眾不劫寡, 富不侮貧, 貴不敖賤, 詐不欺愚. 凡天下禍簒怨恨, 可使毋起者, 以相愛生也. 是以仁者譽之' (《墨子 · 兼愛中》, MX, p. 95).
9. 顏淵問仁, 子曰: '克己復禮為仁. 一日克己復禮, 天下歸仁焉. 為仁由己, 而由人乎哉?' 顏淵曰: '請問其目.' 子曰: '非禮勿視, 非禮勿聽, 非禮勿言, 非禮勿動!' (《論語 · 顏淵》, LY: §12.1).

Here we observe that Confucius incorporates the social code into individual virtues and identifies it with *ren*. However, as the above quotation makes clear, any realization of internal moral values must be precisely controlled to be compatible with the proprieties; and, in the whole context of the *Lunyu*, the proprieties that Confucius pursued were evidently the pre-established social codes of the Zhou dynasty.[10] This is the main reason why the Confucians and Mohists were in a cat-and-dog relationship: the Confucians thought that an ideal society would be realized only when the pre-established social codes were precisely followed, whereas the Mohists thought that the pre-established social codes were mere tools for ruling people in order to preserve vested interests and exploit the weak.

The idea that the practice of any moral value should be subject to the established social codes is also naturally reflected in Confucius' politics. Being asked by Zi Lu 子路, 'What would you do first of all, if the king of Wei 衛 invited you to administer [his state]?,' Confucius answered, 'Definitely, I would undertake the rectification of titles 正名.'[11] Here the 'rectification of titles' has two meanings: firstly, one should hold oneself responsible for one's title, and, secondly, one should not intend to usurp a title that is not allowed by birth. In short, we find Confucius' concept of self to be not yet fully individualized: although the development of individual virtues is emphasized, the practice of these virtues should be subject to pre-established, birth-determined social relationships.

Filial Piety

There is another particularistic value that overrules other values and characterizes Confucianism. When Lord She 葉 said, 'Among my people, there is a very honest man. He gave evidence that his father had stolen sheep,' Confucius answered, 'The honesty among my people differs from yours. [Our] honesty comes about when the father conceals the fault of his sons and the sons conceal the fault of their father.'[12] For two and a half

10. For example, Confucius said, 'The Zhou dynasty took as a warning [the downfall] of the Xia 夏 and Yin 殷 dynasties. [Therefore] its culture was splendid. I follow Zhou!' 子曰: '周監於二代, 郁郁乎文哉. 吾從周' (《論語 · 八佾》, LY: §3.14).
11. 子路曰: '衛君待子而為政, 子將奚先?' 子曰: '必也正名乎!' (《論語 · 子路》, LY: §13.3).
12. 葉公語孔子曰: '吾黨有直躬者, 其父攘羊, 而子證之.' 孔子曰: '吾黨之直者異於是. 父爲子隱, 子爲父隱, 直在其中矣' (《論語 · 子路》, LY: §13.18).

millennia, the Chinese regarded honesty, in Confucius' sense, as a real manifestation of the warmest heart, which is called *xiao* (孝: filial piety). In such a context, Confucius declares this filial piety to be the root of *ren* and recommends gentlemen 君子 to engage in fostering it.[13]

Apart from *li*, discussed above, most of the important Confucian values, such as *ren*, *yi* (義: righteousness or justice), *zhi* (直: honesty), *xin* (信: trust), etc., are universal ones: they are applied to all people regardless of their social status. However, none of them can violate the sanctity of filial piety: as we observed above, to give evidence of others' stealing counts as honesty, but to give evidence of one's own father's stealing counts as immoral. Traditionally, the Confucians branded anyone violating the duty of filial piety as an animal. So Mencius makes a criticism, 'Mr Yang (i.e., Yangzi 楊子) advocated egoism. That is [the behaviour of] those who have no lord. Mr Mo (i.e., Mozi 墨子) advocated universal love. That is [the behaviour of] those who have no father. Those who have no lord or father are animals.'[14]

This particularistic characteristic of *xiao* became axiomatized as the term *qinqinzhishai* (親親之殺: the lesser application of love to others for one's own parents). In the *Zhongyong* 中庸, we can find its stereotype:

> *Ren* (仁: benevolence) is *ren* (人: humanity). For it, to love one's parents is the most important thing. *Yi* 義 is righteousness. For it, to respect the wise is the most important thing. *Li* (禮: propriety) is formed from the lesser application of love [to others than one's own parents] and from the gradation in respecting wise people. If, being a junior, a man cannot satisfy his seniors, he cannot rule his subjects. Therefore, a gentleman must train himself; to train himself, he must serve his parents; to serve his parents, he must know about people; to know about people, he must know about Heaven.[15]

According to these definitions, the Confucian virtues *ren* and *yi* lose their universality, being defined in terms of filial piety with particularistic commands. Therefore, the proprieties are the particularistic

13. 'Gentlemen must be engaged in the root. Once the root is established, *dao* arises [from it]. It is filial piety and obedience to elder brothers which is the root of practising *ren*!' 君子務本, 本立而道生. 孝弟也者, 其爲仁之本與 (《論語 · 學而》, LY: §1.2).
14. 楊氏爲我, 是無君也; 墨氏兼愛, 是無父也. 無父 · 無君, 是禽獸也 (《孟子 · 滕文公下》, MZ: §6.9).
15. 仁者, 人也, 親親為大. 義者, 宜也, 尊賢為大. 親親之殺 · 尊賢之等, 禮所生也. 在下位, 不獲乎上, 民不可得而治矣. 故君子, 不可以不脩身; 思脩身, 不可以不事親; 思事親, 不可以不知人 思知人, 不可以不知天 (《禮記 · 中庸》; ZhoY, p. 887).

manifestations of other universal values, which should be stratified by particularistic motivation, i.e., filial piety.

This shows a basic conception of the Confucian self: a self of universal values is located in the network of particularistic social codes, and this location is justified by the naturalism of the family system. When they cultivated their minds, what was expected to be developed was not the personality but the observance of rules to establish relationships with others, i.e., becoming a proper father/son, a proper king/subject, a proper husband/wife, etc. Since the socially ideal relationship of the Confucians was strictly this-worldly, there was no room for a soteriology pursuing individual freedom in the next world.

Human Nature

As the Chinese word *xing* 性 is the combination of the heart 忄 and birth 生, etymologically it means the nature embedded in one's heart from birth. In Chinese philosophy one's nature is generally regarded as something unchangeable; what we can do through our efforts is to purify our minds and realize the nature that is given to us from birth. So when Confucius sighed, 'Although the natures 性 of people are similar to each other, their practices 習 are far different from each other,'[16] he was distinguishing unchanging nature from the varying development of practice.

Note that Confucius declared that the natures of people are similar 相近, but not identical 一. Before the arrival of Buddhism, except for certain Confucian philosophers who inherited Mencius' view of human nature, the vast majority of Chinese held that each person possesses a different *xing*, although it is quite similar among human beings. In particular, the philosophical Daoists strongly advocated that the variety of natures found in living beings must be respected:

> One who sets [people] right always follows the reality of natural life 性命之情. Therefore, he does not call a man who has four or six fingers deformed. He regards neither a tall person [as having] something redundant nor a short person as lacking [something necessary]. For this reason, although the legs of a duck are short, it is harmful to lengthen them; although the legs of a crane are long, it is disastrous to shorten them. Hence, something long by nature 性 should not be shortened, and something short by nature should not be lengthened.[17]

16. 性相近也, 習相遠也 (《論語 · 陽貨》, LY: §17.2).
17. 彼正正者, 不失其性命之情. 故合者不為駢, 而枝者不為跂; 長者不為有餘, 短不為不足. 是故鳧脛雖短, 續之則憂; 鶴脛雖長, 斷之則悲. 故性長非所斷, 性短非所續 (《莊子 · 駢拇》; ZZJS, p. 317).

From the viewpoint of the Daoists, both the construction of an ideal society and the cultivation of an individual mind must be in accordance with the variety of human nature; nature must not be artificially defined as socially desirable virtues, as the Confucians attempted at that time.

The definition of *xing* by Mencius is remarkable in two respects. Firstly, he rejected the definition of *xing* as all characteristics inherent from birth, but defined it as those that characterize a person as a human being. According to the discussions in the *Mengzi*, the opponent, Gaozi 告子, defines *xing* as [anything] inherent from birth (生之謂性, MZ: §11.3) and insists that the desire for food and sex are the nature [of human beings] (食色性也, §11.4); in contrast, Mencius insists that human nature is benevolence 仁, righteousness 義, propriety 禮 and wisdom 智 (§11.6), which are the fundamental virtues of Confucianism, giving the reason that they are the nature common to and peculiar to human beings (§3.6). In this way of thinking, the second remarkable aspect of his definition of human nature is that all people have the same nature: the human nature of Confucian saints does not differ from that of ordinary people (§11.7).

Confucius was an ethicist rather than a philosopher; we seldom find philosophical arguments to support his ethical propositions. Mencius engaged in a few philosophical discussions in the *Mengzi*. However, the overall teachings of the *Mengzi* reveal that he too remained an ethicist rather than a philosopher. His discussion about human nature is not philosophically systematized; and he himself did not apply the theory to an ontological or epistemological system. Following the heated debates between the Buddhists and Daoists, the Confucians of the Song dynasty (宋: 960–1279) developed an ethical metaphysics, called Neo-Confucianism, and the above definition of human nature by Mencius played a pivotal role in the whole doctrinal system of Neo-Confucianism.

THE INDIVIDUAL SELF

The Popular Belief in Spirits

The ancient Chinese believed that a human being possesses two kinds of spirit. One is *hun* (魂, soul) and the other *po* (魄, psyche). Xiao (2003, p. 51) summarizes the ancient concepts relating to them:

> *Hun* is the mentality controlling thought and understanding; *po* is the mentality controlling our body, speech and movement. Although both of them are mentality, a person in whose mentality the former is predominant and who is therefore not attached to the physical body goes to Heaven after death and becomes a *shen* (神: spirit, deity), whereas a person in whose mentality the latter is predominant and who is therefore attached to the physical body is stuck to the earth and becomes a *gui* (鬼: ghost).

Like other peoples, the Chinese worshipped spirits and ghosts. They thought that although *hun*s and *po*s normally disintegrate after death, certain strong ones are transformed into ghosts or spirits and remain after death; but it was not thought that such spirits exist eternally.[18] They also assumed that some naturally formed ghosts and spirits are not the transformations of *hun* or *po*. Ghosts and spirits were regarded as invisible, but they were believed to exist and wield power over nature and people. However, in philosophical thought, as Graham (1989, p. 15) points out, 'except for the Mohists, no one in ancient China much cared whether consciousness survives death or whether Heaven is a personal God or impersonal principle.' Among the two disregarded topics, the question whether consciousness continues to exist after death has received less attention.

As mentioned above, the preservation of ceremonial observances was the profession of the Confucians, and the service of ancestors was one of the most important ceremonies. However, Confucius himself remains silent on the question of the existence of ghosts and spirits, as did the Buddha on the question of the existence of a Buddha after the *nirvāṇa* without residue:

> Jilu asked about serving the ghosts and deities. The Master answered, 'Not being able to serve people, how could [we] serve the ghosts?' [Jilu] asked, 'May I ask about death?' [The Master] answered, 'Not knowing about life, how could [we] know death?'[19]

This was an influential tendency among philosophers towards the realm of death, prevailing before the arrival of Buddhism. Prior to the arrival of Buddhism, we find no Chinese philosopher presenting a theory of rebirth, much less arguing for the existence of a permanent self.

---

18. For this topic, refer to Li (1995, pp. 198–200).
19. 季路問事鬼神. 子曰: '未能事人, 焉能事鬼?' 曰: '敢問死.' 曰: '未知生, 焉知死?' (論語・先進》, LY: §11.12).

The Concept of Self and Shen 神 *in Philosophical Daoism*

As discussed in Part II, Buddhist soteriology is dependent on Buddhist ontology, which is, in turn, based on its epistemology: the soteriological framework is inseparable from phenomena as they are and as they are experienced. Hence the concept of *nirvāṇa* depends on the concept of self located in *saṃsāra*, which, in turn, depends on the epistemological view of what is real. In cases where a Buddhist regards everything as subject to change, such permanent existence as the *dharma*-body would be regarded as a mere name, signifying nothing in 'reality'. In cases where a Buddhist regards reality as not subject to change, i.e., if he or she regards emptiness (*śūnyatā*) as real, the *dharma*-body would be considered as the real self; therefore, there would be neither birth and death nor *saṃsāra* and *nirvāṇa*, in 'the highest sense'.

The Chinese had no concept of rebirth, or of anything permanent, except for the mystic concept of *dao*. To them, on the one hand, the early Buddhist concept of non-self (無我: *anātman*) was introduced in contrast to the eternalist self (我: *ātman*), and, on the other hand, the Mahāyāna teachings of *dharma*-body, *tathāgatagarbha*, etc., were introduced in contrast to the early Buddhist teachings of suffering, emptiness, impermanence and non-self. Being inclined to Mahāyāna, early Chinese Buddhists understood the complexity of the Buddhist self, utilizing their background knowledge of Daoist ideas, particularly *shen* (神: spirit), which designates the essence of the mind. Being used in Chinese Buddhist texts, the term *shen*, on the one hand, retained its Daoist sense, i.e., the essence of the mind, and, on the other, newly attained the 'Buddhist' idea of a permanent agent going through *saṃsāra*. Before examining the Chinese Buddhist sense of *shen*, I examine the original implications of the term *shen* in Daoist philosophy.

Dao 道

While the Buddhist self is located in *saṃsāra* under the law of karma, a self in philosophical Daoism is located in the universe created and operated by *dao* 道. In Daoist philosophy, *dao* contains the following implications. Firstly, it is not a mere method or principle that phenomena follow: it also designates the power or source that created the universe: '*Dao* produces the one, the one produces the two, the two produce the three and the three produce all things.'[20] Secondly, since it is the source

20. 道生一, 一生二, 二生三, 三生萬物 (《老子》, LZJS: §42).

of the creation, *dao* is naturally assumed to precede the existence of the universe: '*Dao* ... exists forever from the beginning, [even] when heaven and earth did not exist.'[21] Thirdly, *dao* does not disappear after its creation, but pervades all the phenomena that it created, and functions as the fundamental principle according to which all phenomena work. Among these three, the first two cosmogonic implications appear not to have prevailed in the Daoist literature during the pre-Qin period (before 221 BCE). Only particular texts, such as the *Laozi* 老子, explicitly use the cosmogonic implications. After the Confucian Dong Zhongshu (董仲舒: 179–104 BCE) presented a Confucian cosmogony based on Daoist ideas, we can trace the cosmogonic implications of *dao* widely in Chinese thought; after Wangbi (王弼: 226–49) produced a commentary on the *Laozi*, we find the cosmogonic implications explicitly postulated in mainstream Chinese thought.

The *dao* embedded in everything has been designated by various names, such as *li* 理, *de* 德, *xing* 性 and *ming* 命, in different texts. For example,

> 'In the beginning, there was nothing; the nothing had no name. When the one had arisen, the one existed but had no form. When myriad things attain it (i.e., the one) and come into being, it is called *de* (德: virtue). [The *de*] has no form, but it is distinguished; however, since it does not differ [from *dao*], it is called *ming* (命: order).'[22]

We have seen Mencius defining human nature in terms of the basic Confucian virtues: benevolence 仁, righteousness 義, propriety 禮 and wisdom 智 (MZ: §11.6). Instead of such artificial social values, the philosophical Daoists assumed that the complete *dao*, i.e., the principle of nature, is embedded in all beings. Later, integrating Mencius' definition of *xing* (性: nature) and the Daoist concept of *dao*, the Neo-Confucians identified their cosmogonic entity *dao* (or *taiji* 太極) with their traditional values, such as benevolence, etc., and called it *xing* when the *dao* is imbedded in creatures.

Recall the fact that the philosophical Daoists advocated the view that the variety of natures of living beings should be respected as they are, rather than being controlled by artificial social values. Regarding this view, a complicated philosophical question troubled the Daoists, which troubled the Neo-Confucians also: could the variety of nature

21. 夫道 ... 未有天地, 自古以固存 (莊子・大宗師》, ZZJS, pp. 246–7).
22. 泰初有无, 无有无名. 一之所起, 有一而未形. 物得以生, 謂之德. 未形者有分, 且然无閒, 謂之命 (莊子・天地》, ZZJS, p. 424).

be compatible with a single *dao*? In response to this problem, the Daoists stratified phenomena into two ontological/epistemological levels; although the Daoist philosophers did not clearly theorize it, the dichotomy is similar to the Indian one between the conventional truth (*saṃvṛti-satya*) and the highest truth (*paramārtha-satya*). In the conventional sense, as I quoted above, 'although the legs of a duck are short, it is harmful to lengthen them; although the legs of a crane are long, it is disastrous to shorten them'; whereas in the highest sense any differentiation is meaningless:

> 'There is nothing in the world bigger than the tip of a hair [of an animal] in the autumn; Taishan[23] may well be regarded as small [compared to it]. No one lives longer than a person who died as a baby; Pengzu[24] may well be regarded as having suffered a premature death [compared to the baby]. The universe came into being simultaneously with me, and the myriad of things are one with me.'[25]

In daily life and politics, the variety of the nature of creatures is emphasized; however, in the discussion of truth and soteriology, the oneness of *dao* is emphasized.

Being the ontological, epistemological and soteriological gist of Daoism, *dao* is also the principle according to which a ruler should rule his subjects. Hence, an ideal Daoist ruler follows only one practice of ruling: he lets everyone be as he or she is, just as the universe lets everything be as it is. This political *dao* is sloganized as *wuwei* (無為: lit. to do nothing):

> 'Although the universe is vast, its creation is impartial; although there are a myriad things, there is [only] one way to rule them; although there are many people, they can be ruled [only] by a ruler who bases himself on *de*,[26] and accomplishes [his work] in accordance with Heaven. Therefore it is said, '[The way by which a ruler] in far-off times ruled the whole world was *wuwei*, which is nothing but the *de* of Heaven.'[27]

---

23. Taishan 泰山 was considered by the ancient Chinese to be the highest mountain.
24. Pengzu 彭祖 is a legendary figure who was believed to have lived for eight hundred years.
25. 夫天下莫大於秋豪之末, 而大山為小; 莫壽於殤子, 而彭祖為夭. 天地與我並生, 而萬物與我為一 (莊子 · 齊物論》, ZZJS, p. 79).
26. Here, *de* is the *dao* which is embedded in its creatures. See the quotation on p. 161.
27. 天地雖大, 其化均也; 萬物雖多, 其治一也; 人卒雖眾#, 其主君也. 君原於德, 而成於天. 故曰: '玄古之君天下, 无為也, 天德而已矣' (《莊子 · 天地, ZZJS, p. 403).

The similarity between the Daoist concept of *dao* and the Brahmanic concept of *brahman* is noteworthy. In Part II, I quoted a series of epithets of Brahmā, the personified form of *brahman*, from the *Dīgha-nikāya*: 'the Conqueror, the Unconquered, the Only Seer, the Power-wielder, the Lord, the Maker, the Creator, the Best, the Appointer, the Controller, and the Father of all beings that have been born and that will be born.'[28] Among these epithets, those relevant to creation may well be attributed to *dao*, whereas such epithets as 'the Conqueror' do not match *dao*, since *dao* remained impersonal in philosophical Daoism.[29] The epithet 'Seer' for the agent of perception may well be attributed to *shen*, which is the purest embodiment of *dao*. Some features of this cosmogonic implication of *dao* survive in its Buddhist usages and they play a pivotal role in forming the ideas of self.

Qi 氣 *and the Formation of the Mind and Body*

According to philosophical Daoism, everything in the universe is made of *qi* (氣: pristine material or vital energy). *Dao* produces *qi*, and forms everything from it. In daily life, *qi* means gas, air, breath, etc.; in the philosophical context, as Zhang *et al.* (1987, pp. 4–5) summarize, it designates: (1) the original matter of everything, (2) material elements, (3) dynamic phenomena, (4) ether, (5) vitality and (6) moral capacity. Among these, usage (1) designates the arcane substratum of everything; usage (2) refers to concrete but unperceivable material elements; usage (3) refers to concrete and perceivable phenomena; and usage (4) implies that there is no empty space: the whole universe is completely filled with *qi*. With reference to the first four usages, I translate *qi* as pristine material. As for usage (5), *qi* implies the energy of movement and vitality in nature. Due to this implication, *qi* is frequently translated as (vital) energy. *Qi* also has the meaning of (6), since it is the product of *dao* and embedded with *dao*.

The Daoists, as well as other Chinese philosophers, thought that both body (*xing* 形 or *ti* 體) and mind (*xin* 心 or *jing* 精) are made of *qi* 氣.[30]

28. *aham asmi Brahmā Mahābrahmā abhibhū anabhibhūto aññadatthudaso vasavattī issaro kattā nimmātā seṭṭho sañjitā vasī pitā bhūta-bhavyānaṃ* (*Brahmajāla-sutta*, D.I.18).

29. Religious Daoism personalizes *dao*. The personalized *dao* has frequently been called *shen* 神. For the relationship between Buddhism and religious Daoism, see Tang (1973, pp. 104–14).

30. 'Human beings are produced by means of passive *qi* and active *qi*. Through the dominance of passive *qi*, bones and flesh are produced; by the dominance of

Since they regarded the mind also as a product of *qi*, ancient Chinese philosophers may well be regarded as materialists. For them, the body is an accumulation of the coarse form of *qi*, whereas the mind is an accumulation of its essential or pure (*jing* 精) form, so the word *jing* (精: essence, purity) is frequently used to indicate the mind (*xin* 心).[31]

Emphasizing that a human being, as a creature of *dao*, is born with complete *dao*, the Chinese tended to liken a human being to the universe:[32]

> The mind is what is received from Heaven, and the body is what is given by the earth. ... Therefore, the roundness of a head is modelled on Heaven; the rectangle of the feet is modelled on the earth. [Just as] the heavenly body has four seasons, five elements,[33] nine divisions[34] and 366 days, a human being also has four limbs, five organs, nine openings [of the body] and 366 articulations. [Just as] the heavenly body has wind, rain, cold and heat, a human being also has taking, giving, pleasure and anger. Therefore the gall bladder corresponds to clouds, the lungs to air, the liver to wind, the kidneys to rain, and the

---

active *qi*, the mind is produced.' 夫人所以生者，陰陽氣也．陰氣主為骨肉，陽氣主為精神 (《論衡・證鬼》 (王充: 27–97? CE), LHJS, p. 946).

31. '*Jing* 精 is the essence of *qi* 氣. When *qi* is guided, *jing* (i.e., the mind) is generated. Once it is generated, there is thought; once there is thought, there is knowledge. But once there is knowledge, you must stop.' 精也者，氣之精者也．氣 (道)[導] 乃生，生乃思，思乃知，知乃止矣 (《管子・內業》, NY, p. 61).

32. Compare this Chinese account with the following theory of the formation of human beings based on an Upaniṣadic account of creation, as introduced by Frauwallner (1973 [1953], vol. 1, p. 69):

    > According to this doctrine, the fountainhead – the spring of all – being is a primeval entity, the existing Being (*Sat*). This being creates the heat or glowing fire (*tejaḥ*), out of the fire springs the water (*āpaḥ*) and out of water springs the food (*annam*). ... The operation of these primal elements shapes itself in a special way in the formation of the human body. For instance, when they enter the body, they become divided in those parts. Of the food, the grossest constituent part becomes excrement, the middle part flesh, and the finest becomes the thinking organ (*manaḥ*). Of the water, the grossest constituent part becomes urine, the middle part blood, the finest part Breath (*prāṇaḥ*). Of the fire, the grossest constituent part becomes the bones, the middle part the marrow, and the finest part becomes speech (*vāk*).

33. The five elements 五行 are the five states of forces according to the combination of passive and active *qi*, which are represented as wood, fire, earth, metal and water.

34. It is not clear exactly what nine divisions 九解 means. It may be the eight directions plus the centre.

> spleen to lightning. In this way, [a human being] is in mutual influence with the Heaven and earth. However, among these, the heart is lord.[35]

In this sense, the Chinese considered a human being to be a microscopic universe 小宇宙. This close relationship between human beings and the macroscopic universe may be the origin from which the Confucians identified the cosmologic concept of *dao* with the Confucian values of *ren*, etc. For example, the eclectic Confucian Dong Zhongshu announces:

> The bodily form of human beings is shaped in accordance with the celestial rule; the temperament of human beings becomes benevolent in the transformation of the celestial will; the virtuous practices of human beings become righteous in transformation of the celestial principle. … The correspondences of Heaven are found among human beings. The nature of human beings is from Heaven.[36]

Accepting Daoist ontology and cosmology, this eclectic Confucian had already identified Heaven as the social value of Confucianism, and designated it as human nature, although he did not present a complicated theory of *xing* 性 and *li* 理, as the Neo-Confucians did later.

While the similarity between the Daoist concept of *dao* and the Brahmanic concept of *brahman* is conspicuous, we cannot find any similarity between the philosophical Daoist ideas of self and the Brahmanic concept of *ātman*. On the contrary, Daoist ideas are closer to Buddhist ones. As the early Buddhists did not accept any self that is independent of the five aggregates, Daoist philosophers did not assume a self that is independent of *qi*. For them, a person or a self is the totality of the body and mind, which is a temporary construction of the ever-changing *qi*. Hence, there is no more self when the *qi* disintegrates after death:

> 'The life of human beings is [the result of] the accumulation of *qi*. The accumulation [of *qi*] results in life and the scattering [of it] results in death.'[37]

So there is neither a chain of innumerable rebirths nor a permanent self in Daoist philosophy. Furthermore, *qi* itself has never been regarded as

35. 夫精神者, 所受於天也; 而形體者, 所稟於地也. … 故頭之圓也, 象天; 足之方也, 象地. 天有四時・五行・九解・三百六十六日, 人亦有四支・五藏・九竅・三百六十六節. 天有風・雨・寒・暑, 人亦有取・與・喜・怒. 故膽為雲, 肺為氣, 肝為風, 腎為雨, 脾為雷, 以與天地相參也, 而心為之主 (《淮南子・精神》, HNZ, pp. 99–100).
36. 人之形體, 化天數而成; 人之血氣, 化天志而仁; 人之德行, 化天理而義. … 天之副, 在乎人; 人之情性, 有由天者矣 (《春秋繁露・為人者天》, CFYJ, pp. 318–19).
37. 人之生, 氣之聚也. 聚則為生, 散則為死 (《莊子・知北游》, ZZJS, p. 733).

a permanent substance, like the *dravya* of the Vaiśeṣika.[38] The Chinese neither analysed matter to the extreme at which it could not be analysed any further, nor assumed a permanent agent or substance that includes action. The Chinese were satisfied with the unclear concept of *qi* as pristine material and vital energy which condenses or scatters by a natural process.

Shen, *the Essence or Lord of the Mind*

Sizhen Li (2001, p. 30) deduces the original meaning of the word *shen* 神 as 'lightning' from its inscriptions on ancient bronze objects. This sheds light on the most frequent use of *shen* as an adjective referring to supernaturalness, implying overwhelming power with the nuance of difficulty in grasping it: for example, a hypothetical sage, Wang Ni 王倪, in the *Zhuangzi*, announces, 'A supreme person is supernatural 神. [The fire that] burns a big lake cannot make him feel hot; [the coldness that] freezes the rivers Huang and Han cannot make him feel cold.'[39] When *shen* is used as a noun, it usually refers to: (1) a deity or spirit and (2) the essence of mind or the mind in general. In the former case, it is a personification of the supernaturalness; in the latter case, it is an abstraction of the abstruse operation of the mind.

Sporadically, we find *shen* used as a noun referring particularly to the power of creation possessed by *dao* itself or by a person who has realized *dao*:

> There is one thing that can generate [everything]; it is called *shen*. There is one factor that can transform [in every situation]; it is called the capacity to know. Generating with no change in *qi* and transforming with no change in the capacity to know – only a gentleman who grasps the one can do these things. Grasping the one, he can rule all things. A gentleman orders others about, and is not ordered about by others. This is the principle of obtaining the one.[40]

---

38. For the concept of *dravya*, see Dasgupta (1922, vol. 1, pp. 310–19).
39. 至人神矣! 大澤焚而不能熱, 河漢沍而不能寒 (《莊子・齊物論》, ZZJS, p. 96).
40. 一物能化謂之神, 一事能變謂之智. 化不易氣, 變不易智, 惟執一之君子能為此乎! 執一不失, 能君萬物. 君子使物, 不為物使, 得一之理 (《管子・內業》, NY, p. 63). While Roth (NY, p. 62) considered 'one thing' and 'one factor' as grammatical objects, I here regard them as subjects. According to Roth's translation, the first two occurrences of 'one' in 一物 and 一事 refer to a different thing from the later occurrences of 'one' in 執一 and 得一. I regard those occurrences of 'one' as signifying the same object.

When *shen* is used in this particular sense, it refers to a concrete agent in the process of creation: for example, in the 'Production of Water by the Great One' 太一生水 of the *Guodian chumu zhujian* 郭店楚墓竹簡, the bright [manifestation of] *shenming* 神明 acts as the agent of creation: 'The four seasons are the product of *yin* (i.e., the passive *qi*) and *yang* (i.e., the active *qi*); *yin* and *yang* are the product of the bright [manifestation of] *shen;* the bright [manifestation of *shen*] and the whole world are the product of the Great One (i.e., *dao*).'[41] Roughly corresponding to the Upaniṣadic concept of the 'great *ātman*', this *shen* is personified by later religious Daoists as the agent of creation, and named *shangdi* (上帝: God).

As mentioned above, *shen* may refer to the mind in general or to the quintessence of the mind. *Shen* in any sense is composed entirely of *qi*; therefore, when *qi* scatters, even the quintessence of the mind perishes. To illustrate this dependence of the mind on *qi*, the Chinese Daoists employed a simile of fuel and fire:

> When a man dies, his five organs decay. When they decay, there is no basis for accommodating the five constant virtues 五常.[42] The container of knowledge will have decayed; the capacity to know will have disappeared. The body is formed by means of *qi*; [the existence of] *qi* is known by means of the body. There is no fire burning by itself [without fuel] in the world; how could there be in this world a mind 精 that can perceive without a body?[43]

As I discuss in detail below, around the fifth and sixth centuries, there was a heated debate between the Chinese philosophers and Buddhists over the question of whether *shen* perishes after death or continues to exist permanently. The arguments against Buddhism in these debates were heavily dependent on the ideas reflected in the above quotation (Li, 2001, pp. 60–8).

---

41. 四時者, (侌)[陰](昜)[陽] 之所生. (侌)[陰](昜) [陽] 者, 神明之所生也. 神明者・天([阝+亠/匕/土])[地] 者, (大)[太] 一之所生也 (re-quoted from Xiao, 2003, p. 89).
42. The five constant virtues 五常 are benevolence 仁, righteousness 義, propriety 禮, wisdom 智 and trust 信.
43. 人死, 五藏腐朽. 腐朽, 則五常無所託矣, 所用藏智者已敗矣, 所用爲智者已去矣. 形須氣而成, 氣須形而知. 天下無獨燃之火, 世間安得有無體獨知之精? (《論衡・論事》, LHJS, p. 875). We have seen on p. 101 that the same simile is used by the early Buddhists in the *Aggivacchagotta-sutta* (M.I.487), in order to illustrate that there is no permanent self beyond the five aggregates. Here we ascertain that, as far as the concept of self is concerned, the Daoist ideas are quite similar to the Buddhist ones.

However, it is not to be expected that so many philosophical Daoists, in such a vast territory and over such a long period, could have a completely consistent doctrinal system. There were always minority opinions among the Daoist tradition, and some of them became dynamic forces that resulted in the various developments of later thought. As for the concept of *shen*, we sporadically find the philosophical Daoists endowing it with an existential state beyond that of mere *qi*.

> 'Brightness originates from darkness; [the relative] relationship originates from no-form. *Jingshen* (精神: mind) originates from *dao*, the bodily basis 形本 originates from *jing*, and a myriad of things mutually originate from form 形.'[44]

Note that in the above the mind is declared to be born from *dao*. However, it was a general view among the philosophical Daoists, as quoted in notes 30 and 35, that the mind originates from heaven or active *qi*, while the body originates from the earth or passive *qi*. Also, it was generally assumed that bodily materials come first and that the mind emerges later, as the development of human beings from an embryo shows.[45] Contrarily, here the mind is said to originate not from *qi*, but directly from *dao*. When we regard *jing* 精 as an abbreviation of *jingshen* 精神 in the above quotation, just as *xing* 形 is an abbreviation of *xingben* 形本, this means that *dao* creates *shen* and then *shen* creates a myriad of things, which matches the idea reflected in note 41. In this specific case, *shen* is the spirit of *dao* itself. One of the most controversial passages in the *Zhuangzi* announces: 'When our hands finish lighting the firewood, the fire [continues to exist,] moving [from one piece of firewood to another]; there is no extinction of it.'[46]

Here the firewood may represent the bodily basis and fire the essence of life, which can be perfected by the Daoist skill of fostering life 養生, and which is nothing but the Daoist concept of *shen*. This idea does not fit in well with the whole context of the *Zhuangzi*, where the essence of life is also expected to disintegrate after death. However, this minor idea played an important role when the Chinese Buddhists argued against other Chinese intellectuals for the existence of imperishable *shen*.

---

44. 夫昭昭生於冥， 有倫生於无形． 精神生於道， 形本生於精， 而萬物以形相生 (《莊子・知北游》, ZZJS, p. 741).
45. This idea was axiomatized by Xunzi (荀子: 313–238 BCE) as 'After the body is prepared, the mind appears' 形具而神生 (《荀子・天論》, XZJJ, p. 206). Although he was a Confucian, this axiom has frequently been quoted in Daoist arguments against Buddhism.
46. 指窮於為薪, 火傳也, 不知其盡也 (《莊子・養生主》, ZZJS, p. 129).

In addition, unlike the Indian Buddhists in rivalry with Brahmanism, the Daoists proclaimed the existence of the 'true lord,' which is the lord of the body and mind and which can be regarded as the quintessence of self. In the *Zhuangzi*, it is said:

> It seems that there is a true lord, but I just cannot find any indication of it (or him). It is certain that it operates, but I cannot see its form. It is real, but it has no form. … There must be a true lord. No matter whether I grasp its reality or not, there is no loss or increase concerning its true [existence].[47]

There is no doubt that, as the *Huainanzi* articulates,[48] the 'true lord' in the above indicates *shen*. This means that *shen* was regarded as the true agent of thought. So we observe that, although they are inconsistent with the general ideas of philosophical Daoism, there were some minority ideas that made it possible for the Chinese Buddhists to develop an influential conception of self nearer to the Brahmanic *ātman*.

The Daoist Self in Epistemology, Soteriology and Politics

The *Laozi* 老子 begins with the following statement: 'If *dao* can be talked about, it is not true *dao*. If a name can be named, it is not a true name.'[49] Since the single *dao* produces everything, and since everything has the single *dao* embedded in it, the understanding of truth must comprehend both the monistic and the pluralistic aspects of *dao*. However, pluralistic knowledge without an understanding of monistic *dao* is ignorance. Since the word knowledge 智 usually designates a pluralistic understanding of the world without the insight of monistic *dao*, pursuing knowledge is devalued as dangerous and hopeless in Daoist texts.[50] Moreover, pluralistic knowledge can be true only when it is gained by Daoist saints

47. 若有真宰, 而特不得其眹. 可行己信, 而不見其形, 有情而無形. … 其有真君存焉! 如求得其情與不得, 無益損乎其真 (《莊子・齊物論》, ZZJS, p. 55).
48. 'The heart 心 is the lord of the body; *shen* is the jewel of the mind 心.' 心者, 形之主也; 而神者, 心之寶也 << 淮南子・精神 >> (HNZ, p. 103). The Chinese used the word 心 to refer to both the heart and the mind, regarding the heart as the organ of thought. This identification of the heart as the organ of thought had been dominant even among medical practitioners before the modernization of China in the nineteenth century.
49. 道可道, 非常道; 名可名, 非常名 (《老子》, LZJS, p. 3, §1).
50. 'Our life is limited, whereas [the objects of] knowledge are limitless. Pursuing something limitless by means of something limited is dangerous. If one were still engaged in [improving] knowledge, that would be dangerous.' 吾生也有涯, 而知也無涯. 以有涯隨無涯, 殆已! 而為知者, 而矣! (《莊子・養生主》, ZZJS, p. 115).

who have already realized the monistic aspect of *dao*. Therefore, the 'real' knowledge to be pursued by Daoists for soteriological purposes is always accompanied by an understanding of monistic *dao*:

> The knowledge of ancient people must have reached perfection. What is perfection? Some of them thought that from the beginning there is nothing. This knowledge is perfect and complete. There is nothing to be added to this knowledge. After them, some thought that, although there are things, from the beginning there is no distinction. Below them, some thought that, although there is a distinction, from the beginning there is nothing right or wrong. Since rights and wrongs are clarified, *dao* declines; since *dao* declines, favouritism occurs.[51]

Therefore Daoist philosophers rejected the possibility that *dao* is grasped through logical reasoning or linguistic analysis.[52] *Shen*, the Daoist quintessence of the self, is the purest embodiment of *dao*; given the monistic character of *dao*, it is natural that philosophical Daoist epistemology does not allow the grasping of the true self by means of dualistic knowledge.

The concept of *shen* plays a core role particularly in the soteriological system of philosophical Daoism, as the concept of non-self does in Buddhism. It is an agent that undertakes soteriological practices and is an epistemological object that should be understood correctly. The *shen* as a soteriological agent is existentially dependent on a material basis: 'The [bodily] form is the accommodation of life, *qi* is the stuffing of life, and *shen* is the controller of life. If one [of them] fails to play its role, [all of] the three get hurt.'[53] Indeed, in religious Daoism and in Daoist medicine, bodily practice is considered as important as mental practice. However, for philosophical Daoism before the arrival of Buddhism the

---

51. 古之人, 其知有所至矣. 惡乎至? 有以為未始有物者, 至矣, 盡矣, 不可以加矣. 其次以為有物矣, 而未始有封也. 其次以為有封焉, 而未始有是非也. 是非彰也, 道之所以虧也; 道之所以虧, 愛之所以成 (《莊子 · 齊物論》, ZZJS, p. 74).
52. 'From the beginning, *dao* has no distinction, and language has no definite meaning. [While people are] doing so (i.e., are attached to language), discrimination occurs. Let me discuss discrimination: there is left, right, morality, righteousness, distinction, arguments, competition and conflicts. These are the so-called eight virtues. As regards the realm beyond the universe, saints accept its existence but do not discuss it; as regards the realm within the universe, saints discuss it but do not construct arguments.' 夫道未始有封, 言未始有常, 為是而有畛也. 請言其畛: 有左, 有右, 有倫, 有義, 有分, 有辯, 有競, 有爭, 此之謂八德. 六合之外, 聖人存而不論; 六合之內, 聖人論而不議 (《莊子 · 齊物論》, ZZJS, p. 83).
53. 夫形者, 生之舍也; 氣者, 生之充也; 神者, 生之制也. 一失位, 則三者傷矣 (《淮南子 · 原道》, HNZ, p. 17).

soteriological aim, i.e., the realization of *dao*, is possible only through mental practice, particularly through the purification of *shen*.

According to the Daoist philosophers, everyone has *shen* from birth. However, while still alive we may lose it if we are careless of the cultivation of the mind;[54] in addition, while practising properly, we may collect more *shen* from outside.[55] Although it is popularly believed that certain strong *hun* 魂 and *po* 魄 transform respectively into *shen* (神: spirit, deity) and *gui* (鬼: ghost), the majority of Daoist philosophers assume that there is no continuation of life after death. Their soteriology ends with death, no matter whether the aim of the realization of *dao* has been achieved in this life or not.[56] In short, the soteriology of Daoism is restricted to this life and it aims to foster the *shen* that is the essence of *dao* embedded in our minds.

Given that the soteriology aims to foster *shen*, the Daoist process of practice is inevitably dependent on the characteristics of *shen*: being the essential materialization of *dao*, *shen* is neither to be perceived by our senses nor to be known by our intelligence, just like *dao*. Thus, a practitioner should not depend on his senses or intelligence to foster *shen*:[57]

> The quintessence of the ultimate *dao* is [too] deep and dark [to see]; the extremity of the ultimate *dao* is [too] murky and silent [to grasp]. Do not try seeing or hearing, but cherish *shen* in composure. Then the

---

54. Just after announcing, 'The mind is the lord of the body; *shen* is the jewel of the mind,' the *Huainanzi* goes on to say, 'Being overworked without rest, the body falls down; being consumed continuously, the mind is exhausted' 形勞而不休則蹶, 精用而不已則竭 (《淮南子 · 精神》, HNZ, p. 103). For this reason, in the previous quotation from the *Guanzi* 管子, it is said, 'But once there is knowledge, you must stop.'
55. 'If you rectify your bodily posture and keep your observation one-pointed, the harmony of the universe will reach you; if you control your perception and concentrate your intention, *shen* will come and abide [in your body], *de* will be your beauty, and *dao* will be your accommodation.' 若正汝形, 一汝視, 天和將至; 攝汝知, 一汝度, 神將來舍. 德將為汝美, 道將為汝居 (《莊子 · 知北游》, ZZJS, p. 737).
56. Anecdotes about Daoist saints who lived for hundreds of years are frequently found here and there in the Daoist literature. However, before the arrival of Buddhism, I could not find any story about Daoist saints who continued their practice in consecutive lives.
57. Also compare this with the two passages from the *Mahābhārata*, as introduced by Frauwallner (1973 [1953], vol. 1, p. 108): 'One should not comprehend the sound with the ear, nor experience the touch through the skin or know the form with the eyes, nor the taste with the tongue. One should also abstain from all experiences through the smell' (XII, 195, v. 6), and 'As the tortoise again withdraws in itself the limbs which it had stretched out, so should one hold

> body will become sound by itself. One must keep [one's mind] calm and clean. Do not overwork your body or stir up your mind. Then you can live a long time. When there is nothing to be seen by your eyes, to be heard by your ears or to be known by your mind, your *shen* will be protected and your body will live for a long time.[58]

Being the origin of creation, *dao* is regarded as 'ruthlessly equal' to any creature.[59] Therefore, a practitioner who fosters *shen* should be equal to any object, and his or her emotion should remain in equanimity:

> Therefore it is said, 'Sorrow and pleasure defile *de* 德; joy and anger falsify *dao*; affection and dislike fail *de*. Therefore, having no worry or pleasure in mind is the ultimate *de*; being one-pointed without change is the ultimate equanimity; getting on with everything is the ultimate emptiness; having no partial relationship with anything is the ultimate disinterestedness; not being disobedient to anything is the ultimate purity.' ... 'This is the way to foster *shen*.'[60]

Here, we should attend to the fact that removing one's own emotion is closely related to the ideal of universal equality and the monistic aspect of *dao*.

The *shen* and body of a person in the course of practice enjoy a close relationship with all the phenomena of the universe, since all of them are created and pervaded by the single *dao*:

> Saints observe the appropriate [state] of active and passive [*qi*], and discern the benefit of a myriad of things, so that they foster life. Therefore, [saints'] *jingshen* (i.e., the mind) remains peaceful in their bodies, and they enjoy a long life.[61]

---

together the sense-organs through the thinking (*manaḥ*)' (XII, 328, v. 39). This agreement between Daoism and Brahmanism is not to be interpreted as a mere coincidence. We find considerable similarities originating in the features common to Daoist and Brahmanic cosmogony and epistemology.

58. 至道之精，窈窈冥冥；至道之極，昏昏默默. 無視，無聽，抱神以靜，形將自正. 必靜，必清，無勞女形，無搖女精，乃可以長生. 目無所見，耳無所聞，心無所知，女神將守，形乃長生 (《莊子 · 在宥》, ZZJS, p. 381).
59. 'Heaven and earth are ruthless; they regard all things as straw dogs. A sage is ruthless; he regards people as straw dogs.' 天地不仁，以萬物爲芻狗；聖人不仁，以百姓爲芻狗 (《老子》, LZJS, p. 22, §5). A 'straw dog' 芻狗 is a doll in the form of a dog, which is thrown away after being used in ancestor worship.
60. 故曰：悲樂者，德之邪；喜怒者，道之過；好惡者，德之失. 故心不憂樂，德之至也；一而不變，靜之至也；無所於忤，虛之至也；不與物交，淡之至也；無所於逆，粹之至也. ... 此養神之道也 (《莊子 · 刻意》, ZZJS, pp. 542–4).
61. 聖人察陰陽之宜，辨萬物之利，以便生. 故精神安乎形，而年壽得長焉 (《呂氏春秋 · 盡數》, LC, p. 25).

Here we observe that the individual happiness of a Daoist practitioner is attained as a result of pursuing the benefit of the whole universe, since this is the nature of *dao*. Health, longevity and wealth are by-products of mental practice; the ostensible pursuit of worldly happiness is in the integral context of Daoism a personal effort to realize harmonious benefit for the universe.

Not only the practice of fostering *shen*, but also the results of that practice are dependent on the characteristics of *dao*: *shen* in its highest state of Daoist soteriology goes beyond the personality and becomes identical with the monistic *dao*:

> *Jingshen* (i.e., the minds) [of saints] pervades all directions; it reaches all extremes. Its top is as high as Heaven and it coils on the earth. It generates and nourishes a myriad of things. Having no way to describe it, [we] call it Lord 帝. With regard to the pure and unstained *dao*, only *shen* is to be protected. Having protected and maintained it, you will become at one with *shen*. The mind (*jing*) that is one [with *shen*] becomes united with the heavenly order.[62]

This agrees with the idea that *shen* is the spirit of *dao* itself, and is not confined to a personal mentality. In this sense, it is no wonder if a saint who becomes one with *shen* can protect all beings from illness and plague, and cause a rich harvest, when he concentrates his *shen*,[63] although he would reject political engagement in such worldly affairs.

In Part II, I discussed how the fear of death and the desire for eternity affected the concept of self in Indian Buddhism (see pp. 127 ff.). In Daoism, instead of the desire for eternity, we find the desire for a long, healthy life:

> Though doing good, stay away from fame; though doing evil, keep away from punishment. Take the middle way! Then you may protect your body, preserve your life, look after your parents, and live out your natural life-span.[64]

Exaggerating and slightly distorting this art of living,[65] Mencius criticized Yangzi, an important forerunner of the Laozi-Zhuangzi school: 'Yangzi

62. 精神四達並流，無所不極. 上際於天，下蟠於地，化育萬物，不可為象. 其名為同帝. 純素之道, 唯神是守. 守而勿失, 與神為一 . 一之精通, 合於天倫 (《莊子・刻意》, ZZJS, p. 544).
63. 藐姑射山，有神人居焉. ... 其神凝，使物不疵癘而年穀熟（《莊子・逍遙遊》, ZZJS, p. 28).
64. 為善，無近名；為惡，無近刑! 緣督以為經，可以保身，可以全生，可以養親，可以盡年 (《莊子・養生主》, ZZJS, p. 115).
65. For more details about Mencius' distortion, see Graham (1989, pp. 59–64).

adopted egoism. He would not pluck out a hair from his body even if it could benefit the whole world.'[66] However, judging from the whole context of philosophical Daoism, what Daoists advocated was a political individualism. The ostensibly selfish slogan, 'protecting the body and fostering life' 保身養生 is indeed suggested to serve as a fundamental principle for ideal rule:

> Therefore, when there is no choice for a gentleman but to be a ruler, nothing is better than doing nothing [artificial] 無為. After [the way of] doing nothing [is carried out], the reality of natural life becomes stable. Therefore if [a gentleman] thinks his body more precious than sovereignty over the world, he deserves to be entrusted with the world; if he loves his body more than sovereignty over the world, he deserves to be charged with the world.[67]

Since the whole system of philosophical Daoist soteriology, which includes ostensibly selfish aims, is indeed based on large-scale views of life and death, it is unsurprising to find the following view of life stated in an astonishing tone of dispassion: at the funeral of his wife, Zhuangzi was singing a song and pounding on a tub. Huizi 惠子 criticized his discourtesy, but Zhuangzi answered:

> No, it is not so. In the first moments after her death, how could I alone remain ungrieving? However, looking back to the beginning, [I found that she] originally had no life; not only had she no life, but also she had no body; not only had she no body, but also she had no material elements 氣. Suddenly, there was a transformation, and the material elements appeared. When the materials were transformed, [her bodily] form appeared; according to the transformation of her [bodily] form, she came to be born. Now there has been another transformation, and she has come to die. It is [as natural] as the four seasons taking turns. I should confess that I did not understand the fate [of living beings], if I lamented loudly while she lies down peacefully in the immense room (i.e., Heaven and earth).[68]

66. 孟子曰: '楊子取爲我, 拔一毛而利天下, 不爲也' (《孟子 · 盡心上》, MZ: §13.26).
67. 故君子不得已而臨莅, 莫若無為. 無為也而後, 安其性命之情. 故貴以身於為天下, 則可以托天下; 愛以身於為天下, 則可以寄天下 (《莊子 · 在宥》, ZZJS, p. 381). We also find the same sentence '故貴以身於為天下, 則可以托天下; 愛以身於為天下, 則可以寄天下' in the *Laozi* §13 (LZJS, p. 50).
68. 不然. 是其始死也, 我獨何能无概然? 察其始而本无生. 非徒无生也, 而本无形. 非徒无形也, 而本无氣. 芒芴之間, 變而有氣, 氣變而有形, 形變而有生. 今又變而之死, 是相與為春秋四時行也. 人且偃然寢於巨室, 而我噭噭然隨而哭之, 自以為不通乎命. 故止也 (《莊子 · 至樂》, ZZJS, pp. 614–15).

THE PHILOSOPHICAL DAOIST SELF IN CONTRAST TO THE EARLY BUDDHIST ONE

In concluding this chapter, I will analyse the philosophical Daoist ideas of self in comparison with the early Buddhist one. One of the most important differences between the two is that while the early Buddhist one is located in *saṃsāra* under karmic law, the Daoist one is located in the universe created and operated by *dao* without assuming future lives. Speaking in Indian Buddhist terms, the philosophical Daoists were *ucchedavādin* nihilists: instead of pursuing liberation from innumerable rebirths or happy results in future lives, the Daoists pursued mental and bodily happiness in this life. Moreover, while the early Buddhist self is constructed on the basis of the dualism of mind and matter, the Daoist self is constructed on the monogenesis of *qi*: the mind is an accumulation of purer *qi*, whereas the body is an accumulation of coarser *qi*. In addition, it is also noteworthy that while the early Buddhist self is a bundle of the five aggregates without any core, the philosophical Daoist self has an essential core: *shen*.

While the early Buddhists rejected the existence of a permanent creator or operator of the universe, no matter whether personified or not, the Daoists based their ontology, soteriology, epistemology and concept of self on the pivotal concept of *dao*, which functions as the impersonal creator and operator of the universe. Generally speaking, except for personification, the concepts of *dao* and *brahman* share many ontological and epistemological characteristics. Furthermore, *shen*, i.e., the essential core of the self, is regarded as the purest materialization of *dao*. For this reason, it is natural for the concept of *shen* to become close to the concept of *ātman* when the property of permanence is attributed to it, so that it plays the role of the agent going through *saṃsāra*.

There are also coincidental similarities between the early Buddhist and philosophical Daoist ideas of self. Above all, there is no permanent self. *Shen*, the essence of the mind and the core of a self, is also impermanent: it can be enlarged or strengthened by appropriate practices, and lessened by inappropriate ways of life; in addition, in the philosophical discussions no continuation of *shen* as a personal identifier after death was assumed. This important similarity originates in the way of thinking that does not assume a permanent substance. Like the early Buddhists, the Daoist philosophers accepted the change of everything that is perceived, except for *dao*. Hence, it is said:

> The arising of things is as swift as galloping horses. Everything moves in change; in every moment, things become different.[69]

Beneath such differences in ontology, epistemology and soteriology between the two traditions, we find that there is a fundamental difference in the way of thinking. While the Indian Buddhists held fast to the analytical way of thinking, the Daoists had no use for it. In India, the doctrinal development of Buddhism was always justified by means of meditative observations and analytical reasoning: the early Buddhists analytically observed that a self is a successive compound of impermanent components; the Abhidharmists, such as the Vaibhāṣikas and the Sarvāstivādins, analysed or observed temporal and spatial units that cannot be analysed any further; the Mādhyamikas advocated the meditative or analytic knowledge of *śūnyatā*, arguing that any causation is impossible if there is an entity that exists without changing even for a moment; and the Yogācārins provided various logical arguments supporting their observation that there cannot be external objects. In the course of these developments, analytical reasoning was adopted to argue for both the conventional truth and the highest truth. On the contrary, the Daoists devalued analytical thinking in their epistemology and excluded it from proper soteriological method: it cannot catch truth, and, even worse, is a fundamental obstacle to grasping the truth. Instead, they held fast to the mystical insight into *dao* as the proper method for achieving soteriological goals. Generally speaking, the Chinese Buddhists devalued analytical reasoning as a mere tool for establishing the conventional truth, insisting that it cannot catch the highest truth and also that it is the fundamental obstruction to understanding the truth; in this aspect, they followed the Daoists.

In the following chapter, in order to clarify how close the Chinese Buddhist concept of self is to the Brahmanic one, I analyse its characteristics in comparison with the three critical properties of the Brahmanic *ātman*: *sat* (existence), *cit* (consciousness) and *ānanda* (joy). As for the philosophical Daoist self before the arrival of Buddhism, the concept of *shen* implies only the property of *cit*, rather than the other two. The first property cannot be attributed to *shen*, since it is impermanent. The third property does not play any role in philosophical Daoist soteriology or epistemology. As did early Buddhism, the philosophical Daoists emphasized emotional equanimity for the purification of *shen*.

---

69. 物之生也, 若驟若馳, 无動而不變, 无時而不移 (《莊子・秋水》, ZZJS, p. 585).

Chapter 7

NON-SELF BUT AN IMPERISHABLE SOUL IN CHINESE BUDDHIST TRANSLATIONS

In Part I, introducing the translation procedure and analysing the cultural characteristics of Chinese Buddhist translation, I illustrated the cultural atmosphere that allowed the Buddhist translators arbitrarily to insert their opinions in the body of canonical translations. The use of Chinese terms indicating an imperishable soul, such as *hunpo* 魂魄, *shenshi* 神識 and *jingshen* 精神, in Buddhist translations affords a typical example of arbitrary interpolations or adaptations. In this chapter, I aim to demonstrate how the indigenous Chinese ways of thinking influenced Buddhist translation in China, by exploring and analysing the adaptations and interpolations that reflect the idea of an imperishable soul.

NON-SELF 無我

The Chinese Buddhists must have recognized from the beginning that non-self (*anātman*) is the core teaching of the Buddha: the South/Central Asian originals were full of the teaching of *anātman*, and their Chinese translations convey the teaching with clarity. The Buddhist translators in China rendered *-ātman* as *wo* (我: I), *wu* (吾: I), *shen* (身: body), etc., and the negative prefix *an-* as *wu-*無, *fei-*非, etc. In the earliest phase of Chinese Buddhist translation, An Shigao (安世高: fl. 148–71) preferred rendering *anātman* as *feishen* 非身 or *wushen* 無身, and Lokakṣema (fl. 178–189) preferred rendering it as *wuwo* 無我 or *feiwo* 非我. Later, *wuwo* 無我 and *feiwo* 非我 became the standard renderings for *anātman*. Technically speaking, the compounds beginning *wu-* correspond to *anātman* as a *bahuvrīhi* compound, since it means 'having no self' or 'there is no self', whereas the compounds beginning *fei-* correspond to *anātman* as a *karmadhāraya* compound, since it means 'not the self'. However, in general, Buddhist translators in China do not appear to have clearly distinguished between these meanings.

Despite the fact that they had access to the South/Central Asian Buddhist scriptures that are full of the doctrine of *anātman*, and although they indeed translated *anātman* as *wuwo*, etc., we sometimes find Chinese translators adopting controversial renderings or arbitrarily inserting certain terms indicating an eternalist *ātman*. In the following section, I inspect the usages and meanings of the terms that indicate an imperishable soul.

CRITICAL TERMS FOR AN IMPERISHABLE SOUL IN THE TRANSLATIONS

Recall the fact that, in rivalry with eternalism, which dominated India, the critical concern of Indian Buddhists with regard to the concept of self was to explain how a person suffers innumerable rebirths without a permanent agent, so they argued that human beings are mere combinations of impermanent components which are subject to dependent origination. On the contrary, the urgent concern of the early Chinese Buddhists was to argue for *saṃsāra* against all other Chinese intellectual movements, which had no idea of it at all. For this reason, the Chinese Buddhists argued for the existence of an agent that goes through *saṃsāra* according to karmic law. In other words, the early Chinese Buddhists had to adopt a notion of a permanent self in order to explain *saṃsāra*.

Primary Terms

HUN 魂

As introduced in the previous chapter, there was a popular belief among the Chinese that a human being possesses two kinds of spirit: *hun* (魂, soul) and *po* (魄, psyche), and that certain strong *hun*s or *po*s become spirits 神 or ghosts 鬼 after death. In order to help the 'ignorant' Chinese to understand the process of rebirth, the pioneer Buddhists in China adopted the terms *hun* and *po* and enriched their applications: the *hun*s and *po*s of all living beings transfer from this body to another after death; they exist endlessly except when they achieve *nirvāṇa*. However, the existence of *po* is usually ignored in the Buddhist texts unless it is used at the end of the compound *hunpo*, or juxtaposed with *hun* as a couplet, probably because there is no space for two different kinds of soul in Buddhism and because *hun* was regarded as the purer.

As it had been by the Chinese before the arrival of Buddhism, *hun* was also regarded by many Buddhists as an agent of thought. *Hun* is an agent that controls the process of perception or thinking; it is not merely a momentary act of thinking. So *hun* abides even when there is no thinking process going on. One interesting characteristic of *hun* is, the Chinese believed, that there may be thinking going on even when a person has lost his or her *hun*. However, in that particular case the process of thinking is in disorder or insane, since the controlling agent is disconnected from the process. For an example of this use, while the Sanskrit *Buddhacarita* describes Chandaka's return to Kapilavastu shortly after he had taken leave of the Bodhisattva (i.e., Siddhārtha) thus:

> Sometimes he brooded, sometimes lamented,
> sometimes stumbled, and sometimes fell.
> Hence, while going [back] in grief, because of his devotion,
> he did a lot of [sacrificial] acts on the road in desperation.[1]

in the corresponding T192 佛所行讚, Dharmakṣema (曇無讖, 385–433) translates it as:

> Sometimes he was sunk in thought, [sometimes] lost [his] *hun*,
> sometimes faced up and down, and sometimes drooped,
> Sometimes he fell and got up again.
> Crying in grief, he turned back along the road.[2]

The fact that *hun* is the agent for controlling the process of thought is noteworthy: being the agent of thinking, the concept of *hun* fundamentally differs from the Indian Buddhist concept of *vijñāna* (consciousness), which is never an abiding agent of thought, but is a momentary act of thinking. In the system of the eighteen *dhātu*s (elements), *manas* (the mind) is assumed to be the organ of *manovijñāna* (mind-consciousness). However, at least theoretically, *manas* has not been regarded by Indian Buddhists as an abiding entity independent of momentary *vijñāna*. In their theories, Theravāda Buddhists identified *manas* as a kind of momentary *citta* (thinking or thought);[3] Sarvāstivāda Buddhists defined it as one of

1. *kvacit pradadhyau, vilalāpa ca kvacit, kvacit pracaskhāla, papāta ca kvacit, ato vrajan bhaktivaśena duḥkhitaś cacāra bahvīr avaśaḥ pathi kriyāḥ* (BC, p. 67, §6.68).
2. 或沈思失魂 或俯仰垂身 或倒而復起 悲泣隨路還 (T192.4.12b21–22).
3. 'Which factors are the acts of thinking? Eye-consciousness, ear-consciousness, nose-consciousness, tongue-consciousness, body-consciousness, mind-element,

the six *vijñāna*s that occurred immediately before [the present one];[4] and the Yogācārins, such as Vasubandhu, who assumed eight kinds of *vijñāna*, identified *manas* as the seventh *vijñāna*.[5] Generally speaking, for the Indian Buddhists, *manas* or the mind is a sort of *vijñāna* or a mere name that designates the totality of *vijñāna*s and other mental actions; an abiding agent which controls the process of thinking has not been assumed by learned Indian Buddhists.

The Chinese Buddhists adopted this Chinese concept of *hun*, and transformed it into a 'Buddhist' one in order to explain *saṃsāra*: every *hun* of living beings moves to another body for the next life according to its moral deeds in the past. Hence, T555 *Wumuzi jing* 五母子經, which is traditionally attributed to Zhi Qian, announces:

> [After death,] all [components] of the body turn into soil; in responsibility for past deeds, *hun* follows [the results of] skilful and unskilful [karma].[6]

However, this idea is substantially anti-Buddhist in the Indian sense. Since the *hunpo* is the quintessence of the self and since it is the agent of thought, if it transfers from one body to another endlessly, it rather corresponds to the Brahmanic *ātman* which had been thoroughly rejected by the early Buddhists as well as the Mahāyānists. As I will discuss in detail below, while struggling against other Chinese intellectual movements and advocating the theory of *saṃsāra*, the Chinese Buddhists went too far to remain within the boundary of 'orthodoxy' in the Indian Buddhist sense.

Even before the arrival of Buddhism, *hun* was thought possibly to last for a while after death; the density of *hun* may remain strong at the moment of death for certain reasons, particularly for reasons of a grudge. However, it was considered natural for *hun* to disintegrate after death; if it remains as a spirit after death, it is unusual and dangerous. Hence, for the prosperity of a person, a family or a state it was important to appease

---

and mind-consciousness-element': *katame dhammā cittā? cakkhuviññāṇaṃ sotaviññāṇaṃ ghānaviññāṇaṃ jivhāviññāṇaṃ kāyaviññāṇaṃ manodhātu manoviññāṇadhātu—ime dhammā cittā* (Dhs §1187). For detailed information about the operation of *manas* as an act of thinking, see Cousins (1981, pp. 30–9).

4. 'Of the six *vijñāna*s, the one immediately preceding is the *manas*': *ṣaṇṇām anantarâtītaṃ vijñānaṃ yad dhi tan manaḥ* (AbhK, p. 41, §1.17ab).

5. 'The *vijñāna*, called *manas*, has that (i.e., the *ālayavijñāna*) as its object, and has the nature of thinking' (*tadālambaṃ mano nāma vijñānaṃ mananâtmakam;* TrimsV. 50, §5cd).

6. 身皆歸土，魂當所作，隨其善惡 (T555.14.907a13–14).

the spirits that were haunting the neighbourhood due to their grudges. The Chinese Buddhists also maintained this attitude towards ghosts: it is natural for a living being to go to the place of the next life (*gati*) after death, whereas it is unusual and dangerous if it haunts nearby human beings. *Hun* in the Chinese Buddhist scriptures is frequently used to designate those spirits that fail to find a proper place for the next life and haunt nearby human beings. In this usage, *hun* is frequently compounded as *yuanhun* (冤魂: ill-willing *hun*), *youhun* (遊魂: wandering *hun*) or *guhun* (孤魂: lonely *hun*) throughout Chinese Buddhist literature.

SHEN 神

From the beginning of Chinese Buddhist translation, *shen* was widely used to translate both *ṛddhi* (supernormal power) and *deva* (deity). In translating *ṛddhi*, it is usually an adjective, frequently forming compounds such as *shentong* (神通: supernatural power), *shenzu* (神足: the foundation of supernatural power, i.e., *ṛddhipāda*) or *weishen* (威神: mightiness); in translating *deva*, it is usually a noun, frequently forming compounds, such as *tianshen* (天神: heavenly deities) or *dishen* (地神: earthly deities). This Buddhist use accords with the original meaning of *shen* in Chinese literature. Leaving aside such common usage, in this book I pay attention to the use of *shen* that indicates an imperishable soul undergoing endless rebirth, which is a concept neither from Indian Buddhism nor from Chinese thought.

Shen is also used to designate an agent of thinking, as is *hun*. When both terms are used in this sense, *hun* is more frequently used in negative contexts and *shen* in positive ones. So when a person appears insane due to fear or sorrow, it is more frequently expressed as that person having lost his or her *hun*; on the contrary, when a person purifies his or her own mind, *shen* frequently appears as the object of the purification. For example, T212 **Udānavarga-nidāna* 出曜經 (tr. Zhu Fonian (竺佛念: fl. 373–413)) and T213 **Udānavarga* 法集要頌經 (tr. Tianxizai (天息災: fl. 980–1000) states:

> If a man intends to refine his *shen*, [he] has to train himself over and over. A wise man easily graces [his virtues], so is called a world hero. If one is intimate with a wise man, one becomes reposeful without worries.[7]

7. 人欲練其神　要當數修琢　智者易彫飾　乃名世之雄　能親近彼者　安隱無憂惱 (T212.4.743a18–19 and T213.4.792a29–b2). T213 has *lian* 鍊 for *lian* 練. *Lian* 練 is the process of whitening silk by boiling it, and *lian* 鍊 is the process of tempering metal by fire.

Without access to the originals of T212 and T213, we cannot tell exactly which term was employed there for *shen*; however, the overall context indicates that it may render *citta* (mind or thought). The popular Chinese expressions *diaozhuo* (彫琢: chiselling and carving to embellish jade) and *xiushi* (修飾: decorating) show the translators' effort to introduce the Buddhist cultivation of the mind in terms of the Daoist purification of *shen*.

As for the use of *shen* to indicate a permanent agent going through *saṃsāra*, we sporadically find *shen* employed as a rendering of the Indian term *jīva* (life) in the sense of *jīvātman* (an individual permanent self).[8] For example, in the *Pāyāsi-sutta* of the *Dīgha-nikāya*, Prince Pāyāsi visits the venerable Kumāra Kassapa, and argues in various ways that there is no rebirth. As an argument, he describes his experience: he ordered that a criminal should be put in a jar, that its lid should be shut, and then the jar was wrapped in damp skin, covered with damp clay, put in the oven and a fire lit. Being assured that the criminal was dead, they opened the jar and watched to see whether a soul escaped. The prince reports, 'Indeed, we do not see any *jīva* escaping.'[9] Among the three corresponding Chinese translations, T1 *Dīrghāgama* (tr. Buddhayaśas and Zhu Fonian in 413) uses *shen* to render *jīva*: 'Nonetheless, [we] did not see [his] *shen* moving from here to another place;'[10] T26 *Madhyamāgama* (tr. Saṃghadeva in 397–98, proofread and published in 401) renders *jīva* as 'the life of living beings' (衆生生: possibly for *sattvajīva*) or merely 'living beings' (衆生: possibly for *sattva*),[11] and T45 *Da zhengjuwang jing* 大正句王經 (tr. Faxian 法賢: fl. 973–1001) as 'the person or the spontaneous birth for the next life' (後世之人及化生: possibly for *paralokaṃ puruṣañ* (or *pudgalañ*) *ca aupapādukañ ca*).[12] It appears that for normal Chinese readers the expression translated as 'the life of living beings' or 'the person or the spontaneous birth for the next life' does not clearly signify an agent in *saṃsāra*. On the contrary, the rendering *shen* successfully

8. In the tradition of Brahmanism, *ātman* is identified with *brahman*, the impersonal creator and operator of all things. To explain the variety of living beings and the unity between *ātman* and *brahman*, Brahmanic philosophers present two interpretations of *ātman*. The non-dualistic aspect of *ātman* is called *paramātman*, which is identical with *brahman*, and the individual aspect of *ātman* is called *jīvātman*, which creates karmic deeds and suffers the results.
9. *n' ev' assa mayaṃ jīvaṃ nikkhamantaṃ passāma* (D.II.334).
10. 亦不見神有往來之處 (T1.1.44a16–17).
11. 不見衆生生 (T26.1.528c3); 觀視衆生入時出時 (T26.1.528b28).
12. 終不見有後世之人及化生等出入之者 (T45.1.833c2–3).

conveys that sense, although the Chinese reader may infer some implications of *shen* that the Indian *jīva* does not have.

The use of *shen* to indicate an agent in *saṃsāra* started from the beginning of Chinese Buddhist translation. In T607 **Yogācārabhūmi* 道地經, An Shigao (安世高: fl. 148–71) translates the description of the moment of conception as follows: 'At that very moment the father and mother have a seminal emission, and the *shen* immediately reaches it and thinks, "This is my semen." So [the *shen*] is satisfied and gets delight.'[13] Although the original text is missing, the original term corresponding to *shen* is probably *gandharva* or possibly *vijñāna*, *antarābhava*, etc.[14] Whatever the original term may be, learned Indian Buddhists would not have read 'a permanent agent' when they encountered *vijñāna*, etc.; however, well-educated Chinese Buddhists would read a permanent agent when they encountered *shen* in translations, as we can ascertain from their apologetic arguments for the existence of imperishable *shen* 神不滅. By adopting *shen* in the quoted passage, An Shigao may not have intended to indicate a permanent agent, but he may not have fully understood the Chinese implications of *shen*. It must have been his Chinese assistant who recommended the adoption of this term, and who might not have precisely understood the Indian concept of *vijñāna*, etc. This is the starting point from which Chinese Buddhists developed an idea of self that is closer to the Brahmanic *ātman*, though they had no accurate knowledge of Brahmanic doctrines.

However, more frequently, when it indicates a permanent agent in *saṃsāra*, *shen* is not used as a translating word; it is arbitrarily interpolated by translators without any corresponding word in the original texts. For example, T20 *Ambāṣṭha-sūtra* describes the stage of attaining the heavenly eye (*divya-cakṣus*) as follows: 'Through the eye of *dao*, he sees others' *hunshen* [and knows] its origination before birth and its destination after death.'[15] The Pali *Ambaṭṭha-sutta*, the third *sutta* of the *Dīgha-nikāya*, omits this part, since it is a repetition of the corresponding part of the *Sāmaññaphala-sutta*, the second *sutta* of the *Dīgha-nikāya*.

---

13. 父母即時墮精, 神便到意生為是我精, 即可意喜生 (T607.15.234a14–15).
14. There are various ways of interpreting the twelvefold dependent origination. When it is interpreted as twofold karmic causation in three lives, the third factor *vijñāna* is frequently interpreted as the first consciousness at the moment of entering the womb. *Gandharva* and *antarābhava* are intermediate existents in the form of a ghost between the last moment of the previous life and the first moment of the next.
15. 道眼見人魂神生所從來死趣何道 (T20.1.262b9–10).

The corresponding part in the *Sāmaññaphala-sutta* describes this stage: 'With the heavenly eye, which is pure and super-human, he sees living beings passing away and being reborn; he knows whether the beings become mean or noble, ugly or beautiful, and fortunate or miserable, according to their karma. ...'[16] Note that 'living beings' (*satta*) in the Pali *sutta* corresponds to 'others' 人 in the Chinese translation; *hunshen* in the translation is an interpolation by the translator. Unless it is a Vātsīputrīya text, an Indian Buddhist text is hardly expected to contain any word corresponding to the Chinese Buddhist concept of *shen* in such contexts.

Another important use of *shen* is that it is often identified with *vijñāna* (consciousness). We can trace this use of *shen* from the beginning of Chinese Buddhist translation. Lokakṣema presents a compound, *shihunshen* 識魂神, in T418 **Pratyutpanna-buddha-saṃmukhâvasthita-samādhi-sūtra* 般舟三昧經 (tr. in 179). This *shihunshen* must be the translation of *vijñāna* only, since there the five aggregates and four elements are listed: 'form (色, *rūpa*), feeling (痛痒, *vedanā*), apperception (思想, *saṃjñā*), mental activities (生死, *saṃskāra*), consciousness (識魂神, *vijñāna*), earth-element (地, *pṛthivī-dhātu*), water-element (水, *ab-dhātu*), fire-element (火, *tejo-dhātu*) and wind-element (風, *vāyu-dhātu*)' (T418.13.905b17). The first member *shi* 識 of the compound *shihunshen* 識魂神, when used alone, is the standard rendering for *vijñāna*;[17] therefore, the remaining member, *hunshen* 魂神, appears to be an explanation of *shi* or *vijñāna*, inserted by the translator or a later interpreter, for Chinese readers who were unfamiliar with the concept of *shi* or *vijñāna* but understood the meaning of *hunshen*. If the last part of this annotative compound is not a gloss incorporated into the main text in the course of transcription, it illustrates how some of the experts in Indian and Chinese thought within a translation team influenced each other.[18] If it is a gloss, it may

---

16. *so dibbena cakkhunā visuddhena atikkantamānusakena satte passati cavamāne upapajjamāne hīne paṇīte suvaṇṇe dubbaṇṇe sugate duggate yathākammūpage satte pajānāti* ... (D.I.82_25–28).
17. The translation of *vijñāna* as *shihunshen* 識魂神 appears only in T417 and T418 throughout the whole Taisho canon. T417 is also traditionally attributed to Lokakṣema. However, Harrison (1990, p. xvi) argues that T417 is an anonymous abridgement of the Song, Yuan and Ming redaction of T418, into which a long versified passage has been interpolated. Throughout the ten translations whose attribution to Lokakṣema is convincing (see p. 198), we find that *shi* 識 alone is regularly used to render *vijñāna*.
18. For the structure of a translation team led by Lokakṣema, see pp. 11–12. There I introduced the translation team for T224 *Aṣṭasāhasrikā Prajñāpāramitā*

show that many Chinese intellectuals may have not been precisely aware of the momentariness of *vijñāna*.[19]

SHI 識

Recall the discussion in the *Mahātaṇhāsaṅkhaya-sutta*, where the monk Sāti has a wrong view that the Buddha taught, 'This very consciousness runs through *saṃsāra*, not another.' Being summoned and asked by the Buddha, 'What is that consciousness, Sāti?', he replies, 'This, which has speaking and knowing (or feeling), experiences here and there the result of skilful and unskilful actions.' In short, he regards *vijñāna* as a permanent agent undergoing *saṃsāra* and simultaneously as the agent of perception, as do Brahmanic philosophers. Of course, the Buddha rejects his view, calling him 'a fool' (*moghapurisa*), one of the harshest expressions that the Buddha uses in the Pali canon. This harsh expression may reflect the Buddha's serious concern about the misunderstanding. I have introduced some examples in which *vijñāna* is translated not by the standard rendering *shi* but as *shen*. In addition, *shen* and *hun*, along with *shi*, are found in compounds such as *shenshi* 神識 and *hunshi* 魂識, which sometimes translate *vijñāna*, but at other times are arbitrarily interpolated, indicating a permanent agent of perception, i.e., in accordance with the evil view of the monk Sāti. I will introduce and analyse the use of these compounds below.

JING 精

Etymologically, *jing* 精 means 'polished rice', with the emphasized implication of purity. When applied to human beings, it means semen, with the emphasized implication of vitality. Unlike *hun*, *shen* and *shi*, *jing* is seldom used as a noun to indicate an imperishable soul. However, as an adjective, *jing* is incorporated in compounds such as *jinghun* 精魂, *jingshen* 精神 and *jingshi* 精識, and emphasizes the implication of purity and vitality. I will discuss the use of some compounds with *jing* below.

道行般若經. CSZJJ (T2145.55.48c10–16) preserves the colophon to T418. The colophon states that T224 and T418 were translated simultaneously by similar members: the reciter was Zhu Shuofo 竺朔佛, the translator Lokakṣema, the dictator Meng Fu 孟福, and the scribe Zhang Lian 張蓮.

19. In T606 **Yogācārabhūmi-sūtra* 修行道地經 (tr. by Zhu Fahu), we also find *shen* 神 (15.206a9) and *hunshen* 魂神 (15.206a11) as renderings for *vijñāna*. These terms are used to translate the last of the six elements (i.e., earth, water, fire, wind, space and consciousness).

Compound Terms

HUNPO 魂魄

As *hun* 魂 alone may mean 'an abiding agent that controls the process of thought', the compound *hunpo* may also signify the same thing. For example, T449 **Bhaiṣajyaguru-pūrvapraṇidhāna-viśeṣavistara-sūtra* 藥師如來本願功德經 (tr. Dharmagupta: ?–619) states: 'If anyone recites and keeps this *sūtra*, ... In addition, no spectre can take away his or her *hunpo*; even when it is already taken away, [the *hunpo*] immediately returns as usual.'[20] As mentioned above, a person who has lost his or her *hunpo* is expected to become insane. In this specific case, the term does not necessarily imply an agent in *saṃsāra*.

Hunpo is frequently used to indicate an agent in *saṃsāra*. For example, in T581 *Bashi jing* 八師經 (tr. Zhi Qian), the Buddha states in a concluding verse:

> [After death, while] the body decays and turns into earth,
> *hunpo* [goes to the next life], following [karmic] causation.
> Fearing this, I practised *dao* and attained *nirvāṇa*.[21]

Here it is clear that *hunpo* is used to mean an agent undergoing *saṃsāra*. It is interesting that in the same text we find a use of *hunpo* matching the Daoist soteriological context. In another verse of the text, the Buddha states:

> Having sexual desire, one commits impure activities,
> and so becomes confused and loses the right way.
> [As a result,] his *jingshen* and *hunpo* run away;
> his vitality gets hurt and so he dies early.[22]

In particular, 'His vitality gets hurt and he dies early' 傷命而早夭 in the above quotation is a critical Daoist concern, being expressed in typical Daoist terms; furthermore, *jingshen* 精神 and *hunpo* 魂魄 appear to be something that can be condensed or scattered according to the proper or improper conduct of life, as frequently described in Daoist texts. These

---

20. 若復有人誦持此經, ... 亦復不為諸鬼所持奪其魂魄. 設已奪者, 還復如故 (T449.14.403a4–18).
21. 身爛還為土 魂魄隨因緣 吾用畏是故 學道昇泥洹 (T581.14.966a21–22).
22. 婬為不淨行 迷惑失正道 精神魂魄馳 傷命而早夭 (T581.14.965b17–18). Here *jingshen* 精神 and *hunpo* 魂魄 appear to be juxtaposed as two synonyms, actually designating the same entity. In canonical translations, we witness several occurrences of the juxtaposition *jingshenhunpo* 精神魂魄 or *hunpojingshen* 魂魄精神 in this synonymous sense.

uses of *hunpo* mean that the translator correctly understood the Daoist concept of *hunpo* and added a new sense of the agent in *saṃsāra* to that concept, being unaware that the new sense is indeed anti-Buddhist in the Indian sense.

HUNLING 魂靈

Ling 靈 originally meant 'a shaman' as a noun, and 'mystic' as an adjective, and later it came popularly to designate a soul or deity. In canonical translations the compound *linghun* in most cases indicates a soul going through *saṃsāra*. For example, in T152 **(Ṣaṭ)pāramitā-samāsa* 六度集經 (tr. Kang Senghui), a practitioner meditates on dependent origination: 'Since this occurs, that occurs; if this does not occur, that does not occur. Once birth occurs, the troubles of ageing and death must occur. However, *hunling* does not perish but receives [another] body again. If there is no birth, there is no ageing; if there is no ageing, there is no death.'[23] Doubtless, the sentence, 'However, *hunling* does not perish but receives [another] body again,' is an arbitrary insertion of the translator's own view.

Sporadically, we find *hunling* also being used to designate *vijñāna*, etc., not necessarily indicating an agent in *saṃsāra*. T76 *Brahmāyus-sūtra* 梵摩渝經 (tr. Zhi Qian) translates Brahmāyus's questioning of the Buddha: 'Saint, did you cross over [*saṃsāra*] and abide in *nirvāṇa*, leaving the three realms forever? As for your mind (*citta*), thought (*manas*), consciousness (*vijñāna*) and *hunling*, did you extinguish all suffering?'[24] Considering the normal use of the triplet of *citta*, *manas* and *vijñana* in Indian Buddhist scriptures, *hunling* appears not to be a translating word but an annotative insertion by the translator. More interestingly, the aforementioned T212 **Udānavarga-nidāna* states: 'At death, *shen* moves [to another body]. The wind-element leaves [first], and then the fire-element. [Then] *hunling* scatters.'[25] Here, *hunling* is described as an entity that scatters after death, as in philosophical Daoist texts. Furthermore, in this particular case, *shen* and *hunling* appear to

---

23. 有是即得是， 無是不得是． 夫生必有老死之患， 魂靈不滅即更受身． 不生即無老，不老即無死 (T152.3.40c9–12).
24. 仙度處泥洹 永離三界不 心意識魂靈 能滅衆苦不 (T76.1.885b2–3). As for the Sanskrit words *citta* and *manas*, I would translate them respectively as 'thought' and 'mind'. However, when it comes to the Chinese words 心 (for *citta*) and 意 (*manas*), I prefer translating them respectively as 'mind' and 'thought'.
25. 死為神徙, 風去火次, 魂靈散矣 (T212.4.725c18). We find the expression '*hunling* scatters' 魂靈散 also in T609 *Chanyao jing* 禪要經 (tr. anon.; 15.238c22).

be different entities: the former moves to another body, but the latter scatters and is dissipated.

HUNSHEN 魂神

With a few exceptions,[26] *hunshen* almost exclusively indicates an agent in *saṃsāra*. For example, T493 *Anan sishi jing* 阿難四事經 (tr. Zhi Qian) states:

> In the beginning of one's birth, *hunshen* comes [into the body] from the sky. Depending on the parents' *qi* 氣 [that originated from] sexual desire, it forms its own body. It stays in the mother's abdomen for ten months and then is born. Obtaining parents in delight, it comes to be able to maintain life. However, it suffers harsh days of worry and anger. [The body] dies after extreme distress. However, *hunshen* does not perish, but seeks another body.[27]

Along with *hunpo* 魂魄 and *jingshen* 精神, *hunshen* is the rendering that is most frequently adopted to designate an imperishable soul in Chinese Buddhist translations.

I have mentioned that in T417, a work by Lokakṣema, we find the term *shihunshen* 識魂神, in which *shi* (識, *vijñāna*) is annotated by *hunshen* (see p. 184). That same translator uses *hunshen* in the sense of an agent in *saṃsāra* in T362 (Larger) *Sukhāvatī-vyūha* 阿彌陀三耶三佛薩樓佛檀過度人道經: 'Therefore, it naturally happens that, when such beings as hell beings, animals, ghosts, birds and worms change bodily form and move to other bad destinations (*durgati*), their *hunshen* 魂神 and *jingshi* (精識: lit. pure consciousness) of long or short lifespan naturally enter the destination and dwell in a womb in a [new] form.'[28] In

26. At T397.13.236a18, T417.13.899b4, T418.13.905b17, T492A.14.753a21, T495.14.758b26 and T905.18.909c12, *hunshen* is used as an agent of thought with no necessary implication of the agent in *saṃsāra*.
27. 人初來生，　魂神空來，　依因二親情欲之氣，　以成己體．　在母腹中，　十月乃生．得親喜悅，　可得全命．　愁忿之日，　即切絕之，　困極乃終．　魂神不滅，　復更求身 (T493.14.757a14–17).
28. 故有自然泥犁・禽獸・薜荔・蜎飛・蠕動之類, 轉貿身形, 改惡易道, 壽命短長魂神精識, 自然入趣, 受形寄胎 (T362.12.313c19–21). T361 無量清淨平等覺經 is a revised translation by Zhi Qian of T362. At T361.12.295c15, Zhi Qian uses *hunshenmingjing* 魂神命精 instead of *hunshenjingshi* 魂神精識. *Mingjing* 命精 implies pure vitality, whereas *jingshi* 精識 implies pure consciousness. No version of the Sanskrit Larger *Sukhāvatī-vyūha* ([Sukh(L)_Sch] from the Schöyen collection and [Sukh(L)_A] from the Nepali manuscripts) includes a part corresponding to these sentences in T362 and T361.

this case, we can read that *jingshi* (lit. pure consciousness) and *hunshen* are juxtaposed as synonyms in an explanatory way.

JINGSHEN 精神

Jingshen had frequently been used in philosophical Daoist texts as a technical term to indicate the mental agent of thought or the quintessence of the mind; Buddhist translators also kept this sense in their works. For example, in T7 *Mahāparinirvāṇa-sūtra* 大般涅槃經, Faxian (法顯: fl. 413) translates:

> ... Although King Sudarśana possessed 84,000 mansions embellished with jewels, no more than one room [was needed] for the king to stay in. What was needed for his body was merely enough food. However, engaging himself in thinking about [ruling] the world, the king tied his mind to physical affairs. He exhausted his *jingshen* in vain and there was no benefit to his own body.[29]

Here, the expression 'exhausted his *jingshen* in vain and there was no benefit to his own body' is extremely Daoist in character.

In most cases where it indicates a permanent agent in *saṃsāra*, *jingshen* is not a rendering of a specific Indian term, but an arbitrary insertion by translators. Such a use is well illustrated in the example that I quoted at the beginning of this book (see Introduction, notes 1 and 3).

SHISHEN 識神

I have quoted a passage from T1 *Dīrghāgama* in which *jīva*, in the sense of *jīvātman*, is rendered as *shen* (see note 10). In Kumāra Kassapa's refutation, T1 uses also *shishen* 識神 in order to render *jīva*.[30] Here *shishen* is the compound of *shi* 識 and *shen* 神. Given that *shi* alone has been the standard rendering of *vijñāna* from the beginning of Buddhist translation, this implies that the Chinese Buddhists who assumed the existence of an imperishable soul thought that *vijñāna* was the entity to be signified by the Chinese term *shen*. While making this identification, the Chinese translators and readers appear to have been unaware that their view was similar to that of the monk Sāti, who was severely reproached by the Buddha in the *Mahātaṅhā-saṅkhaya-sutta*.

---

29. ... 雕飾寶殿, 八萬四千, 王之所處, 不過一室. 身之所須, 飽足而已. 而王役慮四方, 纏心物務, 徒勞精神, 於身無益 (T7.1.203a2–5). No extant Sanskrit or Pali text (MPS, MPP and MSD) includes a part corresponding to this paragraph in T7.
30. 汝諸眷屬見汝識神有出入不 (T1.1.44a22–23). *'api nu tā tumhaṃ jīvaṃ passanti pavisantaṃ vā nikkhamantaṃ vā?' ti* (D.II.333_25–26).

Buddhist translators in China frequently used *shen* and *jingshen* to render *vijñāna* as the third factor in the twelvefold dependent origination, when interpreted as twofold karmic causation in three lives, i.e., the first consciousness that enters the womb of the expectant mother (see note 14). Moreover, according to early Buddhism and Abhidharma Buddhism, a Buddha or an *arhat* has a last consciousness at the moment of entering the *nirvāṇa* without residue (*nirupadhiśeṣanirvāṇa*), but this is not followed by a first consciousness in the next life. *Shishen* is frequently used to render *vijñāna* in this sense. Therefore, in the *Vakkali-sutta* of the *Saṃyutta-nikāya*, when pointing out the cloud of smoke surrounding the body of the *arhat* Vakkali, who has just committed suicide to avoid the pain of illness, the Buddha announces:

> Monks, this [cloud] is Māra, the evil one, who is looking for the high-born Vakkali's consciousness: 'Where is the high-born Vakkali's consciousness grounded?' However, without his consciousness being grounded anywhere, the high-born Vakkali has entered *nirvāṇa*.[31]

The corresponding T99 *Saṃyuktāgama* (tr. Guṇabhadra in c. 435) translates the passage as follows:

> The Buddha announced to the monks: 'This is the token of evil Māra who is surrounding [the body] and looking for the high-born Vakkali's *shishen*: "Where will it be born?" ' The Buddha announced to the monks: 'The high-born Vakkali committed suicide with a knife, without a remaining *shishen*.'[32]

T99 is a complete translation of a Sarvāstivāda *Saṃyuktāgama*.[33] There *vijñāna* is consistently rendered merely as *shi* 識, except for the four occurrences of *shishen* for *vijñāna*: two of these occur in the above quotation, and the other two occur at T99.2.286b11–17,[34]

---

31. *'eso kho, bhikkhave, Māro pāpimā Vakkalissa kulaputtassa viññāṇam samannesati: 'kattha Vakkalissa kulaputtassa viññāṇam patiṭṭhitan?' ti. apatiṭṭhitena ca, bhikkhave, viññāṇena Vakkali kulaputto parinibbuto' ti* (S.III.124_9–13).
32. 佛告諸比丘: '此是惡魔之像, 周匝求覓跋迦梨善男子識神當生何處.' 佛告諸比丘: '跋迦梨善男子不住識神, 以刀自殺' (T99.2.347b8–11).
33. For this sectarian affiliation, refer to Waldschmidt (1980, pp. 146–7), Mayeda (1985, p. 99) and Willemen (1998, p.8, n.43).
34. 佛告比丘: '此是惡魔波旬, 於瞿低迦善男子身側, 周匝求其識神. 然比丘瞿低迦, 以不住心, 執刀自殺.' 爾時, 世尊為瞿低迦比丘, 受第一記. 爾時, 波旬而說偈言: 上下及諸方 遍求彼識神 都不見其處 瞿低何所之.

which corresponds to the *Godhika-sutta* (S.I.122_10–18).[35] There too Māra looks for the consciousness of the *arhat* Godhika, who has just committed suicide. In the course of translation, some Chinese assistants of Guṇabhadra, who himself barely spoke Chinese (see p. 10), may have read a special implication of *vijñāna* into these specific cases and added *shen* after *shi* to emphasize that special implication, while none of them was seriously aware of the different implications of the Indian term *vijñāna* and the Chinese term *shen*.

SHENSHI 神識

Shishen 識神 and *shenshi* 神識 are combinations of the same terms *shi* 識 and *shen* 神 in a different order, and the two combinations indeed designate the same object, the agent of thought and/or the agent in *saṃsāra*. For example, while T99.2.286b11–17 renders the *vijñāna* of S.I.122_10–18 as *shishen* (see notes 34 and 35), the corresponding T100.2.383a9–15[36] and T125.2.643a7–11[37] render it as *shenshi*. The virtual identity in meaning between *shishen* and *shenshi* in turn strengthens the identification of *shen* as *shi* by some Chinese Buddhist translators. As discussed in the previous chapter, the Daoist concept of *shen* is distinct from the Indian Buddhist concept of *vijñāna*. However, we now witness that the Chinese Buddhists adopted and revised the

---

35. *'eso kho, bhikkhave, Māro pāpimā Godhikassa kulaputtassa viññāṇaṃ samanvesati: 'kattha Godhikassa kulaputtassa viññāṇaṃ patiṭṭhitan?' ti. appatiṭṭhitena ca, bhikkhave, viññāṇena Godhiko kulaputto parinibbuto' ti. atha kho Māro pāpimā beluvapaṭṭuvīṇam ādāya yena Bhagavā ten' upasaṃkami, upasaṅkamitvā gāthāya ajjhabhāsi:*

    uddham adho ca tiriyaṃ disânudisāsv aham
    anvesaṃ nâdhigacchāmi: Godhiko so kuhiṃ gato ti.

36. 佛告比丘: '求 比丘, 以入涅槃, 無有神識, 無所至方.' 爾時, 魔王化形摩納, 而說偈言: 上下及四方 推求求 識 莫知所至方 神識竟何趣
The translator and translation date of T100 *Saṃyuktāgama* in 16 fascs. are unknown. There is a view that T100 is a work of the Mahīśāsakas or the Dharmaguptakas (Mayeda, 1985, pp. 100–1); however, as Waldschmidt (1980, pp. 146–8) pointed out, it appears that T100 is in the tradition of the Sarvāstivāda, like T99.
37. 世尊告曰: '此弊魔波旬, 欲得知婆迦梨神識所在.' 是時, 尊者阿難白世尊曰: '唯願世尊, 說婆迦梨比丘神識為何所在!' 世尊告曰: '婆迦梨比丘神識, 永無所著. 彼族姓子, 以般涅槃. 當作如是持!'
The translatorship of T125 *Ekottarāgama* has been disputed in the East Asian Buddhist tradition. Some Buddhist catalogues attribute it to Dharmanandi 曇摩難提 (fl. 384–91), but others to Saṃghadeva 僧伽提婆 (fl. 383–401). For more information, see Chap. 8, note 16.

concept of *shen* to designate the agent of thought and/or the agent in *saṃsāra*; furthermore, they identified *shen* as *shi*, which is the standard rendering for *vijñāna*. In short, we witness that, although the monk Sāti's view was strongly rejected by Indian Buddhists, it was accepted as orthodox by some Chinese Buddhists.

The single occurrence of *shenshi* in T99 *Saṃyuktāgama* is noteworthy. In the *Mahānāmasutta* of the *Saṃyutta-nikāya*, the Buddha comforts the Śākya Mahānāma, who is concerned about his lack of progress in practice and his destination (*gati*) after death:

> [...] Crows, vultures, hawks, dogs, jackals or various other animals eat it (i.e., your body). However, his mind, which has been trained for a long time by faith, precepts, learning, donation [and wisdom], ascends and goes to an excellent [destination].[38]

The corresponding part of T99 translates:

> After death, this body may be burnt on a fire or thrown in a cemetery. Being rolled about by wind and exposed to sunlight, it finally becomes dust. However, if the mind, thought and consciousness are permeated for a long time with righteous faith, precepts, donation, learning and wisdom, the *shenshi* ascends towards a pleasant place. He will be born in a heaven.[39]

There are numerous occurrences of *citta, manas* or *vijñāṇa* in the *Saṃyutta-nikāya*; however, regularly rendering it as *xin* (心: mind), *yi* (意: thought) or *shi* (識: consciousness), except for the four occurrences of *shishen* 識神 for *vijñāna* (see notes 32 and 34), the translator renders it as *shenshi* 神識 only in this passage. Furthermore, the relative pronoun structure in the Pali text (*yañ cittam ..., tam*) tells us that *xinyishi* is probably rendering *yañ citta-mano-vijñānam* (or *yañ cittam api mano 'pi vijñānam api*), whereas *shenshi* renders *tam* in the original text. In other words, the translator kindly provides readers with the explanation that these Indian Buddhist concepts of *citta*, etc., are identical to the Chinese Buddhist concept of *shenshi*.

---

38. ... *tam idh' eva kākā vā khādanti, gijjhā vā khādanti, kulalā vā khādanti, sunakhā vā khādanti, sigālā vā khādanti, vividhā vā pāṇakajātā khādanti. yañ ca khv' assa cittaṃ dīgharattaṃ saddhāparibhāvitaṃ sīla-suta-cāga-[paññā]paribhāvitaṃ, tam uddhagāmi hoti visesagāmi* (S.V.370_2–7). *Paññāparibhāvitaṃ* appears in the immediately preceding paragraph, so it must appear here also.
39. 若命終時， 此身若火燒， 若棄塚間， 風飄日曝， 久成塵末. 而心・意・識， 久遠長夜， 正信所熏， 戒・施・聞・慧所熏， 神識上昇， 向安樂處， 未來生天 (T99.2.237c3–7).

HUNSHI 魂識

As discussed above, *shi* 識 is usually combined with *shen* in order to indicate the agent of thought and/or the agent in *saṃsāra*. However, it is sporadically also combined with *hun* 魂, as in *hunshi* 魂識. Since *hun* is synonymous with *shen* 神, *hunshi* is also synonymous with *shenshi* 神識 or *shishen* 識神. Hence, as with *shenshi* and *shishen*, it is also used as a rendering for *vijñāna*. For example, in T184 *Xiuxing benqi jing* 修行本起經, an early version of the Buddha's biography, Kang Mengxiang 康孟詳 (fl. 194–9) and Zhu Dali 竺大力 render *vijñāna* as *hunshi*.[40] Unsurprisingly, it is also used to indicate an agent in *saṃsāra*, e.g., '[the monkey] immediately died, and its *hunshi* was conceived in a teacher's family.'[41]

THE REJECTION OF AN IMPERISHABLE SOUL IN THE TRANSLATIONS

As mentioned in Part I, the Chinese Buddhist translation procedure was a process of conversation between many experts from various fields: Indian Buddhist experts provided the basic materials, while bilingual experts did the translation, Chinese literary experts embellished it, Buddhist doctrinal experts checked its doctrinal consistency, and so forth. This unique structure of the Chinese Buddhist translation procedure made it possible for some of its members to interpolate the idea of the imperishable soul, since the Indian experts were unaware of its controversial implications and the doctrinal experts could not detect the serious problems that would result from such interpolations.

However, the procedure also had a system for preventing arbitrary interpolations or controversial adaptations. Some bilingual experts could draw attention to how implications differed between the original terms and their Chinese renderings, and doctrinal experts could point out the inconsistencies which such interpolations or adaptations introduced into the Buddhist doctrinal system. Indeed, as time passed, the Chinese Buddhists' understanding of Indian Buddhism advanced, and this cooperative system of translation became strengthened and

40. 一色像，二痛痒，三思想，四行作，五魂識 (T184.3.471c20–22). T185 *Taizi ruiying benqi jing* 太子瑞應本起經 is a retranslation by Zhi Qian of T184; there (3.478b7–8), Zhi Qian preserves this passage unchanged.

41. 即便命終，魂識受胎於師質家 (T202.4.430a16–17). T202 **Damamūka-nidāna* 賢愚經 was translated by Tanxue weide 曇學威德 and Huijue 慧覺 in 445.

operated more efficiently. As I shall demonstrate in the following chapter, only in the period of archaic translation or in the earliest phase of old translation did the major Buddhist translators add interpolations about an imperishable soul. After that time, we find such interpolations only in the works of minor translators, who did not have sufficient financial support or expertise, and in the Chinese apocrypha.

It appears to be Saṃghadeva and Kumārajīva who created the turning point after which the interpolations of an imperishable soul gradually disappear from Buddhist translations. The Kashmiri Saṃghadeva arrived at Changan 長安 during the reign of Jianyuan 建元 (365–84) of the Former Qin 前秦 dynasty. According to CSZJJ (T2145.55.99b29–100a6 and 63c22–64a28), T26 *Madhyamāgama* was recited by Saṃgharakṣa and translated by Saṃghadeva during 397–98, and proof-read and published in 401. There, while translating *anātman* as *wuwo* 無我 or *feiwo* 非我, Saṃghadeva translates *ātman* in the Brahmanic sense as *shen* 神. For example, while the *Alagaddūpama-sutta* in the *Majjhima-nikāya* states, 'With regard to form (*rūpa*), he sees: "This is not mine, I am not this, and this is not my self",'[42] T26 says, 'All kinds of form, ... all of them are not mine, I am not their belonging, and [they] are not *shen*.'[43] Here, translating *ātman* as *shen*, Saṃghadeva appears to warn the Chinese Buddhists that such concepts as *shen*, prevalent in the Chinese Buddhist literature, are in fact anti-Buddhist.

The great translator Kumārajīva (344–413?) arrived at Changan in 401, and thereafter engaged in Buddhist translation for about ten years. In all his translations, he renders *ātman* in the Brahmanic sense as *shen* 神. Since his translations have been immensely influential among Chinese Buddhists, his identification of *shen* as the Brahmanic *ātman* must have been a sharp warning to them. For example, in his translation of the *Madhyamaka-kārikā*, with the commentary by Piṅgala 青目, he translates *ātman* as *shen* or *wo* (我: I).[44] Given that *shen* had not been used

---

42. *rūpaṃ 'n' etaṃ mama, n' eso 'ham asmi, na m' eso attā' ti samanupassati* (M.I.136).

43. 比丘者，所有色，... 彼一切非我有，我非彼有，亦非是神. 如是慧觀，知其如真 (1.764c15–18).

44. We can find only two instances of the rendering of *shen* for the Brahmanic *ātman* in the translation of the *Kārikā* (§§9.9–10). (Among them, §9.10 does not have *ātman* in the extant Sanskrit *Kārikā*. The term *shen* may have been inserted by the translator.) However, in the translation of the commentary, the use of *shen* prevails. For example, for the translation of *ātman* in §18.1 of the *Kārikā*, he uses *wo*, but for the translation of its commentary part he uses

as a term for translating *ātman* but is a peculiar Chinese term for interpretations or adaptations, and that *wo* had been the standard rendering of *ātman* prior to his arrival, it appears probable that Kumārajīva found the term *shen* being widely misused among the Chinese Buddhists, and felt that it was necessary to issue a warning that the anti-Buddhist concept *shen* must be rejected.

Sengrui 僧叡, the aforementioned disciple of Kumārajīva, criticizes the situation prior to the arrival of Kumārajīva as follows:

> The previously produced Chinese translations seldom mention the emptiness of the nature of *shishen* 識神 (i.e., *vijñāna*), but frequently mention the existence of *shen*. [It was because the translations of] the *Madhyamaka-śāstra* and the *Śata-śāstra* had not yet been produced [by Kumārajīva] in China. Having no reliable mirror [of truth], who would be able to correct it?[45]

Sengrui attributes the disappearance of the misuse of *shen* to the contribution by Kumārajīva, and this attribution appears to be fair.

---

shen. The reason for the different renderings is unclear, and we have no Indian version of this commentary.

45. 此土先出諸經，於識神性空，明言處少；存神之文，其處甚多.《中》·《百》二論文未及此，又無通鑒，誰與正之? (T2145.55.59a5–7).

Chapter 8

A SURVEY OF INTERPOLATIONS AND ADAPTATIONS OF AN AGENT IN *SAṂSĀRA*

In this chapter, by surveying the interpolations and adaptations that reflect the idea of an imperishable soul, I aim to shed light on the chronological development of the Chinese idea of an imperishable soul at the canonical level. The following discussions are based on the chronological survey presented in the Appendix.

THE PERIOD OF ARCHAIC TRANSLATION (FROM THE MID-SECOND CENTURY TO 375)

An Shigao 安世高 (fl. 148–71), who probably came from Parthia, is the first Buddhist translator in China who is known to us. He arrived in China around 147–48;[1] the exact years of his birth and death are unknown.[2] CSZJJ records thirty-five translations of his, with the information that only twenty-eight of these texts were extant at that time. The number of translations attributed to An Shigao increased to 176 in LDSBJ (T2034.49.49c), and T attributes fifty-five extant texts to him. Zürcher (1991) attested sixteen extant texts as his work (see p. 41 above): T13, T14, T31, T32, T36, T48, T57, T98, T112, T150, T602, T603, T605, T607, T792 and T1508.

1. CSZJJ (T2145.55.95a18–19) states that he arrived in China at the beginning of Emperor Huan's 桓帝 reign (147–67); quoting Daoan's catalogue, GSZ (T2059.50.324a24–25) specifies that he was engaged in Buddhist translation for more than twenty years, from 148. KYL (T2154.55.481c3–5) and ZYL (T2157.55.778c18–19) present more details: he was engaged in translation from 148 to 170.
2. Ui (1971, p. 15) estimates that he lived approximately from 117 to 180.

Among the 16 texts, we cannot find a single use of the seven critical compounds. The only adaptation implying an imperishable soul that I could find is the use of *shen* as the agent in *saṃsāra* in T607 **Yogācārabhūmi* (see Chap. 7, note 13). In T607, we also find him rendering, probably, *vijñāna* as *jingshi* 精識. Although *jingshi* is frequently used synonymously with *jingshen* 精神, and although it is used in the context of the continuous process between life and death, we cannot read a necessary implication of an imperishable soul in this specific case:

> Immediately, *jingshi* 精識 perishes in the body, and there are intermediate aggregations. It is just as if one arm of a scale goes up while the other goes down. In this way, a person abandons the dead body and receives the seed of birth, just as, when seeds are sown, stalks grow up from the roots. In this way, in that intermediate period, as soon as the [last] consciousness (*shi* 識) perishes, there occur the five intermediate aggregates without deficiency. It is neither that the [very] aggregates of the dead individual continue to be the five intermediate aggregates, nor that there occur the intermediate five aggregates independent of the five aggregates of the dead individual. Due to the five aggregates of the dead individual, there occur the intermediate five aggregates.[3]

Here, instead of being an imperishable agent in *saṃsāra*, *jingshi* is clearly described as an impermanent existence, although it is unclear why it is rendered as *jingshi* rather than the standard rendering of *shi* only in this context. Traditionally, T151, T729, T732 and T492b are attributed to An Shigao, and they include some terms indicating the agent in *saṃsāra*. However, these attributions are rather dubious. In general, we may say that An Shigao (and his team) did not utilize terms indicating an imperishable agent in *saṃsāra*.

Lokakṣema 支婁迦讖 (fl. 178–89) is the first Mahāyāna translator known to us. His patronymic Zhi indicates his origin from Yuezhi 月支.[4] CSZJJ (T2145.55.95c23–96a7) states that he arrived at Luoyang 洛陽 about the end of Emperor Huan's reign (147–67), whereas GSZ (T2059.50.324b13–21) locates his arrival during Emperor Ling's 靈帝 reign (168–88). His translations T224 *Aṣṭasāhasrikāprajñapāramitā sūtra* and T362 (Larger) *Sukhāvatī-vyūha* had a deep influence on the development of Chinese Buddhism, whose mainstream has been Mahāyāna. CSZJJ

3. 即時身精識滅, 中便有陰, 譬如稱一上一下. 如是捨死, 受生種, 譬如種禾根生雙. 如是中時, 滅識即時, 中生五陰, 具足不少. 死陰亦不中得五陰往, 亦不離死五陰為有中五陰. 有但死五陰故, 中五陰生 (T607.15.233b26–c2).
4. Ui (1971, p. 472) identifies 'Yuezhi' with the Greater Yuezhi.

lists fourteen translations by him, and LDSBJ twenty-one. As mentioned above, the colophons to T224 and T418 **Pratyutpanna-buddha-saṃmukhâvasthita-samādhi-sūtra* 般舟三昧經 provide us with precious information about the structure of the Buddhist translation teams in that embryonic period. Referring to Zürcher's previous research (1991, pp. 298–300), Harrison (1993, pp. 141–68; 1998, 556–7) attests ten extant translations as probable works of his: T224, T280, T313, T350, T418, T458, T626, T807, and (with caution) T624 and T362.

In T362, Lokakṣema uses *hunshen* 魂神 and *jingshi* 精識 in the sense of an agent in *saṃsāra* (see Chap. 7, note 28). We also find *hunshen* used as the annotative ending to *shi* (for *vijñāna*), forming the compound *shihunshen* in T418 (see p. 184). In T362, we find *jingshen* 精神 used in the sense of the agent of thought (12.312b3), but we cannot detect any necessary implication of an agent in *saṃsāra* there. Considering the number of translations by Lokakṣema, interpolations indicating an agent in *saṃsāra* may be ignored as rare exceptions. In short, during this first phase of Chinese Buddhist translation, started by An Shigao and Lokakṣema, we seldom find interpolations reflecting an imperishable soul.

T184 *Xiuxing benqi jing* 修行本起經 is the first half and T196 *Zhong benqi jing* 中本起經 the second half of a version of the Buddha's biography. Following Daoan's (道安: ?–385) catalogue, CSZJJ (T2145.55.16c18) classifies T184 as an anonymous work and attributes T196 to Kang Mengxiang 康孟詳 (fl. 194–99). Zürcher (1991, p. 299) attributes both T184 and T196 to the group of two or possibly three translators: Kang Mengxiang, *Mahābala 竺大力, and *Dharmaphala 竺曇果.[5] The author of T184 appears to be the first translator who systematically utilized terms indicating an agent in *saṃsāra*. In T184, we find *hunling* 魂靈 once, *hunshen* 魂神 twice, *jingshen* 精神 seven times and *shenshi* 神識 once, all used in the sense of an agent in *saṃsāra*.[6] For example, T184 describes the Bodhisattva's attainment of the heavenly eye (*divya-cakṣus*):

> [He] sees other people's *hunshen* being born in [one of] the five destinations (*gati*) according to their own [past] actions: some fall into hells, some fall into [the world of] animals, some become ghosts, some are

5. For the characteristics of the translation work by Kang Mengxiang and his colleagues, see Zürcher (1991, p.284).
6. More research is required into why we cannot find any use of the seven critical terms in T196, unlike in T184.

> born in heavens, some enter a human body; some are born into noble and rich families, and some into mean and poor families.[7]

Here, from many Indian sources, we can infer that *hunshen* may be the rendering of *sattva*. Encountering *sattva*, learned Indian Buddhist readers may read that this temporary compound of impermanent aggregates is succeeded by another compound of aggregates; however, encountering the above Chinese translation, learned readers with a Chinese educational background may envisage that *hunshen*, the essence of a self or the agent of thought, transfers from this body to another body. In this sense, it is a controversial adaptation.

It is noteworthy that the above passages are inherited with no change in the retranslations of the Buddha's biography: T185 *Taizi ruiying benqi jing* 太子瑞應本起經 (3.478b3–6) by Zhi Qian and T186 *Lalitavistara* 普曜經 (3.522a29–b3) by Zhu Fahu, who may be counted as the two most important figures for the dissemination of the idea of an imperishable soul.

The life of **Zhi Qian** 支謙 (fl. 222–53) and the previous research on his work were introduced at pp. 38 f. Also, for the provisional list of his 'authentic' work and candidate texts, see Table 2.3. Among the twenty-five 'authentic' works, we find Zhi Qian interpolating the idea of an imperishable soul in the following eleven translations: T5, T87, T185, T198, T210, T361, T493, T556, T581, T735 and T790. In these texts, he uses six of the seven critical compounds, all but *shenshi* 神識; of the six compounds, he favours *hunshen* 魂神 and *jingshen* 精神. We also find such interpolations in the following three candidate translations: T6, T20 and T507. In addition, T530 **Sumatī-sūtra* 須摩提長者經 and T555B *Wumuzi jing* 五母子經 are traditionally attributed to Zhi Qian, and use *jingshen* and *linghun* respectively to indicate an agent in *saṃsāra*. However, these two attributions are uncertain.

As mentioned above, Zhi Qian did not hesitate to rephrase sentences and interpolate certain words in order to facilitate his Chinese readers' understanding. While his predecessors inserted the concept of an agent in *saṃsāra* by interpolating the term *shen*, etc., Zhi Qian composed creative explanations in addition to the mere use of terms. For example, in the aforementioned T184 *Xiuxing benqi jing* 修行本起經, the authors, Kang Mengxiang *et al.*, translate a servant's explanation of death to the Bodhisattva Siddhārtha as follows:

7. 見人魂神，各自隨行，生五道中：或墮地獄，或墮畜生，或作鬼神，或生天上，或入人形；有生豪貴富樂家者，有生卑鄙貧賤家者 (T184.3471c17–20).

> Death means exhaustion; *jingshen* will leave [this body then]. [At the moment of death,] the four great elements are going to scatter, and *hunshen* becomes unstable. Since wind leaves, breathing halts; since fire is extinguished, the body becomes cold. Wind [leaves] first, fire [goes out] next, and [then] *hunling* will leave. ...[8]

Here, *jingshen*, *hunshen* and *hunling* might be the rendering of *vijñāna*, etc. However, in the aforementioned T185, a retranslation of T184, probably from a new original, Zhi Qian translates the Bodhisattva's utterance, which follows the above explanation of the servant, but is not included in T184:

> How painful death would be! *Jingshen* must be at a loss. Once there is birth, this suffering of ageing, sickness and death must follow. Although everyone is in a fever to [attain worldly benefits], death is impending and reaches him or her. Is it not painful? I see that, although the body of the dead decays and disappears, *shen* does not perish.[9]

Here, the last sentence, 'I see that, although the body of the dead decays and disappears, *shen* does not perish,' must be a creative insertion by Zhi Qian.[10]

Kang Senghui 康僧會 (?–280) is a keen successor of Zhi Qian in the utilization of an imperishable soul. (For a brief biography, see pp. 53–4.) His translation T152 **(ṣaṭ)pāramitā-samāsa* 六度集經 has the same renderings and writing style as Zhi Qian's works. In T152, Kang Senghui uses *hunling* 魂靈 sixteen times and *hunshen* 魂神 twice in the sense of an agent in *saṃsāra*.[11] At T152.3.40c10–11, he also arbitrarily inserts the expression '*Hunling* does not perish' 魂靈不滅, as did Zhi Qian. T206 *Jiu za piyu jing* 舊雜譬喻經 has traditionally been attributed to Kang and uses *hunshen* twice as an agent in *saṃsāra*; however, this attribution is uncertain.

Zhu Fahu 竺法護 (fl. 266–308) also owes much to Zhi Qian in his insertion of the idea of an imperishable *shen*. (For a brief biography, see p. 57.) T attributes 95 extant translations to him, 75 of which are listed

8. 死者盡也，精神去矣. 四大欲散，魂神不安，風去息絕，火滅身冷，風先火次，魂靈去矣 (T184.3.467a7–9).
9. 夫死痛矣! 精神劇矣! 生當有此老病死苦. 莫不熱中，迫而就之，不亦苦乎? 吾見死者, 形壞體化, 而神不滅 (T185.3.474c29–75a3).
10. In T186 *Lalitavistara* 普曜經, a retranslation of T184, Zhu Fahu maintains Zhi Qian's translation: 夫死痛矣! 精神懅矣! 生當有此老病死苦. 莫不熱中, 迫而就之, 不亦苦乎? 吾見死者, 形壞體化, 而神不滅 (3.503a28–b2).
11. There the use of *shishen* 識神 on three occasions does not necessarily indicate an agent in *saṃsāra*.

in CSZJJ. Kawano (1986) provides a list of the 40 *sūtras* whose dates of translation are recorded in the Buddhist catalogues (CSZJJ, FJL, LDSBJ, YCL and KYL), and Suzuki (1995) suggests another list of 40 texts that are certainly attributable to Zhu Fahu (see Table 2.4), as attested by epilogues, colophons and the Buddhist catalogues. Awaiting further research by experts on Zhu Fahu's work, in this book I have to depend on Suzuki's list. We find that Zhu Fahu utilizes certain terms to indicate the agent in *saṃsāra* in T186 *Lalitavistara* 普曜經, the *Tathāgataguhya-sūtra* 密迹金剛力士會 (incorporated in T310 *Ratnakūṭa-sūtra* 大寶積經), T317 **Garbhāvakrāntinirdeśa-sūtra* 胞胎經, T606 **Yogācāra-bhūmi* 修行道地經 and T737 *Suoyu zhihuan jing* 所欲致患經 among Suzuki's 40 texts; we also find such terms in T288 *Dengmu pusa suowen sanmei jing* 等目菩薩所問三昧經 and T770 *Si pukede jing* 四不可得經, which are not included in Suzuki's list but attributed to Zhu Fahu by CSZJJ. In this sense, Zhu favoured *hunshen* 魂神 and *jingshen* 精神. The use of *shenshi* 神識 in Zhu Fahu's work is peculiar and confusing. In many of his translations he seldom used *shenshi* to indicate an agent in *saṃsāra*; in T186 he uses *hunshen* and *jingshen* to indicate an agent in *saṃsāra*, but uses *shenshi* to render *vijñāna*. However, when one reads his translations, *shenshi* appears to imply more meanings than does the Indian use of *vijñāna*. Further research is required to clarify his use of *shenshi*. T611 *Faguan jing* 法觀經 uses *hunshen* to indicate an agent in *saṃsāra*, and has traditionally been attributed to Zhu Fahu; however, this attribution is uncertain.

Faju 法炬 (fl. 290–311) translated T23 *Da luotan jing* 大樓炭經 and T211 **Dharmapada-nidāna* 法句譬喻經. CSZJJ specifies that **Fali** 法立 co-translated T211 with him. In these two translations, they use *hunpo, hunshen, jingshen* and *shenshi* to indicate an agent in *saṃsāra*. T500 *Luoyun renru jing* 羅云忍辱經 and T501 *Shahe biqiu gongde jing* 沙曷比丘功德經 are traditionally attributed to Faju and interpolate the idea of an agent in *saṃsāra*; however, these attributions are uncertain.

In the following translations we find terms indicating an agent in *saṃsāra*, but their traditional attributions are uncertain: T46 *Analü banian jing* 阿那律八念經 attributed to Zhi Yao (支曜: fl. 185), T360 (Larger) *Sukhāvatī-vyūha* 無量壽經 to Saṃghavarman (康僧鎧: fl. 252), T17 *Śṛgālāvavāda-sūtra* 善生子經 to Zhi Fadu (支法度: fl. 301), and T1331 *Guanding jing* 灌頂經 to Śrīmitra (帛尸梨蜜多羅: fl. 317–22).

THE PERIOD OF OLD TRANSLATION (376–617)

Zhu Fonian 竺佛念 (fl. 373–413) was of Chinese origin (from Liangzhou 涼州), despite his patronym Zhu (竺: India). During the Jianyuan reign 建元 (365–85), two foreign monks, Saṃghabhūti 僧伽跋澄 and Dharmanandi 曇摩難提, arrived at Changan, and Zhu Fonian helped with their translation. As I mentioned in Chapter 1, it was the convention to attribute translations to foreign monks even when they merely brought with them the original texts or recited them in the original language. For this reason, although Zhu Fonian was the actual author of many translations, some of them were attributed to foreign monks. CSZJJ attributes only six translations to him; LDSBJ attributes twelve and T thirteen extant translations. However, the colophons of some of the translations attributed to South/Central Asian monks in CSZJJ reveal that these texts are actually translations by Zhu Fonian, so I temporarily regard the following thirteen translations as his: T1, T194, T212, T226, T309, T384, T385, T656, T1464, T1505, T1543, T1549 and T2045.[12]

He uses terms indicating an agent in *saṃsāra* in T1, T212, T309, T384, T385 and T656 among the thirteen texts; and his favourite renderings were *shishen* 識神 and *shenshi* 神識. This denotes that he may have regarded consciousness (識, *vijñāna*) as the nature of the saṃsāric agent. Hence, in T212 **Udānavarga-nidāna*, in translating the story of Māra searching for the location of the monk Godhika's consciousness (see Chap. 7, note 35), he renders *vijñāna* as *shen* 神 and *shenshi* 神識.[13] In another story in T212, he translates, 'Once a person is born, the person is bound to age. Death is also dependent on birth. Living beings drift around the five destinations (*gati*) repetitively, since [their] *shenshi* moves around without stopping.'[14] He also uses *shenshi* to indicate an agent of thought: '[His or her] *shenshi* becomes confused and their minds are distressed.'[15]

---

12. T125 *Ekottarāgama* may also be a translation by Zhu Fonian with the recitation of Dharmanandi, according to my discussion about its relationship with Saṃghadeva. However, since the translatorship remains debated, I temporarily exclude it from his works here.
13. 是時, 弊魔波旬, 馳奔四面, 求覓: 比丘神為生何處? 不知神所生之處. 往至問佛: '奔趣四方, 求覓神識, 不能知處. 求覓拘提, 亦不知處' (T212.4.647b6–9).
14. 人有生分, 必當有老, 死亦由生. 眾生流轉迴趣五道, 亦由神識遷轉不停 (684c24–25).
15. 神識倒錯, 心意煩熱 (729a16).

Zhu Fonian appears to be the last of those major translators who left dozens of skilful translations and frequently interpolated the idea of an agent in *saṃsāra*. After Saṃghadeva (fl. 383–401) and Kumārajīva (fl. 401–13) translated the Brahmanic *ātman* as *shen* 神 or *shenwo* 神我 and highlighted its controversial implications, we seldom find such interpolations in the works of the major translators.

CSZJJ attributes six translations to **Saṃghadeva** (fl. 383–401), four of which are extant: T26, T1506, T1543 and T1550. None of these has any of the seven critical terms for an agent in *saṃsāra*; furthermore, as mentioned above (see p. 194), by rendering Brahmanic *ātman* as *shenwo* 神我 in T26 *Madhyamāgama*, he clearly refutes the Chinese adaptations that indicate an agent in *saṃsāra*. This raises a question regarding the translatorship of T125 *Ekottarāgama*, which has not been agreed among the traditional cataloguers and is still debated among contemporary scholars.[16] Interestingly, T125 has many interpolations of *shishen* and *shenshi* indicating an agent in *saṃsāra*, as favoured by Zhu Fonian. This implies that T125 *Ekottarāgama* is more probably a work of Dharmanandi and Zhu Fonian, or that, if it is indeed a work by Saṃghadeva, it is an early work of his, before he came to notice the Chinese implications of *shen*, etc., i.e., before the translation of T26 in 401.

Among the extant ones of the thirty-five works which are attributed to **Kumārajīva** in CSZJJ, only T208 *Zhongjing zhuan zapiyu* 眾經撰雜譬喻 has a single occurrence of *hunshen* 魂神, indicating an agent in *saṃsāra*;[17] none of the other seven critical terms is found in any of his translations. T35 *Hai bade jing* 海八德經 and T988 **Māyūrividyārājñī-sūtra* 孔雀王呪經, traditionally attributed to Kumārajīva, also respectively use *hunshen* and *jingshen* 精神 with the implication of a saṃsāric

16. CSZJJ attributes the translation of the *Ekottarāgama* only to Dharmanandi (assisted by Zhu Fonian), but later catalogues record both the first translation by Dharmanandi and the retranslation by Saṃghadeva. (The biographies of Saṃghadeva in CSZJJ (T2145.55.99b–100a) and GSZ (T2059.50.328c–29a) do not mention his retranslation of the *Ekottarāgama*.) While the *tripiṭaka*s of the Song, Yuan and Ming dynasties attribute the extant Chinese *Ekottarāgama* to Dharmanandi, K and T attribute it to Saṃghadeva. For discussions by contemporary scholars, see Mayeda (1985, pp. 102–3) and Ono (1936, spec. vol., pp. 78–9).

17. CSZJJ attributes the *Za piyu jing* 雜譬喻經 to Kumārajīva, and the editors of T identify it with T208. However, K does not preserve a corresponding *sūtra*. It is a new addition and attribution by the editors of T. More research is required to verify this identification.

agent; however, the attribution of these two texts to Kumārajīva remains dubious.

Buddhayaśas 佛陀耶舍 (fl. 408–15) did not use any of the seven critical terms in T1428 *Dharmaguptaka-vinaya* (in 410–12) or in T1430 *Dharmaguptaka-prātimokṣa*; however, in T1 *Dīrghāgama*, which Zhu Fonian co-translated in 413, he used *hunshen* 魂神, *jingshen* 精神 and *shenshi* 神識 to indicate an agent in *saṃsāra*. His other translation, T405 **Ākāśagarbhasūtra* 虛空藏菩薩經, uses *shenshi* 神識 once, but it does not necessarily imply an agent in *saṃsāra*. CSZJJ attributes six translations to **Faxian** 法顯 (fl. 413), five of which (T7, T367, T745, T1425 and T1427)[18] are extant. He used *jingshen* to indicate an agent in *saṃsāra* only once, in T7 *Mahāparinirvāṇa-sūtra*. CSZJJ attributes thirteen translations to **Guṇabhadra** (394–468), seven of which (T99, T120, T189, T270, T353, T670 and T678) are extant. He interpolated the idea of a saṃsāric agent only in T99 *Saṃyuktāgama* in 435.

Among the minor translators, Fazhong 法眾 (fl. 397–418) in T1339 *Da fangdeng tuoluoni jing* 大方等陀羅尼經, Zhiyan 智嚴 (350–427) and Baoyun 寶雲 (376–449) in T590 *Si tianwang jing* 四天王經, Tanxueweide 曇學威德 and Huijue 慧覺 in T202 **Damamūka-nidāna-sūtra* 賢愚經 (tr. in 445), Prajñāruci (fl. 516) in T721 **(Saddharma-) smṛtyupasthāna-sūtra* 正法念處經, Jñānayaśa (fl. 556–81) in T673 *Mahāyānābhisamaya-sūtra* 大乘同性經, Jñānagupta (523–600) in T190 **Abhiniṣkramaṇa-sūtra* 佛本行集經 and the **Bhadrapāla-sūtra* 賢護長者會 (incorporated in T310 *Ratnakūṭa-sūtra* 大寶積經), and Dharmagupta (?–619) in T449 **Bhaiṣajyaguru-pūrvapraṇidhāna-viśeṣavistara-sūtra* 藥師如來本願功德經 used some of the seven critical terms indicating an agent in *saṃsāra*.

If the traditional attributions of authorship to Tanwulan 曇無蘭 (fl. 373–96) and Juqu Jingsheng 沮渠京聲 (?–464) are correct, these two may be regarded as major translators who were fond of the idea of an agent in *saṃsāra*. According to these attributions, Tanwulan interpolated an agent in *saṃsāra* in T22 *Śrāmaṇyaphala-sūtra* 寂志果經,

18. CSZJJ, KYL and ZYL designate his translation of the *Mahāsāṃghika-prātimokṣa* as the *Pråtimokṣa* for monks; however, LDSBJ, YJTJ, NDL and DZL designate it as the *Prātimokṣa* for nuns; FJL does not indicate whether it is for monks or nuns. All of these catalogues record that the text in question was co-translated by Buddhabhadra. The present T1426, the *Prātimokṣa* for monks, is attributed only to Buddhabhadra, and T1427, the *Prātimokṣa* for nuns, is attributed to Buddhabhadra and Faxian.

T143 *Yuye jing* 玉耶經, T741 *Wuku zhangju jing* 五苦章句經, T742 *Ziai jing* 自愛經, T743 *Zhongxin jing* 忠心經 and T796 *Jianzheng jing* 見正經, while Juqu Jingsheng did so in T514 *Jianwang jing* 諫王經, T518 *Zhantuoyue guowang jing* 旃陀越國王經, T541 *Foda sengda jing* 佛大僧大經 and T826 *Dizi si fusheng jing* 弟子死復生經. However, these attributions are uncertain. CSZJJ attributes two translations to Tanwulan, while LDSBJ attributes 110; CSZJJ attributes four translations to Juqu, but LDSBJ attributes thirty-six. None of the translations listed above are attributed to the two translators by CSZJJ. Among the translations in which we find some of the seven terms, the attributions of T495 *Anan fenbie jing* 阿難分別經 to Fajian 法堅 (fl. 385–8), T696 *Mohe chatou jing* 摩訶剎頭經 to Shengjian 聖堅 (fl. 420–22), T43 *Devadūta-sūtra* 閻羅王五天使者經 to Huijian 慧簡 (fl. 457) and T383 **Mahāmāyā-sūtra* 摩訶摩耶經 to Tanjing 曇景 (fl. 479–502) remain uncertain.

THE PERIOD OF NEW TRANSLATION (618 ONWARDS)

Xuanzang 玄奘 (602?–664) did not use any of the seven terms, except for a single use of *shenshi* 神識 in T450 **Bhaiṣajyaguru-pūrvapraṇidhāna-viśeṣavistara-sūtra* 藥師琉璃光如來本願功德經. T450 is a retranslation of the aforementioned T449 (translated by Dharmagupta in 615). In the corresponding part of T449 (14.403c19–27), we find three occurrences of *shenshi*. Xuanzang renders the last two merely as *shi* (識: *vijñāna*), but leaves the first as *shenshi*. Considering the significant consistency in the use of renderings by Xuanzang, the original text of T450 may have had different terms for the first *shenshi* and the last two *shi*; otherwise this single occurrence of *shenshi* may be a mistake in the translation process, caused by referring to the previous translation.[19] T451 藥師琉璃光七佛本願功德經 by **Yijing** 義淨 (635–713) is also a retranslation of T499 and T450. While in T450 Xuanzang leaves only the first *shenshi* of the three occurrences in T499, Yijing (14.415c3–11) leaves the first two as *shenshi* and changes the last to *jingshen* 精神, which is a synonym of *shenshi*. Yijing uses *jingshen* also in T593 **Rājāvavadaka-sūtra* 佛為勝光天子說王法經, indicating an agent in *saṃsāra*.

---

19. In his T1562 *Abhidharma-nyāyānusāra-śāstra* (T29.717b18–19), Xuanzang uses the term *shenshi* once. There, however, it does not imply an agent in *saṃsāra*; it means the consciousness (*shi*) of a deity (*shen:* Māra).

Divākāra 地婆訶羅 (613–87) in T187 **Lalitavistara* 方廣大莊嚴經 and in T970 **Sarvadurgati-pariśodhana-uṣṇīṣavijaya-dhāraṇī* 最勝佛頂陀羅尼淨除業障呪經, Dānapāla 施護 (fl. 980) in T1025 **Samantamukhapraveśaraśmi-vimaloṣṇīṣaprabhā-sarvatathāgatahṛdaya-samâvalokita-dhāraṇī* 佛頂放無垢光明入普門觀察一切如來心陀羅尼經, Richeng 日稱 (fl. 1046–73) in T1671 *Fugai zhengxing suoji jing* 福蓋正行所集經, Shaluoba 沙囉巴 of the Yuan dynasty in T925 *Yaoshi liuliguangwang qifo benyuan gongde jing niansong yigui* 藥師琉璃光王七佛本願功德經念誦儀軌 and Vajradhara Dalai Lama 持金剛達賴喇嘛 *et al.* of the Qing dynasty in T927 *Yaoshi qifo gongyang yigui ruyiwang jing* 藥師七佛供養儀軌如意王經 use some of the seven critical terms. Using some interpolations of an agent in *saṃsāra*, T945 **Śūraṅgama-sūtra* 大佛頂如來密因修證了義諸首楞嚴經 is attributed to Pramiti 般剌蜜帝 (fl. 705); however, T945 is possibly a Chinese apocryphon. T412 *Dizang pusa benyuan jing* 地藏菩薩本願經 uses *hunshen* 魂神 in the sense of a saṃsāric agent, and is attributed to Śikṣānanda (652–710); however, this attribution remains dubious.

The following are anonymous translations that interpolate some of the seven critical terms: T156 *Da fangbian fo baoen jing* 大方便佛報恩經, T142B *Yuyenü jing* 玉耶女經, T522 *Pudawang jing* 普達王經 and T687 *Xiaozi jing* 孝子經 appear to be archaic translations. T523 *Wuwang jing* 五王經, T100 *Saṃyuktāgama* 別譯雜阿含經, T596 *Tianwang taizi biluo jing* 天王太子辟羅經, T750 *Shamiluo jing* 沙彌羅經, T396 *Fa miejin jing* 法滅盡經 and T1333 **Saptabuddhaka-sūtra* 虛空藏菩薩問七佛陀羅尼呪經 appear to be old translations. T441 *Foming jing* 佛名經 is probably a Chinese apocryphon dating from the Tang dynasty.

Chapter 9

THE CHARACTERISTICS OF THE CHINESE BUDDHIST CONCEPT OF SELF

In this final chapter, I aim to show that the idea of an imperishable soul became theorized in a more sophisticated way by Chinese Buddhists after the fifth century, while the expressions reflecting that idea started to disappear gradually in the works of the major translators from the time of Saṃghadeva and Kumārajīva, i.e., around the last decade of the fourth century and the first decade of the fifth century. In my terms, the 'systematic' reading of an imperishable *shen* in the first sense had waned by the fifth century, but the reading in the second sense began to flourish from the fifth century. It is notable that, while the use of such expressions in the canonical translations was restricted by the original context of the Indian scriptures, the authors of the independent treatises and Chan analects could freely create their own theory, quoting particular passages from various canonical texts, sometimes regardless of their original context. For this reason, it is in Chinese treatises and Chan analects that we may more clearly detect the purely Chinese Buddhist implications of the concept.

In the corpus of texts composed by Chinese Buddhists, we find many Buddhists refuting other Chinese thought with a strong sense of rivalry, or accommodating it into Buddhist teaching with an attitude of 'arrogant' pluralism. Obviously, Chinese Buddhists developed their own doctrinal systems with clear differentiations from other kinds of Chinese thought, which must be analysed in detail. Nonetheless, for practical reasons, I restrict my research here to illuminating the process of theorization which yielded the peculiar Chinese Buddhist ideas of self. Therefore, even while quoting Buddhist arguments attacking other types of Chinese thought, I would rather focus on the problem of whether the arguments can be considered as Buddhist ones in the Indian sense.

PHILOSOPHICAL DEBATES ON *SHEN*'S IMPERISHABILITY 神不滅

The *Mouzi lihuo lun* 牟子理惑論 has traditionally been attributed to Mouzi and is known as the oldest extant Chinese treatise on Buddhism (see Chap. 1, note 47). Although this attribution is now challenged by contemporary scholars, it remains a good source for observing how Chinese scholars at the earliest stage understood the Buddhist concept of self. Mouzi argues for the imperishability of the soul against his hypothetical adversaries as follows:

> Someone said, 'Buddhists announce, "After death, people are bound to rebirth," but I do not trust it.' Mouzi answered, '[It is our custom that,] when a person dies, the family climb onto the roof and call the person. The person is already dead; so whom do they call?' Another answered, 'They call the *hunpo* 魂魄 of the person.' Mouzi asked, 'If the *shen* 神 of the person returns, he revives. Otherwise, what is the *shen* called?' He answered, 'It becomes a ghost 鬼神.' Mouzi answered, 'Yes, it does. *Hunshen* 魂神 never perishes. Only the body decays. The body is like the roots and leaves of grain plants; *hunshen* is like their seeds. Whatever root or leaf has arisen must fade; however, how could there be an end of seeds? Only when one is enlightened, does [his or her *hunshen*] perish.'[1]

In the history of Chinese philosophical debate, the negation of *saṃsāra* meant the rejection of Buddhist *dharma*. Without *saṃsāra*, there is neither *nirvāṇa* nor a path to *nirvāṇa*. In order to proclaim the veracity of Buddhism, the most urgent task for the early Chinese Buddhists was to disseminate belief in *saṃsāra*. For this reason, the early Chinese Buddhists adopted the slogan, 'The body perishes after death, but *shen* is imperishable,' as shown in the above quotation.

The Daoist philosophers proclaimed that *shen* disintegrates after the destruction of the bodily base, using the simile of fuel and fire (see Chap. 6, note 43), which is likewise used by the early Buddhists in India (M.I.487) in order to illustrate that there is no permanent self beyond the impermanent five aggregates. Unlike the Indian Buddhists, who, in rivalry with other Indian religious movements, had to argue that there is no permanent self beyond the impermanent aggregates, the Chinese

1. 問曰: '佛道言: '人死, 當復更生,' 僕不信此之審也.' 牟子曰: '人臨死, 其家上屋呼之, 死已復呼誰?' 或曰: '呼其魂魄.' 牟子曰: '神還則生; 不還, 神何之呼?' 曰: '成鬼神.' 牟子曰: '是也. 魂神固不滅矣, 但身自朽爛耳. 身譬如五穀之根葉, 魂神如五穀之種實. 根葉生, 必當死; 種實豈有終已? 得道身滅耳.' (T2102.52.3b10–16).

Buddhists in rivalry with other Chinese thought had to argue that there is an imperishable soul beyond this life.

Such an ironical situation is well reflected in Section 5, 'The Expiry of the Body and the Imperishability of *Shen*' 形盡神不滅 (T2102.52.31b10–32b11), of the *Shamen bujing wangzhe lun* 沙門不敬王者論 by Huiyuan 慧遠 (334–416). There, having summarized the Daoist arguments for the termination of *shen* after death, based on the simile of fuel and fire, Huiyuan first pronounces that *shen* is too subtle to be expressed in language, i.e., it is beyond our perception. In other words, rejecting the empiricism of early Buddhism, Huiyuan argued for the existence of an unperceivable agent in *saṃsāra*, whose nature is described as follows:

> *Shen* is responsive to the whole of existence, [completely] autonomous, abstrusely all-comprehensive and nameless. Perceiving things, it operates; depending on calculation, it acts. Although it perceives things, it is not a thing; therefore, while things vanish, it does not perish. Although it depends on calculation, it is not calculation; therefore, while calculation may end, it is infinite.[2]

This means that the abstruse existence of *shen* is temporally endless and its mysterious operation is spatially boundless. Then Huiyuan likens the shift of fire to another fuel to the shift of *shen* to the next body, appropriating the Daoist authority of the *Zhuangzi* (see Chap. 6, note 46).

In the Chinese debate on the concept of *shen*, the focus is on whether or not it perishes after death; ironically, neither the Daoists nor the Buddhists in China were aware that the concept of *shen* per se is heterodox to the Buddhist doctrinal system. Indeed, the Daoists should have pointed out that the concept of *shen* contradicts the Buddhist doctrine of *anātman*, instead of arguing that *shen* perishes after death. Now, by analysing the characteristics of the Chinese Buddhist concept of *shen*, I shall illustrate how far it is incompatible with the Buddhist concept of self that I analysed in Part II.

The adversaries in the debate on the termination or imperishability of *shen* were Chinese intellectuals who followed Confucian values and utilized philosophical Daoist ontology and epistemology. However, with regard to this particular topic, Confucian ethics is irrelevant; they attacked the theory of *saṃsāra* by basing themselves on Daoist ideas or on the previously introduced eclectic theories of Dong Zhongshu. In this section, I call the ideas of the opponents Daoist, even when they are uttered by Confucians.

---

2. 神也者, 圓應無主, 妙盡無名. 感物而動, 假數而行. 感物而非物, 故物化而不滅; 假數而非數, 故數盡而不窮 (T2102.52.31c7–9).

Characteristics of the Chinese Buddhist Concept of Shen

The Chinese Buddhists borrowed the concept of *shen* from philosophical Daoism. However, redefining the concept in a 'Buddhist' way, they modified the meaning of *shen* so that it works as a permanent agent in *saṃsāra*. In this section, I analyse the Buddhist concept of *shen* in comparison with the Daoist one, revealing the incompatibility of such implications with the Indian Buddhist concept of self.

DUALISM

Daoists advocated monogenesis: both the mind and the body are composed of *qi* 氣. In this monogenesis, *shen*, the essence of the mind, is also composed of *qi*. The difference between *shen* and the other mental factors is that it is composed of the purest *qi*. The Daoist philosophers used this monogenesis to attack the Chinese Buddhist doctrine of the imperishability of *shen*: since *shen* has the same ontological basis as matter, it disintegrates when its bodily base is destroyed.

Following the Indian Buddhist dualism between mind and matter, the Chinese Buddhists located *shen* at an ontological level beyond matter, and set out to refute the arguments for the termination of *shen* after the destruction of its bodily base. For example, in Section 3, 'Being against Transformation' 不順化, of the *Shamen bujing wangzhe lun* 沙門不敬王者論, Huiyuan articulates the difference as follows:

> Whatever exists in all directions gets birth from the Great. Although there are a variety of transformations, fine and coarse in myriad ways, only two differences are found in the ultimate sense: the souled and the unsouled. The souled have sensation in their [process of] transformation, whereas the unsouled have no sensation in their transformation. Anything that has no sensation in its transformation has no more birth when the transformation terminates; since its birth is not dependent on sensation, its transformation perishes when its material basis decomposes. Anything that has sensation in its transformation operates according to its perception of objects; since its operation necessarily depends on sensation, it is born incessantly.[3]

Here, Huiyuan agrees with the Daoists that everything originates from the Great, i.e., *dao*. However, he rejects the Daoist view that mind is made of the same material as the bodily base, and insists that the souled are endlessly reborn due to their ontological nature, which is unlike

---

3. 凡在有方, 同稟生於大. 化雖群品, 萬殊精麁, 異貫統極而言, 有靈與無靈耳. 有靈則有情於化, 無靈則無情於化. 無情於化, 化畢而生盡; 生不由情, 故形朽而化滅. 有情於化, 感物而動; 動必以情, 故其生不絕 (T2102.52.30c1–5).

materiality. This ontological dualism of the Buddhist concept of *shen* constitutes its fundamental difference from Daoist *shen*.

EXISTENCE (*SAT*)

As an agent in *saṃsāra*, *shen* exists permanently, both in the conventional sense (*saṃvṛti*) and in the highest sense (*paramārtha*). In the conventional sense, it is regarded as the essence of the mind, popularly named *hunpo* 魂魄, that goes through *saṃsāra*. The great majority of the interpolations and adaptations indicating an agent in *saṃsāra* at the canonical level are used in this sense. In the highest sense, *shen* is frequently identified with *tathāgatagarbha*. Hence, it is said:

> The substratum (*ti* 體) of *nirvāṇa* is *dharma*-body. Investigating this *dharma*-body, [we find that] it is not a very different thing. The bright [manifestation of] *shen* 神明 in the past becomes *dharma*-body now. As the bright [manifestation of] *shen* has been the substratum of endless life and death, the *dharma*-body is also the substratum of all the merit of *nirvāṇa*.[4]

This is the opinion of Lingzheng 靈正, quoted and opposed by Jizang 吉藏 (549–623). Here I am not interested in whose opinion is right, but in how the Chinese Buddhists adopted the concept of *shen* and developed their ideas of self. Lingzheng's identification of *tathāgatagarbha* with *shenming* illustrates a 'systematic' reading which dominated before the time of Zhiyi 智顗 (538–97) and Jizang.

However, after the doctrinal research by Zhiyi and others, it appears that highly educated Buddhist theorists in China obtained proper knowledge of the doctrinal system of Indian Mahāyāna Buddhism. Hence, instead of the problematic definition by Lingzheng, Jizang suggests a 'correct' one:

> Now I shall explain that [the definition by Lingzheng] is not correct. Identifying a substratum 體 with a function 用, [he] does not reach the profound substratum of *nirvāṇa*. Now, [I] identify the substratum of *nirvāṇa* with the correct *dharma* of the middle way.[5]

I discussed earlier (pp. 144 ff.) how the emphasis on the performance aspect of *tathāgatagarbha* puts the soteriological system of Mahāyāna in danger: the attribution of action to an unconditioned entity makes

4. 涅槃體者, 法身是也. 尋此法身, 更非遠物; 即昔神明, 成今法身. 神明既是生死萬累之體, 法 身亦是涅槃萬德之體 (《大乘玄論》, T1853.45.46b16–18).
5. 今明不然. 以用為體, 不及涅槃深體. 今以中道正法, 為涅槃體 (T1853.45.46b19–20).

the 'true' self identical to the Brahmanic one. Here, understanding *shen* as an activity belonging to the realm of the conditioned, Jizang rejects its identity with the substratum of *nirvāṇa*, an unconditioned entity. Instead, Jizang identifies the substratum of *nirvāṇa* with truth (the correct *dharma* of the middle way). This understanding of Jizang is in complete accord with the 'systematic' reading of the Indian Mahāyānists.

Anyway, the present concern is the 'systematic' reading in the second sense, which dominated the period before Zhiyi. In its origin, *shen* is an agent of thought belonging to the realm of the conditioned (*saṃskṛta* in Sanskrit and *yong* 用 in Chinese). To this conditioned entity, the property of permanent existence is attributed. What could be more similar to the Brahmanic *ātman* than the concept of *shen* which is substantialized as *tathāgatagarbha*? This is the pivotal point from which the ideas of self peculiar to Chinese Buddhism developed.

BEING CONSCIOUS (*CIT*)

Being the essence of mind, *shen* is conscious by its nature. Being conscious, it takes specific things or everything in the world as its objects, as Zongbing 宗炳 (375–443) describes in the *Mingfo lun* 明佛論:

> *Shen* refers to the most mysterious among all things ... Why is [*shen*] said to be mysterious? *Jingshen* 精神 simultaneously reaches all directions without limit: up to the sky and down to the earth.[6]

Here the word 'reach' does not refer merely to the possibility of perceiving specific objects. It indicates that *shen* is always connected with everything in the world. Ignorant beings cannot realize such a full capacity of *shen*, whereas awakened ones freely and fully enjoy it. Furthermore, the Chinese Buddhists thought that *shen* takes truth, i.e., *dao* or *dharma*, as its object. The perception of *dao* by *shen* in this highest sense is not a temporary one. Although ignorant beings are unaware of it, everyone's *shen* is by nature always bright in the percipience of *dao*. Hence, the Chinese Buddhists frequently liken *shen* to a mirror, as Zongbing does in the *Mingfo lun*:[7]

---

6. 神也者妙萬物而為言矣. ... 何妙以言乎? 夫精神四達, 並流無極, 上際於天, 下盤於地 (T2102. 52.10a26–27).

7. Compare this with the description of *ātman* in the *Śvetāśvatara Upaniṣad* II.14: 'Just as a mirror stained by clay shines brilliantly when it is well cleansed, so, having seen the nature of *ātman*, it is embodied, becomes single, has accomplished its work, is freed from sorrow' (*yathâiva bimbaṃ mṛdayôpaliptaṃ tejomayaṃ bhrājate tat sudhautam, tad vā 'tmatattvaṃ prasamīkṣya dehī ekaḥ kṛtârtho bhavate vītaśokaḥ*).

> Now, here is a bright mirror covered with grime. If the grime is thin, its reflection is dim; if the grime is thick, its reflection is dusky; if the grime is too thick, it does not reflect. [However,] since the material is bright by nature, it still reflects [the light of truth], even when covered with grime. Although [it reflects] dimly, duskily or not at all, we have to say that [the brightness] does not cease, as the mirror [exists]. Materials are subject to the accumulation of dirt, and become faulty. In principle, people's *shen* is also like that. When untruth begrimes *shen*, there occur fine or coarse consciousnesses. [Impermanent] consciousnesses are attached to [permanent] *shen*. Therefore, although [the body] dies, [the mind] does not perish. Diminishing it (i.e., untruth) by means of [the realization of] emptiness, one must reach the complete elimination [of ignorance] and reach the original [state of] *shen*. This is called *nirvāṇa*.[8]

Here Zongbing clearly distinguishes *shen* from normal consciousness: *shen* is by nature constantly bright in the percipience of *dao* or *dharma*, whereas consciousnesses (*vijñāna*) are temporary existents contaminated by ignorance. The brightness of a mirror may be covered with grime, but it is always in the mirror, no matter whether people can see it or not. In the same way, *shen* is always in the percipience of *dao*, although ignorant beings are unaware of it.

When we synthesize the above characteristics of *shen*, we reach the following understanding: ontologically, *shen* is a permanent existent, both in the conventional sense and in the highest sense. In an epistemological sense, *shen* is the master or controller of consciousness in the conventional sense, and is constant in the percipience of *dao* or *dharma* in the highest sense. Recall the Yogācāra distinction between three types of constancy: the *dharma*-body is permanent (*nitya*) by nature, the enjoyment-body is in consecutive existence without interruption (*aviccheda*), and the creation-body is repetitively (*punaḥ punar*) created (see Chap. 5, note 24). However, no permanent agent is assumed in that explanation: what is permanent is merely truth or emptiness, not the agent of thought or the agent in *saṃsāra*. In this sense, the Indian Mahāyānists could keep their identity distinct from Brahmanism. Contrarily, in Chinese Mahāyāna Buddhism *shen* is a permanent agent of the constant percipience of *dao*. Doubtless it is closer to the concept of the Brahmanic *ātman* than to the Indian Mahāyāna self.

---

8. 今有明鏡於斯, 紛穢集之. 微則其照藹然, 積則其照昢然, 彌厚則照而昧矣. 質其本明, 故加穢猶照. 雖從藹至昧, 要隨鏡不滅以辯之. 物必隨穢彌失, 而過謬成焉. 人之神理, 有類於此. 偽有累神, 成精麁之識. 識附於神, 故雖死不滅. 漸之以空, 必將習漸至盡, 而窮本神矣, 泥洹之謂也 (T2102.52.11b1–7).

Recall my previous analysis that, while the properties existence (*sat*), consciousness (*cit*) and joy (*ānanda*) of the Brahmanic *ātman* are inherited from Upaniṣadic accounts of creation, the permanent self of Indian Mahāyāna Buddhism, such as *tathāgatagarbha*, is a concept retro-abstracted from its soteriological result. In general, the Upaniṣadic accounts of creation first mention the appearance of existence (*sat*) and then describe its self-awareness: 'Here I am!' The cosmogony of philosophical Daoism differs from the Brahmanic one: in philosophical Daoism, no trace of its personification is found. However, in their theory of the formation of the human being, the philosophical Daoists regarded *shen* as an agent of thought by nature. The property of permanence is attributed later by Buddhists to this agent of thought. This is the peculiar characteristic of the Chinese Buddhist conception of self in question.

SHEN AND CREATION

According to the Yogācārins, who assumed no permanent agent, seemingly external objects are images created by momentary consciousnesses, which succeed one another without interruption. However, they did not dare to proclaim that the permanent self such as *dharma*-body, *tathāgatagarbha*, *buddhatva*, etc., produces anything; the destructive implications of any such move are discussed in Section 5.3.[9] On the contrary, the Chinese Buddhists in question identified the 'true' self as a permanent agent of perception. When such an idea is associated with the mind-only theory, the ultimate source of the creation of the external-like world is easily identified with the essence of the mind, i.e., *shen*. This identification is facilitated by the fact that *shen* is the purest embodiment of *dao* in Daoist cosmogony.

T1857 *Baozang lun* 寶藏論, whose authorship has traditionally been attributed to Sengzhao 僧肇 (374–414) but is probably a work produced after the seventh century, describes the relationship between truth, *dao* and *shen* as follows:

> Being spaceless, matchless, boundless and locationless, truth becomes the origin of everything; not to be seen by eyes or heard by ears, without form or colour, and not illusory, [truth] becomes the sense faculty (根門, *indriya*) of the universe (三界, *tridhātu*). ... It has an operation called *shen* 神, and a shape called body 身. Taking no action (無為, *asaṃskṛta*), it is called *dao*; having no attribute, it is called truth. It is named according to the situation; it creates things in accordance with

9. As introduced in Chap. 5, note 49, a few sentences in LAS are rare exceptions to this general tendency.

> the situation. It exists permanently without birth or ageing. Its principle (*li* 理) concurs with all virtues; things are created [by it] by all means. Although [created] things are boundless, the principle [of creation] is ultimately a single *dao*. It can neither be realized nor attained.[10]

In this passage, 'truth' cannot signify Indian Buddhist *dharma* or *satya*, since these cannot have such operations or functions as described in the above passage. Referring to truth, the author of the *Baozang lun* doubtless meant *dao* as envisaged in the context of Daoist cosmogony.

In Part II, I argued that the obliteration of the distinction between the conditioned and the unconditioned was caused by the Mahāyānist ethical demand for Buddhas to perform salvation perpetually. Here we find a further reason for this obliteration in Chinese Buddhism. In the Chinese Buddhism of this 'systematic' reading, *nirvāṇa*, emptiness (*śūnyatā*), Buddha nature (*buddhatva*), the embryo of Tathāgata (*tathāgatagarbha*), *dharma*, truth (*satya*), etc., are identified with *dao*, and *dao* has the *saṃskṛta* property of creating everything as well as the *asaṃskṛta* property of *wuwei* (無為: taking no action). Therefore, being based on the indigenous concept of *dao*, the realm of ultimate truth for these Chinese Buddhists is incompatible with the dichotomy between the conditioned and the unconditioned.

Summing up the philosophical Daoist use of *shen*, I pointed out that, among the three characteristics of Brahmanic *ātman*, i.e., *sat* (existence), *cit* (consciousness) and *ānanda* (joy), it has only the implication of *cit*. Here we see that the Chinese Buddhist concept of *shen* has the implications of *sat* and *cit*; as for *ānanda*, it is seldom described as an attribute of *shen*. However, this does not mean that the Chinese Buddhist concept of self during the fifth and sixth centuries lacks the implication of *ānanda*; the property *ānanda* is frequently associated with the concept of self in the Chinese interpretation of the *Mahāyāna Mahāparinirvāṇa-sūtra*.

The Mahāyāna Mahāparinirvāṇa-sūtra *and the Chinese Buddhist Self*

There were two main ways for the Chinese Buddhists to form their own idea of self in their canon. The first method was adaptation through renderings or interpolations of their opinions in the course of translation.

---

10. 夫真也者，無洲無渚，無伴無侶，無涯無際，無處無所，能為萬物之祖宗. 非目視, 非耳聞, 非形色, 非幻魂, 能為三界之根門. ... 有用曰神, 有形曰身, 無為曰道, 無相曰真. 應物而號，隨物而造. 常住常存，不生不老. 理合萬德，事出千巧. 事雖無窮, 理終一道. 無有證者, 無有得者 (T1857.45.143c15–22).

The second method was to select specific translations and endow them with the highest authority. As an example of the second method, T374 *Mahāyāna Mahāparinirvāṇa-sūtra* [MMP] 大般涅槃經 has been one of the most influential translations for the formation of the Chinese Buddhist concept of self. The idea of self in MMP is mainly concerned with whether or not the Buddha exists after his complete *nirvāṇa* and whether or not all living beings possess Buddha nature. Among the various versions of MMP, there was no disagreement with regard to the first concern: the Buddha does not cease to exist after death. However, there was disagreement about the second concern.

The Chinese Buddhist translators used the term *foxing* (佛性: Buddha nature) to render various Indian terms that corresponded to the concept of Buddha nature: e.g., *buddhatva* (at T228. 8.654c21 by Dānapāla for AṣṭPr, p. 199_21; at T1606.31.748a21 by Xuanzang for AbhS-bh, p. 105_10), *buddhaprakṛti* (at T474.14.531b25 by Zhi Qian and at T476.14.578a21 by Xuanzang for VKN, p. 340_22),[11] *buddhagotra* (at T1522.26.184c22 by Paramārtha for DśBhū, p. 47_5),[12] *buddhadhātu* (at T1611.31.821c27 by Ratnamati for RGV, p. 5_5), etc. The Chinese meaning of Buddha nature bears a similarity to the definition of human nature 人性 by Mencius. As human nature was understood as the nature that characterizes a person as a human being, Buddha nature was understood as the nature or essence which all Buddhas possess and without which no one can be a Buddha. Furthermore, just as the nature of all human beings is defined by Mencius as the sum of the fundamental Confucian values, so that anyone can be a Confucian saint by cultivating these innate values, Buddha nature was expected by the Chinese Buddhist intellectuals to be inherent in all living beings as a storehouse of all values, so that any being can be a Buddha by cultivating this nature.

Following this line of thought, Daosheng 道生 (355–434) criticized the teaching of T376 (MMP), which was translated by Faxian 法顯 in 417–18, since T376 announces that a group of people called *icchantika* do not have the Buddha nature (T376.12.881b23–6). Describing T376 as incomplete, Daosheng proclaimed that the uncorrupted recension of the *sūtra* must teach that all living beings have the Buddha nature. Soon after, another recension of MMP (T374) was translated by Dharmakṣema

11. The present VKN has *buddhasya* instead of *buddhaprakṛtiko*. However, since *dharmaprakṛtikaś* follows it and since the translations by Zhi Qian and Xuanzang have *foxing* and *faxing* (法性: *dharmaprakṛti*) respectively for the two terms, we may infer that *buddhasya* is a corruption of *buddhaprakṛtiko*.
12. For the implications of *gotra*, see Ruegg (1976).

in 421, and it indeed advocates the teaching that all beings, including *icchantikas*, have the Buddha nature. Thereafter, the theory of Daosheng and the teaching of T374 entered the mainstream of Chinese Buddhism. This anecdote illustrates the law of the survival of the fittest among Buddhist translations in China. In the competition for survival, what was the fittest was in great part determined by congruence with the established Chinese way of thinking.

T374 (MMP) formulates the characteristics of the ultimate self in a phrase of four words – permanence 常, happiness 樂, *ātman* 我 and purity 淨 – which has been the most popular catchphrase among the Chinese with reference to the ultimate self.[13] It is taught that while all beings have the same ultimate self of the four properties, only awakened people realize this. T374 explains these four characteristics regarding the two major concerns of MMP as follows:

> All living beings have the Buddha nature. There is no difference between [the three treasures of] *buddha*, *dharma* and *saṃgha*; the three treasures have the nature of permanence, happiness, *ātman* and purity. [Therefore] no Buddha ultimately enters *nirvāṇa*; [all Buddhas] are permanent without change.[14]

However, we should bear in mind that what is taught in a Buddhist scripture may differ widely from what the Chinese readers understood. In T374, the ultimate self of these four characteristics is what should be realized; this ultimate self of permanence, happiness, *ātman* and purity is not the agent of realization, and this is in accordance with the 'systematic' reading introduced in Section 5.3. On the contrary, many learned Buddhists in China during the fifth and sixth centuries, such as Zongbing, regarded the ultimate self, called *shen*, as the agent that possesses and realizes these characteristics. Hence, Zongbing describes the permanent agent of realization as follows:

> [One should] know the permanent root of purification and follow the practice of
> eradication day by day. Incessantly eradicating it (i.e., desire or ignorance), one must
> reach [the state of] 'doing nothing' 無為. When there is no sensual desire and

13. While T374 includes *ātman* in the catchphrase throughout MMP, none of the extant Sanskrit fragments (MMP_H, MMP_K, MMP_L and MMP_SH) attributes the problematic Brahmanic term *ātman* to the ultimate self.
14. 一切眾生悉有佛性. 佛法眾僧無有差別, 三寶性相常樂我淨. 一切諸佛, 無有畢竟入涅槃者, 常住無變 (T374.12.487a16–18).

> when *shen* shines alone, one is faced with no more birth. When there no birth,
> there is no body. The existence of *shen* without body is called the *dharma*-body.[15]

Here the *dharma*-body of the unconditioned is evidently identified with the *shen*, i.e., the conditioned agent of realization. Following this way of thinking, the Emperor Wu 武帝 (464–549) of the Liang 梁 dynasty identified the Buddha nature of MMP as *shen*, as is introduced by Wonhyo 元曉 in the *Yeolban jongyo* (涅槃宗要: *Gist of the* [*Mahāyāna*] *Mahāparinirvāṇa-sūtra*):

> The mind possesses mysterious *shen* whose nature cannot be lost. Since such *shen* of the mind has already been located in the body, [living beings] are different from inanimate things, such as wood or stone. Because of this (i.e., *shen*), one can achieve the fruit of the great awakening. Therefore, [we should] say that the *shen* of the mind is the substantial cause [of Buddhahood].[16]

CHAN BUDDHISM 禪佛教 AND THE CONCEPT OF SELF

Chan 禪 is an abbreviation of *channa* 禪那, which is a transliteration of *dhyāna* (meditation; *jhāna* in Pali). The practice of *dhyāna* was introduced simultaneously with the start of Chinese Buddhist translation: An Shigao translated T602 **Mahānāpānasmṛti-sūtra* 大安般守意經, a guide to breathing (*ānāpāna*) meditation.[17] Thereafter, many manuals on Buddhist meditation were translated into Chinese and attracted the interest of Chinese people. The similarity between Buddhist and Daoist meditation, along with the similarity between the Buddhist doctrine of *śūnyatā* and Daoist *xuwu* (虛無: 'emptiness and nothing'), played a pivotal role in the successful dissemination of Buddhism in China.

Around the time of Huineng 慧能 (638–713), the Chinese had developed Chan Buddhism, whose soteriological methods and theoretical grounds are very different from Indian ones. I here confine myself to my main

---

15. 識能澄不滅之本， 稟日損之學， 損之又損， 必至無為. 無欲欲情， 唯神獨映， 則無當於生矣; 無生則無身. 無身而有神, 法身之謂也 (T2102.52.10c7–10).
16. 心有神靈不失之性. 如是心神已在身内，即異木石等非情物，由此能成大覺之果. 故說心神為正因體 (T1769.38.249a26–29).
17. Among the lost translations by An Shigao, the *Da shiermen jing* 大十二門經 and the *Shao shiermen jing* 小十二門經 are also known as meditation guidebooks. Daoan's prefaces to these two translations are extant: see respectively T2145.55.a14–b18 and T2145.55.45b26–46a13.

theme by analysing the concept of the 'true' self that the Chan Buddhist practitioners aimed to realize. For this purpose I utilize Zongmi's 宗密 (780–841) categorization of various Chan teachings, as illustrated in his *Chanyuan zhuquanji douxu* 禪源諸詮集都序 ('The General Preface to the *Annotated Collection of Chan Sources*': T2015.48.397b1–413b29). The teaching of this preface can be interpreted as being compatible with both the 'systematic' reading by the advocators of *shen* during the fifth and sixth centuries and the reading by the theorists after Zhiyi. I do not attempt here to determine which of these two readings is correct. I merely aim to illustrate that the tradition advocating the imperishable *shen* during the fifth and sixth centuries was vividly alive in the further development of Buddhism after the seventh century.

In the *Chanyuan zhuquanji douxu*, Zongmi categorizes Chan Buddhist teachings into three tenets in comparison with the threefold hierarchy of Buddhist doctrinal systems. The first and lowest one is 'the tenet of eliminating delusion and cultivating the mind' 息妄修心宗. Even in this lowest tenet, the Buddha nature is assumed, as taught in T374 (MMP). However, according to this tenet, the Buddha nature is covered with ignorance that has accumulated over endless time, just like a mirror covered with thick grime. To become a Buddha, a practitioner has to eliminate delusion 妄念 gradually, and, when all the delusion has gone, one is awakened and becomes omniscient (T2015.48.402b21–c3). In this tenet, the self has a pure and permanent core, i.e., Buddha nature, and impure and impermanent factors, i.e., various kinds of delusion. The reason why this tenet is regarded as the lowest is that those who hold it regard deluded thinking or its objects as real entities and attempt to eliminate them. Zongmi classifies the teachings of the masters Zhishen 智侁, Shenxiu 神秀 (605–706), Baotang 保唐 (714–74), Xuanshi 宣什 and others under this tenet.

The second tenet is called by Zongmi 'the tenet of doing away with anything' 泯絕無寄宗. This tenet emphasizes the doctrine of *śūnyatā*. There has been nothing from the beginning; it is not that we eliminate delusion. There is no wisdom, Buddha, living beings, *dharmadhātu* or *nirvāṇa*. By realizing that from the beginning there has been nothing, and not being attached to anything, one can be released from falsehood, which is called liberation (402c3–15). Zongmi placed this tenet above the first one because it teaches that from the beginning there is no delusion or external object. He classifies the teachings of Niutou 牛頭 (594–657), Shitou 頭 (700–790) and Jingshan 徑山 (714–92), as well as others, under this tenet.

The last and highest tenet is named 'the tenet of directly revealing the nature of the mind' 直顯心性宗. This tenet advocates that, no matter whether it appears to be existing or empty, everything is nothing but the true nature 真性. As for the substance of the true nature, it has no attribute and takes no action; as for its operation, it creates varieties of phenomena (402c15–20). Compared to the second tenet, which emphasizes the method of not being attached to anything, this last tenet emphasizes the fact that everything is a complete manifestation of the true nature. This true nature, called *foxing* (佛性: Buddha-nature), *rulaizang* (如來藏: *tathāgatagarbha*), *zhongshengxin* (眾生心: the mind of living beings), *zhenwo* (真我: true self), etc., has the characteristics of permanent existence (*sat*), being conscious (*cit*), being happy (*ānanda*) and creating everything. Although its description became more sophisticated and systematized after the doctrinal development by Zhiyi, this can be perfectly understood in terms of the Chinese Buddhist concept of *shen*, which is the essence of the mind, the purest embodiment of *dao* and the permanent agent in *saṃsāra*.

Zongmi subdivides this highest tenet into two types: the first (402c20–27) is called by later Chan Buddhists *dunwudunxiu* (頓悟頓修: sudden awakening and sudden practice) and the second (402c27–3a10) *dunwujianxiu* (頓悟漸修: sudden awakening and gradual practice). The tenet of sudden awakening and sudden practice proclaims that this current agent of speech, action and feeling [of unenlightened beings] is the very Buddha-nature. This agent is a Buddha from the beginning; there is no Buddha apart from it. We cannot produce a mind in order to practise or eliminate *dao* or evil, which is nothing but the mind. Therefore the soteriology of this tenet is as follows:

> [This true] nature is like space; it is not to be added to or reduced. There is no need to add [virtues]. Once one stops karmic action but fosters *shen* at every time and everywhere, the embryo of sainthood develops and manifests its natural mystery. This is true awakening, true practice and true realization.[18]

The tenet of sudden awakening and gradual practice follows the second tenet, since it rejects the reality of deluded thinking and external objects; however, it differs from the second, since it proclaims that the true nature permanently exists as an agent of thought and creation. Unenlightened beings are unaware of this true nature because of their

18. 性如虛空, 不增不減, 何假添補? 但隨時隨處, 息業養神, 聖胎增長, 顯發自然神妙. 此即是為真悟・真修・真證也 (T2015.48.402c25–27).

ignorance, which is empty in itself. One should first attain the sudden awakening of this true nature and the emptiness of deluded thinking and external objects; then one should gradually remove one's ignorance and desires, being fully aware of their emptiness. When delusions are exhausted by the natural 'practice of non-practice' 無修之修, birth and death are eliminated; once they are eliminated, the serene illumination [of the true nature] manifests itself and its operation is boundless. This [completed true nature] is called a Buddha.

Here it is clear that in Chan Buddhism the realization of truth, no matter whether it is called true nature, Buddha nature, *tathāgatagarbha* or something else, is the realization of the real self, which is the essence of the mind, the true agent of thought and creation, and the permanent agent of the highest awakening. Hence, in his *Zongjing lu* 宗鏡錄, the Chan master Yanshou 延壽 (904–75) quotes and interprets the teaching, 'The Tathāgata's advent in a world is only to show the equality [of everything],' from the **Ratnakāraṇḍaka-vyūha* 文殊師利現寶藏經, as follows:

> Being attached to illusory suffering, one seeks liberation; wishing for the [intellectual] capacity of saints, one attempts practice. However, all these are actions of the illusory self, i.e., discrimination by sensory consciousnesses. For this reason, when the Great Hero appeared [in this world], he showed only the correct tenet: destroying the illusory self, [he] revealed the gate towards the true self; rejecting sensory consciousness, [he] directed [living beings] to the way towards pure consciousness. The true self and pure consciousness are equality [as taught in the **Ratnakāraṇḍaka-vyūha*]. By means of pure consciousness, one eliminates discrimination; [by means of] the true self, one is not attached to the senses. Since discrimination has gone, differences disappear by themselves; since there is no sensory attachment, equality appears by itself.[19]

In short, the concept of self in Chan Buddhism may be regarded as the acme of the development of the Buddhist concept of *shen*. As for the self in the conventional sense, it may be compatible with the various Indian Buddhist theories of self. However, sincere Chan Buddhists should not be deluded by such concepts. Instead, they should realize the true self. This true self is not Daoist, since there was neither a permanent self

19. 夫執妄苦而求離，望聖量而欲修，皆是妄我施為，情識分別．是以大雄垂跡，但示正宗：破妄我，而顯真我之門；斥情識，而歸淨識之道．真我・ 淨識，即平等相，以淨識絕分別，真我無執情．絕分別故，差別自亡； 無執情故， 平等自現 (T2016.48.564c27–65a3).

nor an individual agent of creation in philosophical Daoism before the arrival of Buddhism; it is not Indian Buddhism, since in that there can be neither a permanent agent of thought nor an essence of the mind that creates everything. This unique concept of self has been created through the process of harmonizing Indian Buddhist concepts with Chinese indigenous concerns and ways of thinking.

CONCLUSION

In Part II, I argued that the formation of fundamental doctrines in early and later Buddhism reflects a strong sense of rivalry with Brahmanism: although Mahāyānists developed the concept of *tathāgatagarbha*, they did not make it an agent of perception in a 'systematic' way. In other words, the development of Indian Buddhism was restricted by the need to differ from Brahmanism. However, from the beginning Chinese Buddhists borrowed fundamental terms and theories from philosophical Daoism in order to make Buddhism more easily understood. Of course, the Chinese Buddhists had to reinterpret and redefine the Daoist terms, since the ontological, epistemological and soteriological bases underlying the terms differed fundamentally between Buddhism and Daoism. However, even after this reinterpretation and redefinition, those borrowed terms still maintained some Chinese indigenous implications that are incompatible with the doctrinal system of Indian Buddhism. The term *shen* illustrates a typical development of this trend: although the concept *shen* is redefined and reinterpreted in order to play the role of a permanent agent in *saṃsāra*, it still maintained the Daoist implication of being the agent of thought and the purest embodiment of *dao*. This is an important reason why and an illustration of how the Chinese developed a Buddhism that was peculiar to China.

The Chinese are famous for being practical. In philosophy, their first concern was politics and ethics. Except for the Daoist concept of *dao*, we find hardly any metaphysical discussion among Chinese philosophers before the arrival of Buddhism. As for the concept of self, the Chinese were as empiricist as the early Indian Buddhists. They did not assume any permanent self that they could not perceive. However, when the Chinese Buddhists attributed the property of permanence to *shen* and emphasized its being the embodiment of all the properties of *dao*, the Chinese Buddhist self became transcendental. Since from the beginning the concept of *shen* was adopted in order to explain the Buddhist self and Buddhist truth was identified with *dao*, we may say that the Chinese Buddhists did away with empiricism throughout their history.

When the Indian Buddhists gave up empiricism and proclaimed the highest truth to be beyond our experience, they adopted reasoning (*anumāna*) as a correct means of grasping the truth. However, except for rare cases, such as the Mohists, whose independent movement had already disappeared before the arrival of Buddhism, the Chinese in general thought not only that truth is beyond reasoning, but also that reasoning hinders people from grasping truth. This aversion to reasoning was much stronger in philosophical Daoism. *Dao* is beyond our perceptive and intellectual experience, and is blocked by emotional desire and the logical way of thinking; hence Daoist soteriology is a process of neutralizing emotion and removing logical thought. Chinese Buddhists show the same tendency in their epistemological, ontological and soteriological understanding of self and truth. Although a self in the conventional sense appears to be a mere compound of the five aggregates, there is a real self in the highest sense, which cannot be perceived. To purify the real self and realize *dao*, we have to remove our desire and ignorance; and the latter includes our reasoning. This is not the final result of a long development in Chinese Buddhism; it was inherited from Daoism from the earliest stage of Chinese Buddhism.

The tendency to devalue reasoning as a means of grasping the truth fits with the lack of ontological reductionism in Chinese Buddhism. Indian Buddhists, such as the early Buddhists, Abhidharmists and Yogācārins, proclaimed firstly that the whole is a mere name, whereas its components are real entities, and secondly that the whole cannot have any property that none of its components has. As I demonstrated in Chapters 3 and 4, many of the Indian Buddhist arguments for non-self (*anātman*) rely on this reductionism. In the same contexts, the Indian Buddhists argued that a self as a compound cannot have its own-nature (*svabhāva*) since it is a mere name, whereas the five aggregates and the four great elements, i.e., the real entities comprising a self, have their own-natures. However, the Chinese did not use such reductionist arguments. Before the arrival of Buddhism, the debate about human nature focused on the nature of a person as a whole, rather than any of his/her components. In the context of Chinese philosophy, it appears ridiculous to analyse a person into his/her components and discuss their nature. In this way of thinking, the Chinese Buddhists in general devalued analytic understanding, including reductionism, as mere conventional truth, and pursued the realization of irreducible reality by means of a non-analytic insight.

APPENDIX

This table summarizes my chronological survey of controversial adaptations or arbitrary interpolations indicating an imperishable soul in the body of Chinese canonical translations.

1. I make use of the computerized data of the *Chinese Electronic Tripitaka Collection* by CBETA released in February 2007.
2. I do not attempt to present an exhaustive survey of all the adaptations and interpolations of an imperishable soul; instead, I survey the occurrences of the seven critical compounds that were introduced in Chapter 7: *hunpo, hunling, hunshen, jingshen, shishen, shenshi* and *hunshi.*
3. In counting the occurrences of the compounds, I put the number in parentheses in the following table, if none of the occurrences of a specific term necessarily indicates an imperishable soul.
4. When some of the occurrences of a specific compound indicate an imperishable soul but others do not necessarily do so, I have counted all the occurrences as indicating an imperishable soul.
5. When tabling the results of this survey, I parenthesize the sutra number and shade the line in grey if none of the terms in the translation necessarily indicates an imperishable soul. I retain those translations in the table in order to illustrate all usages of the terms rather than giving a partial impression.
6. The following abbreviations are used in the table:
   apo.: an apocryphon; **at.**: an archaic translation; **attr.**: attributed to; **nt.**: a new translation; **poss.**: possibly; **prob.**: probably; **ot.**: an old translation; **tr.**: translated by; **trad.**: traditionally; **Abh**: Abhidharma literature; **MS**: Mahāyāna scriptures; **NML**: non-Mahāyāna literary works (*jātaka, avadāna*, etc.); **NMS**: non-Mahāyāna *sūtra*; **VAJ**: Vajrayāna literature; **Vin**: *vinaya.*
7. The active years of the translators are given at their first occurrence, and not repeated.

Occurrences of the seven critical compounds that indicate an agent in *saṃsāra*

	魂魄	魂靈	魂神	精神	識神	神識	魂識	Genre	Translator
T1			1	1	7			NMS	長阿含經 tr. Buddhayaśas and Zhu Fonian in 413
T5			1					NMS	佛般泥洹經 tr. Zhi Qian (fl. 222–53)
T6			4	2				NMS	般泥洹經 prob. tr. in Zhi Qian's circle
T7				1				NMS	大般涅槃經 tr. Faxian (fl. 413)
T17				1				NMS	善生子經 trad. attr. Zhi Fadu (fl. 301)
T20			1	2				NMS	佛開解梵志阿經 prob. tr. in Zhi Qian's circle
T22			3					NMS	寂志果經 trad. attr. Tanwulan (fl. 373–96)
T23	4			5				NMS	大樓炭經 tr. Faju (fl. 290–311)
T35			1					NMS	海八德經 trad. attr. Kumārajīva (344–413)
T43			3		1			NMS	閻羅王五天使者經 trad. attr. Huijian (c. 457)
T46			1	1				NMS	阿那律八念經 trad. attr. Zhi Yao (fl. 185)
(T76)		(1)						NMS	梵摩渝經 tr. Zhi Qian
T87		1		2				NMS	齋經 tr. Zhi Qian
T99					4	1		NMS	雜阿含經 tr. Guṇabhadra (394–468)
T100						2		NMS	別譯雜阿含經 anonymous, ot.
(T103)						(3)		NMS	聖法印經 tr. Zhu Fahu (fl. 266–308)
T125				(1)	5	16		NMS	增壹阿含經 tr. Saṃghadeva (fl. 383–401) or Dharmanandi (fl. 383–91)
T142B			1					NMS	玉耶女經 anonymous, poss. at.
T143			1					NMS	玉耶經 trad. attr. Tanwulan
T151			1					NMS	阿含正行經 trad. attr. An Shigao (fl. 148–71)
T152		16	2		(3)			MS	六度集經 tr. Kang Senghui (?–280)
(T154)					(1)			NML	生經 tr. Zhu Fahu
T156				2				NML	大方便佛報恩經 anonymous, poss. at.
(T159)						(1)		MS	大乘本生心地觀經 tr. Prajñā (during the Tang)
(T182B)					(1)			NML	鹿母經 tr. Zhu Fahu
T184		1	2	7			1	NML	修行本起經 tr. Kang Mengxiang (fl. 194–99) and Zhu Dali
T185			2	7			1	NML	太子瑞應本起經 tr. Zhi Qian
T186			2	5		(3)		NML	普曜經 tr. Zhu Fahu
T187				1		1		NML	方廣大莊嚴經 tr. Divākāra (613–87)
(T189)				(1)		(1)		NML	過去現在因果經 tr. Guṇabhadra
T190	1			3				NML	佛本行集經 tr. Jñānagupta (523–600)
(T192)						(1)		NML	佛所行讚 trad. attr. Dharmakṣema (385–433)

	魂魄	魂靈	魂神	精神	識神	神識	魂識	Genre	Translator
(T193)	(1)							NML	佛本行經 tr. Baoyun (376–449)
T198					1			NML	義足經 tr. Zhi Qian
(T200)				(1)				NML	撰集百緣經 trad. attr. Zhi Qian
(T201)				(1)				NML	大莊嚴論經 trad. attr. Kumārajīva
T202				(1)	2		1	NML	賢愚經 tr. Tanxueweide and Huijue in 445
(T203)				(1)				NML	雜寶藏經 tr. Kiṃkara (fl. 465–72) and Tanyao
(T205)					(1)			NML	雜譬喻經 anonymous; poss. at.
T206			2					NML	舊雜譬喻經 trad. attr. Kang Senghui
T208			1	(1)				NML	眾經撰雜譬喻 tr. Kumārajīva
T210		1		3	2			NML	法句經 tr. Zhi Qian and Zhu Jiangyan
T211			4	5	1	(1)		NML	法句譬喻經 tr. Fali (fl. 290–311) and Faju
T212		2	3	7	2	21		NML	出曜經 tr. Zhu Fonian (fl. 373–413)
(T213)						(1)		NML	法集要頌經 tr. Tianxizai (fl. 980–1000)
(T222)						(3)		MS	光讚經 tr. Zhu Fahu
(T245)					(1)			MS	仁王般若波羅蜜經 trad. attr. Kumārajīva; prob. apo.
(T277)						(1)		MS	觀普賢菩薩行法經 tr. Dharmamitra (fl. 356–442)
(T285)				(1)		(11)		MS	漸備一切智德經 tr. Zhu Fahu
T288						1		MS	等目菩薩所問三昧經 prob. tr. Zhu Fahu
(T291)						(1)		MS	如來興顯經 tr. Zhu Fahu
(T292)						(2)		MS	度世品經 tr. Zhu Fahu
T309			1		13	37		MS	十住斷結經 tr. Zhu Fonian
T310						3		MS	大寶積經・密迹金剛力士會 tr. Zhu Fahu
(T310)						(1)		MS	大寶積經・入胎藏會 tr. Yijing (635–713)
T310						21		MS	大寶積經・賢護長者會 tr. Jñānagupta
(T310)						(2)		MS	大寶積經・寶髻菩薩會 tr. Zhu Fahu
T317				1				NMS	胞胎經 tr. Zhu Fahu
T360			1	(2)				MS	無量壽經 trad. attr. Saṃghavarman (fl. 252)
T361			1	(1)				MS	無量清淨平等覺經 tr. Zhi Qian
T362			1	(1)				MS	阿彌陀三耶三佛薩樓佛檀過度人道經 tr. Lokakṣema (fl. 178–89)
T383						2		MS	摩訶摩耶經 trad. attr. Tanjing; poss. ot.
T384				(2)	15	5		MS	菩薩從兜術天降神母胎說廣普經 tr. Zhu Fonian
T385					2			MS	中陰經 tr. Zhu Fonian
T396				1				MS	法滅盡經 anonymous, poss. ot.
(T397)			(1)					MS	大方等大集經・日藏分 tr. Narendrayaśas (490–589)

	魂魄	魂靈	魂神	精神	識神	神識	魂識	Genre	Translator
(T399)						(2)		MS	寶女所問經 tr. Zhu Fahu
(T403)						(1)		MS	阿差末菩薩經 tr. Zhu Fahu
(T405)						(1)		MS	虛空藏菩薩經 Buddhayaśas (fl. 408)
T412			3			(1)		MS	地藏菩薩本願經 trad. attr. Śīkṣānanda (652–710)
(T417)			(1)					MS	般舟三昧經 trad. attr. Lokakṣema
(T418)			(1)					MS	般舟三昧經 tr. Lokakṣema
(T434)				(1)				MS	稱揚諸佛功德經 trad. attr. Kiṃkara
T441	3	1		12				MS	佛名經 anonymous, poss. apo.
T449	(3)					3		MS	藥師如來本願功德經 tr. Dharmagupta (?–619)
T450						1		MS	藥師琉璃光如來本願功德經 tr. Xuanzang (602?–664)
T451				(1)		2		MS	藥師琉璃光七佛本願功德經 tr. Yijing
(T459)						(1)		MS	文殊悔過經 tr. Zhu Fahu
(T477)						(1)		MS	大方等頂王經 tr. Zhu Fahu
(T492A)			(1)					NMS	阿難問事佛吉凶經 trad. attr. An Shigao
T492B				1	1			NMS	阿難問事佛吉凶經 trad. attr. An Shigao
T493			4					NMS	阿難四事經 tr. Zhi Qian
T495			(1)	1	1			NMS	阿難分別經 trad. attr. Fajian (fl. 385–88)
T500			2					NMS	羅云忍辱經 trad. attr. Faju (c. 308)
T501			1					MS	沙曷比丘功德經 trad. attr. Faju
T507		2						NMS	未生冤經 prob. tr. Zhi Qian
T514			2					NMS	諫王經 trad. attr. Juqu Jingsheng (?–464)
T518			1					NMS	旃陀越國王經 trad. attr. Juqu Jingsheng
T522			1					NMS	普達王經 anonymous, poss. at.
T523	1	1		1	(1)			NMS	五王經 anonymous, poss. ot.
T530				2				NMS	須摩提長者經 trad. attr. Zhi Qian
(T534)				(1)				MS	月光童子經 tr. Zhu Fahu
T541		1						NMS	佛大僧大經 trad. attr. Juqu Jingsheng
T555B		2						NMS	五母子經 trad. attr. Zhi Qian
T556	1							NMS	七女經 tr. Zhi Qian
T581	2	1	2	1	(1)			NMS	八師經 tr. Zhi Qian
(T589)						(4)		MS	魔逆經 tr. Zhu Fahu
T590			1					NMS	四天王經 tr. Zhiyan (350–427) and Baoyun
T593				1				MS	佛為勝光天子說王法經 tr. Yijing
T596		1						NMS	天王太子辟羅經 anonymous, poss. ot.
T606	1		2	10				Abh	修行道地經 tr. Zhu Fahu
(T609)		(1)						Abh	禪要經 anonymous, poss. at.

	魂魄	魂靈	魂神	精神	識神	神識	魂識	Genre	Translator
T611			2					NMS	法觀經 trad. attr. Zhu Fahu
(T613)					(1)			NMS	禪祕要法經 trad. attr. Kumārajīva
T656					6	15		MS	菩薩瓔珞經 tr. Zhu Fonian
(T659)				(1)				MS	大乘寶雲經 tr. Mandāra and Saṃghapāla (460–524)
T673						4		MS	大乘同性經 tr. Jñānayaśa (fl. 556–81)
T687		1						NMS	孝子經 anonymous, poss. at.
T696			1					NMS	摩訶刹頭經 trad. attr. Shengjian (fl. 420–22)
(T703)				(1)				NML	燈指因緣經 trad. attr. Kumārajīva
T721				1				MS	正法念處經 tr. Prajñāruci (fl. 516)
T729	3							NMS	分別善惡所起經 trad. attr. An Shigao
T732	2							NMS	罵意經 trad. attr. An Shigao
T735	2		6	2				NMS	四願經 tr. Zhi Qian
T737			1					NMS	所欲致患經 tr. Zhu Fahu
T741					1			MS	五苦章句經 trad. attr. Tanwulan
T742		1						NMS	自愛經 trad. attr. Tanwulan
T743		1						MS	忠心經 trad. attr. Tanwulan
T750		1						NMS	沙彌羅經 anonymous, poss. ot.
(T754)				(2)		(1)		NMS	未曾有因緣經 trad. attr. Tanjing
T770			1					MS	四不可得經 prob. tr. Zhu Fahu
T784		2						NMS	四十二章經 trad. attr. Kāśyapamātaṃga and Zhu Falan (legendary figures of first century)
T790			1					NMS	孛經抄 tr. Zhi Qian
T796						18		MS	見正經 trad. attr. Tanwulan
(T810)						(1)		MS	諸佛要集經 tr. Zhu Fahu
(T813)						(1)		MS	無希望經 tr. Zhu Fahu
T826			2					MS	弟子死復生經 trad. attr. Juqu Jingsheng
(T895A)				(1)				Vaj	蘇婆呼童子請問經 tr. Śubhakarasiṃha (637–735)
(T895B)				(1)				Vaj	蘇婆呼童子請問經 tr. Śubhakarasiṃha
(T899)						(1)		Vaj	清淨法身毘盧遮那心地法門成就一切陀羅尼三種悉地 anonymous
(T905)			(1)					Vaj	三種悉地破地獄轉業障出三界祕密陀羅尼法 trad. attr. Śubhakarasiṃha
T925				(1)		2		Vaj	藥師琉璃光王七佛本願功德經念誦儀軌 tr. Shaluoba
T927				(1)		2		Vaj	藥師七佛供養儀軌如意王經 tr. Vajradhara Dalailama
T945	1	1		4		7		Vaj	首楞嚴經 tr. Pramiti (arr. Ch. 705), poss. apo.

	魂魄	魂靈	魂神	精神	識神	神識	魂識	Genre	Translator
T970							1	Vaj	最勝佛頂陀羅尼淨除業 障呪經 tr. Divākāra
T988				1				Vaj	孔雀王呪經 trad. attr. Kumārajīva
(T999)				(1)				Vaj	守護大千國土經 tr. Dānapāla (fl. 980)
(T1002)							(1)	Vaj	不空羂索毘盧遮那佛大灌頂光 tr. Amoghavajra (705–74)
(T1007)				(1)				Vaj	牟梨曼陀羅呪經 anonymous, poss. ot.
T1025						1		Vaj	佛頂放無垢光明入普門觀察一切如來心陀羅尼經 tr. Dānapāla
(T1092)							(1)	Vaj	不空羂索神變真言經 tr. Bodhiruci (?–527)
(T1099)				(1)				Vaj	聖觀自在菩薩不空王祕密心陀羅尼經 tr. Shihu
(T1138A)				(1)				Vaj	金剛祕密善門陀羅尼呪經 anonymous, poss. ot.
(T1177A)						(1)		Vaj	大乘瑜伽金剛性海曼殊室利千臂千鉢大教王經 trad. attr. Amoghavajra
(T1178)				(1)				Vaj	文殊菩薩獻佛陀羅尼名烏蘇吒 anonymous
(T1190)				(2)				Vaj	聖妙吉祥真實名經 tr. Shi Zhi
(T1191)				(1)				Vaj	大方廣菩薩藏文殊師利根本儀 tr. Tianxizai
(T1278)				(1)				Vaj	迦樓羅及諸天密言經 by Prajñābala, prob. the Tang
(T1290)		(1)						Vaj	焰羅王供行法次第 trad. attr. Amoghavajra
(T1299)		(1)		(1)				Vaj	文殊師利菩薩及諸仙所說吉凶時日善惡宿曜經 tr. Amoghavajra
(T1303)				(1)				Vaj	聖曜母陀羅尼經 tr. Fatian
(T1307)	(2)							Vaj	北斗七星延命經 anonymous, poss. the Tang
(T1309)				(3)				Vaj	七曜星辰別行法 anonymous
(T1312)				(2)				Vaj	難儞計濕嚩囉天說支輪經 tr. Faxian
(T1320)							(1)	Vaj	瑜伽集要焰口施食儀 anonymous
T1331	1			8				Vaj	灌頂經 trad. attr. Śrīmitra (fl. 317–22)
(T1332)				(2)				Vaj	七佛所說神呪經 anonymous, poss. ot.
T1333				1				Vaj	虛空藏菩薩問七佛陀羅尼呪經 anonymous, poss. ot.
(T1336)				(1)		(1)		Vaj	陀羅尼雜集 anonymous, poss. ot.
T1339				2				Vaj	大方等陀羅尼經 tr. Fazhong (fl. 397–418)
(T1340)	(1)							Vaj	大法炬陀羅尼經 tr. Jñānagupta
(T1393)	(1)							Vaj	摩尼羅亶經 trad. attr. Tanwulan

	魂魄	魂靈	魂神	精神	識神	神識	魂識	Genre	Translator
(T1425)					(1)			Vin	摩訶僧祇律 tr. Buddhabhadra (359–429)
(T1450)		(1)						Vin	根本說一切有部毘奈耶破僧事 tr. Yijing
(T1451)			(1)	(2)		(1)		Vin	根本說一切有部毘奈耶雜事 tr. Yijing
(T1507)				(1)				Abh	分別功德論 anonymous, poss. at.
(T1549)				(1)		(1)		Abh	尊婆須蜜菩薩所集論 tr. Saṃghabhūti (fl. 383–98)
(T1562)						(1)		Abh	阿毘達磨順正理論 tr. Xuanzang
(T1633)						(3)		Abh	如實論 tr. Paramārtha (499–569)
(T1646)				(1)				Abh	成實論 tr. Kumārajīva
(T1670A)				(7)				Abh	那先比丘經 anonymous, poss. ot.
(T1670B)				(8)		(1)		Abh	那先比丘經 anonymous, poss. ot.
T1671						1		Abh	福蓋正行所集經 tr. Richeng in 1064

REFERENCES

PRIMARY SOURCES

Indian Buddhist sources

[A] *Aṅguttara-nikāya*, edited by Richard Morris, Edmund Hardy, Mabel Hunt and Caroline A. F. Rhys Davids. 1888–1961. 5 vols: 2nd edn (vol. 1); 1st edn (vols. 2–5). London: Pali Text Society.

[AbhK] *Abhidharmakośa-bhāṣya* (attr. to Vasubandhu). *Abhidharmakośam (Svopajñabhāṣyasahitaṃ Sphuṭārthavyākhyopetaṃ ca)*, edited by Dwārikādās Śāstrī. 1998. Varanasi: Bauddha Bhāratī.

[AbhK-vy] *Abhidharma-kośa-vyākhyā* (attr. to Yaśomitra). *Sphuṭārthā Abhidharmakośavyākhyā*, edited by Unrai Ogihara. 1990. Publishing Association of Abhidharmakośavyākhyā. Tokyo: Sankibo Buddhist Book Store.

[AbhS-bh] *Abhidharma-samuccaya-bhāṣya* (attr. to Asaṅga and Sthiramati). *Abhidharmasamuccaya-bhāṣya*, edited by Nathmal Tatia. 1976. Patna: K. P. Jayaswal Research Institute.

[AṣṭPr] *Aṣṭasāhasrikā Prajñāpāramitā – With Haribhadra's Commentary Called Āloka*, edited by Paraśurāma Lakṣmaṇa Vaidya. 1960. Darbhanga: Mithilāvidyāpīṭhapradhāna.

[BC] *Buddhacarita* (attr. to Aśvaghoṣa). *Aśvaghoṣa's Buddhacarita or Acts of the Buddha*, edited by E. H. Johnston. 1936. Lahore (Reprinted Delhi: Motilal Banarsidass Publishers, 1984).

[D] *Dīgha-Nikāya*, edited by T. W. Rhys Davids and J. Estlin Carpenter. 1890–1911. 3 vols. London: Pali Text Society.

[Dhp] *Dharmapada, Udānavarga*

[Dhp_G] *The Gāndhārī Dharmapada*, edited by John Brough. 1962. London: Oxford University Press (Reprinted Delhi: Motilal Banarsidass Publishers, 2001).

[Dhp_P] *Dhammapada*, edited by Oskar von Hinüber and K. R. Norman. 1994. Oxford: Pali Text Society.

[Dhp_Pat] 'Patna Dharmapada – Part I: Text', edited by Margaret Cone. 1989. *Journal of the Pali Text Society*, **13**: 101–217.

[Dhp-a] *Dhammapada-aṭṭhakathā* (attr. to Buddhaghosa). *The Commentary on the Dhammapada*, edited by Harry Campbell Norman. 1906. 4 vols. London: Pali Text Society.

[Dhs] *Dhammasaṅgaṇi*, edited by Eduard Müller. 1885. London: Pali Text Society.

[Dhsk] *Dharmaskandha. Fragmente des Dharmaskandha: ein Abhidharma-Text in Sanskrit aus Gilgit*, edited by Siglinde Dietz. 1984. Göttingen: Vandenhoeck & Ruprecht.

[DśBhū] *Daśabhūmika-sūtra. Daśabhūmikasūtram*, edited by Paraśurāma Lakṣmaṇa Vaidya. 1967. Darbhanga: Mithilāvidyāpīṭhapradhāna.
[LAS] *Laṇkāvatāra-sūtra. Saddharmalaṅkāvatārasūtram*, edited by Paraśurāma Lakṣmaṅa Vaidya. 1963. Darbhanga: Mithila Institute of Post-Graduate Studies and Research in Sanskrit Learning.
[M] *Majjhima-Nikāya*, edited by V. Trenckner, Robert Chalmers and Mabel Haynes Bode. 1888–99. 3 vols. London: Pali Text Society.
[MMK] *Mūlamadhyamaka-kārikā* (attr. to Nāgārjuna). *Mūlamadhyamakakārikā of Nāgārjuna: The Philosophy of the Middle Way: Introduction, Sanskrit Text, English Translation and Annotation*, edited by David J. Kalupahana, 1986. Albany: State University of New York (Reprinted Delhi: Motilal Banarsidass Publishers, 1991).
[MMP] *Mahāyāna Mahāparinirvāṇa-sūtra.*
[MMP_H] *Mahāparinirvāṇa Sūtra*, in A. F. Rudolf Hoernle (ed.). *Manuscript Remains of Buddhist Literature Found in Eastern Turkestan*. 1916. Oxford: Clarendon Press, pp. 93–7.
[MMP_K] *Sanskrit Fragments of the Mahāyāna Mahāparinirvāṇasūtra: I. Koyasan Manuscript*, edited by Akira Yuyama. 1981. Tokyo: Reiyukai Library.
[MMP_L]: *New Sanskrit Fragments of the Mahāyāna Mahāparinirvāṇasūtra: Central Asian Manuscript Collection at Leningrad*, edited by Grigorii Maksimovich Bongard-Levin. 1986. Tokyo: International Institute for Buddhist Studies.
[MMP_SH] *Sanskrit Fragments of the Mahāyāna Mahāparinirvāṇasūtra: A Study of the Central Asian Documents in the Stein/Hoernle Collection of the India Office Library, London*, edited by Kazunobu Matsuda and Grigorii Maksimovich Bongard-Levin. 1988. Tokyo: Toyo Bunko.
[MP] *Mahāparinirvāṇa-sūtra*
[MPP] *Mahāparinibbāna-sutta* (D.II.72–168) and [MSD] *Mahāsudassana-sutta* (D.II.169–99).
[MPS] *Das Mahāparinirvāṇasūtra*, edited by Ernst Waldschmidt. 1950–51. Berlin: Akademie-Verlag.
[MPS_BV] Grigorii Maksimovich Bongard-Levin and M. I. Vorob'eva-Desjatovskaja (eds), 'New Fragments from the Hīnayāna Sūtras: The *Mahāvadāna-sūtra* and the *Mahāparinirvāṇa-sūtra*', in *Pamiatniki indiiskoi pis'mennosti iz TSentral'noi Azii*. 1990. pp. 208–44.
[MSA] *Mahāyānasūtrālaṃkāra* (attr. to Asaṅga), edited by Surekha V. Limaye. 1992. Delhi: Indian Books Centre.
[MSD] see under [MPP] above.
[MVibh] *Madhyānta-vibhāga-śāstram* (attr. to Asaṅga, Sthiramati and Vasubandhu), edited by Ram Chandra Pandeya. 1971. Delhi: Motilal Banarsidass.
[RGV] *Ratnagotravibhāga* (attr. to Maitreya). *The Ratnagotravibhāga: Mahāyānottaratantraśāstra*, edited by E. H. Johnston. 1950. Patna: The Bihar Research Society (Reprinted 1991, edited by H. S. Prasad. Delhi: Sri Satguru Publications, pp. 51–197).
[S] *Saṃyutta-Nikāya*, edited by Léon Feer. 1884–98. 5 vols. London: Pali Text Society.
[SP] *Saddharmapuṇḍarīkasūtram*, edited by Paraśurāma Lakshmāna Vaidya. 1960. Darbhanga: Mithila Institute of Post-Graduate Studies and Research in Sanskrit Learning.
[Spk] *Sārattha-ppakāsinī* (attr. to Buddhaghosa). *Sārattha-ppakāsinī: Buddhaghosa's Commentary on the Saṃyutta-Nikāya*, edited by F. L. Woodward. 1929–37. 3 vols. London: Pali Text Society.
[Sukh(L)] *Sukhāvatī-vyūha* (Larger)
[Sukh(L)_A] *Sukhāvatīvyūha*, edited by Atsuji Ashikaga. 1965. Kyoto: Librairie Hozokan.

[Sukh(L)_Sch] *Larger Sukhāvatīvyūhasūtra*, in Paul Harrison, Jens-Uwe Hartmann and Kazunobu Matsuda (eds), *Manuscripts in the Schöyen Collection. III: Buddhist Manuscripts*. 2002. Oslo: Hermes Publishing, pp. 179–214.

[Sv] *Sumaṅgala-vilāsinī* (attr. to Buddhaghosa). *The Sumaṅgala-vilāsinī: Buddhaghosa's Commentary on the Dīgha-Nikāya*, edited by T. W. Rhys Davids, J. Estlin Carpenter and William Stede. 1968–71. 2nd edn. 3 vols. London: Pali Text Society.

[TriṃśV] *Triṃśikā-vijñapti-kārikā* and *Triṃśika-vijñapti-bhāṣya* (attr. to Vasubandhu and Sthiramati). *Triṃśikā-Kārikā & Bhāṣya*, in *Vasubandhu's Vijñapti-mātratā-siddhi with Sthiramati's Commentary*, edited by Krishna Nath Chatterjee. 1980. Varanasi: Kishor Vidya Niketan, pp. 27–134.

[Ud] *Udānavarga*, edited by Franz Bernhard. 1965. Göttingen: Vandenhoeck & Ruprecht.

[Vibh] *The Vibhaṅga: Being the Second Book of the Abhidhamma Piṭaka*, edited by Caroline A. F. Rhys Davids. 1904. London: Pali Text Society.

[ViṃśV] *Viṃśatikā-vijñapti-kārikā* and *Viṃśatikā-vijñapti-vṛtti* (attr. to Vasubandhu). *Viṃśatikā-Kārikā & Vṛtti*, in *Vasubandhu's Vijñapti-mātratā-siddhi with Sthiramati's Commentary*, edited by Krishna Nath Chatterjee. 1980. Varanasi: Kishor Vidya Niketan, pp. 1–26.

[Vin] *The Vinaya Piṭakaṃ: One of the Principal Buddhist Holy Scriptures in the Pāli Language*, edited by Hermann Oldenberg. 1879–83. 5 vols. London: Pali Text Society.

[Vism] *Visuddhimagga* (attr. to Buddhaghosa). *The Visuddhi-magga of Buddhaghosa*, edited by Caroline A. F. Rhys Davids. 1975. London: Pali Text Society (Original publication: 1920–21 in two volumes, PTS).

[VKN] *Vimalakīrtinirdeśa: Transliterated Sanskrit Text Collated with Tibetan and Chinese Translations*, edited by Taisho daigaku sogo bukkyo kenkyujo. 2004. Tokyo: Taisho daigaku shuppankai.

Other Indian sources

[BĀUp] *Bṛhadāraṇyakopaniṣat*, in *Eighteen Principal Upaniṣads*, edited by V. P. Limaye and R. D. Vadekar. 1958. Poona: Vaidika Saṃśodhana Maṇḍala, pp. 174–282.

[ChUp] *Chāndogya Upaniṣad*: *Chāndogyopaniṣat*, in *Eighteen Principal Upaniṣads*, edited by V. P. Limaye and R. D. Vadekar. 1958. Poona: Vaidika Saṃśodhana Maṇḍala, pp. 68–173.

[ŚvUp] *Śvetāśvatara Upaniṣad. Śvetāśvataropaniṣat*, in *Eighteen Principal Upaniṣads*, edited by V. P. Limaye and R. D. Vadekar. 1958. Poona: Vaidika Saṃśodhana Maṇḍala, pp. 283–300.

Chinese Buddhist sources

[CSZJJ] *Chu sanzang ji ji* 出三藏記集 (T2145; compiled by Sengyou 僧祐 in *c.* 515).

[DNL] *Datang neidian lu* 大唐內典錄 (T2149; compiled by Daoxuan 道宣 in 664).

[DZL] *Dazhou kanding zhongjing mulu* 大周刊定眾經目錄 (T2153; compiled by Mingquan 明佺 *et al.* in 695).

[FJL] *Fajing lu* 法經錄 = *Zhongjing mulu* 眾經目錄 (T2146; compiled by Fajing 法經 *et al.* in 594?).

[GSZ] *Gaoseng zhuan* 高僧傳 (T2059; compiled by Huijiao 慧皎 in 519? or in 522?).

[GYTJ] *Gujin yijing tuji* 古今譯經圖紀 (T2151; compiled by Jingmai 靖邁 after 664).

[K] *Korean Tripiṭaka. Goryeo daejanggyeong* 高麗大藏經, edited by Dongguk Daehakgyo. 1957. 48 vols. Seoul: Dongguk Daehakgyo.

[KYL] *Kaiyuan shijiao lu* 開元釋教錄 (T2154; compiled by Zhisheng 智升 in 730).

[LDSBJ] *Lidai sanbao ji* 歷代三寶紀 (T2034; compiled by Fei Changfang 費長房 in 597).

[T] *Taisho shinshu daizokyo* 大正新脩大蔵経, edited by Junjiro Takakusu and Kaikyoku Watanabe. 1924. 85 vols. Tokyo: Taisho shinshu daizokyo kankokai.

[XGSZ] *Xu gaoseng zhuan* 續高僧傳 (T2060; compiled by Daoxuan 道宣).

[YCL] *Yancong lu* 彥琮錄 = *Zhongjing mulu* 眾經目錄 (T2147; compiled by Yancong 彥琮 *et al.*).

[YJTJ] *Gujin yijing tuji* 古今譯經圖紀 (T2151; compiled by Jingmai 靖邁 in 664-5).

[ZYL] *Zhenyuan xinding shijiao mulu* 貞元新定釋教目錄 (T2157; compiled by Yuanzhao 圓照 in 800).

[ZZL] *Zongli zhongjing mulu* 綜理眾經目錄 (being incorporated in CSZJJ; compiled by Daoan 道安 in *c.* 374–85).

Other Chinese sources

[CFYJ] *Chunqiu fanlu yizheng* 春秋繁露義證 (attr. to Zhongshu Dong 董仲舒; comm. Yu Su 蘇輿), edited by Zhe Zhong 鍾哲. 1992. Beijing: Zhonghua shuju 中華書局.

[HNZ] *Huainanzi* 淮南子 (attr. to An Liu 劉安; comm. You Gao 高誘), in *Zhuzi jicheng* 諸子集成, vol. 7, edited by Guoxue zhengli she 國學整理社. 1954. Beijing: Zhonghua shuju 中華書局.

[LC] *Lushi chunqi* 呂氏春秋 (attr. to Buwei Lu 呂不韋; comm. You Gao 高誘), in *Zhuzi jicheng* 諸子集成, vol. 6, edited by Guoxue zhengli she 國學整理社. 1954. Beijing: Zhonghua shuju 中華書局.

[LHJS] *Lunheng jiaoshi* 論衡校釋 (attr. to Chong Wang 王充; comm. Hui Huang 黃暉 and Pansui Liu 劉盼遂), edited by Zhonghua shuju 中華書局. 1990. Beijing: Zhonghua shuju 中華書局.

[LY] *Lunyu* 論語 (attr. to Confucius 孔子), in *Shisanjing zhushu* 十三經注疏, edited by Zhonghua shuju 中華書局. 1936. Shanghai: Zhonghua shuju 中華書局.

[LZJS] *Laozi jiaoshi* 老子校釋 (attr. to Laozi 老子; comm. Qianzhi Zhu 朱謙之), edited by Zhonghua shuju 中華書局. 1984. Beijing: Zhonghua shuju 中華書局.

[MX] *Mozi xiangu* 墨子閒詁 (attr. to Di Mo 墨翟; comm. Yirang Sun 孫詒讓), edited by Yikai Sun 孫以楷. 1986. Beijing: Zhonghua shuju 中華書局.

[MZ] *Mengzi* 孟子 (attr. to Mencius 孟子), in *Shisanjing zhushu* 十三經注疏, edited by Zhonghua shuju 中華書局. 1936. Shanghai: Zhonghua shuju 中華書局.

[NY] *Neiye* (attr. to Guanzhong 管仲), in *Original Tao: Inward Training (Nei-yeh) and the Foundations of Taoist Mysticism*, edited by Harold David Roth. 1999. New York: Columbia University Press.

[XZJJ] *Xunzi jijie* 荀子集解 (attr. to Xunzi 荀子 *et al.*), in *Zhuzi jicheng* 諸子集成, vol. 2, edited by Guoxue zhengli she 國學整理社. 1954. Beijing: Zhonghua shuju 中華書局.

[ZhoY] *Zhongyong* 中庸, in *Liji zhushu* 禮記注疏 of the *Shisanjing zhushu* 十三經注疏, edited by Zhonghua shuju 中華書局. 1936. Shanghai: Zhonghua shuju 中華書局.

[ZZJS] *Zhuangzi jishi* 莊子集釋 (attr. to Zhuangzi 莊子), edited by Qingfan Guo 郭慶藩; amend. Xiaoyu Wang 王孝魚. 1961. Beijing: Zhonghua shuju 中華書局.

Translations of primary sources

Graham, Angus Charles. 1978. *Later Mohist Logic, Ethics, and Science*. Hong Kong: Chinese University Press.

Harrison, Paul M. 1990. *The Samādhi of Direct Encounter with the Buddhas of the Present: An Annotated English Translation of the Tibetan Version of the Pratyutpanna-Buddha-saṃmukhâvasthita-samādhi-sūtra with Several Appendices Relating to the History of the Text.* Tokyo: International Institute for Buddhist Studies.

Horner, I. B. 1954. *The Collection of the Middle Length Sayings: Majjhima-Nikāya,* London: Pali Text Society.

Kalupahana, David J. 1986. *A Path of Righteousness: Dhammapada: An Introductory Essay, Together with the Pali Text, English Translation and Commentary.* Lanham, MD: University Presses of America.

Keenan, John P. 1994. *How Master Mou Removes Our Doubts: A Reader-Response Study and Translation of the Mou-tzu li-huo lun.* Albany: State University of New York Press.

La Vallée Poussin, Louis de, and Leo M. Pruden. 1988–90. *Abhidharmakośabhāṣyam.* 4 vols. Berkeley, California: Asian Humanities Press (Original publication *L'Abhidharmakośa de Vasubandhu.* Brussels: Institut Belge des Hautes Études Chinoises, 1971–72).

Ñāṇamoli, Bhikkhu, and Bhikkhu Bodhi. 1995. *The Middle Length Discourses of the Buddha: A New Translation of the Majjhima Nikāya.* Boston: Wisdom Publications.

Norman, K. R. 1997. *The Word of the Doctrine: Dhammapada.* Oxford: Pali Text Society.

Olivelle, Patrick. 1996. *Upaniṣads.* Oxford: Oxford University Press.

Rhys Davids, T. W., and Caroline A. F. Rhys Davids. 1899–1921. *Dialogues of the Buddha.* 3 vols. London: Pali Text Society (Reprinted: Delhi: Motilal Banarsidass Publishers, 2000).

Ui, Hakujyu 宇井伯壽. 1971. *Yakukyoshi kenkyu* 訳経史研究. Tokyo: Iwanami shoten.

SECONDARY SOURCES

An, Yang-Gyu. 1998. 'Buddhology in the Mahāparinibbāna-Suttanta and Its Commentary – With an Annotated Translation of Buddhaghosa's Commentary', DPhil thesis, Faculty of Oriental Studies, University of Oxford.

Asayama, Yukihiko 朝山幸彦. 1993. 'The connection between Zhiqian's translation method and his own life experience', 支謙の「訳経の仕方」と伝歴, *Journal of Indian and Buddhist Studies* 印度学仏教学研究, **42**(1): 236–42.

Bareau, André. 1991. 'The notion of time in early Buddhism', in H. S. Prasad (ed.), *Essays on Time in Buddhism.* Delhi: Sri Satguru Publications, pp. 1–12 (first published in *East and West* (1957), **7**: 353–64).

Bhattacharya, Kamaleswar. 1973. *L' Ātman-brahman dans le bouddhisme ancien.* Paris: École française d'Extrême-Orient.

Bhattacharya, Kamaleswar. 1989. 'Brahman in the Pali Canon and in the Pali commentaries', in H. S. Prasad and N. H. Samtani (eds), *Amalā Prajñā: Aspects of Buddhist Studies: Professor P. V. Bapat Felicitation Volume.* Delhi: Sri Satguru Publications, pp. 15–32.

Bodhi, Bhikkhu. 1998a. 'A critical examination of Ñāṇavīra's "A note on Paṭiccasamuppāda". (I)', *Buddhist Studies Review,* **15**(1): 43–64.

Bodhi, Bhikkhu. 1998b. 'A critical examination of Ñāṇavīra's "A note on Paṭiccasamuppāda". (II)', *Buddhist Studies Review,* **15**(2): 157–81.

Bucknell, Roderick S. 1999. 'Conditioned arising evolves: variation and change in textual accounts of the *Paṭicca-samuppāda* doctrine', *Journal of the International Association of Buddhist Studies,* **22**(2): 311–42.

Collins, Steven. 1982. *Selfless Persons: Imagery and Thought in Theravāda Buddhism.* Cambridge: Cambridge University Press.

Cousins, L. S. 1981. 'The *Paṭṭhāna* and the development of Theravādin Abhidhamma', *Journal of the Pali Text Society*, **9**: 22–46.
Cousins, L. S. 1992. 'Vitakka/Vitarka and Vicāra', *Indo-Iranian Journal*, **35**(2–3): 137–57.
Cousins, L. S. 1996. 'Good or skilful?—Kusala in canon and commentary', *Journal of Buddhist Ethics*, **3**: 136–64.
Cousins, L. S. 1998. 'Nirvāṇa', in Edward Craig (ed.), *Routledge Encyclopedia of Philosophy*, 10 vols. London: Routledge, vol. 7, pp. 8–12.
Dasgupta, Surendranath. 1922. *A History of Indian Philosophy*. 5 vols. Cambridge: Cambridge University Press (1st Indian edn. Delhi: Motilal Banarsidass, 1975).
Duerlinger, James. 2003. *Indian Buddhist Theories of Persons: Vasubandhu's 'Refutation of the Theory of a Self'*. London: Routledge.
Feng, Youlan. 1952. *A History of Chinese Philosophy*, tr. Derk Bodde, 2 vols. 2nd edn. Princeton: Princeton University Press (reprinted Delhi: Motilal Banarsidass, 1994).
Frauwallner, Erich. 1973. *History of Indian Philosophy*, tr. V. M. Bedekar. 2 vols. Delhi: Motilal Banarsidass Publishers (Original publication: *Geschichte der indischen Philosophie*. Salzburg: Otto Müller Verlag, 1953).
Gombrich, Richard F. 1984. 'Notes on the Brahmanical background to Buddhist ethics', in H. Saddhātissa *et al.* (eds), *Buddhist Studies in Honour of Hammalava Saddhātissa*. Nugegoda, Sri Lanka: Hammalava Saddhātissa Felicitation Volume Committee, pp. 91–102.
Gombrich, Richard F. 1990a. 'Recovering the Buddha's message', in Tadeusz Skorupski (ed.), *Buddhist Forum*, vol. 1. London: School of Oriental and African Studies, University of London, pp. 5–20.
Gombrich, Richard F. 1990b. 'How the Mahāyāna began', in Tadeusz Skorupski (ed.), *Buddhist Forum*, vol. 1. London: School of Oriental and African Studies, University of London, pp. 21–30.
Gombrich, Richard F. 1992. 'The Buddha's book of Genesis?', *Indo-Iranian Journal*, **35**: 159–78.
Gombrich, Richard F. 2006. *How Buddhism Began: The Conditioned Genesis of the Early Teachings*, 2nd edn. Abingdon: Routledge.
Graham, Angus Charles. 1989. *Disputers of the Tao: Philosophical Argument in Ancient China*. Chicago: Open Court.
Harrison, Paul. 1993. 'The earliest Chinese translations of Mahāyāna Buddhist sūtras: some notes on the works of Lokakṣema', *Buddhist Studies Review*, **10**(2): 135–77.
Harrison, Paul 1998. 'Women in the pure land: some reflections on the textual sources', *Journal of Indian Philosophy*, **26**(6): 553–72.
Hartmann, Jens-Uwe. 1989. 'Fragmente aus dem *Dirghāgama* der Sarvāstivādins', in Fumio Enomoto *et al.* (eds), *Sanskrit-Texte aus dem Buddhistischen Kanon: Neuentdeckungen und Neueditionen*. 4 vols. Göttingen: Vandenhoeck & Ruprecht, vol. 1, pp. 37–68.
Hartmann, Jens-Uwe. 2004. 'Contents and structure of the *Dīrghāgama* of the (Mūla-)Sarvāstivādins', in *Annual Report of the International Research Institute for Advanced Buddhology at Soka University* 創価大学國際仏教学高等研究所年普, vol. 7, pp. 119–37.
Harvey, Peter. 1986. 'Signless meditations in Pāli Buddhism', *Journal of the International Association of Buddhist Studies*, **9**(1): 25–52.
Harvey, Peter. 1995. *The Selfless Mind: Personality, Consciousness and Nirvāṇa in Early Buddhism*. London: Curzon Press.
Hukaura, Masahumi 深浦正文. 1938. 'Yakukyo no seki' 訳経の制規, *Nikka bukkyo kenkyukai renpo* 日華仏教研究会年報, **3**: 260–80.
Hwang, Soon-il. 2006. *Metaphor and Literalism: The Doctrinal History of Nirvana*. London: Routledge.

Jaini, Padmanabh S. 2001. 'The Sautrāntika theory of Bīja', in *Collected Papers on Buddhist Studies*. Delhi: Motilal Banarsidass Publishers, pp. 219–37. (First published in *Bulletin of the School of Oriental and African Studies* (1959), **22**(2): 236–49.)

Jurewicz, Joanna. 2000. 'Playing with fire: The *Pratītyasamutpāda* from the perspective of Vedic thought', *Journal of the Pali Text Society*, **26**: 77–103.

Karunadasa, Y. 1987. 'Anattā as via media', *Sri Lanka Journal of Buddhist Studies*, **1**: 1–9.

Karunadasa, Y. 1996. *The Dhamma Theory: Philosophical Cornerstone of the Abhidhamma*. Kandy: Buddhist Publication Society.

Kawano, Satosi 河野訓. 1986. 'On the translations of Buddhist sūtras by Dharmarakṣa' 竺法護の訳 経について, *Journal of Indian and Buddhist Studies* 印度学仏教学研究, **35**(1): 72–4.

Lamotte, Étienne. 1980. 'Conditioned co-production and supreme enlightenment', in Somaratna Balasooriya (ed.), *Buddhist Studies in Honour of Walpola Rahula*. London: Gordon Fraser, pp. 118–32.

Lancaster, Lewis R. 1969. 'The Chinese translation of the *Aṣṭasāhasrikā-Prajñāpāramitā-Sūtra* attributed to Chih Ch'ien 支謙, *Monumenta Serica (Journal of Oriental Studies)*, pp. 246–57.

Li, Sizhen 李似珍. 2001. *Xingshen, xinxing, qingzhi: Zhongguo gudai xinshenguan shuping* 形神・心性・精志—中国古代心身观述评. Nanchang: Jiangxi renmin chubanshe 江西人民出版社.

Li, Xingling 李幸玲. 1995. *Liuchao shenmiebumielun yu fojiao lunhui zhutizhi yanjiu* 六朝神滅不滅論與佛教輪迴主體之研究, in *Guoyan suoji* 國研所集, vol. 39. Taibei: Guoli shifan daxue guowen yanjiusuo chuban 國立師範大學國文研究所出版.

Mayeda, Egaku. 1985. 'Japanese studies on the schools of the Chinese *Āgamas*', in Heinz Bechert (ed.), *Zur Schulzugehörigkeit von Werken der Hīnayāna-Literatur*. Göttingen: Vandenhoeck & Ruprecht, pp. 94–103.

Meisig, Konrad. 1993. 'On the archetype of the *Ambāṣṭasūtra*', *Wiener Zeitschrift für die Kunde Südasiens*, **36** (Supplementband): 229–38.

Nakamura, Hajime. 1955. 'Upaniṣadic tradition and the early school of Vedānta as noticed in Buddhist scripture', *Harvard Journal of Asiatic Studies*, **18**(1): 74–104.

Nattier, Jan. 2003. 'The ten epithets of the Buddha in the translations of Zhi Qian', in *Annual Report of the International Research Institute for Advanced Buddhology at Soka University*, pp. 207–50.

Norman, K. R. 1991. 'A note on *attā* in the *Alagaddūpama-sutta*', in *Collected Papers*, 7 vols. Oxford: Pali Text Society, vol. 2, pp. 200–9. (First published in *Studies in Indian Philosophy (Memorial Volume for Pandit Sukhlalji Sanghvi)*. Ahmedabad: L.D. Institute of Indology, 1981, pp. 19–29).

Norman, K. R. 1993a. 'Death and the Tathāgata', in *Collected Papers*, 7 vols. Oxford: Pali Text Society, vol. 4, pp. 251–63. (First published in *Studies in Buddhism and Culture (In Honour of Professor Dr. Egaku Mayeda)*, Tokyo, 1991, pp. 1–11).

Norman, K. R. 1993b. 'Theravāda Buddhism and Brahmanical Hinduism', in *Collected Papers*, 7 vols. Oxford: Pali Text Society, vol. 4, pp. 271–80. (First published in Tadeusz Skorupski (ed.), *Buddhist Forum*, vol. II, Tring: Institute of Buddhist Studies, pp. 193–200.).

Norman, K. R. 1996. 'Mistaken ideas about Nibbāna', in *Collected Papers*, 7 vols. Oxford: Pali Text Society, vol. 6, pp. 9–30. (First published in *Buddhist Forum III*, Tring: Institute of Buddhist Studies, 1994, pp. 211–25.)

Norman, K. R. 1996. 'Pāli translations', in *Collected Papers*, 7 vols. Oxford: Pali Text Society, vol. 6, pp. 156–70. (First published in *Buddhist Studies Review* (1989), **6**(2):153–65.)

Oldenberg, Hermann. 1991. *The Doctrine of the Upaniṣads and the Early Buddhism*, tr. Shridhar B. Shrotri. Delhi: Motilal Banarsidass (Original publication: *Die Lehre der Upanishaden und die Anfänge des Buddhismus*, Göttingen, 1915).

Pak, Hae-dang 박해당. 1992. 'The understanding of man in early Chinese Buddhism' 중국초기불교의인간이해, in *White Lotus: A Collection of Buddhist Studies* 백련불교논집. Haein-sa: 백련불교문화재단, vol. 1, pp. 93–127.

Park, Jungnok. 2008. 'A new attribution of the authorship of T5 and T6 *Mahāparinirvāṇa sūtra*', *Journal of the International Association of Buddhist Studies*, **31**(1/2): 339–67.

Ruegg, D. Seyfort. 1976. 'The meanings of the term gotra and the textual history of the *Ratnagotravibhāga*', *Bulletin of the School of Oriental and African Studies*, **39**(2): 341–63.

Ruegg, David Seyfort. 1989. *Buddha-nature, Mind and the Problem of Gradualism in a Comparative Perspective: On the Transmission and Reception of Buddhism in India and Tibet*. London: School of Oriental and African Studies, University of London.

Schmithausen, Lambert. 1987. *Ālayavijñāna: On the Origin and the Early Development of a Central Concept of Yogācāra Philosophy*. Tokyo: International Institute for Buddhist Studies.

Schmithausen, Lambert. 2005. *On the Problem of the External World in the Ch'eng wei shih lun*. Tokyo: International Institute for Buddhist Studies of the International College for Postgraduate Buddhist Studies.

Suzuki, Hiromi 鈴木裕美. 1995. 'On the translation terminology used in the old translation period sūtras' 古訳経典における訳語について: 竺法護訳出経典を中心として, *Journal of Indian and Buddhist Studies* 印度學佛教學研究, **43**(2): 198–200.

Tang, Yongtong 湯用彤. 1973. *Han-Wei-Liangjin-Nanbeichao fojiaoshi* 漢魏兩晉南北朝佛教史. Taibei: Xinwenfeng chuban gongsi 新文豐出版公司 (Original publication Changsha, 1938).

Tokuno, Kyoko. 1990. 'The evaluation of indigenous scriptures in Chinese Buddhist bibliographical catalogues', in Robert E. Buswell (ed.), *Chinese Buddhist Apocrypha*. Honolulu: University of Hawaii Press, pp. 31–74. (Reprinted Delhi: Sri Satguru Publications, 1992.)

Van Buitenen, J. A. B. 1964. 'The Large Ātman', *History of Religion*, **4**(1): 103–14.

Waldschmidt, Ernst. 1980. 'Central Asian sūtra fragments and their relation to the Chinese *Āgamas*', in Heinz Bechert (ed.), *Die Sprache der ältesten buddhistischen Überlieferung*. Göttingen: Vandenhoeck und Ruprecht, pp. 136–74.

Willemen, Charles, Bart Dessein and Collett Cox. 1998. *Sarvāstivāda Buddhist Scholasticism*. Leiden: Brill.

Williams, P. M. 1974. 'The translation and interpretation of the twelve terms in the *Paṭiccasamuppāda*', *Numen*, **21**(1): 35–63.

Xiao, Dengfu 蕭登福. 2003. *Daojia daojiao yu zhongtu fojiao chuqi jingyi fazhan* 道家道教與中土佛教初期經義發展. Shanghai: Shanghai guji chubanshe 上海古籍出版社.

Zhang, Liwen 张立文 *et al.* 1987. *Qi* 气. Beijing: Zhongguo renmin daxue chubanshe 中国人民大学出版社.

Zhang, Liwen 张立文 *et al.* 1993. Xin 心. Beijing: Zhongguo renmin daxue chubanshe 中国人民大学出版社.

Zhong, Zhaopeng. 1996. 'Lun jingqishen' 論精氣神, *Daojia wenhua yanjiu* 道家文化研究, **9**: 201–24.

Zürcher, E. 1972. *The Buddhist Conquest of China: The Spread and Adaptation of Buddhism in Early Medieval China*, 2nd edn. Leiden: Brill.

Zürcher, E. 1991. 'A new look at the earliest Chinese Buddhist texts', in Koichi Shinohara and Gregory Schopen (eds), *From Benares to Beijing: Essays on Buddhism and Chinese Religion in Honour of Prof. Jan Yün-Hua*. Oakville, Ontario: Mosaic Press, pp. 277–324.

DICTIONARIES AND CATALOGUES

Akanuma, Chizen 赤沼智善. 1967. *Indo bukkyo koyu meishi jiten* 印度佛教固有名詞辭典. Kyoto: Hozokan 法蔵館.

Ci, Yi 慈怡. 1989. *Foguang dacidian* 佛光大辭典. Foguang chubanshe 佛光出版社.

Editorial Committee for the *Hanyu dacidian*. 2001. *Hanyu dacidian* 汉语大辞典. Hanyu dacidian chubanshe 汉语大辞典出版社.

Editorial Committee for the *Zhongwen dacidian* 中文大辭典編纂委員會. 1968. *Zhongwen dacidian* 中文大辭典. Zhongguo wenhua xueyuan chubanbu 中國文化學院出版部.

Edgerton, Franklin. 1953. *Buddhist Hybrid Sanskrit Grammar and Dictionary* [BHSD]. 2 vols. New Haven: Yale University Press.

Lancaster, Lewis R. 1979. *The Korean Buddhist Canon: A Descriptive Catalogue*. Berkeley: University of California Press.

Mochizuki, Sinko 望月信亨 and Zenryu Tsukamoto 塚本善隆. 1954–58. *Bukkyo daijiten* 佛教大辭典. Tokyo: Sekai seiten kanko kyokai 世界聖典刊行協會.

Monier-Williams, Monier, Ernst Leumann and Carl Cappeller. 1899. *A Sanskrit-English Dictionary: Etymologically and Philologically Arranged with Special Reference to Cognate Indo-European Languages*, new edn. Oxford: Clarendon Press.

Ogiwara, Unrai 荻原雲來. 1964. *Kanyaku taisho bonwa daijiten* 漢訳對照梵和大辞典. Tokyo: Suzuki gakujutsu zaidan 鈴木学術財団.

Ono, Genmyo 小野玄妙 and Maruyama, Takao 丸山孝雄. 1936–78. *Bussho kaisetsu daijiten* 佛書解說大辭典. Tokyo 東京: Daito shuppansha 大東出版社.

Rhys Davids, T. W., and William Stede. 1966. *The Pali Text Society's Pali–English Dictionary* [PED]. London: published for the Pali Text Society by Luzac.

ELECTRONIC SOURCES

Chaṭṭha Saṅgāyanā CD [VRI_CD], version 3.0. Vipassana Research Institute, 1999.

Chinese Electronic Tripitaka Collection [CBETA] CBETA 電子佛典集成. Chinese Buddhist Electronic Text Association 中華電子佛典協會. February 2007.

Electronic Dictionary of Buddhist Studies [EDBS] 佛学电子辞典, version 3.5.30. Zhonghua fodian baoku 中华佛典宝库.

INDEX

Page numbers in **bold** indicate tables.

Aba jing 43
Abhidharmakośa-bhāṣya (Vasubandhu) 22–3, 107
Abhidharmic theories 104–10
Ambāṣtha 28–36
Ambāṣtha-sutra 4
attribution of 42–62
interpolations in 28–36
translation of 44
Amozhou jing 30
An Shigao 38, 39, 41, 48, 196–7
translation of Chan 218
translation of non-self 177
use of *shen* 183
An Xuan 40
Analects 153
analytical thinking, *see* reasoning
Ānanda 115
anātman, *see* non-self
anti-Brahmanism 84–90, 141
in Abhidharmic theories 105
in Mahāyāna Buddhism 143
anumāna 105–6, 108, 109
archaic translation 11–13
arhats 8, 99
attainment of 103
Godhika 191
Vakkali 190
Aṣtasāhasrikā Prajnāpāramitā 11, 40, 111
ātman, *see* self
atoms 120

Bai Yan 46, 55–6
Baoyun 204
'barbarian' dynasties 13
Beal, S. 77
being conscious (*cit*) 212–14
benevolence 153–6
Bhattacharya 81–2
on immortality 129
Bhikkhu Bodhi 78, 79
Bhikkhu Ñāṇamoḷi 78, 79
bipeds 24–5
bliss, *see* happiness
Bo Fazu 56–7
Bodhi, *see* Bhikkhu Bodhi
bodhisattvas 112, 113, 118, 198–9
on death 200
nirvāṇa without abiding 135
body images 31, 33
Brahmā 86–7
brahman 84, 85–8
in Abhidharmic theories 105
vs. *dao* 163
definition of *karman* 68
vs. immortality 129–31
origin of *ātman* 141–2
as synonym of *dhamma* 89
use of 90
Brahmanism, defined 84
brahmins 28, 30–1, 33, 34, 89
nihilism 66
Buddha 7–8, 125
and brahmin pupil/master 28–36
on complete pleasure 132
on consciousness 185
on death 192
on dependent origination and *dhamma* 91
on emptiness 115
epithets of 24–5, 52, 54, 55, 89
on eternalism 69–70, 88
on experience 92–6
on *hunpo* 186
on immortality 127–8
imperceptible form of 102
interpretation of karma 68
nature 216–17, 219, 220–1
on nihilism 66
parinirvāṇa 126–7
in *Prajñāpāramitā* literature and Mahāyāna theories 112

and salvation 134–8, 139–40
on self and five aggregates 70, 71, 79–80
state of self after *nirvāṇa* 101–2
on suffering 73–4
on Vakkali 190
Buddhayaśas 12, 14, 27, 30, 204–5
Buddhist catalogues 38–40

cakkavatti dhammiko dhammarājā 50–1, 54
causation 75, 77, 107, 117
Chan Buddhism 218–22
Chandaka 179
Chinese concept of self
before Buddhism 151–75
in Chan Buddhism 218–22
characteristics of 210–15, 223–4
debates on imperishability 208–9
development of imperishable soul 196–206, 215–18
early Buddhism *vs.* Daoism 175–6
imperishable soul in translations 178–95
Chu sanzang ji ji (Sengyou) **39**, 40, 43, **44**, 45, 46, 52–62; *see also Zongli zhongjing mulu* (Daoan)
concept of reality 143–4
Confucianism 32, 152, 153
human nature 158, 165
see also Confucius; Mencius; Neo-Confucianism
Confucius 151
on death and ghosts 159
as an ethicist 158
on filial piety 155–6
ideal society 155
on *ren* 153, 154
on *xing* 157
consciousness 26, 179–80, 197
and dependent origination 72, 73
experience of 91
as part of the five aggregates 51, 70, 71
as part of the Stages 15
and *shen* 213
translations of 184–5, 189–91
see also mind-consciousness; store-consciousness
correct reasoning 105–6, 108, 109
[corrupted] flows 102–3
Cousins, L. S. 29
craving 102
creation
Buddhist doctrines *vs.* Brahmanic ideas 86–8, 141–2
Daoists' view on 160–1, 163, 166–7, 175, 214
Indian *vs.* Chinese Buddhism 214–15
creation-body 136, 140, 141

dao (way) 151–2, 160–3
and early Buddhism 175–6
and knowledge 169–70
and *qi* 163–4
and *shen* 166–9, 171–3, 208, 209, 212, 214–15, 219, 223–4
Daoan 41, 42, 45, **47**
translation theory 6–8, 9
Daohan 12
Daoism 32, 152
vs. early Buddhism 175–6
natures of beings 157–8, 163–74
see also dao (way)
Daosheng 216, 217
Datang neidian lu (Daoxuan) **39**, 43, **44**
de 172
death
Confucius' view on 159
Daoists' view on 167, 168, 171, 174
translations of 199–200
Death (Māra) 71
dependent origination 18–19, 72–4, 90, 144
in Abhidharmic theories 107
and *dhamma* 91, 144–7
see also karma, law of
deva api manusyan draksyanti, manusya api devan draksyanti 17–18, 18n
dhamma
in Abhidharmic theories 106, 108–9
Chinese translation of 77
and dependent origination 144–7
interpretations of 74–7, 89, 91
dharma-body 136, 139–41, 143, 211
Dharmaguptaka Vinaya 12
Dharmapada
adaptations of 25–6
translators of 9–10, 46
Dharmaskandha 19
dhyāna, see meditation
Dīgha-nikāya 26–8, 29
direct observation 122
Dīrghāgama 12, 29
Dong Zhongshu 161, 165
dualism 210–11
dvipadôttama 24–5

egoism 133
empiricism 91–6, 224
in Abhidharmic theories 105–6, 108
in *Prajñapāramitā* literature and Mahāyāna theories 111, 114, 118
in Yogācāra theories 119
emptiness 112, 114–17, 124
and dependent origination 145–7
without abandonment 138
emptiness concentration 114–15

enjoyment-body 136, 140, 141
eternal death, fear of 128
eternalism 83–4
  and Buddhism's immortality 127–8
  rejection of 68–70, 74, 93, 95–6
ethics 134, 139, 152, 155
'everything' 92–6, 107, 108–9
existence (*sat*) 211–12
external objects 121–2, 124

fa 77
Fajian 205
Faju 60–1, 201
Fali 60–1, 201
family lineage 28–9, 31–2, 33–5
Fanzhi aba jing 43, **44**
Faxian 27, 204, 216
Fayong 43, **44**
Fazhong 204
Fei Changfang 39
feiwo, *see* non-self
feixinghuangdi 50–1, 54
filial piety 33, 35, 49, 154, 155–7
fire imagery 90
five aggregates 51–2, 54, 55, 91, 110
  and everything 93–4
  in *Prajñāpāramitā* literature and Mahāyāna theories 118
  and self 70–2, 80
five precepts 49
Fo kaijie fanzhi aba jing 30, 43, **44**
four achievements of practitioners 51, 58–9
four knowledges 135–6
four noble truths 66, 73, 91, 100–3
  impermanence/permanence of 143
  and rational egoism 133
foxing 216–17, 219, 220–1
Fundamental Stages 15

Gaozi 158
genesis, *see* creation
ghosts 159, 181
Gombrich, R. F. 90
Graham, A. C. 159
Great Qin emperor 12
gui (ghost) 159, 181
Gujin yijing tuji (Jingmai) **39**, 43, **44**
Guṇabhadra 10, 19, 142n, 190–1, 204

happiness 75, 76, 95
  and experience 95–6
  and *nirvāṇa* 130–3
Harrison, P. 40, 42, 198
Harvey, P. 78
hermeneutic tradition 81
higher knowledge/truth 92, 109, 143–4, 162
honesty, Confucius' view on 155–6
Hongfusi Temple 14
Horner, I. B. 78
Huijian 205
Huijue 204
Huineng 218
Huiyuan 209, 210
Huizi 174
human body
  Daoists' view on 164–5, 170–4
  early Buddhism *vs.* Daoism 175–6
  whole and parts 98
human nature 157–8, 161, 163–9, 216–17
hun (soul) 158–9, 178–81, 186–93; *see also* Chinese concept of self
hunling 187–8, 198, 200
hunpo 181, 186–7, 201, 208
hunshen 54, 188–9, 208
  as Chinese interpolation 51, 184
  use of 198, 199, 200, 201, 203, 204
hunshi 193

icchantika 124, 216, 217
ideal society 153, 155
ideation 115–16
immortality, and *nirvāṇa* 127–33
imperishable soul, *see* Chinese concept of self
intention 116

jianai (universal love) 154
Jijiaye 27
jing (essence, purity) 164, 185
jingshen 197, 212
  as Chinese interpolation 1, 51
  Daoists' view on 168, 173, 186
  use of 198, 199, 201, 203, 204, 205
  see also shen
jingshi 188, 197, 198
jīva 182–3
Jizang 211, 212
Juqu Jingsheng 204, 205
Jurewicz, J. 90

Kaiyuan shijiao lu (Zhisheng) **39**, 43, **44**
Kalupahana 74, 75–6
Kang Mengxiang 193, 198, 199–200
Kang Senghui 38, 53–4, 61, 200
karma
  ethicization of 68
  law of 66, 67–8
  and store-consciousness 122–4
  see also dependent origination
Karunadasa, Y. 97
  on *dhamma*s 106
  levels of reality 109
Kawano, S. 201
kinds of visible object 22–4
knowledge 135–6, 169–70
kongyixianse 22–4

Kumārajīva 194, 203
death 13n
on Indian languages 5
translation works 13, 17–18, 19–20, 21

'lady of beautiful thighs' 26–8
Lamotte, É. 73
Lancaster, L. R. 40–1
Laozi 169
'large *ātman*' 141–2
Legalism 152
li (ceremony, propriety) 153, 154, 156–7
liangzuzun 24–5
Lidai sanbao ji (Fei Changfang) **39**, 43, **44**
life of beings 110
linghun 199; *see also hun*(soul); *hunling*
Lingzheng 211
Lokakṣema 11, 20, 48, 197–9
attribution to 38, 40, 41, 42, 46
translation of non-self 177
translation of *vijñāna* 184
Lunyu (*Analects*) 153

Mahāparinirvāṇa-sūtra
non-self 1
translators of 46, 56–7, **62**
Mahāyāna Mahāparinirvāṇa-sūtra 216
Mahāyāna theories 111–19
manas 75–6
manojava 76–7
Māra 190, 191
meditation 92, 108, 115, 131
and store-consciousness 124
see also Chan Buddhism
Mencius
as an ethicist 158
on filial piety 156
on *ren* and *shu* 153
on *xing* 158, 161
on Yangzi 173–4
Meng Fu 11
mental objects 94, 100
metres, loss of 5, 19–20
middle way 74, 80, 84, 117, 144–7
mind (*xin*) 98, 164
mind-consciousness 94
mind-only theory 74, 75, 119, 121–2, 124
mingxingzu, see vidyā-caraṇa-saṃpanna
Mohism 152; *see also* Mozi
moral value 134–9, 152, 155
Moteng 8n
Mouzi 208
Mozi
ideal society 155
on *jianai* 154
Mencius' comment on 156

Nāgārjuna 111–12, 117, 145

Ñāṇamoḷi, *see* Bhikkhu Ñāṇamoḷi
Nattier, J. 46, **47**
on translators 40, 41, 42, 55
Neo-Confucianism 158, 161
new translation 11, 14–16
nibbāna, see *nirvāṇa*
Nie Chengyuan 59
nihilism 66–7, 74, 83–4
and *nirvāṇa* 69
nirvāṇa
in Abhidharmic theories 108–9
of Buddha 126–7
in Chinese Buddhism 211, 212, 213
and nihilism 69
path leading to 100–3
as synonym of immortality 127–33
two kinds of 99
without abiding 135–8
in Yogācāra theories 125
non-self 84, 102, 150
Chinese translations of 177–8
Norman, K. R. 67–8
Buddhist doctrines *vs*. Brahmanic ideas 90
on immortality 129
on mind 74, 75–6
use of *brahman* 90

old translation 11, 13
Oldenberg, H. 85–6, 138–9

Pañcasikha 26–7
Pañcaskandha, see five aggregates
Paramārtha 22
parinirvāṇa 126–7, 128
Pauṣkarasārin 28–36
Pāyāsi, Prince 182
perfection of wisdom 112, 113
permanent self, *see* eternalism
phenomena
and *dhamma* 91, 108
three characteristics of 90, 120–1
pleasure, *see* happiness
po (psyche) 158–9, 178–9
Poṭṭhapāda 95
practitioners of the two vehicles 135
Prajñapāramitā literature 111–19
Pratītyasamutpāda, see dependent origination
pristine material, see *qi* (pristine material or vital energy)
propriety (*li*) 153, 154, 156–7
pudgala 105
Puguang 23–4
Pūraṇa Kassapa 67

qi (pristine material or vital energy) 151, 163–7, 168, 170, 210

reality, concept of 143–4
reasoning 176, 224; *see also* correct reasoning
recitation 12n
reductio ad absurdum 117
reductionism 97–8, 224
- in Abhidharmic theories 106–7
- in *Prajñapāramitā* literature and Mahāyāna theories 111
- in Yogācāra theories 119–20

ren (benevolence) 153–6
Rhys Davids, T. W., and Caroline A. F 27–8, 131
Rockhill, W. 77

Sakkapañha-sutta 26–8
Śākya clan 29, 30, 31–5
salvation 135–8
Saṃghadeva 194–5, 203
saṃsāra 66, 67, 88, 175
- Chinese explanation of 178, 211

sanbuyi 7–8
Sāriputta 91, 114
Sāti 185
(Ṣaṭ)pāramitā-samāsa 54, **62**
Schmithausen, L. 121
scribes 12, 12n, 14, 21
self
- in Abhidharmic theories 104–10
- basic principles 83–98
- and Buddhist soteriology 65
- critical features of 66–74
- interpretation of 78–82
- and *nirvāṇa* 127–48
- in *Prajñapāramitā* literature and Mahāyāna theories 111–19
- state after *nirvāṇa* 101, 102
- in Yogācāra theories 119–25
- *see also* Chinese concept of self; non-self

Sengrui 5, 17–18, 195
Sengyou 37–8, 40, 42, 45
Sengzhao 12, 214–15
seven treasures of the wheel-turning king 50–1, 54, 60–1
She, Lord 155
shen 166–9
- characteristics of concept of 210–18, 223–4
- debates on imperishability of 208–9
- and early Buddhism 175, 176
- as a soteriological agent 170–3
- translations of 194–5
- use of 181–5
- *vs. vijñāna* 26
- *see also jingshen*

Shengjian 205
shenqu 26
shenshi 191–2
- use of 198, 199, 201, 202, 203, 204, 205

shenwo 203
shi
- use of 188, 189, 191–3, 197, 205
- *vs. vijñāna* 26, 185

shihunshen 184, 198
shishen 189–91, 202, 203
shu 153
signless concentration 114–15
Sizhen Li 166
skilful actions 67, 136–7
soul, *see hun* (soul)
sounds 9
Sthiramati 120
store-consciousness 119, 123–4, 125, 136, 148
Subhūti 112, 113, 118
suffering 75, 76
- in Brahmanic sense 129
- cessation of the origin of 99–103
- elimination of 73–4
- four noble truths 66, 73, 91
- impermanence of 71
- in *Prajñapāramitā* literature and Mahāyāna theories 113
- and reductionism 98
- whole aggregate of 72

Sun He 11
Sun Quan 48
Suzuki, H. 57, **58**, 201
syntax 18–19
systematic reading 74–83

Tanjing 205
Tanwulan 204, 205
tathāgatagarbha 140–2, 143, 220–1
- Chinese explanation of 211
- praise of the activity of 144–8

Temple Hongfusi 14
threefold body 135–6, 139–40
translation
- interpolations and adaptations ix, 4, 5–6, 24–36
- linguistic characteristics 5, 17–24
- periods of 196–206
- procedure 9–17, 20, 193–4
- theories 6–9

translators 21
- attribution to 9–11
- comparison of 52–62
- interpolations and adaptations 4, 193, 197–206
- and truth of the Buddha 8
- verification of 37–42
- *see also* individual persons

trilakṣaṇa 90
twelvefold dependent origination 18–19

ucchedavādin 175
Uddālaka Āruṇi 84–5
Ui, H. 45–6, **47**, 56
  on translation 38, 39
unconditioned skilfulness 136–7
universal love 154
universe 164–5
unskilful actions 67
upāyakauśalyagatiṅgata 20–1, 21n

Vaccha 101
Vajirā 71
Vakkali 190
Van Buitenen, J. A. B. 141–2
Vāseṭṭha 89
Vasubandhu
  on correct reasoning 105–6
  defines *dhamma* 108
  on kinds of visible object 22
  on self 107–8, 121–2, 138
Vasudeva, Somadeva 29
Vātsīputrīyas 105
verses 5, 19–20
vidyā-caraṇa-saṃpanna 25
Vighna 9–10, 46
vijñāna, see consciousness
vyapetavijñana 26

Wang Ni 166
Wangbi 161
Willemen, C. 77
Wonhyo 218
word order 18–19
Wu Emperor 218
wushiben 7
wuwei 162, 174, 217
wuwo, see non-self

Xiao, *see* filial piety
Xiao Dengfu 158–9
Xiao jing 33
xin (mind) 98, 164
xing 157–8
Xu Jingzong 14–16
Xuanzang 205–6
  translation of *Dharmaskandha* 19
  translation of kinds of visible object 22–4
  translation of *upāyakauśalyagatiṅgata* 21
  translation team 14–16
  translation theory 8–9
Xulai jing 55–6, **62**

Yan Yuan 154
Yancong lu/*Zhongjing mulu* **39**, 43, **44**
Yangzi 156, 173–4
Yanshou 221
Yao Shuang 12
yi (righteousness) 156
Yijing 30, 205
yin and *yang* 167
Yogācāra theories 119–25
Yogācārabhūmi 14–16

Zengzi 33
Zhang Liwen 163
Zhang Shaoan 11
Zhenyuan xinding shijiao mulu (Yuanzhao) **39**, 43, **44**
Zhi Mindu 41
Zhi Qian 4, 30
  attribution to 38, 40–1, 42–8
  comparison with other translators 52–62
  and *Dharmapada* 10
  style of translation 48–52
  translation of imperishable soul 199–200
  translation of *upāyakauśalyagatiṅgata* 21
  translation of *vijñāna* 26
Zhiyan 204
Zhonggong 153
Zhongjing mulu (Yancong) **39**, 43, **44**
Zhou dynasty 153, 155
Zhou Tili 11
Zhu Dali 193, 198
Zhu Fahu 57–9, 57n, 200–1
Zhu Faji 59
Zhu Fonian 12, 13, 27, 30, 202–3
Zhu Jiangyan
  and *Dharmapada* 10, 46
  translation of *vijñana* 26
Zhu Shixing 59–60
Zhu Shulan 59–60
Zhu Shuofo 11
Zhuangzi 166, 168, 169
  on knowledge and *dao* 170
  on *shen* 172
  on *wuwei* and death 174
zhuanlunshengwang 50–1, 54
Zi Lu 155
Zibi 11
Zigong 153
Zongbing 212–13, 217–18
Zongli zhongjing mulu (Daoan) 6, **39**, 43, **44**
Zongmi 219–21
zu 24–5
Zürcher, E., on translations 41–2, 45, 196, 198

www.ingramcontent.com/pod-product-compliance
Lightning Source LLC
Chambersburg PA
CBHW070758230426
43665CB00017B/2414
* 9 7 8 1 8 4 5 5 3 9 9 7 9 *